Going, Going ... Ca

Terry —

Hope you enjoy reading
this book as much as
enjoyed writing it.

Jason Gonzales

Going, Going ... Caught!

*Baseball's Great Outfield Catches
as Described by Those
Who Saw Them, 1887–1964*

JASON ARONOFF

Foreword by Dave Anderson

McFarland & Company, Inc., Publishers

Jefferson, North Carolina, and London

LIBRARY OF CONGRESS CATALOGUING-IN-PUBLICATION DATA

Aronoff, Jason.
Going, going...caught! : baseball's great outfield catches as described by those who saw them, 1887–1964 / Jason Aronoff ; foreword by Dave Anderson.
p.   cm.
Includes bibliographical references and index.

ISBN 978-0-7864-4113-6
softcover : 50# alkaline paper ∞

1. Baseball—United States—History.   2. Baseball—Defense—United States—History.   3. Fielding (Baseball)—United States—History.
4. Baseball players—United States—Biography.   I. Title.
GV863.A1A78   2009   796.357'640973—dc22   2008052178

British Library cataloguing data are available

On the cover: Giants centerfielder Willie Mays, 1956 (Associated Press)

Manufactured in the United States of America

McFarland & Company, Inc., Publishers
Box 611, Jefferson, North Carolina 28640
www.mcfarlandpub.com

Acknowledgments

There are many people to thank for their help on this project.

For giving me encouragement to pursue the subject of great catches, for his nearly six decades of keen observations on baseball and other sports, and for writing the foreword to this book, I especially want to express my gratitude to Dave Anderson.

The assistance of the workers in the microfilm rooms at the Buffalo and Erie County Public Library and at the New York Public Library was invaluable. The reference librarians and the people in the Inter-Library Loan Department at the Buffalo and Erie County Public Library were unfailingly helpful.

Jim Mones and Jeff Roth at the *New York Times* Photo Archives, Lisa Nelson and Tom Gilbert at Associated Press Wide World Photos, Jessica Poblete, Kim Strong, and Kim Apley at Corbis, and Angela Troisi of the *New York Daily News* tracked down photos in which I had interest.

The following people provided significant assistance: Merri-Todd Webster of the Enoch Pratt Free Library in Baltimore, Maryland; Joy Holland, Susan Aprill, June Koffi and Lisa DeBoer of the Brooklyn Collection at the Brooklyn Public Library; Bill Chase of the Fine Arts and Special Collections Department at the Cleveland Public Library; Amy Starr Degnan of the Steele Memorial Library, Elmira, New York; Julie Able of the Indianapolis-Marion County Public Library; Ron Tetrick of the Kokomo-Howard County (Indiana) Public Library; Sheila Nash of the Los Angeles Public Library; Tiffany Berry of the Sayre (Pennsylvania) Public Library; Charles Brown of the St. Louis Mercantile Library; Kate Adams and Susan Scupin of the St. Louis County Library; Richard Hanrath of the Schaumburg (Illinois) Township District Library; Bill Stout at the Temple University Library; Steve Moskowitz of the Trenton Public Library; Ben Prestianni of the Wilmington (Delaware) Public Library; and Wendy Bish-McGrew of the Guthrie Memorial Library in Hanover, Pennsylvania.

Todd Gustafson at the George Eastman House in Rochester, N.Y., provided me with information about the capability of cameras to take action shots of outfielders in the pre–1930 years. Margaret Goodbody of the Washingtoniana Division, District of Columbia Public Library, and Don Wentworth of the Carnegie Library of Pittsburgh took an interest in the topic of my work and added pertinent information beyond my original requests.

Reference librarians and/or microfilm librarians at the following institutions graciously answered many questions I asked: Atlantic City Public Library; Harold Washington Library in Chicago; Public Library of Cincinnati and Hamilton County; Cleveland Public Library; East Shore Area Library, Daupin County Library System, Harrisburg, Pennsylvania; Milwaukee Public Library; Newark (New Jersey) Public Library; University of Michigan Graduate Library; Waukegan (Illinois) Public Library; and especially the Free Library of Philadelphia.

Patricia Kelly, Bill Burdick, Bill Francis, Gabriel Schechter, and the librarians of the Baseball Hall of Fame in Cooperstown, New York, found photos and data that I had hoped to find but didn't think was actually available. Steven Gietschier and James Meier at *The Sporting News* archives gave me leads and data that were helpful. Mr. Gietschier of *The Sporting News* and John Kuenster of *Baseball Digest* were generous about the use of material from those publications. Thanks also to the proprietors of the *SPORT* magazine archive, who are keeping *SPORT* magazine alive online at www.TheSportGallery.com.

John Seitter, executive director of the Camden County (New Jersey) Historical Society, Christopher Carden, former director of the library and special collections at The Bostonian Society, and the staff of the Missouri Historical Society tracked down information which expedited my work. Cindy Clark and Alice Kane, both in Boston, and Elizabeth Shook and Ed Schmidt in St. Louis were thorough in the library work they provided.

The search for the Dummy Hoy catch led me to the following helpful people: in Des Moines, Iowa, Robert Mapes, and several reference librarians at the Des Moines Public Library; in Duluth, Minnesota, Mike Grossman at the Duluth Public Library; in Eau Claire, Wisconsin, Kathy Herfel of the Eau Claire Public Library, and Frank Smoot of the Chippewa Valley Museum; in La Crosse, Wisconsin, Bill Peterson of the La Crosse Public Library; in Milwaukee, Erin Elliott of the Milwaukee Public Library, and the DITTO Department at the same library; in Minneapolis, Natalie Hart of the INFORM Research Services Department of the Minneapolis Public Library; in Oshkosh, Wisconsin, Jeremiah Miller and Scott Cross at the Oshkosh Public Museum, and several reference librarians at the Oshkosh Public Library; and in St. Paul, Sue Pummill and Ron Paulson of the St. Paul Public Library.

The following players had vivid memories of events from over 50 years ago: Mel Clark, Carl Erskine, Ernie Johnson, Al Luplow, Bobby Morgan, Steve Ridzik and Don Thompson.

Jo-Anne Carr, archival assistant at Holy Cross University, sent me information on Jigger Statz from his time as a student at Holy Cross. Nods of appreciation go to Al Harriman for his editorial suggestions and to Darryl Swanson for his fine drawings.

Writers John Holway, Jack Lang, Russell Schneider, and Dave Anderson provided different vantage points on great fielding efforts they have seen or written about. Mike Einstein afforded me the opportunity to share his father's (Charles Einstein) early collaboration with Willie Mays that showed the depth of the great ballplayer's thinking about his sport. The three *Fireside Book of Baseball* volumes that Charles Einstein edited remain among the greatest books ever put together on baseball.

As kids, Bob Kandle, Lou "Wick" Wickward and Warren Elliott were almost always available for throw-and-catch sessions and baseball talk. Harold Goldstein's next-door narrow backyard, across a public alley and onto the Welch-Kandle family's driveway served as the local "ball field."

My brothers Remy and Ethan routinely give me encouragement and new perspectives. In 1952, our father, Remington, with several other men, founded the Little League program of Millville, New Jersey, so boys interested in baseball could have an organized outlet. Our mother, Doris, supported our participation in constructive activities whether or not they involved sports.

In 1962, a shared interest in baseball trivia led to a long friendship with Harvey and Judy Finkel. For decades I have engaged in many hours of conversations on the Cleveland Indians with Steve Loveland and Bill Loveland. Steve's wife and Bill's mother, Junetta

Loveland, a Tribe fan too, liked the playing and managing styles of Lou Boudreau and Mike Hargrove.

My wife Debby, a longtime Indians fan, has understood my fascination with the topic of this book and withstood the time I have taken to complete it. If I had been nearly as diligent a worker as our daughters Jenny, Nell, and Amy, I would have finished it years ago. For their wonderful humor and their support, I am grateful.

Finally, I would like to acknowledge the generous courtesy of the following for allowing me to use materials in the book:

The *Boston Herald* for quotations from Will Cloney, Ed Costello, Bill Cunningham, Ed Cunningham, Henry McKenna, Arthur Sampson and Burt Whitman of the *Boston Herald*; and John Drohan of the *Boston Traveler*. Reprinted with permission of the *Boston Herald*;

Articles by Bob Maisel reprinted courtesy of the *Baltimore Sun* Company, Inc. All rights Reserved;

The *Detroit Free Press* for quotes from articles by Charles P. Ward, Hal Middlesworth and staff writers. Reprinted by permission of the *Detroit Free Press*;

Quotations from Sam Greene's September 17, 1957, article "Tuttle's Catch Greatest Since 1934, Says Rowe" reprinted with permission of *The Detroit News*;

The *Minneapolis Star-Tribune* for quotations from *Minneapolis Star* writer Bob Beebe; and from *Minneapolis Tribune* writers Halsey Hall and Joe Hendrickson. Reprinted with permission of *Minneapolis Star-Tribune*;

The *Star-Ledger* (Newark) for quotations from Michael Gaven and Murray Robinson of the *Newark Star-Eagle*; Joe Reichler of the *Newark Star-Ledger*; and Charley Feeney and Jack Lang of the *Long Island Press*. All are property of the *The Star-Ledger* (Newark);

The *Philadelphia Inquirer* for quotations from Stan Baumgartner, Sam Carchidi, Frank Dolson, and Allen Lewis of the *Philadelphia Inquirer*; and Grant Doherty, Joe Greenday, and Stan Hochman of the *Philadelphia Daily News*. Reprinted with permission of *The Philadelphia Inquirer* & *Daily News*;

Potomac Books for a quote from Tony Castro, *Mickey Mantle: America's Prodigal Son* (Washington, D.C.: Brassey's, 2002). Used by permission of Potomac Books, Inc. (formerly Brassey's, Inc.);

The *St. Louis Post-Dispatch* for quotes from writers Bob Broeg, James M. Gould, Neal Russo, Babe Ruth, J. Roy Stockton, Herman Wecke and Ed Wray. Reprinted with permission of the *St. Louis Post-Dispatch*, copyright 1934, 1936, 1941, 1942, 1950, 1961;

The *Washington Post* for quotations from *Washington Post* writers Bob Addie, N.W. Baxter, and Herb Heft; and from the *Washington Star* writer Burton Hawkins. Reprinted with permission of *The Washington Post*;

W.W. Norton & Company, Inc. for quotations from John J. McGraw, *My Thirty Years in Baseball* (New York: Boni and Liveright, 1923);

The *San Francisco Examiner* for permission to use quotations from *Examiner* writers Charles Einstein, Curly Grieve, Walter Judge, and Harry Jupiter;

Sports Publishing LLC for permission to quote from Jack Buck, with Rob Rains and Bob Broeg, *Jack Buck: "That's a Winner"* (Champaign, Illinois: Sagamore Publishing LLC, 1997);

and Temple University Press for permission to use quotations from Robin Roberts and C. Paul Rogers III, *The Whiz Kids and the 1950 Pennant* (Philadelphia: Temple University Press, 1996).

Table of Contents

Foreword
by Dave Anderson

For as long as baseball has been played, the great hitters, the great pitchers, and the great managers have had their pages in the literature of the sport, but the beauty of this book is that Jason Aronoff mined a subject never before explored: great catches by outfielders.

Mined is the word. He had to dig into the dusty decades of newspapers large and small long before videotape preserved great catches for all of us to see. Some of the early catches by famous and obscure outfielders were not even frozen in time by a camera, but they were described, often at length as well as in admiration, in the next day's newspaper. Those words, along with whatever old photos were available, are what Jason mined.

But what makes a great catch?

Over more than 50 years covering major-league baseball, from the Brooklyn Dodgers of the fifties to the Yankee–Red Sox rivalry of today, my definition of a great catch involved the outfielder having to cope with catching a spinning ball coming out of the glare of a sunny sky or out of the background of shaded spectators, but also with the outfielder's possible collision with at least one of three objects: the wall or fence, the grassy field itself, an outfield teammate.

Another factor is the importance of the stage, especially the World Series, a post-season championship or division playoff, or a pennant-race situation.

As memorable as Willie Mays' over-the-shoulder catch of Vic Wertz's drive to deep center field in the old Polo Grounds has proved to be, its stage was the 1954 World Series, with television cameras and dozens of newspaper and wire-service photographers there to record it, and reporters to write about it. As dazzling as the catch was, the stage increased its fame. Basically, all Mays had to do was turn, run, look back over his shoulder and catch the ball. The center field bleachers weren't that close. Neither were either of his outfield teammates. And the ground was not a factor.

But the catch happened on baseball's grandest stage, the World Series, and Willie Mays, one of baseball's grandest centerfielders, made it happen. Had he made the same catch during a routine mid-season game, would it be remembered as fondly, or as often? I doubt it.

I've never tried to rate any outfielder's catch as "the greatest," but like you and any other credible baseball fan, I'm entitled to select the greatest catch *that I've seen at a game*, not broadcast live on television or on videotape. More than fifty years later, it remains Duke Snider's full-speed sprint and Spider-Man climb up the 12-foot left-center field wall at old Shibe Park in Philadelphia to rob Willie (Puddin' Head) Jones of an extra-base hit, if not a home run, that would have won the game for the Phillies. Instead, it was the final out in the Brooklyn Dodgers' 12-inning victory.

I'm sure you have your favorite greatest catch, and you may find it here among the dozens of gems that Jason Aronoff has mined. You'll enjoy comparing them.

Dave Anderson is a Pulitzer Prize–winning sports columnist for The New York Times.

Preface

A failed effort to get a photograph of a great catch I remembered from my childhood in the mid–1950s led to this book celebrating some of the greatest catches outfielders made between 1887 and 1964. My interest in great catches began with a catch that Duke Snider made in 1954, a catch which some of those of us who saw it contend was "the greatest." I saw it on a small-screen, black-and-white television set. I was eleven at the time, and was a Brooklyn Dodgers fan.

I lived in Millville, New Jersey, which was and is in Philadelphia Phillies territory. My older brother Remy was the only Dodgers fan I knew among the mostly loyal fans of the Phillies' Whiz Kids teams of the early fifties. He had been a Dodgers fan for several years by the time I began to take an interest in major league baseball in 1952, and, from his example, I too became a Dodgers fan.

Any time the Dodgers were playing the Phillies on television, Remy and I tuned in. One of those times was on Memorial Day 1954. Over all the years from that day until 2001, I recalled little except that the game was exciting, and that Duke Snider robbed Willie "Puddin' Head" Jones with a great catch on the wall at Shibe Park. After I read Duke Snider's autobiography, *The Duke of Flatbush*, I again recalled having seen the 1954 Memorial Day catch. In the book, Snider described it as "my best catch ever." The book did not have a photo of the catch.

In his 2001 autobiography, *Zim*, Don Zimmer mentioned the great catch in Philadelphia by his teammate Snider. In July 2001, I bought a copy of the September 1955 *SPORT* magazine with Duke Snider on the cover. In the story on Snider by Al Stump, the Memorial Day 1954 catch again was mentioned. At this point, I wanted more than ever to see a picture of the catch. I began to do library searches, newspaper searches, and Web searches without success.

I called Dave Anderson of the *New York Times*, who wrote about the catch for the *Brooklyn Eagle* in 1954. He said he didn't remember any wire photos of the catch coming across his desk at the *Eagle*. Without hesitation and spontaneously, Dave said Snider's catch was the greatest catch he had ever seen. He spoke about the catch as if it had happened yesterday. It was still vivid in his mind after almost fifty years. His comments and the other information I had on the catch caused me to feel that such an extraordinarily athletic event, which flabbergasted its viewers, should be known beyond the dwindling number of people who saw it.

There are many contenders for the "greatest catch ever" accolade. The claim here is that Snider's catch, and others, should be recognized as examples of athletic bursts at the highest level sports has to offer.

Locating the Catches

There have been a few formal listings of great catches. For most years in the 1880s, the *New York Clipper*, a weekly newspaper, gave summaries of the best fielding of the year. Given that players during the 1880s either used no glove or half-fingered gloves basically covering the hand's palm, the catches briefly described in the *Clipper* summaries must have had fans buzzing. Because playing without gloves was commonplace, one-handed catches were referred to as "one hand" or "left hand" or "right hand" catches as opposed to "gloved hand" or (later) "bare hand" catches.

Among the outfielders singled out for praise in the 1880s were Jim Lillie of Buffalo and later Kansas City; Mike Mansell of Pittsburgh; Jim Fogarty, Ed Greer, and Ed Andrews of the Philadelphia Athletics; Joe Sommer of Baltimore; Mike Dorgan of New York; and Joe Hornung and Dick Johnston of Boston

Joe Hornung was a heralded left fielder. Under "Fielding Feats of 1885," The *New York Clipper* of February 6, 1886, included the following comments about Hornung:

Hornung of the Boston Club is generally acknowledged to have no peer as a left-fielder, and his fine form last season in that position is shown by the fact that he made only twelve errors—most of them excusable ones—in ninety-eight championships games. It would take too much space to give all his clever fielding plays, and we need mention only.... In the Boston-New York game June 26 Caskins struck a terrific liner to left-field, apparently impossible for Hornung to catch. He ran, however, at full speed a long distance, and leaping high in the air, succeeded in taking with one hand the ball just as it was spinning like a shot over his head. It was one of the finest catches ever seen on the Boston grounds, and he was repeatedly compelled to acknowledge the hearty applause for the wonderful feat.

The editors of *Baseball Digest* twice called for readers to write about great catches they had seen. Contributors were given $25 if their article was used. The first time this was done was in 1949 and 1950, and the second time in 1961 and 1962. (See Appendix A for one catch that wasn't.) *Baseball Digest* has regularly had articles about great fielding. The most systematic coverage of great fielding occurred in two of Herbert Simons' *Baseball Digest* articles, one in the December 1964–January 1965 issue, and the other in the December 1967–January 1968 issue. In the first issue, Simons wrote about the 23 greatest plays of the year in the major leagues, and, in the second issue, the 25 greatest plays of the year.

Most of the catches described in this book were located through some mention of them in newspaper articles, biographies of players, books by former players, or in other baseball books.

The time frame of this book is from 1887 to 1964. That span begins with the date of the first of the particular catches about which others have commented, and concludes with Duke Snider's retirement, the demolition of the Polo Grounds in New York, and with what arguably may have been the last of Willie Mays' greatest catches. Also, by 1964 the landscape of major league baseball included the relocation of old-guard franchises in Boston, St. Louis, Philadelphia, Brooklyn and New York to other cities. During the 1950s, after fifty years of stability among major league franchises, five franchises moved, four to the west, and one to the east. First, the Boston Braves left Boston for Milwaukee after the 1952 season. The St. Louis Browns moved to Baltimore after the 1953 season. The Philadelphia A's went to Kansas City after the 1954 season. Both the Giants and the Dodgers moved to the West Coast after the 1957 season.

The new landscape in the early 1960s included Minnesota and new franchises in New York, Washington, Los Angeles, and Houston. It also included, beginning with the opening of RFK Stadium in Washington in 1962, a new kind of multi-purpose, impersonal, less fan-friendly stadium with uniform outfield dimensions and fences. Over the next ten years this kind of stadium also was built in St. Louis, Houston, Atlanta, Philadelphia, Cincinnati, Oakland, and Pittsburgh.

Significant about these new ballparks was the loss of the idiosyncrasies of outfields and outfield fences with which players in earlier decades had to contend and try to conquer. No longer could a player race out to a "483 ft." sign to track down a fly ball. No longer could a player make plays off oddly angled and multi-surfaced walls game in and game out. After 1970, only a few of the ballparks built in the first two decades of the twentieth century remained to challenge the outfielders.

The new ballparks of the 1960s and 1970s did not stop major league outfielders from making great catches, some perhaps greater than the ones discussed in this book. But that story, after 1964, remains for someone else to pursue.

PART I. HISTORICAL BACKGROUND

• ONE •

A Great Play, "The Greatest," Photography, and Sportswriters

Great catches are a natural part of baseball, and each generation has players who make great catches, and who have fans and sportswriters saying that this or that particular catch is the greatest they have ever seen. The catches reported in this book represent a small sampling from the realm of all the outstanding catches in professional baseball history. This book makes no pretense to be a comprehensive search for the greatest catches across all the games played since baseball began. Even if one wanted to be comprehensive, the effort could consume a lifetime of often frustrating reading among millions of articles written in newspapers about games that have occurred in hundreds of cities and dozens of leagues.

In addition, it is likely that thousands of outstanding catches have been made since the time baseball began. And, of all those catches, many—maybe even most—went unreported, especially in the early years of the sport when newspaper coverage often was brief. Many other great catches have been reported with too few details to tell how outstanding they were.

A serious limitation is finding credible and regular reports on games in the Negro and Latin leagues. We must take it for granted that outfielders in the Negro and Latin American leagues made spectacular catches. However, it is difficult to find the documentation that tells us what they did in the field. Players like Cool Papa Bell and Oscar Charleston were among those who undoubtedly made catches that made spectators scratch their heads in amazement. At the beginning of his book, *The Complete Book of Baseball's Negro Leagues: The Other Half of Baseball History*, John Holway comments on the difficulty of getting information about Negro League games. Many newspapers did not cover the games and there were no official scorekeepers for some games.

Holway does cite some catches by Negro League players, particularly one by Spotswood Poles in Detroit in 1909, which will be presented later, and one by Oscar Charleston. Dave Malarcher, who played in the outfield with centerfielder Charleston on the Indianapolis ABCs, told John Holway about the greatest catch he ever saw, one made by Oscar. Holway wrote:

> ABC right fielder Dave Malarcher said he and George Shively fielded only foul balls, that Oscar Charleston caught everything else. Charleston had a weak arm, thus played a shallow centerfield, as did Tris Speaker of the Red Sox. But, no one remembered seeing a fly ball hit over his head. Malarcher recalled the greatest catch he ever saw: "The batter hit the ball to deep center, way back, way over Charleston's head. He turned and ran like he was going to catch a train, he just flew back there. He ran so fast he just overran it. As he turned, it was falling behind him, and he caught it just before it hit the ground. It was marvelous. Marvelous" [117].

7

In his book *Blackball Stars: Negro League Pioneers,* Holway notes that Malarcher told him the catch by Charleston came in Dave Malarcher's rookie year, 1916, and occurred in a game against the New York Cubans in Kokomo, Indiana. Dave Malarcher's recollection of this one catch may be the only glimpse available of Oscar Charleston's inventory of great plays.

The catches cited here are ones that spectators have said were great catches, some greater than anything else the viewers had seen. As will be evident, the view of "greatest" is fluid and subject to change even by the same expert witnesses.

A Great Play

A definition of a great play is in order when discussing great catches. Branch Rickey, one of the most fertile minds baseball has ever had, provides a worthy definition. In his book *American Diamonds,* he has a short section titled "The Great Play." Rickey wrote:

> Who can really define a great play among professionals? Is that point that marks greatness somewhere beyond infinity? Or is greatness in the field a relative thing compared to what other players can do? I think it is the supreme effort on a play where the out is made or the score averted on a ball that is on the razor edge of the line of possibility. It is a combination of reflex, chance, speed, control, brains, and sheer ability that succeeds when there is only one way to make a play. Over the years, sometimes when you see such a play you cannot believe it. But you know how great it is and you never forget it [182].

The play has to be one which nobody else, or nearly nobody else, would make. Outfielders without some of the traits Rickey lists can make spectacular plays. However, the plays were spectacular *for them* because they were not expected to make the plays. A number of times the sportswriters noted a "fine" or even a "spectacular" catch by an outfielder known to be relatively slow afoot, or by a fielder who could not jump very high off the ground when leaping for the ball against an outfield fence.

In addition, players with all these traits need the right opportunities to make the catches. This is what Branch Rickey called "chance." Someone has to hit the ball to a place where the impossible becomes a possibility. At times, the field has something about it that makes the catch seem both impossible and possible at the same time. Willie Mays' catch of Vic Wertz's drive in the 1954 World Series occurred in a stadium, the Polo Grounds, which had a deep center field fence. Mays could run full out for a considerable distance. Wertz had to be able to hit a bullet to a deep part of the field, which he did. Many of the fans in the Polo Grounds that day didn't realize that Mays' instant and precise calculations about the ball's trajectory and speed would enable him to make the catch.

"The Greatest"

A major part of the allure of baseball is the possibility that when one goes to a game a fielder will make a wonderful catch. This frequently happens. Once in a lifetime of attending games, a fan might see a catch that will be far greater than any other he or she has ever seen.

The words "the greatest" are, or should be, the ultimate compliment for a person or for a person's achievement, just as the words "the fastest" or the "strongest" indicate the ultimate for other achievements. Whereas the words "the fastest" and "the strongest" are quantifiable and usually can be readily validated across time, "the greatest" is much more subjective. Debates about who is the greatest player of all time, and what was the greatest this or that in each sport, will go on and on. In this book, the contention is that there have been some catches in baseball that are transcendent, and that are therefore among "the greatest."

As will be evident, there is a wide range of opinion across the years. Since many people quoted are experts, one must take their words seriously. When people who have been connected with baseball for decades say a catch or play was the greatest they ever saw, then we know these men are comparing that particular catch with catches made by hundreds of outfielders in thousands of games across decades. A person who has been watching thousands of games for thirty or forty or fifty years and who declares a catch to be "the greatest" is someone whose opinion is to be highly valued.

Photography

The photographic equipment necessary to take pictures of outfielders in the act of making catches in games was available at least as far back as the second decade of the twentieth century. Whether it was too costly to have photographers use such equipment or whether it was not a priority with the sports photo editors at the newspapers, it appears that it was not until 1942 that a picture of a major league outfielder in the act making a catch was taken and shown widely. An Associated Press wire photo of the Yankees' Charlie Keller robbing the St. Louis Cardinals' Terry Moore of a home run in the fourth game of the 1942 World Series may be the first photograph showing an in-game catch by an outfielder.

Today a great catch can be seen over and over because games are televised and videotaped. Since the advent of videotape technology there have been many great catches caught on tape. However, almost none of them have been as memorable to as many fans as the catch and throw Willie Mays made in the 1954 World Series on the Indians' Vic Wertz's long shot. Even though fans have left ballparks buzzing about catches Paul Blair, Garry Maddox, Devon White, Jim Edmonds, Kenny Lofton, Torii Hunter, Ken Griffey Jr., Andruw Jones, Grady Sizemore, or Coco Crisp and other more recent outstanding outfielders have made, few, if any, of these catches have received the attention and accolades that Mays' catch and throw against the Indians received.

In 1954, regular season games usually were televised on weekends and holidays and were shown on the stations in the cities that had the major league franchises. There were few permanent photographic records of the regular season games that were televised. The All Star game and the World Series games received the kind of attention that would yield a permanent record. But before 1954 and for many years thereafter, most great catches in regular season games did not get photographed.

Prior to the advent of games presented on television, and especially with the development of videotaping technology, only people at the ballpark would see a great outfield play when it occurred. Vivid accounts by radio sportscasters could give radio listeners a good idea of a great play. The most consistent accounts about the great catches prior to the age of videotape were those from baseball writers for newspapers. Videotape, and the boom in daily sports shows featuring replays from every game played, now enable tens of millions of viewers the opportunity to see great fielding feats.

Beginning with the 1949 World Series, photographers with telephoto lenses began to capture outfield action more purposefully. From 1942 to 1948, other than Charlie Keller's catch in the 1942 Series, the only World Series catch of significance that has appeared in pictures was Al Gionfriddo's catch of Joe DiMaggio's long drive in 1947, even though there were a number of other outstanding catches by outfielders in the World Series of those years.

In the 1949 Series' last game, the Brooklyn Dodgers' Duke Snider made two outstanding catches on the Yankees' Joe DiMaggio, one leaping at the fence and one running in. Photos of both appeared in the newspapers. After 1949, some photographers who covered the games for the major newspapers and wire services became skilled at getting photos of fielders at critical moments. One of those skilled men was Ernest Sisto of the *New York Times*, who was a pioneer in capturing the dramatic shot of an outfielder at the moment the ball was caught. Despite the skills of Sisto and a number of his colleagues, most of the great catches during regular season games between 1950 and 1964 were not photographed. If outfielders were fortunate enough to get in World Series games from 1949 on, then there was a good chance their great catches would be photographed.

Even after photographers began to take outfield shots during regular season games, a single shot usually did not do justice to the totality of a great play. Such a play is a series of actions and reactions that single shots cannot usually capture: the outfielder's reaction to the ball as it leaves the bat, as the ball is in the air, as the fielder is running, as the ball descends, as the outfielder prepares to catch it, as he actually makes the catch, and as he throws the ball in. This sequence is best caught with motion picture cameras focused on that fielder and on the ball. The sequence of still photographs showing Willie Mays' great catch in the 1954 World Series helps make the catch, after more than fifty years, the most memorable baseball catch for many fans. However, the film does a better job of conveying the thrill of the chase Willie made to get to the ball.

Sportswriters

The bulk of the information in this book comes from the reports of newspaper writers who gave us many ways to "see" the same great events. Readers will find a wide range of writing styles among the writers. The range in part results from the different backgrounds from which the writers came. Today it is expected that sportswriters attend journalism schools in order to work on newspapers. When baseball began, and for almost a hundred years thereafter, there were many nonacademic routes that could lead to a regular job reporting on baseball and other sports.

Some of the early sportswriters did have college backgrounds. One was William B. Hanna, who, after graduating from Lafayette College in 1878, worked at the *Kansas City Star* in the 1880s before going to New York around 1890. Before 1900 he worked for the *New York World*, the *New York Press*, and the *New York Herald*. He then worked for sixteen years at the *New York Sun*, before returning to the *Herald*. Hanna passed away in 1930.

The *New York Times'* Roscoe McGowen did not have academic credentials. In addition to his chores on the family farm, McGowen began writing for a country weekly in Illinois at the age of 11 in 1897. At 13 he no longer attended school and began working full-time at the country newspaper. After leaving that paper, he worked as railroad telegrapher and a train dispatcher, then a wire operator for the Associated Press and the United Press, and then took a job as an editorial columnist for the *Rock Island* (Illinois) *Argus*. While with the Rock Island paper, he contributed to the *Chicago Tribune*. The *Tribune's* publisher saw those contributions and later hired McGowen to write editorials for the *New*

York Daily News. McGowen also covered the Brooklyn Dodgers for the *Daily News.* He worked for a year for the *Brooklyn Standard* before joining the *New York Times* in 1929. He covered the Brooklyn Dodgers for most of his thirty years at the *Times.*

Sportswriters of the period we are considering varied widely in their attention to fielding. Part of this was due to space limitations of their newspaper. Some newspapers devoted more space to baseball games than did other newspapers, and thus could say more about defensive plays if they were inclined to do so. Baseball writers have been obligated to discuss offensive performances more often than defensive plays. Manufacturing runs is the most essential thing teams do to win games, and baseball writers usually had to tell about how the runs were scored. Thus, they had to be economical in the details they could give about the fielding plays. Many outstanding catches simply did not get mentioned, or if mentioned, were limited to a word, e.g., "spectacular." Some baseball writers routinely made a point of informing their readers about outstanding fielding plays. Other writers included information about great fielding plays only when the plays were pivotal in the games, or if the catches were so spectacular that they could not be omitted. Such spectacular plays defied any usual description and often had to be compared to another great play which old-timers had seen.

Some papers did not publish on Sundays, and on Mondays the writers for these papers tended to discuss the Sunday games more than the Saturday games. Also, for many years before night games were played, some afternoon/evening papers tried to get some results of that afternoon's games, but did not have enough time or space in the paper to do more than give the scores by innings. These papers' baseball writers had to compete against the writers for morning papers who had all the previous afternoon's results in hand, and who had time to do a thorough job. The advent of night baseball reversed this process and put pressure on the writers for morning papers to meet tight deadlines.

The work of these baseball writers enables us to judge the greatness of what players did across the decades. When debates about the greatest centerfielders of all time blossomed in the late 1930s and in the 1950s, there were writers quoting people who had seen the best players in their primes, and writers who had seen and covered the players from the different eras, some from before 1900. The greatness of the catches and plays I cite are based on the descriptions and evaluations the baseball writers put in their newspaper articles and on the descriptions from people the writers quoted. Like many players presented below whose defensive feats should be more widely known, the work of the earlier sportswriters, now mostly forgotten, should be more widely known. This book is a tribute to those writers.

TWO

Ballparks: Disputes, Dimensions, Quirks, and Crashes into Concrete

One advantage that major league outfielders had from about 1910 through 1952 was that they played many games a year in essentially the same seven or eight parks, and did so year in and year out. This gave them a chance to get to know the idiosyncrasies of the turf, the fences, and the distances involved.

The earliest ballparks essentially were imposed on open fields with the spectators standing or sitting around the area designated for the players. As baseball became a popular spectator sport in the 1860s, the parks became enclosed or partially enclosed, and consisted of wooden stands behind home plate and along the first and third base lines, and either standing room or a few rows of bleachers in the outfield. Some late nineteenth-century and early twentieth-century fields still included open areas behind the outfielders so people with horses and carriages could watch the games.

In 1862, Brooklyn's Union Grounds became the first enclosed playing field. After this, it became a logical business move for owners to charge people to get in to watch the games. In 1862, the first admission price at the Union Grounds in Brooklyn was ten cents. Within twenty years of the beginning of the sport, owners began to understand the profits to be made.

The *New York Clipper Annual* for 1891 includes a note telling how the ticket price was used not only to generate profits, but was used to control the size of the crowd.

> The Athletics in 1866 played all the strongest clubs in the country, and were defeated only twice, once by the Atlantics of Brooklyn and once by the Unions of Morrisania. The first game between the Athletics and the Atlantics for the championship took place Oct. 1, 1866, in Philadelphia, the number of people inside and outside the enclosed ground being estimated as high as 30,000, it being the largest attendance known at a baseball game. Inside the inclosure the crowd was immense, and packed so close that there was no room for the players to field. An attempt was, however, made to play the game; but one inning was sufficient to show that it was impossible, and, after a vain attempt to clear the field, both parties reluctantly consented to an adjournment. The postponed game was played Oct. 22, in Philadelphia. The price of tickets was placed at one dollar, and upwards of two thousand people paid this "steep" tariff of admission, the highest ever charged merely for entrance to the grounds, while five or six thousand more witnessed the game from the surrounding embankments. Rain and darkness obliged the umpire to call the game at the end of the seventh inning, the victory remained with the Athletics by the decisive totals of 31 to 12.

Admission charges were also used to reduce the number of unsavory people who came to the games to be disruptive and who prevented others from enjoying the athletic contest. In addition, in the mid–1870s another measure was adopted to keep the nonpaying and the unruly elements out of the park.

The first commercial use of barbed wire, in 1874, was to keep livestock in confined areas. It didn't take baseball owners long to find a use for this new invention. In his book *Diamonds*, Michael Gershman includes the reproduction of a postcard from 1876 promoting the use of barbed wire by owners of baseball clubs to keep nonpaying spectators out of the viewing area. The postcard, sent out by the manufacturers of the wire, shows the barbed wire atop the fence surrounding Boston's South End Grounds. On the reverse side of the postcard is a testimonial from N. F. Apolonio, the president of the "Boston Base Ball Association," attesting to the value of barbed wire in increasing the revenues for the team. At least one other owner followed Mr. Apolonio by installing barbed wire on the top of the outfield fence. In *Ballparks of North America*, Michael Benson noted that in the 1890s the Washington Senators' ballpark had "barbed wire on top of the outfield fence—presumably to keep freeloaders from sitting up there" (407).

Another reason for the use of barbed wire could have been to keep fans off the playing field. In *Where They Ain't*, Burt Solomon wrote about the barbed wire fence at the Washington field in 1897: "Three rows of barbed wire ran across the top, six feet off the ground, to keep the cranks in the bleachers from storming onto the field" (114). As the owners began to build larger stadiums with high walls and tightly controlled entry points, there was no need for barbed wire to keep nonpaying and rowdy people out.

Despite the bowler hats and the suits the men routinely wore, giving them a respectable appearance, many men who began flocking to the games in the 19th century gave a high level of verbal abuse to home team players when they performed poorly, to players for the rival teams, and to umpires whose decisions were perceived to be unfavorable to the home team. It must have been intimidating for the players to have the fans so close to the field, and especially to have essentially no barriers between the fans and the field. In *Ballparks of North America*, Michael Benson comments on the fans' proximity to the field in his discussion of pre–1890s parks. What he wrote could have applied to some parks after the turn of the twentieth century:

> When crowds on the field threatened to overwhelm games, policemen were assigned to keep fans back as far as possible. With no law authority present, fields of play tended to shrink as the game went on. Fans, giving themselves breathing room and a better view, inched closer to the outfielders' backs [253].

In addition to fans encroaching onto the field of play, there were direct threats to players and umpires from the fans. Making a mistake or even a play perceived to be a mistake could lead to taunts and threats from the spectators. Crowd control was a major issue in the early days of baseball.

In 1897, in nearly all games, only one umpire worked the game. Not only did he have to be concerned with the whereabouts and the unruliness of the crowds, he had to be concerned with the whereabouts and the threatening behavior of some players. In addition, the umpire had to try to make decisions on multiple events happening at the same time on the field. His failure to see all the simultaneous events at times led to missed calls that fans and players turned into disputes. There were times when threats from fans passed beyond nasty name-calling and spilled onto the field. For example, on May 15, 1897, the *New York Times* carried a report of a game between Philadelphia and Louisville, which the visiting

Philadelphia club won by a 7 to 1 score. The brief article was titled ATTEMPTED TO MOB UMPIRE, and subtitled "Crowd from Bleachers Break into the Field and Attack Umpire Sheridan." The *Times'* account of the game was as follows:

> Frazer's [Chick Fraser] wildness in the first inning, and the home team's inability to hit Fifield, was the cause of its defeat to-day. Umpire Sheridan made two or three questionable decisions against the Louisville team, and a crowd from the bleachers broke into the field and attempted to mob him during the fourth inning. The police protected him and succeeded in preventing trouble.

Less than three months later, in early August, Sheridan quit umpiring for a while because he could no longer endure the abuse he was taking on the field.

The unidentified writer of the "Notes Of The Game" section in the *New York World*, after the April 30, 1897 game between Baltimore and New York, commented on the behavior of some fans:

> The Baltimore crowds are the unfairest on the National League circuit, with the possible exception of Cincinnati. Hundreds of hoodlums sit on the bleachers and stands and endeavor to outdo each other in foul and abusive attacks on visiting teams. Instead of making an attempt to check this disorderly conduct the policemen seem to encourage it. ...Cincinnati excels in that the ruffians at those grounds go to the extreme of throwing beer glasses.

Some Cincinnati fans had been practicing throwing beer glasses for over a decade. The *New York Times* reported that, in an August 29, 1886, game between Pittsburgh and Cincinnati, "a few hoodlums" were responsible for throwing a dozen beer glasses on to the field to protest the umpire's decision.

The beer glasses in Cincinnati led to an ugly scene involving an umpire during an August 4, 1897, game. The umpire of the game between Cincinnati and Pittsburgh was Tim Hurst, who only three days earlier had punched Cincinnati's catcher, Heinie Peltz, who in turn hit Hurst in the mouth. During the game on August 4, the Cincinnati fans were irate because they felt Hurst had blown a call. A Cincinnati player was running to second base for an apparent double when the Pittsburgh second baseman pulled the Cincinnati runner down. Hurst evidently didn't see the takedown because he called the Cincinnati runner out instead of awarding him second base.

Just after this event, several fans tossed beer glasses onto the field. Hurst felt that one glass landed too close to him, and evidently was intended for him. He picked up a glass and threw it into the stands, hitting a Cincinnati fireman over the right eye and causing a cut that required six stitches to close. Hurst was arrested and charged with assault and battery. Later, as quoted in the August 7, 1897 *Cincinnati Enquirer*, Hurst said he was just throwing the glass back off the field and did not intend to harm any one. Hurst also said, "Umpires have been getting all the worst of it in the West this year, and we have frequently been assaulted."

The *Cincinnati Commercial Tribune* writer on August 5 told about the chief reason beer glasses usually could be found on the field near the stands: "It has been customary for persons sitting on the seats under the grand stand known as 'rooters row' to throw the glasses after they are empty out on the field so that the waiters can collect them without disturbing the crowd during the game."

A number of writers covering major league baseball were disgusted with the way unruliness was interfering with the games and blamed the owners for not taking a stand against the offending behavior. In his August 5, 1897, column, just after the incident involving Hurst, C.W. Zuber of the *Cincinnati Times-Star* summarized the disgust:

Authorities on base ball are getting worked up over the manner in which the game is actually being "fought" out in all that the word implies. Scraps are so numerous that a person having a knowledge of upper cuts, left-hand jabs, punts, ducks, etc., etc., finds more to interest him in ball games than does your genial fan, who knows the good, clean game of base ball alone and can not see why or where pugilism and rowdyism figures in.

The *Cincinnati Enquirer's* unidentified writer also made several comments about the umpiring situation:

It is high time the league was doing something about its umpires. As the system of the big league now stands it is a howling farce. As a sample of its inconsistencies the East now has three umpires, while Tim Hurst is the only regular official west of the Alleghanies. The wild and wooly is left to do the best it can.

Substitute umpires won't do. It is an outrage to ask visiting teams and spectators put up with them.

More money is lost to the game by bad umpires than it would take to bear the expenses of the double umpire system.

The idea of a two-umpire crew at games had been discussed before, but no action had been taken. For example, in an August 11, 1886, letter to the editor of the *New York Times*, "An Onlooker" wrote that two umpires working a game could help bring about an end to the verbal abuse directed at umpires and the need for the umpire to require a police escort to get off the field at the end of the game so as "to escape the violence of a mob." The writer went on to say that the single umpire had more duties to perform in order to manage a game than he could accomplish, and that this inability to simultaneously monitor all the events on the field, and the fans, too, was leading to the widespread disrespect of umpires.

In 1910, even after more than one umpire worked each game, it still was apparent that crowds were affecting the way games were played. In the July 19, 1910, *Boston Traveler*, an evening paper at the time, Harry J. Casey told of that day's crowd for the Red Sox–Detroit Tigers games. He began his article by telling about the crowd:

The record-breaking crowd of the season turned out for a double-header for Detroit and the Speed Boys. President Taylor estimated the crowd at 22,000 and there was [*sic*] fully 3,000 outside of the grounds clamoring for admission. Owing to the large crowd, ropes were stretched across the outfield, and Managers Donovan and Jennings decided that a hit into the crowd would be good for two bases.

As he described the inning-by-inning events, Casey started the Red Sox half of the second inning with:

The crowd had increased so that play was held up while the police and the players, the latter armed with baseball bats, tried to keep the fans from crowding the playing space. The players with both teams were forced out of their dugouts and had to sit along the baselines. More police were sent for. For a few minutes the crowd refused to give way, but when they saw that there would be no more baseball unless they gave the players more room, they edged back a few feet. The players got a long rope, and by tieing [*sic*] one end to a post and pulling at the other end, managed to get the crowd back a little.

The doubleheader was played at the Huntington Avenue Baseball Grounds, where the Red Sox played until the end of the 1911 season. When the ballpark opened in 1901, its capacity was 9,000. In the third game of the 1903 World Series at the Huntington Grounds, overcrowding had a similar effect on the ability of the players to play. In the seven years after 1903 Red Sox officials had learned little about how to control the size of the crowds.

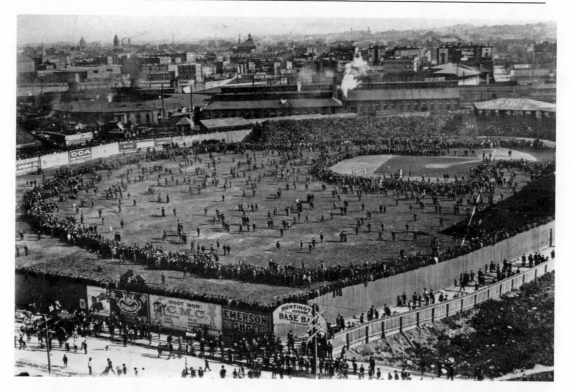

This photograph, taken before game three of the 1903 World Series between the Red Sox and Pittsburgh at Boston's Huntington Avenue Baseball Grounds, shows one of the most extreme examples of a lack of crowd control. In a stadium designed for 9,000 fans, well over 20,000, many of whom did not pay to get in, overwhelmed the security people. Fans were standing just off the foul lines and just behind the outfielders' backs even though the crowd pushed in the outfield distances several hundred feet.

Even some of the ballparks built from 1909 to 1915 continued to host games in which fans essentially were sitting or standing on the outfield grass and in front of the outfield walls. Policemen standing just in front of the fans acted as crowd control agents. This was especially the case for World Series games, when either temporary seating was put in the outfield area, or extra thousands were allowed to stand in what, during the regular season, was the perimeter of the outfield. As had been the case for many years, these additional areas for fans not only considerably shrunk the area of the playing field, but also put potentially volatile fans nearer to the players.

Outfield Distances and Quirks

Twelve major league parks were built between 1909 and 1915. Most of these parks had very generous outfield dimensions. The oddly shaped Polo Grounds, opened in 1911, was the exception, due to its short left and right field lines. At most of the other parks, even hitting down the lines, a batter had to be powerful to hit a ball out in fair territory. In some parks, like the Polo Grounds and Forbes Field, parts other than center field also had the long distances. For example, the longest point from home plate in Forbes Field was left of center field, a distance of 462 feet in 1909 and 457 feet later.

Ebbets Field's original center field distance is the most incongruous compared to what it was in its last several decades. Left field shrank from an original distance of 419 feet when the park opened in 1913, to 384 feet in 1931, and ended at 348 feet in 1957. What began in 1913 as a difficult park to drive a ball out of became a good park for hitters by the 1940s.

Philadelphia's Shibe Park's center field distance from home plate was 515 feet when the park opened in 1909, and fluctuated between 447 feet and 468 feet for most of the years it was used. The 1909 distance to center at Shibe Park was a short poke compared to the 550 feet to the deepest corner of center field at Braves Field when it opened in 1915. Even more impressive at Boston's Braves Field were the distances down the left and right field foul lines, both at 402 feet. The long distances encouraged inside-the-park home runs in 1915, and, to be sure, it was an exciting thing see. In 1921, thirty-eight home runs were hit at Braves Field the entire year, and thirty-four of them were inside the park home runs. In that same year Babe Ruth himself hit a record fifty-nine home runs, not one of them being an inside the park homer.

As was the case in other parks built before 1916, the outfield distances at Braves Field also became shorter. Evidently, in the late 1920s the Braves' owners finally conceded that the home runs sailing out of the other major league parks was something fans would want to see at Braves Field too. In 1928 the distance down the left field line became 320 feet, and the distance down the right field line became 364 feet. It wasn't until 1941 that the long distance in center field dropped to 401 feet.

Special mention should be made of the Polo Grounds, as it was there that a number of the greatest catches were made. The outfield distances went to extremes. During its history, the left field line extended 279 feet from home plate. The second deck down the left field foul line jutted out over the field and was only 250 feet away. The right field line was a similar case, with the distance across most of the stadium's history being just under 258 feet. The distances curved dramatically outward so that the onfield, in-play bullpen in left center field was about 450 feet out, and the bullpen in right center was about 445 feet away from the plate. Center field had an extension past the curve of the rest of the outfield. The back part of that extension was at times as far as 505 feet, though during Willie Mays' time as a New York Giant from 1951 through the 1957 season it was usually between 480 and 483 feet.

The extended center field area included the steps up to each team's second story clubhouse. The steps were in play and were located along the side walls to the left and right of straightaway center field. From 1921 on, the Eddie Grant Memorial was situated just in front of the wall in straightaway center field. It was a monument dedicated to a former Giants ballplayer who was the first major league ballplayer killed in World War I. The Grant Memorial monument was a granite slab resting on a concrete base. On the granite slab was a bronze plaque with information about Eddie Grant. The monument was five feet tall, and the slab was about thirty inches across. In the history of the Polo Grounds, no one ever hit a ball out of the playing field in dead center. Balls were hit to the steps to the clubhouses, to the Eddie Grant Memorial, and very near the wall in straightaway center. Philip Lowry, in *Green Cathedrals*, mentions the different dips and rises in the outfield at the Polo Grounds. He wrote, "the outfield was slightly sunken. A manager standing in his dugout, could only see the top half of his outfielders. At the wall, the field was 8 feet below the infield" (198).

Most of the parks built from 1909 through the mid–1920s had some unusual outfield features that made them tricky for the fielders to play. Even in symmetrically drawn parks, the fence heights, the fence compositions, the placement of scoreboards, the placement of flagpoles on the fields near the center field fence, and the placement of fan seating varied and had a bearing on the play of the outfielders.

Even fans seated outside of the stadium dramatically changed the tasks of hitters and fielders in at least one major league ballpark. The Philadelphia Athletics' management grew tired of the owners of the two-story row houses across the street from Shibe Park's 12-foot right-field wall allowing hundreds of fans to view the games from their windows and roofs. Especially during the World Series in which the A's played, the windows and roofs of those residences were filled with fans who may have had better seats than did some of the paying customers. In 1935, after enduring the rooftop viewers for 26 years, the A's built the wall up to 34 feet and eliminated the rooftop views of the field. The new fence, called the "spite fence" by the former rooftop fans across the street, fence changed the way batters approached right and right center field, and outfielders now had to play balls off the sections of angled corrugated metal of which the fence was constructed.

At Ebbets Field, from right center through right field, there was a 38-foot tall-wall of different angles and materials that led to caroms coming off at many unusual angles. The bottom half of the wall was concave, with the bend being at the nine-and-a-half-foot point. The bottom half was made of concrete. The top half was a nineteen-foot screen. This wall was complicated in 1932 by the addition of a scoreboard that was about 50 feet wide by 35 feet tall; it jutted out five feet from the wall and had its left and right sides angled at 45 degrees. Part of the Dodgers' success in the late 1940s through the mid–1950s was due to the ability of their right fielder Carl Furillo and centerfielder Duke Snider to master the intricacies of their parts of that wall. Furillo's magnificent throwing arm and his precise knowledge of the angles at which balls were likely to come off the wall intimidated many National League batters from taking more than a single on balls hit off the wall in right field or in right center.

At Crosley Field in Cincinnati, there was an upward slope that rose four feet over the last fifteen to twenty feet to the outfield fence. This steep angle made the outfield a picturesque one for fans. However, for outfielders moving toward the wall trying to make a catch, the area could be a tricky one. The incline at Crosley Field also could serve as a warning to the outfielder that he was nearing the fence. Until the widespread adoption of warning tracks near the outfield fences in the late 1940s, outfielders had to depend on knowing where they were, or on another outfielder yelling and warning them that they were nearing the fence in their pursuit of the ball.

Concrete Walls and Crashes: Earle Combs, Terry Moore, and Pete Reiser

In contrast to the expansive center field areas in the Polo Grounds, Forbes Field and Yankee Stadium were the more compact center field areas in other ballparks. For many years players for the St. Louis teams, the Brooklyn Dodgers, the Chicago Cubs, and the Cincinnati Redlegs had to be concerned with the location of the fences as they pursued fly balls. In Brooklyn, the longest distance was 393 feet to the center field wall. In Chicago's Wrigley Field, the ivy-covered center field wall was 400 feet away. At Cincinnati's Crosley Field, the longest distance, off to the right of center field, was 387 feet.

The smaller fields constrained many outfielders who might have been making great running play after great running play on balls hit behind them but had to stop and watch balls fly over the fence. Outfielders had to learn the distances and gauge the speed and arc

After years of seeing thousands of nonpaying rooftop fans across the street from the 12-foot-high right field fence at Shibe Park, the Philadelphia A's owners, in 1935, built the fence to 34 feet tall. The new fence not only prevented the rooftop fans from seeing the games, it also changed how outfielders played their position as balls came careening off the angles of the corrugated metal that faced the upper part of the new fence.

of the batted ball so they would not collide with the walls, especially in the year after a park's outfield dimensions were shortened. Most outfielders learned to stop short of the walls, and learned when and how to play balls off the walls. Others learned to vault up the walls to catch balls well above their heads.

Many ballparks completed after 1908 had outfield walls made of concrete. The failure of outfielders to know where they were in relation to the concrete wall could have tragic consequences. Some players had frightening collisions with walls. Three outstanding players were among the victims of such collisions.

Due to a collision with an unforgiving concrete outfield wall, Earle Combs's career was essentially ended. Thirty-three years old at the time of the crash, Combs had been a member of one of the greatest outfields in baseball history. Flanked by Bob Meusel in right field and Babe Ruth in left field, Combs had been a speedy ball hawk who made many wonderful catches. Several of those catches occurred in one game, as Harry Cross of the *New York Times* noted in his account of the July 12, 1925, Yankees–White Sox game in Chicago, which Chicago won 3 to 0. Cross wove the fielding of Combs into his colorful description of the game's key events:

Teddy Lyons, an estimable young man from Texas, gave the Yanks a whitewash shower this afternoon, embarrassing Miller Huggins's carefree lads by a score of 3 to 0. Some 32,000 Middlewesterners sat in at the pitching picnic and approved of every ball that Teddy chucked. Five hits was the sum total of safe hits the Yank bats produced, and the hitting ambitions of Ruth, Meusel, Gehrig and the other sluggers were held in check.

Standing out among the few noteworthy things the New Yorkers did was the versatility of Earl [*sic*] Combs, the Tennessee school teacher, in centre field. Earl covered the middle terrace like a heavy dew and made catches off Kamm, Lyons and Falk which smacked of the uncanny. He had eight putouts, and not one was a cinch.

Sam Jones did the deceiving for the Yanks and made the Sox behave fairly well except in the fourth, when a single by Manager Collins and doubles by Hooper and Schalk eased a couple of runs over. The other unit came in the fifth on a perfect squeeze by Mostil and Collins.

The tossing contribution of Lyons was close to being a work of art. In no inning did two hits dovetail. He kept the hits wider apart that a couple of enemies. The only serious bruise to his service was promulgated by Combs, who helped himself to a couple of two-baggers.

Pee Wee Wanninger was the only Manhattan citizen who got a chance to see what third base looked like. In the third, he singled, went to second on Jones' sacrifice and arrived at the third corner on Dugan's grounder to third. Pier No. 3 was a dark secret to the other Yanks and they kept away as if it was quarantined.

The first big moment of the game came in the opening session, when Ruth arrived at the bat. The moment was not furnished by the Babe, however, but by Earl Sheely, who took his life in his hands to stop a bullet-drive from the Bambino's club. He stopped the ball, but how he retained all of his anatomy is a mystery. He not only corralled the ball but also got Ruth out in the bargain.

Earl Combs emblazoned the second inning with a highly sensational catch of Willie Kamm's Texas Leaguer. He ran a whole city block to nab the ball and nabbed it on the end of his index digit. It furnished the third out of the inning and was deeply disappointing to Bib Falk, who was on third impatient to score.

The Sox became alarmingly active in the fourth. Eddie Collins instigated the uprising by shooting a single to left and Sheely, trying to bunt, popped to Bengough. After Falk died at first Harry Hooper doubled to right, pushing Collins over. Kamm drew a ticket and Schalk punched a double along the left field foul line, scoring Hooper. Ted Lyons ended the bad news by hoisting a fly to Combs.

The Sox concocted a gorgeous squeeze play in the fifth. Mostil doubled to left and traveled to third on Davis's sacrifice. With Collins at the bat Mostil came tearing down the third base line as Jones was serving the ball, and Eddie lightly tapped it and Mostil romped over, Collins succumbing, Jones to Gehrig. A great play, the squeeze, when it works like that.

Baseball clubs which can win ballgames are no novelty in the national diversion, but few clubs can lose 'em so artistically as the Yanks.

It's worth going miles to see a boy like Combs perform. No matter what the rest of them are doing Earl is playing ball every minute from the first to the twenty-seventh putout.

Diminutive Benny Bengough has been doing a lot of fancy catching. Two foul tips collided in no gentle manner with the big toe on Benny's left pedal today and he hopped around on one foot like a flamingo.

Earl Sheely, who stopped Ruth's hard-hit ball in the first inning, was the White Sox's first baseman.

In an article devoted mostly to Combs the day after the game Harry Cross reported on, the unnamed writer for the *New York Telegram* wrote, "and so much was talked yesterday about Master Combs. That chap ... made eight catches in yesterday's game. Three were made in such a way that the fans were excited to the wildest kind of cheering."

Almost two years later, on May 17, 1927, in a game in which the Yankees defeated the Tigers in Detroit, Combs made yet another sensational catch of a long drive to deep center

field by Bob Fothergill. The next day the *New York Times'* James R. Harrison wrote of Combs' catch, "crash, not to say, wham! But Combs dashed back, stuck up his glove beyond his right shoulder, and made one of the dizziest catches ever seen in these or any parts."

In his book *Murderer's Row*, G.H. Fleming cited James R. Harrison's comments about Combs's catch on Fothergill and then parenthetically added, "No outfielder covered ground faster and better than Combs, who was sometimes called 'the Kentucky greyhound' and could run a hundred yards while wearing a baseball uniform in ten seconds flat" (149).

Combs had begun to slow down a bit by 1934. He was shifted to left field early in the season and Ben Chapman took over the center field position. The still speedy Combs was playing left field on July 24, 1934, not center field as he had played nearly all his years as a Yankee. On that

Along with outfield mates Babe Ruth and Bob Meusel, centerfielder Earle Combs was part of one of the best outfield trios in the history of baseball. In 1934, late in his career, the speedy Combs ran with great force into the concrete outfield wall in St. Louis.

day, Combs uncharacteristically lost track of where he was in relation to the concrete outfield wall in St. Louis. The *New York Sun's* James M. Kahn devoted most of his article to the collision and its aftermath:

His brilliant career ended for the season, and possibly forever, Earle Combs, the Yankee veteran outfielder, lay in dangerous condition in St. John's Hospital here today with a fractured skull and a broken collarbone, suffered in the seventh inning of yesterday's game with the Browns. Running at full speed, he crashed into the concrete wall which fronts the left field bleachers at Sportsman's Park. Unsparing, as always, of his efforts to win, he was trying to spear Harlan Clift's triple, which decided the game in favor of the Browns.

In thus ending a decade of major league service, which placed him among the best outfielders of all time, the silver-thatched Kentuckian completed a cycle. In 1924, he began his career calamitously by breaking his ankle trying to score the winning run in a game with the Indians in Cleveland. In trying to save yesterday's game, he finished his fine service even more disastrously. Dr. Robert F. Hyland, St. Louis Surgeon and club physician of the Cardinals and the Browns, in whose care Combs has been placed, doubts that Earle will ever play ball again. Certainly any possibility of his playing again this season is out of the question. He will have to remain in St. John's Hospital indefinitely, since he is a condition too serious to be moved.

Though knocked unconscious by his headlong crash into the concrete barrier, Combs regained his senses after being borne into the Yankee clubhouse by his team mates, and had not relapsed into a coma upon being removed to the hospital. This was pointed out as a favorable sign in the outfielder's condition by Dr. Hyland, who said that the greatest danger in retarding the complete recovery of Combs lay in the possibility of a hemorrhage following the fracture. His injury was described as a linear fracture of the left temporal bone, which is that region on the left side of the head, between the ear and the forehead.

The seriousness of Combs' injury was immediately apparent from the time he crashed into the wall. Every eye in the park was riveted on him, for the play marked the turning point in the ball game. Leading by the scant margin of 2 to 1 as the Browns came up in their half of the seventh, the Yanks saw their lead threatened by successive passes to Strange and pinch-hitter Garms, batting in place of George Blacholder. With the temperature at 110.2, the hottest day in St. Louis history, Johnny Murphy was wobbling about in the pitcher's box having difficulty in finding the plate. Clift, who followed Garms, worked the count to 3 and 2, and then banged the "cripple" in an arching line straight for the left center field wall.

Just as straight, Combs turned and sprinted after the drive in a desperate and reckless try for a catch. Since he was running from left field toward center, he did not have his head turned directly toward the wall, but ran toward it at an angle. Running as hard as he could go, he crashed into the concrete with his left side, his upraised gloved hand just meeting the ball as it hit the wall and bounded back into the playing field.

The impact flung Combs back on the grass, where he lay motionless. It was evident that he was seriously hurt. With Strange and Garms running around the bases and Clift pounding after them, Ben Chapman, who had been drawn over on the play, retrieved the ball and flung it to Jack Saltzgaver at third base to hold Clift from scoring. Then he dashed over to his team mate and was immediately joined by players from both clubs. A group of players carried Combs into the Yankee clubhouse. Dr. Leo Bartels, who was watching the game from the stands, hurried into the clubhouse, where, after about five minutes, the silver-haired veteran came to.

Combs regained consciousness, groaning about the pain in his left shoulder. He had no recognition of what had happened and kept asking his team mates, who stood about fanning him with towels, what had happened. He had no idea of what inning it was, who had hit the ball or that he had banged into the wall. He continued to complain about his shoulder and about his knee, which were badly scraped and bruised from the contact with the wall. He did not complain about his head, and it was first thought that a possible broken shoulder as the worst of his injuries.

His shoulder was so painful that he could not slip out of his uniform shirt, which was cut off him. He was removed in an ambulance to St. John's Hospital, where X-ray pictures, taken last night, and a more thorough examination disclosed the true nature of his injuries.

The accident to Combs cast a pall over the Yankees which had them walking about their hotel today like men in a daze. A modest, even-tempered fellow, with a cheerful, unquenchable spirit, Combs has been the most popular man on the club with his team mates. Both Miller Huggins, his first manager, and Joe McCarthy, who developed Combs in Louisville and sold him to the Yankees in 1923 for $50,000, had on innumerable occasions called him the player with the "greatest disposition" in baseball. He always played the game out to the last notch, a characteristic which led to his tragic accident.

Manager McCarthy, Babe Ruth and most of the players spent hours at the hospital last night. There was nothing they could do, but they hung around the quiet, darkened halls with the pathetic futility of people who want to help in a helpless situation. The Babe was deeply moved and mumbled, "Well, that's the end of the Yankees."

In the next day's *New York Times*, in an uncredited article, it was noted that Combs's condition still was critical, and that he was resting comfortably. The hemorrhaging he had overnight had subsided. Thus, an operation to deal with the hemorrhaging was unnecessary.

Dan Daniel, sportswriter for the *New York World-Telegram*, admired the playing ability of centerfielder Combs. Daniel had written that Combs was the best centerfielder in the history of the Yankees' franchise. Daniel was in St. Louis the day Combs collided with the wall. He described what the doctors were doing for Combs, the collision, and tried to explain what might have contributed to Combs crash. Among other things, Daniel wrote:

> Baseball has seen many bad accidents, but none quite like that which laid Combs low yesterday. Other outfielders have crashed into walls and fences. But none came into a collision with the speed, utter abandon and unseeing eagerness which carried the New York star into the concrete at Sportsman's Park.
>
> Contributing factors in the accident were the newness of left field duties to Combs, who for ten years played only in the more expansive and protected areas in center, and the terrific heat.

Dan Daniel did not pursue either of those topics further in that article. However, in his "Daniel's Dope" column of the same day he did talk about the heat:

> It was ridiculous to play baseball yesterday. It was bad enough on Monday, when the official temperature was 109. But yesterday St. Louis set a new record of 110.2, and in the Yankees dugout it was as hot as it ever could be in the tropical jungles of Africa.
>
> True enough, major league baseball players are athletes and should be in shape to play under all conditions. But, the withering heat yesterday simply defied human effort, and the game should have been postponed.
>
> The local club had no precedent for such action, as no contest ever had been called off on account of excessive heat. But that was the time to set a precedent.
>
> Baseball is serious business, especially for those who play it in the majors, and those who pay the salaries. But it is not so serious that it must be played in temperatures which invite trouble.

Just before he gave his thoughts about the extreme temperature, Daniel wrote about Combs's collision:

> No accident ever suffered by a member of the Yankees was so severe as that which claimed Combs.
>
> The New York club had had its share of broken legs and of minor mishaps. But to see a man with Combs' speed crash into concrete the way he did makes one go cold.
>
> It was a miserable climax to a miserable trip, marked by defeats and terrific heat.

In 1935, Earle Combs did come back to play in 89 games, and hit .282. He retired after the 1935 year. He was a career .325 hitter.

Four years after Combs charged into the wall in St. Louis, the St. Louis Cardinals' Terry Moore, one the best centerfielders of all time, lost track of where he was on the same field. The *New York Times*' John Drebinger described Moore's crash in a game against the New York Giants on June 11, 1938, which ended in a 2 to 2 tie due to rain in the ninth inning. In the sixth inning, Alex Kampouris sent a high blast to left center field that Moore sprinted to get. Drebinger wrote of the result, "Ball and runner smashed into the wall simultaneously. The mishap occurred a few feet from where Earle Combs, Yankee outfielder, suffered a skull fracture three years ago." Terry Moore was taken to the hospital and was found to have had a concussion. He recovered from his bout with the wall and continued to play at a high level for years to come.

Earle Combs was voted into the Hall of Fame in 1970. Terry Moore learned from his crash into the wall in St. Louis and continued to have a very productive major league career. Moore made an inventive catch in 1941 that showed he had learned how to approach concrete walls to make a catch.

Unlike Earle Combs, Pete Reiser will not be voted into the Hall of Fame. Reiser, an extraordinarily talented player, had his career shortened by perhaps the most injuries and illnesses ever to beset a major league player. These injuries and illnesses took an enormous toll on his body. Several of the worst injuries were caused by Reiser's collisions with concrete walls. Over Reiser's years in Brooklyn several New York writers chronicled his exploits as a wonderful player and his injuries and illnesses. The *New York Times'* Roscoe McGowen was especially attentive to Reiser's physical state, and many of his updates follow.

Even in his first full, and spectacular, 1941 season, Reiser was often injured. After the first day of training camp on February 15, 1941, the *New York Times'* Roscoe McGowen indicated his concern about Reiser's physical state: "Like Mel Ott of the Giants, Reiser must take extra precautions against charley horses, so he has been ordered to moderate his running and be careful about quick starts and stops for some time." Less than three weeks later, on March 4, Reiser sprained his ankle. According to McGowen, while doing a drill on a cut-off play, "young Pete Reiser dashed up the steep incline leading to the clubhouse, stepped on a loose rock and turned his right ankle."

In one of the last exhibition season games, on April 10 in Wilmington, Delaware, against the Yankees, Reiser pulled a muscle in his side while fouling off a ball, and had to leave the game. On April 23, he was hit on the cheekbone by the Phillies' Ike Pearson, and was supposed to be out of action for two weeks. This beaning followed the very serious beanings the Dodgers' Ducky Medwick and Pee Wee Reese had absorbed in 1940.

On May 8, 1941, while making a catch of a ball hit by the St. Louis Cardinals' Enos Slaughter, Reiser was temporarily dazed after running into the metal gate in center field in Ebbets Field. He had to leave the game. On June 15, Reiser sprained his ankle sprinting to first trying to beat out a hot smash he had hit to the first baseman. On August 4, Durocher did not play Reiser because Reiser had flare-up of his sciatic nerve in his right hip. He then went into the hospital for several days because of the sciatic nerve problem. On August 10, after getting back into the lineup, Reiser and two of his teammates were hit within two innings by the Boston Braves' relief pitcher Richard Merriwell Errickson. Reiser and his teammate Dolph Camilli were hit in the head, but the damage was not as bad as it could have been because they were wearing protective helmets in their hats.

On September 10, Pete had an aching right wrist. Since he had trouble swinging the bat, he was replaced in the first game of the doubleheader against the Chicago Cubs. On September 27, while throwing a ball from the outfield to home plate during practice before the game against the Phillies, Reiser felt something snap in his elbow, and was rushed to the clubhouse for an examination. No serious injury was found.

All these things went wrong, yet 1941 was Reiser's greatest year by far. At age 22, he won the National League batting crown with a .343 average, and led the league in slugging percentage, doubles, triples, and runs scored. He led the Dodgers to the National League pennant.

The next year, 1942, was to be pivotal in Reiser's career. In late May, he was out of action for more than a week with a wrenched muscle in his side. On June 2, he was five-for-five at the plate against the Pirates. After his last hit, he bruised his left instep when he stepped on catcher Al Lopez's mask as he raced for home on an infield grounder. In an article dated July 3, 1942, the *New York Post's* Jerry Mitchell expressed optimism about Pete Reiser's year. The title of the article was "Reiser Is Exception To Second-Year Jinx." Although Mitchell's text about Reiser continued the optimistic outlook, there still was one injury to report:

> Just as surely as the Dodgers seem on their way to a second pennant in succession, so does one of the best of them—Pete Reiser—appear to be headed for his second straight batting championship.

Reiser's average as he faced the happy prospect of hitting against Philadelphia pitching in today's single game and tomorrow's two, was a robust .348-best in the league.

Out of the order because of a damaged wrist when the Dodgers dropped in here for a night game last Monday, and used only briefly in Tuesday's game with the Braves, he's able and ready to continue his attempt to win the batting title all over again.

The kind of jinx that routinely beset Reiser was of a different variety than Jerry Mitchell had in mind. In 1942 Reiser's jinx had little to do with being bested by wily pitchers who discovered his weaknesses, but instead had almost everything to do with being prone to injury and with his failure to monitor the location of his body in confined spaces. An example of his proneness to injury was apparent when Reiser hit himself in the right ankle with a bat at the 1942 All Star game.

The major blow to his career occurred on July 19 in St. Louis. Martin J. Haley of the *St. Louis Globe-Democrat* described how the injury occurred:

> A highly dramatic finish ended the nightcap when Enos Slaughter, leading off the last part of the second overtime round, hit a tremendous home run inside the park to right center.
>
> Brooklyn's centerfielder, the St. Louis boy, Pete Reiser, last year's National League batting champion, made a spectacular effort to snare the far-flung drive but failed.
>
> Racing far back at top speed, all unmindful of the wall, Reiser stretched high and grabbed the ball with his glove at the 405-foot mark, but just as it appeared as if he made a clean catch, the back of his head struck the concrete a fearful blow.
>
> The impact caused his arm to strike the wall forcing the ball out of his glove and across the turf toward the flag pole.
>
> Although dazed by the collision, Reiser, after staggering several steps, rushed after the leather and started a relay toward the plate, but Slaughter beat it home for his seventh circuit clout of the season.
>
> Immediately the fans swarmed onto the field, and as other spectators started a cushion barrage into center field, Right Fielder Stanley Bordagaray of the Dodgers rushed to Reiser's side and held Pete up. Other Dodgers also hurried to the scene, and they led Pete off the field through thousands of spectators.
>
> After a brief rest and first aid treatment in the Brooklyn dressing quarters, Reiser was removed in an ambulance to St. John's Hospital for X-ray and further treatment.

Elsewhere in the *Globe-Democrat*'s sports pages was a note about Reiser having been diagnosed with a brain concussion after his collision with the wall.

In his article about the game, James M. Gould of the *St. Louis Post-Dispatch* wrote about the impact of the Reiser injury on the pennant race that year, a race in which the Cardinals were a contender to supplant the Dodgers as the National League champions:

> As a result of the three victories for Southworth's men, the Dodgers' lead has been cut to six games—a margin not impossible to overcome with more than 60 games remaining on the schedule. Moreover, Slaughter's homer may have done more to hurt the Dodgers' chances than just a defeat, for Pete Reiser, the best of Brooklyn's hitters and tops in the National League, may be lost for a while.
>
> Reiser made a gallant try for Slaughter's long wallop almost to the 422-foot mark in center. The ball landed in Pete's glove just as he crashed into the wall. Reiser staggered a bit, but made the relay in to Reese, who threw to the plate, but too late to get Slaughter. Brooklyn players rushed out to help him and he walked off the field under his own power, but it was decided to send him to a hospital where X-rays could be taken to determine the extent of his injuries.
>
> The loss of Reiser just at this stage of the race might make all the difference between a flag and second-place money for the Dodgers.

Pete Reiser was one of the most gifted baseball players ever, but repeated injuries and bad decisions on the baseball field prevented him from realizing his true potential.

Gould's predictions were correct. The Cardinals went on to have an outstanding season, and passed the Dodgers on the way to National League and World Series championships. The Cardinals won 106 games, just two more than the Dodgers. The 104 wins for the Dodgers was an amazing total given that Reiser was a shell of himself as a player after pounding into the concrete wall.

Tom Meany, in a 1942 *Saturday Evening Post* article (condensed and reprinted in the July 1946 *Baseball Digest*), wrote that Joe Medwick, who was the left fielder when Reiser crashed into the wall, said that if Pete had held on to the ball it would have been the greatest catch he had ever seen. Medwick played next to Terry Moore in St. Louis from Moore's rookie year in 1935 until early in the 1940 season, when Medwick was traded to the Dodgers. He had seen centerfielder Moore make many remarkable catches, including a spectacular bare hand catch in 1936.

On August 4, Reiser was out with an upset stomach. On August 5 the *New York Times'* Louis Effrat reported that Reiser had sat out another game, writing, "This time ... it was a headache. It seems that Reiser still gets dizzy spells, a reaction of his collision with the concrete wall at St. Louis recently." The next day, McGowen noted that Reiser had missed three straight games and that the Dodgers were worried about his condition. On August 7, McGowen gave an update of the aftermath of Reiser's collision: "Pistol Pete Reiser's indisposition apparently is more serious than first thought. Secretary John McDonald advised that Reiser 'who has been suffering headaches and nausea, has been under the care of Dr. Charles Weeth, Brooklyn physician, and probably will be out of uniform for a few days.'"

Reiser returned to the lineup by mid–August, and was nearly hurt in a pre-game warm-up on August 18. According to McGowen, "Medwick, trying his hand at hitting fungoes alongside Chuck Dressen before the game, missed beaning Reiser, who was working out around third base, by a hair. 'Take that bat away from him, Charley,' yelled Durocher, 'before he does hit him.'"

On August 22, Reiser made a circus catch in the second inning. Later in the game he was replaced because he had a bad leg. Just six days later, he had to be replaced in the second inning because he was ill. The next day the *Times'* McGowen wrote that Leo Durocher was going to rest Reiser for several days because he was obviously not well and he was playing poorly. McGowen gave Reiser's assessment: "Pete said his injury, which occurred 'about two weeks ago,' causes a pain that starts just inside his left thigh and runs clear up into his left side." The next day the Dodgers sent Reiser to Johns Hopkins Hospital for at least two days so he could get a check-up for his pulled leg muscle. Reiser did get back in the Dodgers' line-up after several days, but his woes at the plate continued. On September 28, Roscoe McGowen noted in the *Times* that Reiser had not had a hit in his last 14 times up.

Before he was hurt chasing the Slaughter drive, Reiser was headed toward an even better year than his impressive 1941 year. He was hitting .383 before the crash in St. Louis, and hit .200 over the last two months to finish at .310. His fielding also suffered, as he had blurry vision and was dizzy at times. Reiser, along with almost everyone else, including team officials and physicians, did not fully understand, or want to understand, the seriousness of the injury suffered in St. Louis.

Although no one would know it in the days and months that followed the collision with the concrete wall in St. Louis in 1942, Reiser was never to return to the consistently spectacular form he had displayed in 1941 and into July of 1942. His career was far from over, and he still made occasional plays in the field, at bat, and on the bases that showed how extraordinary a player he was. Periodically he gave his managers, coaches and teammates hope that he would be the one to lead them to championships.

Pete Reiser was in the Army from 1943 through 1945. Reiser's injury woes as a ball player continued in the service. Playing a game during this period, while chasing a foul fly ball, he broke through a temporary fence and fell 25 feet down an embankment, dislocating his right shoulder.

Upon his return for the 1946 season, hopes were high for Reiser and the Dodgers. On May 19, Reiser hurt his right shoulder. On May 21, Roscoe McGowen noted that Reiser would be sidelined for several days due to the shoulder injury, and added, "Peter, who normally throws right-handed though a portside hitter, practiced throwing with his left before the game."

A cautionary hint to Dodger fans was issued by McGowen in the July 11, 1946, *New York Times*. In a game against the Cubs in Wrigley Field, Reiser was chased back to the fence. McGowen wrote, "There was a breathless moment as Pistol Pete Reiser raced back to the left field wall to pull down Johnson's long drive." McGowen does not tell exactly why the moment was "breathless." It could have been because the drive might have had a major bearing on the outcome, or it could have been because Reiser was heading at a rapid rate into the wall for another crash.

Reiser had another bout with a wall on August 1, 1946, while playing left field. This time it was the Ebbets Field wall that stopped his forward momentum. The *New York Times'* Joseph M. Sheehan reported the action:

In a futile attempt to snag Whitey Kurowski's long double in the fifth inning, Reiser crashed into the left-field wall, cracking his head against it so hard that he was knocked unconscious and had to be carried off the field on a stretcher. He was taken to Peck Memorial Hospital for observation with what preliminary diagnosis established as a slight concussion and will remain there for two or three days.

On September 1, 1946, Reiser went to the hospital with a bout of pleurisy. On the 14th, Reiser left the game before the start of the second inning because he aggravated a "charleyhorse" on a successful dash across home plate.

On September 10, 1946, in his *New York Times* column, Arthur Daley wrote about the Dodgers spirited challenge to the Cardinals, who then were just two games ahead of the Dodgers for the lead in the National League. He seemed to especially enjoy commenting on Reiser's play, which had improved noticeably.

Reiser has gone crazy again. The mercury-footed outfielder has had a moral relapse and gone larcenous once more, stealing bases by the gross lots. He creates such an undercurrent of excitement in the stands whenever he moves onto the base paths that the opposing team immediately gets a mass case of the jitters. He's the only man in the game who can upset the opposition entirely by doing no more than stand a few feet off base, a quizzical, mischievous grin on his face.

In the September 25 *New York Times*, Roscoe McGowen wrote, "Pete's recurring miseries have been almost as painful to Durocher as they have been for Reiser. 'He makes such a lot of difference when's he's in there,' Leo has said repeatedly."

Just a day later, McGowen had to write about the end of Reiser's season in an 8–1 victory over the Phillies. "The speed boy and powerhouse hitter, plagued all year with sundry ills and injuries, eliminated himself in the first inning. Pete slid back into first base, caught his foot on the bag and suffered a fractured fibula in his left leg."

The *Brooklyn Eagle*'s Tommy Holmes told of the play that ended Reiser's season and recounted some of the injuries Pete had had over his years with the Dodgers. In his column he commented on Reiser's luck: "In any event, this was a rough ending to a rough season for a fine young ball player who hasn't had any luck but bad since 1941 when Reiser, as a freshman, led the National League in hitting."

Elsewhere on the *Eagle*'s sports page Holmes wrote, "There never has been a day this year that Reiser was in 100 percent sound shape to play baseball, yet he batted .283 in 121 games, hit 11 homers, batted in 71 runs and led both leagues in stolen bases with 34 thefts.... He stole home seven times, a performance unequalled in major league history." Also on September 26, the *New York Journal-American*'s Michael Gaven said Reiser had been out of the lineup during the year as a result of nine separate injuries.

On September 28, the *Times'* McGowen offered hope for the next year, 1947: "It is believed that an off-season operation to remedy the sternal separation, a memento of his ball-playing service in the Army, and that he will be as good as new next year." During the off-season, Reiser did have a successful operation on his right shoulder, which indicated that he would be able to throw well again.

In 1947, Jackie Robinson joined the Dodgers. He quickly became a major force as a player. His presence on the Dodgers would give Brooklyn two of the most daring and exciting players in the big leagues—he and Reiser, both 28 years old.

In an April 6, 1947, exhibition game with the Dodgers' top farm team, the Montreal Royals, Reiser showed that he might really be healthy again. The *Times'* Roscoe McGowen related the happy news, and indicated that Reiser was going to resume being a force for the Dodgers in the coming season:

Fielding Lou Welaj's single on a bad hop and with Campanella rounding second base, Pete let go the kind of throw to third that no one has seen him make in five years. As the ball took off on that long "furillo hop" directly to Arky Vaughn, Durocher came off the bench with a bound, grinning broadly and waving to the writers in the press box. He wanted to make sure that everybody had seen the old Reiser overhand whip—the arm that cut down many an ambitious runner in the Brooklyn pennant year of 1941.

Reiser several times has thrown hard in warm-ups, but the question as to whether he could cut loose in the stress of an actual game had not been answered until today. That one throw was almost a written guarantee that Pete is completely ready once more and Durocher obviously felt that way.

The "furillo hop" refers to a throw that the strong-armed young outfielder Carl Furillo had perfected. In a July 24, 1953, article in the *Brooklyn Eagle*, Dave Anderson described the hopping ball that Furillo could throw so powerfully:

> Furillo is just part of the Dodgers' vacuum-packed defense, but that arm makes him something special, the same way Billy Cox and Gil Hodges handle their gloves or Duke Snider takes flight for the leaping and diving catches.
>
> Next time you see one of Furillo's throws, notice the top spin. The ball hits the infield grass, then actually picks up speed as it skips another 20 feet about three feet off the ground and pops into the waiting glove.
>
> Fresco Thompson, now a vice-president of the Dodgers, remembers Furillo when he was just a kid playing left field for him then the manager of Reading in the Interstate League in 1941.
>
> "Carl was my only right-handed throwing outfielder, so I had him in left field," reminisced Thompson. "And he really had those third-base coaches scared. Everybody stopped running as soon as Furillo got the ball.
>
> "We played almost all night games and there'd usually be some dew on the grass. So Furillo's throws would skid off that grass and one time he knocked the glove right out of the catcher's hand.
>
> "Paul Chervinko, remember him, he was catching. And he had his glove up waiting for the throw. Furillo bounces it off the wet grass, it flies up, hits the glove and the glove and the ball went flying."

Just three days later on April 9, 1947, Reiser lost one of his greatest supporters, his manager, Leo Durocher, who was suspended for a year by Happy Chandler, the commissioner of major league baseball. An accumulation of things deemed detrimental to baseball led to Leo's suspension. Burt Shotton replaced him.

On June 4 at Ebbets Field against the Pirates, Reiser yet another time failed to understand where he was in the outfield. The gifted player's defective internal compass again led him into a concrete wall while he was traveling at full speed. Roscoe McGowen filled in the details in the June 5 edition of the *New York Times*:

> Reese added a fifth run batted in the eighth, but his joy was dampened, as was that of the entire crowd, because Pete Reiser, Reese's pal, crashed into the centerfield wall and was detained in Swedish Hospital.
>
> Reiser's accident occurred in the sixth inning when Culley [*sic*] Rikard exploded a terrific drive directly toward the centerfield wall. Pete, as he had done many times in the past, went for the ball without regard to barriers.
>
> Just before he crashed head-on the ball nestled into his up-flung glove—and miraculously stayed there for one of the most dramatic putouts in the game's history.
>
> Players from both teams rushed out, greatly concerned about this well-liked and brilliant player, whose career has been dogged by disaster. Shortly a stretcher was hurried out and Pete was carried off the field for the third time since he became a Dodger.

The *New York Journal-American's* Michael Gaven wrote of the concern the Dodgers' leaders had for Reiser's health: "They know that eventually he is going to be seriously hurt.

As long as they play baseball inside closed walls Pete is going to run into them. He is that kind of player. Concrete barriers mean nothing to him when he is in quest of a fly ball, as some 32,287 witnesses to last night's crash will acquiesce." After recounting several more of Reiser's injuries, Gaven recounted Reiser's runs into walls: "Throw in the four crashes into the walls, one in St. Louis and three in Brooklyn and you have the hard luck player of all time."

In the *Times* on June 6, McGowen reported that Reiser did not have a fracture, but did have a concussion and lacerations. He added that Reiser would be "all right in a week." The *New York Times'* Arthur Daley also wrote about Reiser's collision with the wall in his June 6 column:

> If Branch Rickey still hopes that his Dodgers will win the pennant, the Mahatma should order all future games played on the Parade Grounds. It's the only guaranteed method of keeping Pete Reiser sound of limb. As soon as a wall encloses a field, it's a certainty that Pistol Pete will some day crash into it and the Brooks can't win any championship without the services of their spirited and talented young outfielder.
>
> The reckless Reiser cracked up again on Wednesday night but, fortunately, it wasn't as violent a collision as he had with the centerfield wall in St. Louis back in 1942....
>
> His only salvation might be a trade to the Giants so that he could roam freely in those vast Polo Grounds centerfield pastures. However, it's certain that this step-child of Dame Fortune still would come to grief. For the first time in history someone would belt a home run into the bleachers and Pistol Pete would butt his head against the barrier trying to catch the ball.
>
> If Reiser were lucky, he'd become one of the greatest ball players of all time. Being congenitally unlucky, however, he'll probably never make it.

The Parade Grounds to which Daley referred was in Brooklyn. Harold Seymour, fondly recalled the Parade Grounds as a place where he grew up in the twenties playing baseball on the unfenced fields:

> The ball-playing center was the Parade Grounds. That vast, rectangular open area in the heart of Flatbush was ringed by twenty-one baseball diamonds.... There never was enough space to accommodate all the teams that sought permits for a diamond from the parks department. Thousands of people turned out to watch and often wager small amounts on the teams, and each of the outstanding ones among them was cheered by its own ardent followers....
>
> Contact with baseball was therefore well-nigh inescapable for Brooklyn boys. They grew up in an environment pervaded by the game.... The game supplied a common interest that brought into a relationship that required them to judge one another primarily on merit and thereby helped them develop mutual respect despite cultural differences.
>
> The cohesive value of baseball was particularly important in a polyglot city like Brooklyn. In my own neighborhood in Flatbush, for instance, there dwelled within the radius of a few blocks boys of English, Irish, Scottish, German, Italian, Austrian, Spanish, Swedish and Chinese extraction, as well as Protestants, Catholics, and Jews. All of them played baseball side by side and against each other on the sandlots and in schools [457–458].*

Arthur Daley was incorrect in his assessment that the Dodgers could not win without a healthy Reiser. Daley, and most other people, did not know how well the Dodgers' farm system's scouts had done their work. During the three-year period of 1946 through 1948, the nucleus of the great Dodger teams of 1949 through 1956 was put in place. The 1947 team was a strong one, and gave the Yankees a spirited challenge before losing in the World Series. Jackie Robinson, from his 1947 rookie season on, was a major catalyst in

Harold Seymour, Baseball: The Golden Age (New York: Oxford University Press, 1971). Used by permission of Oxford University Press.

moving the Dodgers from a strong team to a dominant team, something that had been expected to continue after the talented Reiser's emergence in 1941.

In the June 5 *Brooklyn Eagle*, Harold C. Burr made a plea for Dodger President Branch Rickey to help Reiser:

> President Branch Rickey should provide Pete Reiser with more protection at home. Either the outfield wall should be rubberized so the daring young man would bounce off it or a gravel path constructed at the base of the stands. He would feel the gravel under his spikes and be warned that he was in a danger zone.
>
> Pete means too much to the Dodgers to permit him to continue to risk life and limb. There's a dirt rim around the outfield at Briggs Stadium, Detroit that answers the same purpose as gravel.

Over the next three days *Brooklyn Eagle* writers Burr and Lou Niss made the case for the Dodgers' leaders to do something about the concrete wall at Ebbets Field. In the June 6 paper Lou Niss wrote about several ideas that came from fans and from the Dodgers front office: "Everything from rubber to radar was pondered and the Brooklyn Baseball club is giving it more thought than the fans. And the solution may be rubber." Niss went on to talk about the three most likely solutions—a rubber facing on the concrete, a terrace going up to the fence, and a 20-foot wide gravel or dirt track in front of the fence. Terraces were thought to cause players to misjudge balls in the air and to lead to sprains and turned ankles. Gravel or dirt warning tracks were not deemed sufficient to stop the speedy, hard-charging and single-minded Reiser. Niss discussed a United States Rubber product called Koylon that would be relatively inexpensive, then about $15,000, to use as a facing on the concrete. He concluded that "Rubber seems the most logical answer and it would require no more than a three-inch thickness to take care of hard running outfielders. This would be cemented to the walls and it is said would almost entirely absorb the shock of a player hitting the wall full force."

On June 7, the *Eagle*'s Harold C. Burr gave an update:

> They are going to try and make Ebbets Field safe for Pete Reiser. President Branch Rickey has received two bids to rubberize the wall so that Pete will bounce off it harmlessly. The Dodger brass hats will hold a meeting Tuesday to decide on the park's new out field face.
>
> President Branch Rickey was for building a grass terrace to slow up Reiser. Somebody else suggested a chicken wire fence until Coach Ray Blades testified that he once got his spikes in such a screen and broke his leg.

Lou Niss's article on June 8 told of the Dodgers' idea of broadening the protective facings or other warning methods from Ebbets Field to all National League parks. He added a new possible solution: "Another suggestion is a canvas fence about a foot or so in front of the wall with the poles to which the canvas is attached rigged so that they give under pressure." Niss continued on to criticize owners who moved fences in to get more home runs. He listed some of the players, one being Earle Combs, who suffered serious injuries at fences, and noted that many other players have been badly shaken up in their runs into fences. Implicit in the discussions about the need for protecting Reiser was the belief that he was not going to change, that he would continue to be at risk to run into a concrete wall at a high rate of speed.

The June 4 crash was to have the same effect on Reiser's year as the 1942 crash in St. Louis. Reiser would become a part-time player and have difficulty being a consistent contributor to the Dodgers' success. After the June 4 crash it was apparent that the hopes Leo Durocher had for Reiser in early April had faded to the point that Reiser would be almost a marginal player in the latter half of the 1947 season. It again was apparent that he had not learned to take his eye off the ball and to make objective, precise calculations about where he was in relation to the fence. He seemed caught up in his speed and the flight of the ball.

This inability to know when he was in danger of colliding with walls was apparent to his teammates even in practice. In his book *Bums*, Peter Golenbock quotes Ralph Branca, who played with Reiser during Pete's last three years in Brooklyn, and who admired Reiser's prodigious all-around baseball talents. Branca said that Reiser was so fearless that, even in batting practice when he was in the outfield shagging flies, other players had to yell at him to keep him from charging into the outfield wall.

On June 17, 1947, Roscoe McGowen of the *New York Times* wrote about Reiser's almost incredible bad luck, which was not to end. "Having begged off on flying to Johns Hopkins to see a couple of doctors, Pete was in uniform here today and standing in center field when Clyde King, chasing a fungo fly, crashed into Pete, who was knocked down. Later he was helped to the clubhouse, but there was no serious injury."

On June 27, McGowen updated Reiser's condition, writing that "Pete Reiser will not play for at least two weeks. Dr. James G. Arnold Jr., Baltimore neurologist, has ordered Pete home to St. Louis to rest for a fortnight, but he said his condition wasn't serious enough for hospitalization." On July 22, McGowen wrote, "Pete made a desperate attempt chasing Young's homer in the third of the opener and he said afterward in the clubhouse, 'something seemed to slip out of place in my left shoulder, but it slipped back in again.' Trainer Harold Wendler said Pete would be all right in two or three days and would work out every day meanwhile." McGowen's chronicle on Reiser's condition continued on August 8: "He became dizzy last night when he misjudged two fly balls which started Boston rallies, but didn't think he had got too much sun yesterday afternoon. He and Mrs. Reiser spent a great part of the day at the beach."

Despite his physical problems, Reiser played aggressively. On July 13 against the Reds, he tried to score from second base an infield grounder. On August 19, after he thought St. Louis pitcher Al Brazle had thrown purposely at his head, Reiser then twice tried to bunt so Brazle would have to come into the base line to field the ball so Reiser could knock him over. On July 21 against the Cincinnati Reds, Pete tried to score from second on a wild pitch. He was just nipped at the plate, but he collided with the Reds' ace pitcher Ewell Blackwell, who was shaken up on the play. On September 9, he crashed into Cubs' first baseman Eddie Waitkus after hitting a grounder to the second baseman Ray Mack. Reiser went down for several minutes. It was feared he was injured, but this time just had the wind knocked out of him.

Reiser's year should have ended in the third game of the World Series against the Yankees when, on an attempted steal, he broke his ankle colliding with Phil Rizzuto. On October 4, the *New York Times*' Roscoe McGowen reported the damage:

> Pistol Pete Reiser probably will not play again in the series as a result of his slide into second base in the first inning of yesterday's game.
> The X-rays of his ankle were negative but Pete has a bad sprain and, Dr. Harold Wendler said, "will play only by some miracle tomorrow."

Reiser suited up the next day, and at a crucial time in the ninth inning he was sent up to pinch-hit, with the Dodgers trailing 2–1 and Yankees pitcher Bill Bevens pitching a no-hitter. The count on the lame Reiser reached three and one when the runner on first, Al Gionfriddo, stole second. With two out and fearing the powerful Reiser might get a pitch to hit a long way, Yankee manager Bucky Harris ordered Bevens to intentionally walk Reiser. Dodger manager Burt Shotton put Eddie Miksis in to run for Reiser. Gionfriddo and Miksis then scored the tying and winning runs on the Dodgers' only hit of the day, a dramatic double by Cookie Lavagetto.

Thus Reiser, who later said that on the day he sustained the injury doctors at the hospital told him his ankle was broken and not sprained, was part of two miraculous events at Ebbets Field that day—the come-from-behind Brooklyn victory with a single out remaining, and, according to Dr. Wendler, Reiser playing at all.

At age 28, during the 1947 season, Reiser played in 110 games, batted .309, and stole 14 bases, down from his league-leading 34 the year before. He never was to play in more than 84 games a year, bat higher than .271, and steal more than 4 bases a year in his remaining five years in the major leagues. He played in 64 games for the Dodgers in 1948, then played two years with the Boston Braves, one with the Pirates, and finished his major league career in Cleveland in 1952. Over ten years he had a career average of .295, and stole 87 bases.

In 1948, the Dodgers' management installed a warning track in front of the outfield fences and padded the walls at Ebbets Field. However, the failure to take these actions sooner, coupled with the management's other poor decisions about how to protect their best player, contributed to an erosion of the once-glorious talents Reiser possessed. Reiser's tendency to ignore the whereabouts of the outfield walls, his injuries, and the lost potential overshadows Reiser's abilities as a fielder and thrower. He was a very good fielder and thrower who made many spectacular plays in the outfield. In his 1942 *Saturday Evening Post* article "Pistol Pete" (condensed and reprinted in the July 1946 *Baseball Digest*), Tom Meany commented on Reiser's speed in the field and his strong throwing arm, saying that "His exceptional speed enables him to challenge even Terry Moore for ground-covering honors, while his steel arm ranks with those of the throwing DiMaggios."

Although no catch by Reiser received the notoriety of the catches presented later, his speed and daring led to many spectacular catches during his time as a Dodger, many of them noted by the baseball writers who covered the Dodger games. It is possible that a remarkable catch he made in the June 4, 1947, game on the ball the Pirate's Cully Rikard hit would qualify as a truly great catch, but it was overshadowed by yet another Reiser run into a wall. The *New York Times'* Roscoe McGowen called the catch on Rikard "one of the most dramatic putouts in the game's history."

McGowen's colleague at the *Times*, John Drebinger, covered the Giants-Brooklyn game on April 19, 1947. He had high praise for a catch Reiser made that day:

> Just how much difference Reiser makes in the Dodger line-up came forcefully to light in the second when Pistol Pete came tearing in like something shot out of a gun for Gearhart's low line drive and with a skidding slide caught the ball inches off the ground. Not since the nimble-footed Jigger Statz patrolled center for the Dodgers years ago had a Brooklyn outfielder made a catch like that at the Polo Grounds.

The *Brooklyn Eagle*'s Harold C. Burr called Reiser's catch of Gearhart's drive a "startling circus catch." Burr also wrote that later in the game Reiser "was limping on his injured ankle." The day after Reiser's terrific catch against Gearhart, McGowen gave another indication of the health problems Pete had and of how gifted a player he was:

> "Pete Reiser will play, I'm sure," said the white-haired Shotton. "He's so much better than anybody else, even if his leg isn't good, that he will play if at all possible." Shotton said Pete had worn a boot on his weak and sore ankle at the Polo Grounds yesterday and would wear

one again tomorrow to protect him against a new injury. This means the Pistol has changed his mind about using any support, as he previously had been convinced he should neither tape the ankle nor wear anything else on it. "I don't think it will heal as fast," said Reiser, "with anything hindering the circulation."

On August 4, 1947, McGowen wrote about what he felt was Reiser's best catch of the year, in a 4–2 Brooklyn victory over the Boston Braves: "Reiser ... had come up with the most glamorous catch of the night or of the season when Frank McCormick opened the eighth with a low, vicious liner to left center. Pete raced over and speared the ball in his gloved hand inches from the ground and while sliding on his back."

In his 1975 book *Nice Guys Finish Last*, written with Ed Linn, Leo Durocher shared his thoughts on Reiser's abilities. Durocher thought that Reiser might have been the best baseball player he ever saw. He believed that Reiser had more power than Willie Mays and could throw at least as well. Reiser was the fastest runner he ever saw on a ball field and was an outstanding, daring base runner. However, due to all of Reiser's injuries, Leo acknowledged that Pete never fulfilled his enormous potential.

In 1941, Reiser was timed in the hundred-yard dash in training camp in Havana. While wearing his baseball uniform and his baseball spikes, Reiser reportedly was timed at 9.8 seconds running 100 yards. In 1941, the world's record was 9.4 seconds. If the timing was accurate, Reiser had close to world-class sprinting speed.

In his 1958 *True* magazine article (reprinted in *The Second Fireside Book of Baseball*, edited by Charles Einstein), after going through a list of the injuries Reiser sustained and asking the unanswerable "What if he hadn't been hurt?" question, W.C. Heinz offered another writer's thought of Reiser's level of play among ballplayers he'd seen. "'I didn't see the oldtimers,' Bob Cooke, who is the sports editor of the *New York Herald Tribune*, was saying recently, 'but Pete Reiser was the best ballplayer I ever saw'" (190).

Even when players were vigilant about the location of the concrete walls as they prepared to catch long fly balls, injury could ensue. In *The Pastime in Turbulence: Interviews with Baseball Players of the 1940s*, Brent Kelley asked Chuck Diering, "What do you consider the major change that's taken place in baseball since you began playing in 1941?" Among other things, Diering said:

I think it's the ballparks that's made the game change so much. I think the grass fields make better games for spectators.

We played against concrete walls, so you had to play the game differently in going to get the ball. Today they're all padded and soft. I broke my arm in Sportsman's Park, ran into the wall going after the ball. Bases loaded, fly ball hit my way out there and I could see I was going to catch it, but the wind carried it a little. I caught the ball, but I had one more step and I crashed into the wall and I broke my arm.

In my day you had to learn to play ricochets off the walls. You had a lot of angles and you had to learn the caroms in different parks. Today the ball hits the wall and it dies right there [272–273].

THREE

The Dead Ball, the Lively Ball, the Long Ball, and Gloves

The Dead Ball and the Lively Ball

Along with the outfield distances, the fences and the fans, another factor with which fielders had to contend was the balls put in play. Prior to 1910 a baseball consisted of a rubber center, yarn wound around that center, and a horsehide cover that was stitched together around the center and the yarn. Before a machine was developed around 1890 to wind the yarn tightly and in a uniform manner, balls wound by hand were of various tensions and were easily misshaped by the pounding the balls took during games. The winding machine increased the uniformity of the new baseballs, but the balls were still "dead" for several reasons.

First, the innermost core of a baseball before 1910 was made of rubber. The rubber went out of shape as the ball was struck, and returned to shape while in flight, thus working against the flight. Cork-center balls were first introduced into regular season major league games in 1911, and the improved results were immediate. The cork centers did not distort as much as rubber upon contact with a bat, and were more resilient than the rubber centers over the course of a game. Averages climbed and home runs increased, although not like the increase that was to occur less than ten years later after Babe Ruth made the switch from pitcher to full-time outfielder.

Second, despite the new "lively" ball introduced in 1911, the baseball tradition of keeping a single ball in play as long as possible meant that, after several innings, the ball was beaten up, less compact, and less lively than it was at the beginning of the game. The ball's yarn was wound by machine to be resilient, but after taking a pounding for several innings, the yarn often became misshapen, and the horsehide cover became scuffed and dirty early in the game. Batters in the 1911 to 1920 era had trouble hammering the mistreated balls to distant parts of the ballparks. Thus, outfielders had fewer chances to make spectacular catches.

In their book *Cincinnati's Crosley Field*, the authors, Greg Rhodes and John Erardi, quote one of Edd Roush's comments about baseballs in the pre–1920 years. Roush was an outstanding hitter and one of the National League's premier fielders, especially for Cincinnati from 1916 through 1926. "'The ball wasn't wrapped tight, and lot of times it'd get mashed on one side,' said Roush. 'I've caught many a ball in the outfield that was mashed flat on one side. Come bouncing out there like a jumping bean. They wouldn't throw it out of the game, though. Only used about three or four balls in a whole game'" (55).

Third, not only were the pre–1920 balls misshapen after being used inning after inning, they frequently were not dry. In his book *Mitts*, William Curran makes the point that prior to the ban on the spitball, the balls were heavier in part due to the moisture on them. He wrote that Edd Roush found the wetter, heavier balls more difficult to throw than they were after the ban on the spitball.

In 1920, the year Babe Ruth revolutionized the game by belting 54 home runs, it appeared that another lively ball had been introduced. A combination of things began favoring batters more, including the encouragement for umpires to eliminate balls that were cut, scuffed and dirty and to keep fresh balls in play across all the innings of a game. Whatever the reasons, there was an increase in the number of good baseballs which batters could drive longer distances.

In his 1923 book *My Thirty Years in Baseball*, John J. McGraw, the New York Giants' manager, wrote the better part of a chapter about how the lively ball and the long ball changed the strategies in playing baseball. His book was written just after the Giants had won two consecutive World Series. Despite this feat, McGraw said he enjoyed the World Series winner he guided in the "deadball" year of 1911 because that team, built around speed, steals, bunts, and the hit and run gave him more enjoyment to see and to manage. He wrote, "The great loss to me, after all, is the thrill that I got out of seeing men shoot down the base paths, one after another, until they had stolen their way to a win. That was baseball—the kind of baseball that I learned to love when I got my first job" (210).

Manager McGraw noted that the practice of umpires throwing out balls that were discolored and battered first occurred in the American League after Ray Chapman was killed in 1920 by a ball thrown by Carl Mays. McGraw wrote:

> I am told that someone had objected to the ball that day, but the umpire did not see fit to throw it out.
> Instead of going as intended, the ball "sailed" and Chapman was hit. Since then the umpires take no chances. In a way one can not blame them [209–210].

In 1925, two years after McGraw's book was published, the lively ball and the difficulties pitchers were having adapting to it and to rule changes were still topics of interest. The *New York Sun*'s Frank Graham interviewed Mike Gonzales, then a catcher for the Chicago Cubs, and titled the July 13, 1925, article "Gonzales Defends Pitchers." Graham's article began:

> Mike Gonzales, dean of the corps of Cuban players in the United States, tossed an interview over his shoulder as he warmed up Elmer Jacobs during the Cubs' batting practice at the Polo Grounds before yesterday's game.
> "What's the matter with present day pitchers? Nothing," he said. "The pitchers of to-day are as good as the ever were, or at least in the time I have been playing ball in this country. That the pitching isn't as good is due to the lively ball and the restrictions placed on pitchers. The pitchers of a few years ago had an entirely different kind of ball to use and there wasn't much they couldn't do to it either. They used paraffin and oils, rosin, tobacco juice, dirt and saliva. Also, they would scuff the cover with their fingers or slice it with their nails. Nowadays the pitchers not only have a 'rabbit' ball but there is a new one put in every few minutes and they cannot doctor it. Even the spitball pitchers are fast disappearing.
> "Then, the fact that it is easier to hit the ball than it used to be has brought a change in the style of hitting. Remember how many choke up hitters there were? How often do you see a choke hitter now? All the boys grip the bat at the end and take a full swing. Bring back the old ball and let the pitchers work on it a little and you'll see the number of home runs cut down almost to nothing. The batters again would be on the defensive and a good many of them would start choking their bats once more. The pitchers, as I have said, are just as good as they ever were, but they haven't got a chance."

At the time of the interview, Gonzales was 32 years old. Mike Gonzales got into his first major league game in 1912 and played seventeen years in the majors.

The discussions about the "lively ball" continued through the twenties as the averages and the home run totals rose. The peak year for hitters, and especially in the National League, was 1930, a year when the league batting average was an astronomical .303. In the National League that year a total of 892 home runs were hit; in 1928 the total home runs were 610, and in 1929 there were 754. In 1920, National Leaguers had hit a total of 261 home runs. By contrast, the American League players hit 483 homers in 1928, 595 in 1929, and 673 in 1930.

The high National League offensive totals in 1930 led the league's officials to do something to curb the explosion of offense. The league officials decided to change the ball. A *New York Times* article by John Drebinger on February 4, 1931, was titled "National Adopts Less Lively Ball," with the first subtitle "League, at its Annual February Meeting, Acts to Put Curb on Home-Run Hitting." About this development Drebinger wrote:

> According to President John A. Heydler, who produced one of the new balls in evidence after the meeting, its essential difference from the sphere that has been bouncing over fences in the past lies in its covering, which has been made much heavier. In addition to this, the stitching is now raised instead of being countersunk as heretofore, and is also to be of slightly heavier material.

Just below this article about the National League's use of a new ball was an article about the American League's version. The American League also was going to use a ball with a heavier stitch that would not only enable the pitcher to get a better grip, but would give the ball more resistance against the wind, thus reducing the distance it would travel.

By late June 1931, National League president Heydler called the "less lively ball" a success. He noted that significant decreases in runs scored, home runs, and the number of batters hitting over .300 led to more competitive games, and attendance was still high despite the Depression.

The experiment was a clear success for the National League officials. By the end of the 1931 season, the league batting average dropped to .277, and the home run total dropped from 892 to 492. It would not be until the 1949 season that the batters in the National League would exceed the 1930 total of home runs. It wouldn't be until the following year, 1950, that American League hitters would exceed the 1930 National League's home run total.

For the purposes of this book, the "lively ball" after 1920 not only produced more long balls for home runs, but more balls outfielders had to chase for long outs. The chases and subsequent catches have produced many thrilling events for fans.

The Long Ball

Because of the grind-it-out kind of offense the game had established in the late 19th century, and because of the lack of uniformly solid balls in play throughout the games during the decade from 1909 to 1919, long drives from most batters at the Polo Grounds and other parks were not common worries for outfielders. Most batters continued to choke up on the bat and to place the ball to get on base so runs could be manufactured by other similarly placed hits, by stolen bases, by bunts, and by hit and run plays.

Relatively few home runs were hit prior to the introduction of the lively ball for league play in 1911, and that continued to be the case during much of the following decade. For example, the leading home run hitter in the National League in 1909 was the New York Giants' Red Murray with 7 homers, and in the American League, Detroit's Ty Cobb with 9. In 1911, the first year of the new lively ball, the National League's home run leader was Cincinnati's Frank Schulte with a career-best 21. In the American League that year the home run king was the Philadelphia A's Frank Baker with 11.

Between 1911 and 1918 only one other player hit more home runs than Schulte's 21, and that was the Philadelphia Phillies' Gavvy Cravath, who hit 24 in 1915. Between 1913 and 1919 Cravath led the league in home runs five more times, twice with 19 (1913 and 1914), twice with 12 (1917 and 1919), and once with 8 (1918). Cravath's highest home run years were the exceptions among major league batters. The other leaders in home runs hit between 8 and 12. In the American League in 1918, Babe Ruth, in 317 at-bats, tied for the most home runs with the A's Tilly Walker. Both had 11 home runs. Walker had 414 at-bats. In 1918, Ruth also had a 13–7 pitching record.

In 1919, the last year Ruth pitched, he had a 9–5 record. In 432 official at-bats he hit 29 home runs. The next highest home run total in the American League was Tilly Walker's 10 in 456 at-bats, and in the National League, the leader was Cravath with 12 in 214 at-bats. Cravath, an outfielder, also was the Phillies' manager for the second half of the season.

The disparity between Babe Ruth and the rest of the players as home run hitters was even more magnified in the 1920 season when Ruth, now with the Yankees as a full-time outfielder, clouted 54 homers in 458 at-bats, while the next highest American League total was George Sisler's 19 in 631 at-bats. The National League leader was Phillies' Cy Williams with 15 in 590 at-bats. Babe Ruth had more home runs than did the entire rosters of each of fourteen of the fifteen other major league clubs.

By the beginning of the 1920 season Ruth already was so dominant a long-ball threat that writers were reaching for new ways to describe his blasts. An example of this came from the unidentified writer for the *New York Times* whose account of the May 1, 1920, Yankees–Red Sox game included:

Babe Ruth sneaked a bomb into the park without anybody knowing it and hid it in his bat. He exploded the weapon in the sixth, when he lambasted a home run high over the right field grand stand into Manhattan Field. This was Babe's first home run of the championship season, and it was a sockdolager. The ball flitted out of sight between the third and fourth flagstaffs on the top of the stand. Ruth smashed it over the same place when he broke the world's home run record last season. The only other citizen who has even slapped the ball over the stand was Joe Jackson, a few seasons back.

When Ruth didn't crack a long ball, it was "news." In a Yankees victory over the White Sox on May 12, 1920, at the Polo Grounds, Ruth had a long home run and a single in the game. The unidentified *New York Times* writer, under the subtitle "Ruth Condescends to Single," gave that hit a paragraph:

Ruth's greatest achievement yesterday wasn't the home run. In the seventh inning of the game Ruth completely forgot himself and hit a single to center field. It is a good thing there is no home run hitters union, for if there was Ruth would probably be heavily fined for making such a puny hit.

Five years later, after a March 29, 1925, exhibition game against Brooklyn in Montgomery, Alabama, doubles Ruth hit merited special attention. Twelve thousand people filled every nook and cranny of the ballpark to see Ruth and the Yankees. John Kieran, writing in the *New York Herald Tribune*, told of Ruth's drawing power and of the long balls he hit.

From far and near the city and country folks stormed the turnstiles in their anxiety to wel-come G. Herman Ruth and the other stars to the city which was the cradle of the Confeder-acy. While the Babe knocked no home runs for the assembled multitude he slammed out a pair of two-baggers and made several sterling catches afield. The customers were all satisfied that Mr. Ruth is easily the greatest ball player in the world, and there were no demands made for the money back. Not only was a new attendance mark set in honor of the Babe, but all former records for the selling of peanuts and pop were smashed beyond recognition.

Later, Kieran wrote more about the doubles.

The two-base hit that Ruth smote in that first inning climbed an embankment in right field and came to a stop just 497 feet from the plate. An official ran out immediately and marked the spot for future reference.

The next time Ruth came to bat Dick Cox moved to a position 450 feet from the plate in right field and awaited developments. The result was a line double to the same area.

Before the end of 1920, Ruth had begun to revolutionize the way the offensive game of baseball was played, and in so doing, he also revolutionized the way outfielders had to play their positions. Outfielders now had to be ready to run long distances more frequently to chase down balls purposely driven to the fences or to run far forward to get balls hit just beyond infielders' territory.

Just as his first season (1962) as manager of the New York Mets was about to begin with a game at the Polo Grounds, Casey Stengel reminisced with Arthur Daley of the *New York Times* about a time before Ruth was in the major leagues. In Daley's April 15, 1962, "Sports of The Times" column, Casey told Daley that his team, the Brooklyn Dodgers, played an exhibition game at a Baltimore racetrack against the Baltimore Orioles, then a minor league team. Babe Ruth was just out of school and was pitching for the Orioles. According to Casey, Ruth fanned eleven Dodgers. Casey said, "And could he pitch!"

The first time Ruth batted he hit a ball far over Casey's head in center field for a triple. Brooklyn's manager, Wilbert Robinson, gave Casey the "what for" for not playing deep enough for Ruth. The next time Ruth came to the plate, Casey moved fifty feet further back. Again Ruth poked one over Stengel's head. Because he didn't think Casey was far enough back on the second long ball hit by Ruth, "Uncle Robbie," as manager Robinson also was known, fined Casey.

Because of that early encounter with Ruth the batter, and because in the 1922 World Series Bill Cunningham caught a Ruth drive to the deepest part of the Polo Grounds, when Casey played center field in the 1923 World Series against the Yankees, he played Ruth extremely deep. He told Daley, "But I made a ketch [*sic*] on the Babe at the same spot and I didn't have to run none at all. I was practically leanin' against the Grant mon-ument in front of the clubhouse which is because I knew who Mister Ruth was and what he could do...."

Casey's tale of his catch on Babe Ruth's long, very high drive in the 1923 World Series was true. Like Bill Cunningham's catch on Ruth in the 1922 World Series, Casey was nearly at the longest distance inside the Polo Grounds, about 480 feet away from home plate, when he caught the Babe's blast. In his article in the October 12, 1923, *New York Tribune*, Grant-land Rice confirms Casey's story. It should be noted that Rice refers back to the 1922 Yan-kees vs. the Giants World Series in which Ruth was only two-for-seventeen at the plate and had no home runs.

As the buoyant Babe crossed the plate with his second home run in consecutive innings the haunting October ghost of 1922 had been chased back to the grave for permanent burial. In two games he had hit nothing shorter than a triple. In the second game they had walked him twice with other home runs on the verge of bubbling out. When he came to bat the last time in the ninth inning he had a third home run primed for everything but direction. Casey Stengel was back again and after putting Mudville on the map once more Casey didn't care to see the old town's glory overshadowed by too wide a margin. So he moved back to a spot in right center that left his back resting comfortably against the stands.

From his distant habitation he could still see the plate, faint and far away. Ruth, in attempting to cut his third wallop more to the right, was a trifle late in his timing. He met the ball squarely, but it sailed straight for Casey Stengel's waiting hands. Turned a few rods to the left this blow also would have landed high up in the right field seats for the greatest record ever made.

In his inning-by-inning report of the game in the *Tribune*, Joseph Val wrote that Stengel caught the ball in center field.

How Ruth's already legendary feats with a bat had changed the game for all the opposing defensive players was apparent by the end of the 1921 season. For example, in reporting the Cleveland-Yankees game on September 23, 1921, an unnamed sportswriter for the *Cleveland Plain Dealer* devoted most of his article to how hard Ruth hit the ball.

The first quarter of the four-game series between New York and Cleveland, a series that is expected to decide the American league championship, went to New York, 4 to 2, for the reason that Babe Ruth can hit the ball harder than any other man connected with the national game, possibly harder than any man living. As a result, New York now leads by nine points.

Before the contest started, Tris Speaker, Cleveland's crippled manager, declared there was only one way to pitch to Ruth when he had a chance to break up a game. That way, he explained, was to give him four wide ones. Speaker meant, of course, if Ruth were at bat with men on he would have to be so treated. Naturally, as no one was on when Ruth came to bat, Stanley Coveleskie disdained, to his sorrow, to purposely pass the demon slugger except the first time up.

He pitched to him the other three times and how Ruth did slam that ball. He did not hit it out of the lot, but he might just as well, for he all but put three Cleveland infielders out of commission and turned each of his efforts into a two base hit.

Apparently, the Indians underestimated the ability of this man Ruth to land on the ball. Boston players say they have beaten Ruth out of many a hit by playing an unusually deep infield. Cleveland, however, today played Ruth as they would any other batter. That is, the infield did, while the outfield went way to the limits. Consequently, when Ruth smashed three hits through the inner defense, the outer guards had no chance to stop the king of swat from reaching second.

Cleveland was leading, 2 to 1, in the fourth inning when Ruth smashed the ball to short. Sewell ran up a few steps and the ball bounded off the famous turtle back infield, caromed off Sewell's hand and rolled to center. Joe Wood, playing deep, was able to get the ball to second about a fifth of a second after Ruth reached the same station. Then Ruth scored on Pipp's drive.

Ruth was up again in the sixth, again with one out. This time he hammered the ball at Wamby. Bill stuck out his hand and tagged the ball, but all the good it did was to deflect the ball into short center and cause Bill to wonder if his hand was still attached to his wrist. Result—another double for Ruth. He then proceeded to score all the way from second when Meusel got a Texas leaguer to left, Meusel taking second on Jamieson's useless throw to the plate and scoring when Pipp singled to center.

Ruth went to bat for the last time in the eighth inning. Coveleskie pitched one strike to him. The next was inside. Ruth hooked his drive and all but killed Doc Johnston. The ball bounced off Johnston and Elmer Smith gave chase as Doc took inventory of his fingers. Result—another two-sacker. Meusel's sacrifice and Pipp's long sacrifice fly then put Babe across the plate for his third tally of the game.

In short, Coveleskie was all to the good when pitching against human beings. But Ruth is not human—not when he grasps that big bat in his hands and swings.

From the sportswriter's account, Ruth's influence was noted: the outfielders played far back on him, thus permitting short balls to be doubles, and the infielders had to be wary of the balls coming at them as a result of Ruth's powerful stroke. (The "Wamby" the writer mentioned was the Indians' second baseman, Bill Wambsganss, now best known for turning in an unassisted triple play in the 1920 World Series.) Prior to the Ruth revolution, many outfielders tended to play close to the infield, knowing that many, if not most, of the hitters were concerned with simply punching the ball into gaps away from fielders, and were not able to get enough power on the overused and abused, and thus softer, ball to drive it to the deepest parts of the ballparks.

Before Ruth revolutionized the game with his long-ball hitting, the most notable exception to the punch-hitting game was Joe Jackson. In his book *Shoeless Joe and Ragtime Baseball*, Harvey Frommer notes a particularly long home run Jackson hit off Russ Ford of the Yankees on June 4, 1913. Frommer quotes Jackson's teammate Jack Graney, who played in the outfield for the Cleveland Indians from 1909 until 1922. Graney said Jackson golfed a low spitter out of the Polo Grounds that day and added: "And remember that the ball was a lump of coal in those days" (43).

Sportswriters were amazed at what Jackson had done. They had never seen any ball hit that was comparable. The unidentified writer for the *New York Post* said:

> Joe Jackson's skyrocket homer in the second inning was worth the price of admission all by itself. This wiry athlete put his whole body into one of Ford's fast ones and shot the bulb not merely into the lower tier of the right-field grandstand, which is a fairly common occurrence; not into the second tier, which is a less common occurrence, but far and high above the top of the cement structure which divides the Polo Grounds from Manhattan Field. When last seen, the ball was sailing southeast by south, full canvas set, in the general direction of Bermuda and the West Indies.

One of the subtitles in the June 5, 1913, *New York Sun* was: "Among Other Slugging Feats Joe Jackson Loses Ball in the Sky." The article's author had fun describing the Jackson homer.

> Joe Jackson made a colossal four bagger. Before the game an airship rode overhead through the aerial sea and Jackson's homer went that high. It cleared the roof of the grandstand and was variously reported to have come down in places all the way from Manhattan Field to Governor's Island. Maybe it stayed up in the clouds. It was hard to see what did become of it.
> Cy Seymour poled a home run into Manhattan Field once, but that was before the lofty stadium was erected. A home run or two also has been driven across the left field fence to the L tracks, longer drives perhaps than Jackson's, but none was as high as the mighty wallop of the big gun from Cleveland. The ball was hit off Ford....
> Jackson's home run was all the hitting done by the Naps in the second and when Joseph touched the plate the orb was just passing the Big Dipper.

The Cleveland team was referred to as the "Naps" after the Hall of Fame second baseman Napoleon Lajoie became their manager (1905 to 1910), and even after that as he continued to be a stellar player for the team (1911 to 1914).

On June 6, Sam Crane of the *New York Evening Journal* wrote an article that compared the Jackson blast to other long home runs he had seen going back to back to 1880, first as a player and then as a writer. Of Jackson's home run, he wrote:

> There were two other circuit clouts made, but, while they were hard hits, they were not patches on "Jolting Joe's" jab that cleared every sky high obstacle in the Polo Grounds and in the immediate neighborhood for miles around. The ball landed somewhere. There is no doubt of that, for Sir Isaac Newton's statement that everything that goes up must come down is still considered sufficient authority to bank on even in these baseball days when "up in the air" is considered a permanent ascension.

Yes, siree, Joe Jackson's wonderful wallop was a record-breaker. It the longest drive ever made on the Polo Grounds, either to right field, centre field or to left field....

After telling of other long balls he had seen hit, Sam Crane returned to Jackson's drive.

I have seen—well, all those great hits and many more—but I will come down to earth now and take my hat off to Joe Jackson of the Clevelands for making the longest lick I ever saw—and that was yesterday.

The sportswriters for Cleveland papers were astounded by Joe Jackson's prodigious home run. About the blast, a "staff" writer for the *Cleveland Press* wrote:

"You can put it down that Jackson's home run yesterday was the hardest and longest drive in the history of baseball," said manager Birmingham today....

Jackson's home run went over the top deck of the stand, which at that point is about three hundred feet from the plate. The stand is about seventy feet high, and Jackson's smash went about twenty-five feet above that on a slant line, disappearing in the distance. The drive on a line is approximated at 360 feet.

Joe Birmingham was Cleveland's manager from 1912 to 1915.

The *Cleveland Plain Dealer* included a picture of the Polo Grounds. A dotted line was added showing the path of the ball Jackson hit. Under the picture more about the distance the ball traveled was included.

The exact distance from home plate to the section of the stand at the Polo Grounds over which Joe Jackson hit his famous home run yesterday was measured after the game and found to be 303 feet. The stand at that point is about ninety feet high and the ball went fully thirty feet over the top of it.

Figuring out the problem under the supposition that the distance from the plate to the stand is 303 feet and that the ball cleared the stand at 100 feet from the ground, the ball carried more than 500 feet.

It is without question the longest hit ever made on the famous New York grounds.

The article written about the game was by Henry T. Edwards, who told more about what Jackson had done.

Joe Jackson's smash, however, was remarkable. It was wonderful. It was phenomenal, as it cleared the roof of the stand by fully thirty feet and dropped far out in a vacant lot to the south of the Polo Grounds. When it disappeared from the view of the spectators it was close to 120 feet in the air. Blows into the right field stand are not infrequent, but this was the first time it was ever hit over the top, and it must be remembered that this is a high double decker. It is probably ninety feet from the ground to the roof. Above are slender flagpoles, one every thirty feet or so. It cleared even these staffs.

Joe DiMaggio, in his 1949 book *Lucky to Be a Yankee*, referred to something that made Jackson a hitter unlike others. DiMaggio first noted what the outstanding catcher Mickey Cochrane said was DiMaggio's secret as a hitter. DiMaggio quoted Cochrane:

I'll tell you how it is. It's the way he keeps those wrists cocked until the final stages of his swing, They are still cocked up to the last foot or so—then he turns them loose at exactly the right moment and the right spot. It's like a steel spring at work, or some form of explosion. The natural tendency is to hit too soon. In this respect, it's the same in baseball as in golf. DiMaggio seems to wait much longer than anyone I ever saw, before he puts the final slash from those wrists. I think that's the secret [144].

DiMaggio continued about wrists:

Most of the experts placed the secret of all great hitters to wrist action and timing. Cy Perkins, who used to catch and coach for Detroit, the Athletics and the Yankees, called Joe

Jackson the greatest hitter of all time. "Jackson had the best wrists in baseball. He had wrists like steel and knew how to use them. Better than Ruth's or Cobb's or Speaker's. He had a flick of the wrist that no one else ever had—including Joe DiMaggio. He was lean and loose— never tightened up. He could take his time. He was never in a hurry. That's the answer" [144].

There were players during the 1911 to 1918 years who could hit long balls, but many of those players often choked up on their bats for better bat control and tried to hit the ball with a level swing that sent it into gaps between the fielders. Joe Jackson held the bat near the end and often swung level and hard to drive the balls on a line into the distant areas of the outfield. Outfielders could not play Jackson as shallow as they could most batters. Once Babe Ruth became a regular batter, he tried for more than line drives. He took a long, fast swing from low to high that was designed to drive the ball high and far.

On most batters before 1919, and for several years thereafter, as the rest of baseball caught up with Ruth's unprecedented ability to hit long drives, Tris Speaker and others could afford to play shallow in the outfield. Speaker's first full major league year was 1909 with the Boston Red Sox. Thus he played ten years before Ruth's long-ball revolution began in earnest in 1919.

Ruth's home run production from 1919 on was so spectacular compared to what had come before him that owners, seeing the potential to draw more fans, put an emphasis on long-ball hitters and away from hitters who tried to slap the ball into gaps. This long-ball emphasis in turn led to outfielders playing deeper for batters trying to hit the long ball. The distances of the outfield fences became more of a concern for both the batters and the outfielders. The outfielders became more vigilant about having to cover more ground behind them in ways they had to do only with a few batters prior to 1920. The outfield defense was no longer mostly a sideways defense or a dash in toward the infield. It also became a retreating defense, especially in ballparks with deep outfields. Centerfielders had to have the ability to go straight back quickly and to cover the left- and right-center field areas in the deepest parts of the ballparks.

The long ball also produced more opportunities for long sprints in toward the infield that outfielders often turned into thrilling shoestring catches. Being fast and having outstanding anticipation based on the pitcher's pitch and the batter's swing became even more valuable commodities for outfielders to have after Ruth opened up the power game and forced outfielders to play deeper.

Ruth's influence also spread to the bats and how they were used. Bats that had barrels with circumferences only somewhat wider than the handles began to be replaced by bats with slender handles and more wood at the barrel end. Ruth used heavy bats, 47 to 50 plus ounces, that were not especially tapered at the handle end. However, like Joe Jackson, he gripped the bat at the end of the handle and was able to generate a high bat speed. In addition to gripping bats closer to the handle's end, hitters began to use lighter bats that would enable them to generate even more bat speed through the swing and thus propel the balls longer distances

Gloves

Just as the athleticism and tallness of a player makes a difference in completing a great catch, so too does the size of a baseball glove. Some great catches involved the longest stretch possible to get at a ball. Over the past fifty years, photos of fielders making catches have shown the ball visible near the end of the leather at the tip of the glove as if it were ready to pop out. Such catches probably could not have been made in an earlier day when the glove size or the glove design would not have enabled the fielder to touch the ball or to hold onto the ball if his glove got to it.

Until the mid–1880s, many great catches could not have been made at all because many players didn't wear gloves. Although gloves (primitive by today's standards) were available by the mid–1880s, some players considered it unmanly for fielders to wear gloves. Prior to the use of gloves of any sort, players in the field had to develop ways to catch batted or thrown balls that minimized the damage to fingers and hands. Given the high speeds with which balls could be thrown or batted, it became an art to catch balls in unprotected hands.

Among other things described in the 1868 book *The American Game of Base Ball: How to Learn It, How to Play It, and How to Teach It*, was "Fly Catching." This description gives an idea of what fielders had to do when catching a ball with their bare hands.

> A ball player, in order to learn to catch a ball well, should study the theory of catching, as well as avail himself of constant practice. The theory of catching is as follows: A ball hit up into the air by a bat or thrown up by hand, falls to the ground with the same speed it left the bat or the hand. Taking this fact into consideration, therefore, it will be seen that in attempting to catch a ball falling swiftly to the ground, to stop its progress with the hands abruptly results in either its rebound from the hand, or, if held, in its causing injury or pain to the hands. But a ball falling can be stopped without pain and held firmly, by so timing the movement of the hands as to grasp it as it falls, and allowing the hands to check its progress gradually instead of abruptly. Toss a ball up, by the way of trial, and, as it falls, bring your hands together horizontally and time the movement so that your hands will close on the ball at a right angle to the line of its fall, and the moment the ball is grasped let your hands fall with a spring-like movement, and if this is done properly the progress of the swiftest ball can be checked without any pain or injury to the hand. But if the hands are placed in such a manner, when about to catch the ball, as simply to resist its progress abruptly, then all the force of the blow is imparted to the hands. The only way to catch a swiftly batted or thrown ball without risk of severe pain or injury from the catch, is to grasp the ball in such a manner as to yield to its progress and to check it gradually and not abruptly [40–41].

Many players learned this technique to catch balls hit or thrown at them. However, catching a ball speeding through the air at 75 to 100 miles an hour with one's bare hands, or catching a wickedly hit ground ball, with this technique must have been extremely difficult and painful.

The first players to need something to protect their hands were catchers, whose hands were subject to the most frequent pounding from tipped balls, and especially by balls thrown by strong-armed pitchers. During the 1870s and the 1880s catchers were tinkering with various kinds of small gloves and paddings to save their hands from being mangled. The *New York Clipper Annual of 1891* included a brief note that indicates the perilous nature of a catcher's life before the mid–1880s: "Frank Flint caught in all but one of the one hundred and twenty-one games played by the Indianapolis Club in 1877, this being a great fielding feat for those days, when masks, heavy gloves and chest protectors were not generally used as now."

First basemen were the next people who needed something to cushion the blow from balls flung with great speed from the other infielders.

Opposite: This advertisement for former star pitcher Albert Spalding's company showed the latest innovations in gloves available to catchers. It appeared in the book *The Art of Pitching & Fielding*, which was written by Henry Chadwick and published in 1886.

SPALDING'S TRADE MARKED CATCHERS' GLOVES.

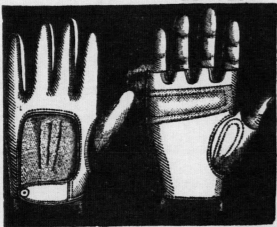

After considerable expense and many experiments, we have finally perfected a Catchers' Glove that meets with general favor from professional catchers.

The old style of open backed gloves introduced by us several years ago is still adhered to, but the quality of material and workmanship has been materially improved, until now we are justified in claiming the best line of catchers's gloves in the market. These Gloves do not interfere with throwing, can be easily put on and taken off, and no player subject to sore hands should be without a pair. We make them in ten different grades, as follows:

No. 000.—Spalding's Special League Catchers' Gloves. Full left hand, back stop glove, made of the heaviest Indian-tanned buckskin, the very best that can be procured. The full left hand glove is extra padded, and sole leather finger tips, to prevent the low curved balls from breaking or otherwise injuring the fingers. The right hand glove is made with open back and fingerless, thoroughly padded........................Price per Pair, $5 00

No. 00.—Spalding's League Regulation Catchers' Gloves, made of extra heavy Indian-tanned buck, and carefully selected with reference to the hard service required of them. This Glove has full left hand, as shown in the illustration, with fingerless right hand, well padded, and warranted........................Price per Pair, 3 50

No. 0.—Spalding's League Catchers' Gloves, made of extra heavy Indian-tanned buck, and carefully selected with special reference to the hard service required of them, open back, both hands fingerless, well padded, and fully warranted........................Price per Pair, 2 50

No. 1.—Spalding's Professional Gloves, made of Indian-tanned buckskin, open back, well padded, but not quite as heavy material as the No. 0............Price per Pair 2 00

The above Gloves are Trade Marked and fully warranted.

AMATEUR CATCHERS' GLOVES.

To meet the demand for a cheaper grade of Gloves, we have added the following line:

No. A.—Full Left Hand Catchers' Gloves, equal to most professional gloves in the market..............Price per Pair, $2 50

No. B.—Amateur Gloves, made of buckskin, open back, well padded, and adapted for amateur players..........Per Pair 1 50

No. C.—Practice Gloves, made of light material, open back, well padded..Per Pair 1 00

No. D.—Junior Gloves, open back, a good glove at the price " 75

No. E.—Cheap open back glove............................... " 50

No F.— "   "   "   "   .... " 25

☞ Any of the above Gloves mailed postpaid on receipt of price. In ordering, please give size of ordinary dress gloves usually worn.

A. G. SPALDING & BROS.,

108 Madison St., CHICAGO.   241 Broadway, NEW YORK,

Gloves became more prominent after Albert Spalding, a great pitcher turned first baseman and soon-to-be-baseball equipment magnate, decided to wear a glove in 1877. Spalding's influence in wearing and promoting gloves for sale in his sporting goods store helped make the glove an acceptable addition for others to wear in a game.

There were players who considered the glove a sissy's tool and who insisted on going barehanded. The last infielder to go gloveless was Cincinnati's second baseman Bid McPhee, whose final year as a barehanded performer was 1895. McPhee already was an outstanding fielder without a glove, but with a glove he later set a fielding percentage mark that stood for almost thirty years. Not surprisingly, fielding became far superior with the use of gloves. Instead of almost two errors being made for every ten chances, within ten years of McPhee's last stand, the average became about a half an error for every ten chances.

From leather palm mitts, to leather which did not reach to the end of the fingers in the first gloves worn in 1870, to gloves which extended to the ends of the fingers and slightly beyond, to padded gloves, and to gloves with longer fingers, the progression of gloves moved forward to protect the hands better and enable fielders to make more plays. The gloves made before 1920 did not have leather laces between the fingers. In 1919, Bill Doak, who pitched for the St. Louis Cardinals, designed a glove with an increased thumb size and laces between the thumb and first finger. The lacing created a web which enabled fielders to snag, and trap and hold balls in their gloves in ways they previously could not. With Doak's new glove, a ball could be caught without necessarily smacking into, or very near, the palm of the glove. His invention, patented in 1922, was improved upon over the next 35 years, with sturdier leather pieces between the thumb and the index finger, and laces between the other fingers being added.

In his book *Glove Affairs*, Noah Liberman contends that the evolution of gloves was slow from the first gloves in the mid–1870s until 1957, and that the modern glove was introduced in 1957 with the Wilson A2000 model. The move to the Wilson glove design was such a huge leap forward that gloves used in 2008 bear a striking resemblance to the 1957 original. The Wilson glove had a deep, already formed pocket, more webbing to better snare balls, and longer, more flexible fingers to clutch and hold the ball. These features made the glove an essential factor in players' gathering in hard-hit grounders, liners, and balls driven to the deepest parts of fields.

Infielders, excepting first basemen, tend to have shorter gloves and like to have a wider and shallower pocket so they can gather in more ground balls and because they want to be able to get rid of the ball quicker. Some players, especially outfielders and first basemen, now have gloves up to an inch longer than the maximum major league standard of 12 inches. Even with the standard in place, major league officials have permitted the use of the longer gloves.

Liberman told about Willie Mays' glove when he made his famous catch on Vic Wertz in the 1954 World Series. He wrote, "Willie Mays made 'the Catch' in 1954 with a Harvey Haddix pitcher's model, a little over 11 inches long" (100).

Early in his career Willie Mays worked to get subtle edges that would help him become a more productive player. One of those advantages had to do with how he used his glove. In his 1955 book *Born to Play Ball* (written with Charles Einstein), Mays wrote about this.

> I worked to perfect a first-baseman-type hold on my glove. That divides the glove into two parts—the thumb part and the rest of the mitt. The thumb and the rest of the fingers hold their parts in a sort of pincer grip, at the very heel of the glove. The rest of the hand isn't in the glove at all. That means the hand is used only to control the glove. The pocket where the ball hits doesn't have any of me in it at all.

The purpose of this isn't to keep my hand from hurting when a hard liner smacks in there. The purpose is, instead, to add two or three inches of reach onto my gloved hand [88–89].

Balls caught by ballplayers extended to their fullest before Doak's invention would generally be more easily caught in the longer, webbed gloves of the present-day player. In addition to the longer glove length, the fact that many present-day ballplayers are taller and have a longer reach makes balls that would have been impossible for earlier players to catch now catchable. Conditions have changed, but a great catch then was a great catch no matter what has happened since.

PART II: THE CATCHES

FOUR

The Greatest Catches Up to 1900

1887—Dummy Hoy

It is highly unlikely that the catch Dummy Hoy made will ever be equaled in a baseball game.

William Ellsworth Hoy was called "Dummy" because he was deaf, and, as a consequence of his deafness, had a very limited range of vocal expression, a range that in most cases did not permit him to communicate through spoken language. The word "dumb" has been used to refer to those who cannot communicate through spoken language, and each of the early deaf baseball players at one time or another was nicknamed "Dummy."

It should be noted that Hoy himself said that he did use speech to let his teammates in the field know when he was going to catch a ball. He is quoted in the *New York Clipper Annual of 1893* as writing:

> the main point is to avoid a possible collision with ... players who surround me in the field going after a fly ball. Now, whenever I take a fly ball I always yell: "I'll take it," the same as I have been doing for seasons past, and, of course, the other fielders will have to let me take it. Whenever none of these men hears me yell, it is understood that I am not after the ball, and they will govern themselves accordingly, and take it, silence being construed to mean a sign for others to take it, while a yell from me is a sign that I'll take it myself, see?

Hoy was born with normal hearing, but contracted spinal meningitis at age two and lost his hearing. When he was 10, his parents sent him to the Columbus, Ohio to attend the Ohio School for the Deaf, from which he graduated as the valedictorian at age 18. Also known as Bill Hoy, he began his major league career in 1888, and played 14 years for six franchises. He was one of the best fielders and throwers in the majors. As a hitter he averaged .288 over his years in the big leagues. He also stole 514 bases. In his final professional baseball season in 1903, at the age of 42, he played 211 games for the Los Angeles team in the Pacific Coast League. He was five feet, four inches tall and weighed about 150 pounds during his playing days. Dummy Hoy died in 1961 at the age of 99.

The unusual catch was made while Hoy was with the Oshkosh team of the Northwestern League, for which he played in 1886 and 1887. The 1886 team finished third in a six-team league. The 1887 team won the Northwestern League title just edging out their nearest rival, the Milwaukee Cream Citys. In 1886, Hoy played in right field, and 1887 he was Oshkosh's centerfielder. Exactly when and where he made the catch are not clear, though the evidence points to 1887 as being the likelier year.

In *Baseball's Famous Outfielders*, Ira Smith began his section on Hoy with:

> A horse and buggy should have been credited with an assist on a spectacular play Dummy Hoy made soon after he joined the Oshkosh club of the Northwestern League in 1886.
>
> Newspapers around the country printed and reprinted the story about the play. Here's how it appeared in the *New York Clipper*:
>
> A high fly was hit that looked as if it was going over the right field fence, along which out-of-town spectators had their teams and rigs stationed. Hoy went after the ball and, as he ran, saw it was going to be high and far out. As a matter of fact, it was coming down where a horse and buggy were standing. The clever out fielder deliberately leaped on the shaft of the buggy and reached out stretched for the ball over the horse's head, despite the restiveness of the animal.
>
> He froze to the ball and put the batter out, thus saving a home run [22–23].

This drawing of Dummy Hoy appeared in the *New York Clipper Annual* of 1893.

Obviously, Ira Smith places the great catch early in Hoy's first year with Oshkosh, in 1886. However, the same text Ira Smith used about Hoy was included in the *New York Clipper Annual of 1893* and was preceded by the following two sentences: "He is an excellent batsman and a bold base runner, ranking high each season in both these important departments. Hoy has made many clever catches, the most sensational perhaps, being in a championship contest at Oshkosh, in 1886." In the 1880s, when there weren't post-season games to determine league championships, writers referred to regular season games as "championship games." Smith's statement that newspapers around the country carried an account of the catch may not be fully accurate either. The newspapers in Oshkosh and the other cities with teams in the Northwestern League did not give a report of Hoy on the shaft of a buggy when he made a catch.

As can be noted from the following sampling from newspaper accounts of Northwestern League games in 1886 and 1887, specific details of the outstanding catches often were not given. In 1886 Dummy Hoy was singled out a number of times for his fine defensive work. The writer for the May 30, 1886, *Duluth Tribune*, in telling of a 5–2 Duluth win over Oshkosh, said: "Hoy at right, carried off the honors for them yesterday, both at the bat and in the field." Later, the writer referred to Hoy as "the nimble right fielder." The writer for *Duluth Tribune* of July 14, 1886, reported, "Hoy, who is a deaf and dumb man, is one of the best men in the nine. He succeeded in knocking in three or four two baggers and a three bagger and in catching several flys, after having to run quite a distance. He also did good work in the field." Three days later, on July 17, 1886, the baseball writer for the *Minneapolis Tribune* told of an outstanding fielding play by Hoy in a 6–1 Oshkosh win

At New York's Polo Grounds before the turn of the twentieth century the outfield served as a place for people to park their horses and buggies and watch the game. It was in such a setting in 1887 that Dummy Hoy chased after a long fly ball and ascended a buggy's rigging to its horse and caught the ball.

in Minneapolis. "For the visitors Hoy caught a fly in right field after a long run—one of the prettiest catches yet seen on the ground."

In the September 24, 1886, *Eau Claire Daily Leader*, in telling about Eau Claire's 5–3 victory over Oshkosh, the writer's comments about the game included, "Hallstrom, the great Swedish wonder (?), was hit all over the Chippewa river and only the excellent fielding and unusual lucky catches of Hoy and Burns saved the Oshkosh club from the humiliating score being presented to them by the Eau Claires." The details of the "unusual lucky catches" were not given.

In 1887, Hoy continued to excel in the field and at bat. Hoy's fielding was mentioned a number of times by the writers for different newspapers, but none of the comments indicate that Dummy Hoy made a catch in the vicinity of a horse. In his May 24, 1887 report of the game between Oshkosh and Des Moines at Des Moines, the baseball writer for the *Iowa State Register* said, "The running catch of Hoy in centerfield was the feature of the game for the visitors." On June 2, Milwaukee defeated Oshkosh by a 5 to 2 score. The *Saint Paul and Minneapolis Pioneer Press* writer reported, among other things, "The features of fielding were elegant, running catches in the out field by Burns and Hoy." Burns was Oshkosh's left fielder.

In the account of Oshkosh's June 7 17–11 victory over Des Moines, the *Pioneer Press* writer noted, "Hoy, Ellis and Laroque made brilliant running catches." Ellis was Oshkosh's right fielder and Laroque was Des Moines' third baseman. On July 4, 1887, in a 13–6 Oshkosh loss to Milwaukee, Hoy was one of three players cited by the *Pioneer Press* for making "beautiful catches." On July 20, the *Pioneer Press* writer, in telling of a 6–5 Oshkosh victory over St. Paul, said, "Hoy, Burns and Murphy caught very handsome flies." On August 26, the *Pioneer Press* account of the game between Oshkosh and Des Moines, which

Oshkosh won 11–1, commented, "the features were elegant fly catches by McCarthy, Hoy, Whitely and Van Dyke." McCarthy was Oshkosh's right fielder, and Whitely and Van Dyke were outfielders for Des Moines. Later in that same series Dummy Hoy made another noteworthy catch. The reporter for the August 31, 1887, *Iowa State Register* wrote, "Hoy's wonderful running catch of Alvord's hit to deep center deserved all the applause it received."

In the *Pioneer Press*'s September 18, 1887, account of the St. Paul-Oshkosh game of the day before, a 6–3 Oshkosh win, the writer paid Hoy a high compliment: "In the ninth, Cleveland's three-bagger and home after a magnificent catch by Hoy of Burch's hit to the fence corner, gave St. Paul its third run." He ended his report of the game with "Hoy, Burch and Murphy made beautiful running catches." Burch and Murphy were St. Paul outfielders.

Two years in a row in mid–September Dummy Hoy made a catch which led a writer to issue comments that were not frequently made then. In 1886, the Eau Claire writer said he made an "unusual lucky " catch. In 1887 Hoy made a "magnificent" catch.

On October 16, 1887, the *Pioneer Press* did a cover story on the Oshkosh team, the champions of the Northwestern League. There was a sketch and a paragraph of the manager, Frank Selee, and of each player. Of Hoy, the writer said, "He covers center field, and his easy, graceful manner of capturing flies made him many friends. He possesses excellent judgment, and is a very fast runner."

Hoy's own account of the famous catch was in a document, which is part of his file at the National Baseball Hall of Fame, assembled by the Helms Athletic Foundation to support a bid to have Hoy elected to the Hall of Fame:

> In the old days, baseball fans were permitted to drive their horses and buggies inside the parks, encircling the outfield. In one game in which I played, under such conditions, a ball was batted deeply into center-field—with a buggy being its destination. I ran back fast, hopped onto the shaft of the buggy, and made a desperate stab for the ball. I was as surprised as anyone else inside the park when I looked up into my glove and found that the ball finally came to rest in my clutched, padded fingers.

Hoy's account has the ball going to center field. Although he could have ranged over from right field to catch a ball hit to center field in 1886, it is more likely that he already was in center field, the position he played in 1887.

The Helms information had undated quotes from a St. Louis baseball historian, Thomas Lonegran:

> William Hoy, when he played for the St. Louis Browns, in the American Association, was one of the brainiest ball players I ever saw. Every time I had an opportunity to see Hoy play, I would take advantage of it.
>
> Hoy was as swift as a panther in the field. I have seen balls hit for singles that would have been doubles or triples with other players fielding them. With men on bases, Hoy never threw to the wrong spot. Hoy was a "Cobb" on the bases. I never saw him picked off base. He led the National League in base-stealing in 1888. Hoy, a deaf mute, didn't bother about coaches. He did his base-running on his own.

The use of hand signals for indicating whether the pitch was a ball or a strike has been attributed to Dummy Hoy's request for the umpires to give him a clear indicator of what the pitch was. Given that umpires in the major leagues did not begin to use arm and hand signals until about 1906, after Hoy had retired, it seems unlikely that his presence on the field directly led umpires to use such signals. From early in his career, Hoy's teammates signaled balls or strikes to him when he was batting. After Minneapolis defeated Oshkosh 7–2 in Minneapolis on August 18, 1886, the *Minneapolis Tribune*'s unidentified reporter wrote, "Of the Oshkosh players, special attention was directed to Hoy, he being a deaf mute.

When at the bat some other member of the nine stands and holds up fingers for balls and strikes, and at times very vigorous signs are made use of."

After playing for Oshkosh, William Ellsworth Hoy went on to play major league baseball for teams in Washington, Buffalo, St. Louis, Cincinnati, Louisville, and Chicago in the American League.

August 31, 1896—Bill Lange

Bill Lange was one of the greatest baseball players of the 1890s, and perhaps one of the best players of any era. At almost six feet, two inches tall and about 200 pounds, he was a big man in a time of generally shorter men. He was a swift and daring runner who would intimidate infielders on the base paths, and he was an outstanding fielder.

In early 1911, Fred Tenney, then the manager of the Boston Braves, did a series of articles for the *New York Times* on players who had been the best at different positions around the ball field. In his February 26, 1911, article, Tenney included Bill Lange among the top centerfielders he had seen. Among other things, Tenney wrote:

> Probably he was the largest man who ever attempted to play the game. A veritable giant in stature, as well as possessing ability to play baseball, a very fast runner, fine fielder, good hitter, he made a great reputation as a daring base-stealer with a slide that eluded the best of basemen.

After a seven-year career in the majors with the Chicago Colts, and still in his prime as a player, Lange quit baseball to go into real estate and insurance in California.

The catch Lange made on August 31, 1896, in a game against the Washington Senators has become somewhat legendary, and the legend involves his speed and power. Although the articles the day after the catch do not support the legend, the catch is a worthy one to report.

Jim Kaplan, in his book *The Fielders*, tells about the legendary catch. The big, speedy Lange made the catch after a long run in which he reportedly cracked though the outfield fence and onto the street. Kaplan cites Arthur Ahrens's comments about the catch in the 1980 *Baseball Research Journal*, in which Ahrens noted that Lange's great catch occurred after boards in the left field fence had been knocked out to allow an injured player to get to a hospital on the other side, an event which was written about at the time.

The writer for the September 1, 1896, *Washington Post* described the event. Washington's left fielder Selbach was apparently responsible for what later became the legend of a player breaking through an outfield fence. Chicago's first baseman, George Decker, tried to catch an errant throw from his pitcher. The powerful throw struck Decker on the left wrist and broke it. The *Washington Post*'s writer added:

> ...the big first baseman writhed in pain. Tom Brown examined the injured arm and advised Decker to hurry over to the Freedmen's Hospital, which he did.
> Selbach followed Decker to the left field fence that separates the park from the hospital grounds. A ladder rested against the fence, but the player couldn't mount it. Selbach used the ladder for a battering ram, and shoved a row of boards from the fence, through which Decker passed and made his way to the hospital. Physicians found that the wrist bone was broken.

Thus, on that day it was Selbach who broke through the fence, Decker who went through it, and most likely not Lange going through it after a catch.

In the September 1, 1896, *Washington Evening Star*, the game's reporter wrote:

As usual, little Willie Lange was the feature of the afternoon's play. It seemed as if the all the big fellow had to do was get his hands on the ball, no matter what the position or the distance covered, and an out would be registered. The flies captured off Farrell's and DeMontreville's bats bordered on the sensational, and would have gone safe on any other fielder. The big fellow also ran bases in marvelous style, pilfering three and going out at third on a decision which could have been given either way and been correct.

The *Washington Post*'s reporter was even more laudatory about the catch.

In the tenth Lange accomplished one of the most miraculous feats in fielding ever witnessed on a ball field, and it is no exaggeration to say that this catch of Lange's trumped any of the efforts of such fielding bright lights as Mike Griffin or Dick Johnson [*sic*] and Jimmy Fogarty, when that pair of phenoms were in their glory. The performance of Lange's happened in the tenth inning.

De Montreville [*sic*] sent the ball on the line with terrific force to deep center field. As it approached Lange the big outfielder gauged it in a flash of a moment, and turning, ran toward the center-field, his stalwart figure flitting over the ground, propelled by those wide strides of the Lanky Bill. He was back to the ball as he ran, but his head was veered around and, turning after he had measured his distance with marvelous accuracy, raised his rangy arms and caught the ball. From the grandstand it looked as if Lange had covered almost half the distance spanned by the ball. The crowd arose and cheered him lustily, the players on the Washington bench joining in the applause while Uncle Anson raised his head and greeted Bill with a courteous bow.

Later in the article the author described Lange's catch on Farrell in the sixth.

Farrell drove a hard liner to left center. The ball soared toward the bulletin board, and as visions of a three-bagger danced in the heads of the fans, Bill Lange advanced on a hard run and pulled down the sphere.

Still later, the author gives another, briefer account of Lange's catch on DeMontreville.

Next occurred the phenomenal play of Bill Lange's. De Montreville raised the ball on the line to deep center, and Lange by a burst of speed and dive in the air pulled down De Mont's fly, and saved Lush from scoring the winning run, as Monty was the third out.

The *Chicago Tribune*'s baseball writer also was enthusiastic about Lange's catch.

Lange scored another of his marvelous plays, and every man who saw this last great feat in fielding is willing to swear that the big centerfielder is the greatest all-around player in the profession. It was at one of the many close stages of the game when everything depended on the outcome of a single play.

In the tenth inning the Senators had a man on third base and two men out. Selbach hit a terrific drive to center field. It was not a fly, but low liner, with speed and straight as a bullet. Lange was deep in the field, but the instant the ball left the bat he turned and ran for the fence. He did not look up until the ball nearly overtook him. To the crowd it looked like a neck and neck race. He seemed to be following the ball as a boy chases a butterfly, waiting for it to come into reach. As the ball passed over his left shoulder he sprang into the air. He fell on his head and shoulders and rolled over on his back, holding the ball as high as he could reach his right hand.

He gave the ball the advantage of a flying start and won the race. The crowd forgot the game and prejudice. The applause and cheering lasted until long after Lange had walked in from the field and took his seat on the bench.

The *Chicago Tribune* writer reported that Selbach hit the ball that Lange caught. The other two accounts have DeMontreville as the batter. Given the accounts of the game in the two Washington papers, clearly DeMontreville hit the ball. Selbach led off the eleventh inning for Washington, walked, and later scored the winning run, the only run of the game.

In a 1944 article in the *Chicago Daily News*, Lange himself contributes to the confusion about his great catch by referring to the wrong date, and by identifying Selbach as the batter. The title of the article was "My Biggest Baseball Day," with the subtitle "It Was July, 1896, When Lange Saved Game for Colts with Great Catch." On the date noted, Chicago played at home against Washington, and there was no mention in Chicago papers of a spectacular catch by Lange on anyone. The details Lange gives of his catch, other than having Selbach as the hitter, fit those given for the game on August 31, 1896. Lange himself did not say he broke through a fence. He said he "crashed off the fence."

The next paragraph in the *Daily News* article, a parenthetical one, gives one explanation for the legend of Lange breaking through the fence: "(Editor's note: Griffith relates that Lange's impact (he was a huge 220-pounder) was so terrific that the fence caved in and Bill was literally out of the park, but that he held the ball in plain sight of the umpire.)" The "Griffith" referred to was Clark Griffith, who pitched for Chicago on the day Lange made this spectacular catch. Griffith should be considered a reliable witness even though the newspaper accounts of the game do not mention that part of the fence went down after Lange made the catch and supposedly tumbled into it.

In an August 2, 1950, obituary column in *The Sporting News* about Lange's passing on July 23, Griffith again was quoted. By 1950, Griffith, then the owner of the Washington Senators, was one of the elder statesmen in baseball. He had seen baseball's greatest players from the early 1890s to the time Lange died.

> When informed of his death, Clark Griffith, president of the Washington Senators, said: "I played ball with Bill Lange on the Chicago National League club for some eight years. I have seen all the other great outfielders—Speaker, Cobb, DiMaggio—in action, and I consider Bill Lange the equal of, if not better than, all outfielders of all time. There wasn't anything he couldn't do."

Later in the article, the author mentions Lange's base running.

> Considered one of the greatest base runners of all time, Lange, in 1896, stole 100 bases, a feat the great Ty Cobb later failed to equal. Ty's best mark was 96 in 1915. In his seven years with the Chicago team, Big Bill pilfered 515 sacks.
>
> Here's what Honus Wagner once said about the Californian: "I'll never forget the first time I tried to put the ball on Lange. He pulled the prettiest hookslide I ever saw, and there I was, standing sort of foolish-like, with the ball, nowhere near him."

Almost a year after Lange made the great catch in Washington, he made another sensational catch in Chicago against Cincinnati on July 27, 1897. The *Chicago Tribune's* sportswriter described the tense game's first extra inning:

> The head of both batting lists were carded to start the round. The crowd stood upon its feet and yelled for victory. Burke came up and smashed a liner straight into Lange's mitt, while the crowd went into paroxysms of joy. Then Hoy drove the ball fiercely across first base. The multitude stood awed while Anson moved and by a quick jump hauled in the flying sphere and ran—actually and really ran—to first and beat the dummy out. Corcoran was next, and the fates of the struggle hung on him. He smote the ball hard and squarely, and shot it out over the wind billows, dancing along toward the clubhouse like a swallow through a gleam of light.
>
> Lange was after it. He tore across at the top of his terrific speed, skimming the ground, turned half around, stretched, and hauled in the ball, finishing his plunging run by staggering and falling until he brought up against the fence.
>
> The crowd went into a frenzy of excitement....

The writer for the *Chicago Times-Herald* was as enthusiastic about the catch as the *Tribune's* reporter:

Then Lange signaled his return to the game by one of those catches for which he is noted. Corcoran pushed the ball out between right and center for what appeared a triple or possibly a home run. "Bill" was after it without ado. With hands stretched far in front of him, he got the ball when it was about the level of his waist, stumbled a few times, partially recovered himself, lost his balance again and finally fell against the fence in front of the field seats.

The following scene was one of the wildest of the season. The pride of soubrettes has made as good catches this season. Decker's performance Sunday equaled, if not exceeded it, but the play came at a time when the excitement was already at fever heat. The bleachers rose en masse and cheered, and the "cranks" in the stand climbed on the seats and waved their hats. Not until Lange had doffed his cap three times were his admirers appeased.

Chicago won the game in exciting fashion when Bill Everitt, the first batter up for the Colts in the tenth inning, hit a home run to win the game by a 4 to 3 score.

Although newspaper reports from the Washington papers in 1896 do not indicate that Bill Lange knocked over the outfield fence by crashing into it, other reports, particularly Clark Griffith's, are hard to dismiss. What cannot be debated is Bill Lange's great fielding play in Washington on August 31, 1896.

In the 1944 *Chicago Daily News* article, Lange recalls an article written by Hugh Fullerton, an early baseball writer, who is in the Hall of Fame as a writer. Lange wrote:

> A few years ago, Hughie Fullerton wrote a magazine story about my play on Selbach's drive and called it the greatest catch of all time, taking precedence over the one Willie Keeler made off the slanting fence in Baltimore; Hughie Jennings' sensational catch of a foul and several that Tris Speaker made.

May 10, 1897—Willie Keeler

Hall of Famer Willie Keeler is most famous today as the man whose record forty-four consecutive game hitting streak was broken by Joe DiMaggio in 1941, and as the man who said, "Hit 'em where they ain't."

In the 1890s Keeler was the one of the best all-around players, if not the best player, in major league baseball. He was an expert batter and base runner, and a peerless outfielder at his right field position. He was one of the fastest runners in major league baseball. In October, after the 1896 season, he reportedly was timed at 10.25 seconds in the hundred-yard dash. (Keeler's teammate, Joe Kelley, had the same time in that race.) The winning time in the 100-yard dash at the 1896 national championships was 10.2 seconds. In his book *Baseball in Baltimore: The First Hundred Years,* James H. Bready wrote that the footing was muddy the day of the race. No matter what the conditions of Keeler's dash, the results indicate that he and his outfield partner Kelley had great speed for those times.

After Willie Keeler died on January 1, 1923, John McGraw, his former teammate on the dominant Baltimore Oriole teams of the mid–1890s, was quoted in the *New York Times* of January 3. McGraw said that Keeler was one of the best fielders in the history of baseball and, as a batter, could place balls better than anyone McGraw had ever seen. McGraw added, "He was also the fastest man going down to first base I ever watched on the ball field. That was in his prime when it was child's play for him to beat out bunts and infield grounders."

In the space of about ten days early in the 1897 season, Keeler made two catches which demonstrated his outstanding skills as a fielder. The first catch was on April 30 against the New York Giants in Baltimore. The headlines for the game in *Baltimore Sun* were:

Keeler the Wonder.
Makes a Hit Every Time, Scores Three of the Five Runs
BUT HE DOES NOT STOP THERE
Cavorts Up a Fence and Takes a Fly Ball in the Air

The *Sun*'s account of the game opened with:

That little baseball marvel, Keeler, had no rival yesterday as the star performer in the Oriole cast and the principal factor in the second victory of the champions over the New Yorks. Without detracting from the credit due "Wizard" Hoffer for the masterly game he pitched, it can be safely said that without the wonderful batting, base-running, and fielding of Baltimore's great little right fielder there would be a different tale to tell of yesterday's game at Union Park.

Keeler hit safely every time he came to bat, made four of Baltimore's nine hits, three of the five runs, stole three of the four stolen bases, and under the old rules would have had two more.

Besides all this, he made the most sensational catch seen at Union Park this season, which cut off at least one run and perhaps more. The catch was a record-breaker. It occurred in the fourth inning and robbed Beckley of a double at least. Beckley picked out a good one, caught it right, and it went sailing for the right-field fence. Keeler was after it like a flash, as usual.

He kept ahead of it until he got to the fence and had to stop. Then he saw that the ball, if let alone, would strike the boards above his head. He made a running jump on the fence and caught the ball. As he took it one foot was on the side of the fence and the other dangling in the air. When he returned to terra firma with the ball in his hand there was a perfect roar of applause.

The unidentified writer for the *New York Herald* wrote the following about Keeler's catch:

"Little Willie" Keeler, who honors Brooklyn with his place of residence, probably robbed the New York Club of a victory. It was in that fateful fourth inning again, when the score stood 1 to 0 in Baltimore's favor. "Yakey" Beckley got one just to his liking and sent the ball curving to right field. Keeler followed it back, and just as the ball was about to hit the fence about eight feet from the ground that great little player jumped two feet into the air and picked the ball off the boards as if it were a grub and he a woodpecker. In making the catch he skinned his hand on the fence.

Master batter Willie Keeler is shown in his prime with his glove in his back pocket and choking way up on the bat to best control where he will hit the pitched ball.

In a "Notes of the Game" section on the sports page of the *New York*

World, the unidentified author commented about others' reactions to Keeler's defensive efforts.

> The Baltimores have the grandest player in the league in little Willie Keeler. The boy is simply wonderful in every branch of the business. He jumped and picked a hit of Beckley's right off the fence yesterday, cruelly robbing Jake Beckley of a two-sacker. Jake fairly wept as he returned to the bench, and all hands sympathized with him. They've all been robbed by the same fellow.

The *Baltimore American*'s writer lauded Keeler's role in being the dominant player in the game.

> Willie Keeler was the hero, the bright particular star of the game, and it rested with him to arouse all the latent enthusiasm that was in the crowd. He did it, too, but, then, who could help being enthused over such work as was done by this great little right fielder yesterday. If he did not win the game for the Champs who did? Three of the five runs scored by them were his, four of the nine hits made by them were also his, and his again was the most thrilling and sensational play seen at Union Park in many a day.
> No wonder the cranks stood up and yelled until they were hoarse. Keeler had been playing in when Beckley, the mighty, strode to the plate, and brought his bat into such violent contact with one of Hoffer's fast ones that the ball went whizzing through the air like a shot toward the right field fence. Everybody thought the ball was easily over the fence, and Beckley was well on his way toward third base, when Willie Keeler, by a great run back, threw himself against the fence and nailed the ball on the very boards. It was a great catch, and easily the feature of the game.

Later in the description of the game's highlights, the *American*'s writer noted that Keeler "by the most daring kind of base running" scored from second base on a wild pitch. Another indication of Keeler's speed was included in a "NOTES OF THE DIAMOND" section. The writer said that three "of Keeler's hits were infield balls that no other man on the team could have beaten out but him."

Better known than his catch on April 30 in New York is the catch Keeler made in Washington in a 13 to 5 Orioles loss to the Senators. The catch came on May 10, 1897, and, like Dummy Hoy's catch while standing on a buggy, is unlikely to be duplicated.

The *Baltimore Sun*'s account of the game included the following about Keeler's catch: "Jennings played great ball, and Keeler made a phenomenal catch of DeMontreville's fly in the first inning, taking the ball above his head against the wire screen in right field." Not only was the *Sun*'s account incomplete, but possibly incorrect in its claim that the ball was hit by DeMontreville. Other accounts say Selbach hit the ball.

The *Baltimore American*'s writer called Keeler's catch on Selbach "the most remarkable" in a game which "abounded in plays of the sensational kind." The writer did not comment on the barbed-wire hazard Keeler had to go through, but did say Keeler caught the ball "as it was disappearing in the bleachers."

Neither the *Baltimore American*'s nor the *Baltimore Sun*'s account was as complete or as accurate as the accounts in the Washington papers. The *Washington Post* gave two accounts of the catch. The first was:

> In the first inning Willie Keeler, the lilliputian phenom of the Orioles, buncoed Al Selbach out of a home run. Selbach shot a liner to the bleachers, but Keeler stopped the passage of the sphere by shoving his left arm into the barbed wire netting, and his mitt froze to the ball. Willie's escape from scratching his hand on the barbed wire was as marvelous as his catch.

The second account read: "Selbach slammed a liner to the bleachers, and the midget wonder, Willie Keeler, advanced on a side run, flung his left arm over the barbed wire fence, and clung to the ball."

The term "midget wonder" and other references to Keeler's size came about because Keeler was about five feet, four and a half inches tall and weighed about 140 pounds. Although Keeler was shorter than many of his contemporaries in the major leagues, players then were shorter than the players of today. In 1900, a five foot, eight inch man would have been about at the average height.

The *Washington Evening Star* described Keeler's catch this way:

> As a start off little Willie Keeler ... made a break for the bleachers as Selbach's hard-hit fly was sailing in that direction. Nine players out of ten would have been content to make the try for the ball, but in the face of the obstacles represented by a barbed wire fence, the nimble little fielder jumped in to the air against the fence, shoved out his left hand and the ball stuck. The play was undoubtedly one of the nerviest and most skillful that has been pulled off at National Park.

The *Washington Morning Times* was even more generous in its account.

> Selbach then came up and after fouling off a few, smashed the ball to right field seemingly safe for a home run. Just as the Spalding [ball] was looping over the wire fence up jumped "Wee Willie" Keeler, and with one hand stuck up, grabbed the sphere and held it tight. It was an astounding piece of fielding, the like of which will hardly be seen this season or any other. The little Birdie was repeatedly applauded for the feat.

The Keeler catch in Washington is referred to in at least three other places. Ira Smith, in his 1954 book *Baseball's Famous Outfielders*, dates the catch in 1895 and identifies the pitcher as Charley Abbey. In his 1988 book *John McGraw*, Charles Alexander tells of a catch in Washington that McGraw called the greatest catch he ever saw. Alexander puts the date as June of 1898, and describes a sliding, bare-hand catch in foul territory and into the barbed wire. The earliest mention is the one McGraw himself offers. McGraw's description differs from the one Alexander gives.

Twenty-six years after the catch, in his book *My Thirty Years in Baseball*, McGraw recalled it as the most spectacular catch he had ever seen. Some of McGraw's recollections do not fit with the accounts in the Washington papers of the day after the game in 1897, but his memory comes from being on the field with Keeler that day, and despite the thousands of catches that he had seen, Keeler's catch was still a special one for him. In 1923, McGraw tells of the hard-hit ball by the Washington batter and where it went:

> On the top of the railing in front of the right field bleachers there were three or four strands of barbed wire, just a little higher than the outfielder's head. It seemed sure that the ball would clear this barbed wire.
> Willie Keeler started with the crack of the bat and got to the fence in time, but it looked as if the ball would go into the stand over his head. That's what it did—almost.
> Seeing the predicament, Willie leaped in the air and fearlessly stuck his bare hand between the strands of barbed wire. The ball struck in his hand and he held it. He held it, despite the painful cutting of his hand as he dragged it back over the sharp barbs. That catch was talked about for months. I have never seen another one like it. It showed marvelous judgment of distance, accuracy and unusual courage [166–167].

It should be noted that since Willie Keeler was left-handed thrower, the bare-hand catch McGraw describes would have been made in his left hand.

In Fred Tenney's 1911 assessment of the best right fielders, Willie Keeler was the best. In the *New York Times* of March 5, 1911, Tenney, then the manager of the National League's Boston team, wrote:

> The name of Willie Keeler brings to one's mind the diminutive size of this baseball "giant," for years, probably the best-known and best-liked of all ball players. Popular everywhere,

praised everywhere, lauded by the newspapers and fellow-players, yet he remained the same quiet, gentlemanly, unassuming chap. A wonderful fielder, very fast runner, sure catcher, and strong thrower, coupled with an extraordinary ability with the bat, he was the type of ideal fielder. Apparently he could hit and place a ball in any part of the field he desired. Woe to the infielder who started to cover the bag when "Wee Willie" was batting, as he invariably would place the ball just where the fielder had been. This faculty made him a wonderful workman in the run and hit play. He started playing at third base, and his hitting was so strong that both New York and Brooklyn secured him, only to pass him up when it was discovered he was left-handed. Wise Hanlon took him, immediately placed him where he belonged, and developed him into a star of the first magnitude.

Fred Tenney began his major league career in 1894 for Boston, and, for most of his years in the league, was a first baseman.

A catch attributed to Keeler, but difficult to document, was included in *Touching Second*, a book by John J. Evers and Hugh S. Fullerton. That 1910 book, reprinted in 2005, included a description of the catch probably entered by the sportswriter Fullerton. As presented, the catch is an unusual one and one which most likely would have drawn the mention of other writers who covered the game. However, a search of the reports of games played between Baltimore and Boston, the opponents Fullerton paired, and between the players noted—Keeler, the fielder, and Chick Stahl, the Boston player who supposedly hit the ball Keeler caught—was not fruitful.

The account in *Touching Second*, which unfortunately does not provide a date for Keeler's catch, follows:

> That Baltimore crowd, a team of only fair players winning by dash, nerve and courage, gave many exhibitions of individual daring, but one of the greatest was the feat of "Wee Willie" Keeler on the home grounds. Right field on the Baltimore grounds of those days was the terror of visiting players. It was down hill, rough and weedy, and back of it was a high fence, peculiarly constructed for advertising purposes. Inside the fence sloped at an angle of about 65 degrees, being straight on the outer side. Boston was playing there late in the season in which the two teams had their frantic struggle for the pennant, and late in the game, with runners on bases, Stahl drove a long fly to right that seemed likely to win the game for Boston. Keeler, one of the fleetest men in the business, seeing the ball was going over his head, leaped upon the slope of the fence and started to run along it, going higher and higher, and just as the ball was going over the fence he caught it. His momentum carried him along the incline and before the big crowd realized he caught the ball, he was running along the top of the fence, and then, holding the ball aloft, he plunged over and fell outside the grounds. Probably never a ball player received such an outburst of applause as he did when he climbed over the fence and tossed the ball to the infield [249–250].

FIVE

1900–1919

August 9, 1909—Spotswood Poles

In his book *The Complete Book of Baseball's Negro Leagues: The Other Half of Baseball History*, John Holway notes the August 10 *Detroit Free Press*'s coverage of the game in which Spotswood Poles made an outstanding catch. The catch by Poles is one of the few catches by a black player that was documented in any detail prior to the integration of major league baseball in 1947. Poles's catch came in the first of three games played in Detroit between the Leland Giants from Chicago and the Philadelphia Giants, the team for which Poles played.

At the time Poles made the catch he was nineteen years old and already was a standout fielder in part because of his speed. In his book *The Biographical Encyclopedia of the Negro Baseball Leagues*, James A. Riley reports that one time in spring training, the five feet, seven inch Poles ran the 100-yard dash in less than ten seconds, a phenomenal time then. Riley also noted that one of the greatest managers, the New York Giants' John McGraw, would have selected Spotswood Poles to be one of four black players to break the color barrier in the major leagues.

The unidentified *Detroit Free Press* writer was not shy about praising the efforts of the players on black teams. Several times he indicated that some of these players were as good as any who ever played on the Bennett Field turf, which included players on the Detroit Tigers and other major league teams. For example, he wrote, "The Quakers tore off some defensive plays that would have done credit to any club that cavorted on the park."

One of the things that impressed the writer was the throwing arms on the field, especially Pete Hill's.

> Both clubs have a number of fine throwers, and in fact every man in the fracas seemed to have a wing. Hill lined one to the plate in the third on Poles' sacrifice fly that would have beaten any runner in the game. Had not the catcher let it get away, the sprinter from third would have been out by a block.

Later he wrote of the Chicago pitcher Walter Ball:

> The latter, a right-hander, was ordered to get a pair of right-hand hitters next in order. Without any warming up, he turned loose a curve ball and a fast one that were beauty brights. The fast one in particular is an offering that a lot of leaguers would like to have in their repertoire. It apparently jumps six inches.

Ball's catcher, Bruce Petway, also came in for praise. He was compared to Lou Criger, a veteran major league catcher who was a defensive standout for the St. Louis Browns in 1909: "One man who looks every inch a player is Petway, the catcher of the Philadelphians.

The Philadelphia Giants' Spotswood Poles, in a photo probably from around 1910, was one of the greatest players of all time.

In build this chap is a ringer for Lou Criger, and in receiving and throwing the likeness isn't so poor."

However, it was Poles's catch which most brought the *Free Press* writer to his feet. He wrote:

The big noise of the day in the way of run-savers was the catch by Poles in center field. Wright, the Leland shortstop, met a fast one right on the nose and started it on a line to the flagpole. Poles set sail with the crack of the bat, running at right angles to the course of the ball, made a leap high in the air just as he got under it, and came down with the pellet clutched in his gloved hand. A more spectacular bit of fielding never has been seen on the lot. The ball was a potential home run when it started, and there are few outfielders in the game who would have speared it.

One of the subtitles for the article was: "Poles Features With One-Hand Catch of Ball Headed for the Flagpole." This indicates that Spotswood Poles had to be wary of colliding with the flagpole that was then in the field of play. Poles's great catch did not prevent his team from losing to the Lelands 3 to 1.

There was another article in the *Free Press* sports page on August 10, 1909, telling that the Leland Giants were going to meet a high-level amateur team from Detroit following the series with the Philadelphia team. The anonymous author of the article appears to have been the same person who wrote about the Leland Giants–Philadelphia Giants game from the day before. He made it very clear about the caliber of players the Negro teams had:

The Leland Giants have at times beaten some of the best clubs in the country, including a number of league aggregations. Several of their men would be in the big leagues if they belonged to the Caucasian race, notably Rube Foster, who is considered among the best pitchers in the world, barring nobody. He has worked against some of the leading batsmen of both leagues and they have found his offerings as vivid a proposition as anything in the hurling line ever cut loose.

This drawing is a reproduction of an August 10, 1909, *Detroit Free Press* cartoon by "Schroeder" that shows Spotswood Poles, who played for the Philadelphia Giants, making a catch against a hitter from Chicago's Leland Giants. This cartoon was one of the few published images, if not the only one, showing a great player from the early black baseball teams making a sensational play (drawing by Darryl Swanson, North Collins, N.Y.).

August 16, 1909—Red Murray

John "Red" Murray was one of the New York Giants' fleet outfielders who often tracked down balls that others thought were sure hits. Although he made many fine catches in his career, including several in the 1912 World Series against the Boston Red Sox, Murray's most storied catch was one he made in Pittsburgh (then "Pittsburg") shortly after Forbes Field opened in 1909.

The August 16 game was a pitchers' battle between the Giants' Christy Mathewson and the Pirates' Vic Willis. Red Murray was the Giants' right fielder. The *New York Times*' writer titled his article "MATHEWSON TWICE SAVED BY MURRAY," and wrote:

> New York ought to send a big delegation to Philadelphia to cheer Red Murray when he appears in that city with the rest of the Giants tomorrow, for today, first by a good double play and later by one of the most magnificent catches ever made in baseball, he saved Christy Mathewson from a second defeat at the hands of the Pirates. Murray's play retired the locals with Leach and Wagner on second and third, and the score 2 to 2. Had it not been made the result would have been at least 4 to 2 in Pittsburg's favor, for the fly, if uncaught, must have been a triple. [Giants manager John] McGraw's great little outfielder achieved his feat in the nick of time, as the game was stopped by the end of that round—the eighth— by a downpour that made resumption of play out of the question.
>
> That it did not reach the ground was astounding. It was careening to Seymour's territory, far out of Si's reach. Tommy and Hans were pounding the paths homeward from the crack of the bat, and Miller was hotfooting from first to second when the catch was made. New Yorkers in the grand stand had their hearts in their throats. Apparently the game had been snatched from the Giants, the Pirates having tied in

The New York Giants' John "Red" Murray, shown here around 1912, was a consistently outstanding fielder, and made his most famous catch in Pittsburgh in 1909 while rain and lightning were in the skies above him.

> that inning. Eleven thousand local rooters roared as if the pennant's fate hinged on the outcome of the afternoon's sport. If ever a fly looked safe, that fly did.
>
> But all that time young Murray was legging it athwart the sward. He ran so fast he looked like an inverted Y with the upper end dipped in the sunset's hue. Fielders in the past may have sprinted as fast before, but none present could name them offhand. Red's spurt was glorious. It took him from a deep point in his own position way inside Si's bailiwick. Not until he was well inside the middle of centre field did the spectators begin to reckon the chance of his getting under the ball. Up to that moment everybody had taken it for granted the smash was a three-bagger, and a good many figured it a homer. Well that rain came down. No ordinary baseball crowd could stand much more in an afternoon after such ball as that. Murray's catch was a fine climax to a game which, flawless on the part of New York, was brilliant on the other side, despite three errors. 'Tis no light task to hammer Christy Mathewson almost out of the box. Yet that was what the Pirates were doing again when Murray saved the Boy Wonder in that grueling eighth.

In the article Murray was called "McGraw's great little outfielder." Murray was not that "little." He was five feet, ten and a half inches tall, and weighed about 190 pounds.

The *New York Times* writer omitted a couple of details which made Murray's catch even more remarkable. In the *Pittsburgh Gazette Times*, the unidentified writer added those details:

> When it was announced that Mathewson would pitch, the spectators burst into applause, but this was nothing to the demonstration enacted when the Pirates tied the score in the eighth inning. At that time there were dark clouds that nearly touched the ground. Forks of lightning gamboled above head and thunder rolled with a boom that made everybody duck his head between his shoulders.

After describing the events leading to Leach's at-bat, the *Gazette Times'* writer continued:

> Leach ... hit for two bases and again the crowd cut loose. It was too much of a picnic to keep quiet and the spectators did not lessen their enthusiasm. Clarke went out to Bridwell on a fly. That silenced a few, but when Wagner was deliberately given his base on ball by the great Mathewson, the air was again shaken and splintered by huzzas. While raindrops big as plates were falling and a mystic darkness began to envelop the park, Miller hit for a home run. The crowd went mad. It yelled itself hoarse and went through antics that would give an alienist [psychiatrist] an easy line on the witness stand.
>
> Then suddenly the noise ceased, and a hand-clapping followed it, because it was not a home run, but it was caught by Red Murray not three feet off the ground. Murray stuck out his naked hand and the ball stuck in it. He was on a dead run and probably never knew the ball hit it, that is the naked hand. The play retired the side, and the rain came down in "torrents."
>
> The rain lasted for thirty minutes, flooding the entire field. Then Umpire Klem gingerly, finding his way, declared the game off.

The unidentified writer for the *Pittsburgh Press* centered his story on Murray's catch. His article was titled "Spectacular Catch by 'Red' Murray Robs Pirates of Victory," and subtitled, "Yesterday's Battle Between Giants and League Leaders Ends in a Tie, Under Unprecedented Conditions." He went on to write:

> Amid such a scene as was probably never before witnessed on a ball field, the contest between the Pirates and the Giants at Forbes Field yesterday afternoon came to a close after eight innings of play, with the score a tie at 2–2.
>
> The Pirates were robbed of victory by "Red" Murray, a New York outfielder who, under exceedingly adverse conditions, made one of the most spectacular catches ever pulled off anywhere, when he grabbed Jack Miller's long fly, ending the inning with two fleet-footed Pirates on the bases.
>
> When the eighth inning opened, the storm which had been brewing for an hour broke in all its fury. The wind whistled, the lightning flashed, the thunder crashed and the rain descended. The score was 2 to 1 in New York's favor. Willis and Mathewson were the opposing slabbists. The Giants were quickly retired in their half, and Pittsburg came to bat. The New Yorkers were playing for rain. They resorted to all sorts of tactics to delay the game until the rain should descend in such torrents as to make the continuance of the game impossible. But the storm king was a Pirate fan, and he held off for a few moments.
>
> It was Vic Willis' turn to bat, but Manager Clarke sent Hyatt to the plate. The big fellow opened the inning by cracking out a long triple. The crowd fairly yelled itself hoarse, and paid no attention to the ominous signs overhead. Then Jap Barbeau sent Hyatt across the plate with the tying run on his long fly to [Giants centerfielder] Seymour. Tommy Leach caused another outburst of enthusiasm from the 10,000 fans when he clouted a two-bagger. Manager Clarke tried hard to advance him, but flied to Bridwell. Wagner was wisely passed up by Mathewson. That brought Jack Miller to bat. The fans implored him to "kill it." Jack swung

viciously twice and missed. Then over came another shoot. Darkness was settling in, and for a moment the fans thought he had fanned. Then the ball was seen rising, rising ever rising far out over the heads of the waiting fielders. Cy Seymour never saw the flight of the sphere. Several of the Giants threw up their hands in discouragement. But "Red" Murray had his eye on the ball. Leach and Wagner had both crossed the plate, and Miller was rounding third when the most wonderful catch ever seen at Forbes Field was pulled off, Murray getting the sphere in his bare hand after a long run. The inning was over and the Pirates had been robbed of victory, for in a moment the storm broke with renewed fury, and the umpires called time. They waited half an hour, and then the game was declared off.

Although the author of the *Press* report might have exaggerated a few things, that Murray's catch was a great one seems beyond dispute. It is likely the ball was wet and dirty, and it probably was very difficult to see the ball given the rain, the lightning, and the darkness at that time of the day.

April 13, 1911—Dode Paskert

In the second game of the 1911 season, George "Dode" Paskert of the Philadelphia Phillies made a catch the likes of which most spectators had never seen. The writers for the New York papers were unanimous in their praise of what Paskert had done.

The unidentified writer for the *New York Times* wrote:

In the eighth inning George Paskert, the Phillies' centre fielder, made one of the most remarkable catches ever seen at the Polo Grounds. When the ball left Snodgrass's bat and went winging into left center field, it was as fine a looking home run as you ever saw. With the crack of the bat Paskert turned and ran toward the fence. His chances of reaching the ball were worth about a nickel. On, on Paskert galloped. His right arm was stretched as far as it would go, and he made a desperate leap, as if leaving the earth forevermore. The ball just about met his finger tips. The bare right hand squeezed the bulb and Paskert kept on running. Everybody in the stands thought the ball had rolled to the fence and Snodgrass kept on pushing around the bases.

The umpires were dumbfounded and didn't know what had happened. Paskert came running in and when he reached the diamond, he tossed the ball into the air from the hand where it had stuck.

The writer for the *New York Herald* saw Paskert's catch this way:

The game was much livelier than on the opening day, as full of action as one of those tragedies which costs one thirty cents to see. But the one feature which stood out was a catch made by Paskert, another Cincinnati acquisition of recent sending. It was one of the best catches ever made on the field. Two men were out in the eighth inning and Devore was on first when Snodgrass hit the ball on a line between left and center fields. It looked to be good for a home run, or at least three bases. Paskert started after it, but it looked as hopeless as chasing rainbows. Back he ran, back, back, back, with the ball. Then he half turned, stuck out one hand, the nude one, spearing the ball. The howl died on the lips of the ten thousand. The ray of hope had flashed across the game like a meteor across the summer sky and was gone. But the ten thousand were good sports, for with the death of the yell of triumph, a shout of appreciation sprang to their lips. Paskert was applauded to the echo.

Damon Runyon of the *New York American* wrote:

A fellow who goes by the name of Paskert ... pulled the audience right out of their seats in the eighth inning when, with Devore on first, Snodgrass aimed one at the safety razor sign, which is about as far as you can hit 'em without killing a bleacherite. Paskert grabbed it with his bare hand right off the edge of a cloud, and came running in with the ball when most people were supposing it was still on its way.

Elsewhere on the same *New York American* sports page was another description of Paskert's catch in which the unidentified author said:

Paskert showed the most wonderful catch ever seen on the Polo Grounds. It was in the eighth inning. Devore was on first with two out, when Snodgrass caught one of Rowan's fast ones with all his force on the end of his bat. The ball shot out on a low line to left centre. With the crack of the bat Paskert turned his back and raced madly toward the wall. He was seen to leap wildly and clutch furtively with his bare hand, but no one dreamed he had the ball. He raced on almost to the fence in his mad career, then sprinted back as fast as he could around Magee's pasture and tossed the sphere to Lobert. He had killed an extra base hit on a one in a million chance.

The *New York Sun*'s account of the game, probably written by William Hanna, told more about Paskert's contribution.

Two ex–Reds did a lot toward beating the Giants. One was the muscular Rowan, the other was the lissome Paskert. The Giants made but three hits off Rowan and Paskert was the whole outfield in himself. He captured eight fly balls. Anything in his domain between second base and the rear wall was his. All was grist that came to his voracious mill. He blossomed like a green bay tree and smothered sky high hoists with annoying avidity. In addition he busted the ball for a two bagger and a single.

The pernicious Paskert made a catch in the eighth inning which struck the crowd dumb. It was a first cousin to a miracle. Devore was on first when Snodgrass drove a furious liner to left centre. The hit was good for a home run unless something phenomenal intervened, but Paskert was the phenomenal something. He wheeled and ran swiftly for the ball. When he came within negotiable distance he reached out as far as he could with his bare hand, and all strung out as it were, his fingers entwined themselves around the whistling ball.

Snodgrass, with no thought that the ball could be caught, was tearing around second base and Devore was at the plate. He stood there in amazement when he saw his mates getting ready to go on the field—it was the third out. Then he turned and saw Paskert and [left fielder Sherry] Magee both racing in full tilt and Doolan slapping Paskert on the back. Paskert never stopped running from the moment of the catch until he reached the bench.

In 1911 in New York, Philadelphia's George "Dode" Paskert made a spectacular catch that led one writer to say facetiously the sparks off Paskert's catch caused the old wooden stands at the Polo Grounds to burn down later that day.

The impetus carried him further out, then he made a detour and came in. "Grand larceny!" exclaimed the fans, also "For the love of Mike!"

The *New York World*'s account of the game included more information about the scene around Paskert's catch.

In the eighth inning Rowan opened up a trifle and passed Josh Devore. Doyle lifted to Lobert, and then Snodgrass cut loose a liner that looked like a sure triple, if not a homer.

Paskert made a dash for the sailing pellet, stuck out his ungloved hand and speared the ball. He kept on the dead run, in a circle, and didn't throw the ball until he was near third.

In the mean time, Devore was legging it for home, with half the crowd yelling like mad, thinking Paskert had missed the catch. [Right fielder John] Titus, also confused, was tearing like an automobile for the centre field fence, looking for the ball. Josh Devore's expression after he crossed the plate and finally "dropped" was a study.

The unidentified writer for the *New York Evening Telegram* put the Paskert catch on high ground.

Although it is "some early" to discuss the question of the "best ever" in baseball, the committee of the present is willing to make a unanimous decision that the one hand catch which was made by Paskert of Snodgrass' liner yesterday afternoon, was one of the best of its kind ever seen on the Polo Ground, or any other well broken and well-behaved ground.

We do not know who was included in the "committee of the present," but presumably the author was talking about his colleagues in the press box, some of whom most likely had been reporting on baseball from the 1880s on.

After noting the outstanding game the Phillies' Jack Rowan pitched against the Giants' pitching star, Christy Mathewson, the unidentified writer for the *Philadelphia Inquirer* gave his account of Paskert's catch.

The Phillies new hurler, however, was not by any means the hero of the conflict. Paskert, the honey boy, who gained that name because he is such a sweet ball player, got into the spotlight by making the greatest catch ever seen on the Polo Grounds and by making six other captures that were in the nature of pippins. In the eighth spasm the former Red camped on the trail of Snodgrass' long welt, which everyone thought would blossom into either a triple or a home run, and made a back-handed and bare handed capture of the crack.

Also among the "committee of the present" in the press box that day early in the 1911 season was the young writer Fred Lieb, then at the beginning of his career as a baseball writer. Over the next sixty-six years, Lieb would rank Paskert's catch near the top of the best catches ever made. In his 1977 book *Baseball as I Have Known It*, Fred Lieb wrote that Paskert's catch was "one of the greatest catches I have seen in seven decades of watching big league games."

Although he was not identified, it was Lieb who wrote the *New York Press*'s account of the game in which Paskert made the great catch:

Devore trudged to first in New York's half of the inning, and then Snodgrass hammered a smoking drive to left centre. It was meant for a clean triple or homer, and ninety-nine times out of a hundred it would have been. But Paskert was on the job and scooped the ball in with his bare fin. Covering ground with the speed of an express train, Paskert made a sideward lunge, threw out his hand and the ball stuck therein. It was one of the greatest catches ever made on Manhattan soil. The drive easily would have sent in Devore, and might have started a batting rally.

In his "Cutting the Plate" column in the May 3, 1927, *New York Post*, Lieb recalled the Paskert catch. He wrote:

In scoring some three thousand or more ball games, I have seen many great catches. Three catches stand out strongest in my mind. One was made by Dode Paskert, playing with the Phillies, against the Giants in the second game of the 1911 season. I recall the game as the old wooden stands at the Polo Grounds burned down the night after the contest, perhaps set on fire by the sparks from Paskert's catch.

One of the other two catches Lieb singled out was a shoestring catch made by the Yankees centerfielder Elmer Miller on a ball hit by Cleveland's Tris Speaker in a game late in the 1921 season. The other catch, which Lieb considered the greatest, was Harry Hooper's catch in the last game of the 1912 World Series.

The day Lieb's column appeared, Lieb saw another catch in a Brooklyn-Giants game which, in his article the next day, he put into the same class as Dode Paskert's catch in 1911. Jigger Statz made the catch on May 3.

The 1911 Paskert catch was again the subject of discussion in 1930. In a May 8, 1930, article included in Paskert's clipping file at the Baseball Hall of Fame, an unidentified writer said:

Recounting the greatest catch he ever saw, Fred Lieb puts it down to the credit of George (Honey Boy) Paskert for the Phillies in a game at the Polo Grounds in May 1911, the day before said Polo Grounds burned down. Fred is right about that catch, but wrong about where it was made. The New Yorker who hit the ball Paskert snared while on the dead run and with his back hand did not hit it to right, and John Titus was not the other Phil outfielder who pursued it. The ball was hit to left and Sherwood Magee went after it with Paskert. It was a smoky or foggy day and first no one could tell who made the catch, for the ball was between the two. Paskert made the catch. Lieb says it was the greatest one he ever saw; I say the same, Bill Hanna says the same, and the man who traveled after the ball with Paskert, said the same. He was Sherwood Magee. He and I were talking about it in 1925 in Syracuse.

Bill Hanna, now pursuing the collegians, must have been seeing ball games since 1883, for he recalls the Kansas City Unions, who were functioning in 1884. He wrote in the *New York Sun* the next day, this was the greatest catch of them all. I watched my first baseball in 1884—saw only a few games then—but I saw baseball steadily after 1886, and the Paskert capture was far away the wonder catch. Dick Johnston used to make spectacular annexations out in the suburbs, so did Jim McAleer, so did Walter Brodie, but the Paskert capture was the catch of the century....

The unidentified author points out three men whose skills as outfielders have been long-forgotten, but who deserve to be remembered: Dick Johnston, Jim McAleer, and Walter Brodie. The following comments about these players come from the clipping files at the Baseball Hall of Fame.

Dick Johnston played from 1884 to 1891. An article from the mid–1880s, and probably from Kingston, New York, included comments about him as a player.

Was born at Rondout, Ulster co., N.Y. in 1863, soon after his father left home for the service; at the age of sixteen years he began to be noticed as a ball tosser and played with the best amateur clubs of Kingston. In 1882 and '83 he played with the Kingston Leaders, a semi-professional club, and made so great a record that he was engaged by the Manager of the Richmond, Va., Club.... As a centre fielder, we are informed, "Dick" covers more ground than any other fielder in the League, possibly, with the exception of Hanlon, of the Detroits. Johnston is also a very fast sprint runner, and some of his fly catches are simply marvelous; as a baserunner he excels, and time and again his fleetness of foot has enabled him to make base-hits out of balls that would have been sure outs with most players. As a batter, he stands 42 out of 120, with an average of .262. Richard is one of the League's youngest players, and gives bright promise to be the leading fielder in the League. He is called the "Phenomenal Fielder of the League."

After he died on April 4, 1934, an article about Dick Johnston was written in the *Kingston Daily Leader.* That article discussed his prowess as a fielder.

> Signing with Boston in 1885, Mr. Johnston remained with that club through the season of 1889. His remarkable ability to bring down fly balls soon earned him fame throughout the country, and many baseball authorities rank him among the top notch outfielders of all time. It was said of him that he covered as much ground as Tris Speaker did in a later day, and Speaker is considered par excellence among outfielders. In the days when he played the fields were not as large as they are today, and in one particularly important game Mr. Johnston is reputed to have climbed a small fence to pull down a fly ball and incidentally win the game.

Jim McAleer played major league baseball from 1889 to 1903. In an April 30, 1931, newspaper article after McAleer's death, the writer told about McAleer's baseball playing days, his role as a major league manager, as an owner, and as an organizer of the American League. He also told of his fielding ability.

> Starting his major baseball career with Cleveland McAleer was regarded as one of the greatest outfielders the major leagues ever produced ... in the opinion of Billy Evans. It was McAleer back in the '90s, who was the first outfielder to chase a long fly ball without keeping an eye on it while he was running.
>   McAleer, once he saw a ball sailing up to go over his head, would estimate with uncanny accuracy where it was going and he would race with all his speed to that spot, not looking backward over his shoulder. Almost invariably this great player was waiting for the ball ahead of the time when it came within distance to catch.
>   "There are a lot of big league outfielders who still haven't learned that trick," Evans said.

Billy Evans was a major league umpire and a long-time writer on major league baseball.

In his assessment of the best centerfielders up to 1911, Fred Tenney, who played for Boston's National League team for sixteen of his seventeen years in the majors, made McAleer the first one he discussed in his February 26, 1911, article in the *New York Times.*

> McAleer of Cleveland, with his super-human eye for angles, poor batter, but what a fielder! He is one of those gifted readers of angles who could turn with the crack of the bat, run like a deer to the spot where the ball would land, turn just as it seemed that he must be hit by the ball, and make an easy, graceful catch. How it is done, even he would be as a loss to tell for, apparently, he never glanced at the ball after it left the bat until he turned for the catch. Truly, the result seemed almost beyond the power of reason. It had to be done so quickly that it must have been sort of an instinct. For many years Jim was a tower of strength in the defensive work of his team. The rest of his club were such hard hitters that it could afford to carry along a fielder of his wonderful capabilities, even though a weak batsman.

Walter "Steve" Brodie played from 1890 to 1902. With the Baltimore Orioles in the mid–1890s, along with Joe Kelley, the left fielder, and Willie Keeler, the right fielder, Brodie was part of one of the best group of outfielders in baseball history.

In a document assembled by a group of people arguing for Brodie's induction into the Hall of Fame are a number of items from a scrapbook kept by Brodie's wife Carrie. Three of them are quotes, one by a *Baltimore Sun* writer, C.M. Gibbs, another one by his former manager, Ned Hanlon, and one by Rodger Pippin, the Sports Editor of the *Baltimore Sun.* The quote from C.M. Gibbs was:

> In center, Steve Brodie was one of the greatest ball hawks of all time. As a matter of fact I cannot recall ever seeing him drop a fly ball if it were possible to get his hands on it. One of his favorite stunts (in practice) was to run with the ball and, watching it over his shoulder, throw one hand behind his back and make the catch. I never saw any other player even attempt this.

The Hanlon quote follows:

> In the outfield, the Yanks have Ruth, Coombs, and Meusel. Splendid gardeners. Ruth, I consider, a grand player in every way. But consider this trio against Keeler, Kelley, and Brodie, all great ground coverers, fast and splendid hitters. Brodie to my mind, was one of the greatest judges of a fly ball in the game. He knew by intuition where a ball was going as soon as it was hit, and was off at full speed at the crack of the bat.

Rodger Pippin cites the opinions of a longtime Baltimore baseball fan:

> One vote for Walter (Steve) Brodie, of the old Orioles, of the National League, as the greatest of all outfielders from a defensive standpoint, is cast by George Mallonee, well known member of the Baltimore Country Club and Rolling Road Golf Club. George having seen all of the great players of the last half century, rates Brodie above Tris Speaker and Joe DiMaggio. He relates that he has seen Brodie, in a championship game, catch a fly ball behind his back. No player, in George's opinion, could judge a fly ball as well, has such sure hands, or could cover more ground.

To return to our main topic, Dode Paskert was not just a one-catch wonder. He was an outstanding fielder, and was so for a long time. In a 1917 article in Paskert's file at the Hall of Fame, an uncredited author tells of Paskert's durability, and his ability as a fielder. The article was written under the title "Paskert Is Star at the Age Which Drops Other Players Out of League."

> Paskert will be thirty-six years of age on August 28 next, and is now playing his fourteenth season in professional baseball....
> Paskert has never been regarded as one of the great hitting stars of baseball, though by no means a weakling with the stick. But in point of pure defensive ability—the art of racing reasonable distances in every direction and dragging down the long wallops—it is doubtful if baseball has ever seen a better outfielder than Dode. There have been many who could go as far in one certain direction and capture 'em, but combining the ability to go in any direction Dode probably outclasses the field. He excels Strunk in going back after the long ones over his head; he is better than Speaker in going to his left, and he can go further than Cobb in any direction.
> The remarkable thing about Paskert at thirty-six years of age is that he has lost none of the use of his legs, and is still able to race just as far over the grass and pull down the hits or circle the bases at full speed without even breathing hard, or suffering from trembling in the legs such as other players begin to be affected with as years roll along. He is never even attacked by charley horses, never suffers from sprained tendons, and never has to tape his legs as a result of the strain of continual service, as many players ten years younger frequently have to do.

Amos Strunk was an outfielder with the Philadelphia A's in 1917. He began in the major leagues with the A's in 1908 and finished his career in the majors in 1924.

A year later, on June 14, 1918, Paskert did it again. He made another bare-hand catch. In the June 15, 1918, *New York Times*, the unidentified writer described the 7–0 win of the New York Giants over the Chicago Cubs at the Polo Grounds. Paskert was a member of the Cubs when he made his catch on Walter Holke.

> The Cubs introduced a couple of fielding plays which were as fine as spilt satin. In the third Dode Paskert romped a couple of city blocks and speared Holke's terrific drive with his bare hand. Holke was brazenly robbed of another hit in the sixth when Charley Hollocher, who is a rare work of art at short stopping, grabbed a blazing liner on the dead run and turned it into a double play by catching Kauff off second.

Dode Paskert's catch on Holke merited a special box in a New York paper. The outlined box, in the Hall of Fame's file on Paskert, was titled "A REAL STAR," and didn't have a writer's name above the article.

Dode Paskert still ranks among the greatest of outfielders. Certain critics recently declared that the Cub star was beginning to go back, but in the games against the Giants the Southerner has given the lie to such statements. His great catch of a liner from Holke's bat in the third inning of Friday's game was one of the choicest bits of fielding ever glimpsed at the Polo Ground and showed Dode to be still the fleet footed, keen eyed outfielder he always has been. He grabbed Holke's hurtling wallop out of the air with his bare right hand after a heart-breaking run and shut off a menacing rally by the Giants.

Fred Lieb, who so admired Paskert's 1911 catch that he saw in his first year as a writer for the *New York Press*, now was a reporter for the *New York Sun*. Although he didn't rate this catch on Holke's liner at the same level as the one in 1911, he still was impressed by what Paskert had done, calling it "spectacular" and a "bright gem."

In the *New York World*, the sportswriter Monitor also told of Paskert's grab.

In the third inning Walter Holke hit a long, low liner to left centre. It looked for all the world like another inside-the-grounds home run, but Dode Paskert raced far toward left, stuck out his bare hand while going at top speed and speared the ball. It was a catch of the most sensational kind.

October 10, 1912—Josh Devore

Outstanding catches were made in the 1912 World Series by right fielders Josh Devore of the New York Giants and Harry Hooper of the Boston Red Sox. This hotly contested Series may have been the best one ever for outfield play. In addition, outfielders Red Murray and Fred Snodgrass of the Giants and Duffy Lewis of the Red Sox made outstanding catches. Baseball's greatest centerfielder at that time, Tris Speaker of the Red Sox, played but was hobbled by an injured ankle during the Series.

The catches by Josh Devore in the third game and Harry Hooper's crucial catch in the eighth game were both decisively important. Devore's catch ended an exciting 2 to 1 game and prevented a Red Sox victory. Hooper's catch prevented the Giants from adding a run that could have brought the game to a conclusion in nine innings in the Giants' favor.

The *Boston Daily Globe*'s T.H. Murnane wrote about Devore's catch:

[Hick] Cady swung and met the ball on the center, and it went shooting out between right and center, with Snodgrass and Devore tearing for the ball at top speed.

A mighty shout went up from Boston fans, for it looked like a 50-to-1 shot that neither fielder could reach the fast traveling ball. Devore was tearing down the field, and while under a full head of steam he leaped into the air, and, with hands extended over his head and his back to the infield, he came out of the air with the ball. It was now that the New York fans cut loose with wild cheers.

It was one of the most sensational finishes ever witnessed on a ball field; a great bid for the game; and a wonderful piece of fielding.

This was the third game to have a sensational finish—all being games in which the public was given enough thrills to last a lifetime.

Tris Speaker wrote a column in the *Boston Daily Globe* after the third game in which he had the following to say about Devore's catch:

The catch Devore made for the windup of the game was as good as any I ever saw. I did not think that it would be possible for him to get it, and when the ball went off Cady's bat I thought the game as good as won for Boston.

Devore played the ball well, although he did not have much choice in that respect. All he could do was to leg it for all he was worth and get to the ball. And how he did leg it! He made the catch while in a very awkward position, but he made it, and that is what saved the game for the Giants.

As might be expected, the *New York Times* had more to say about Devore's catch:

A brilliant catch by Josh Devore, as the little outfielder was racing like mad toward the right field fence in the ninth inning at Fenway Park this afternoon, brought to a sudden close a tumultuous rally by the Red Sox and saved the game for New York, giving them a 2 to 1 victory in the third seething game of the world's series.

When the ball left Cady's bat with a resounding thud and went on its screaming flight the Giants were in the lead by a score of 2 to 1, because up to that time the sturdy Red Sox batters had quailed and fallen before the masterly pitching of "Rube" Marquard; but two Boston Red Sox runners were on second and third, crouched like sprinters waiting for the starter's pistol. There were two out, and a safe hit meant a Boston victory. Is it any wonder that the crowd was inflamed to a condition of hysterical emotion?

Cady's tremendous smash soared between centre and right fields. It was high above the heads of Devore and Snodgrass, and the howling mob of fans behind the low outfield fence watched hungrily for the white ball to drop in their midst. Hendriksen, running for Stahl, and Wagner, on the bases, had started home pellmell, and the Boston runner was almost on the heels of the shortstop while the sphere was still in the air.

Wild Flight of Devore

In the deafening din Devore had been forgotten. He was running faster than he had ever run in his life toward the fence, with one eye peeking keenly over his left shoulder. No one dreamed he could ever reach the ball. The Boston crowd was already celebrating a second victory and counting the series won. The bands were blaring, the bass drums were rumbling, and the cymbals were crashing. The grandstands and bleachers were afire with the waving flags.

Devore continued his wild tearing dash. Little Josh knew what that crisis meant. If the ball got away he would have to listen to the hoots, the jeers, the cries of joy from the jubilant Red Sox horde. On the other hand, he could see himself running to the clubhouse to be surrounded by victory-intoxicated men. On and on he kept in the daring, desperate attempt. One last glance over his shoulder, and he saw the ball about to whizz over his head, seemingly out of reach. But in the instant he gathered all the power in his frame and leaped forward with both hands stretched up.

The mob was rushing toward the gates wildly heralding the Red Sox victory, for more than half the spectators thought that the ball had dropped safely into the crowd. But that sphere

In the third game of the 1912 World Series, Giants centerfielder Josh Devore made a frantic run to catch a ball that would have meant victory for the Boston Red Sox and, for at least a day, made him a hero in the eyes of Giants fans and the New York baseball writers.

was firmly clutched in "Josh's" hands, and he will save it as long as he lives and his children and his children's children will be told over and over again how he vaulted into the azure and saved the good name of the Giants.

That was the last out of the ninth inning and the end of the most nerve-racking rally in the series which already seethed with feverish excitement. If the other games of the series are like the first three New York and Boston will fill all the nerve sanitariums with their citizens.

The *New York American* had columns by the Giants' battery the day of Devore's catch, Rube Marquard, New York's pitcher and Devore's roommate, and catcher John ("Chief") Meyers. Both told a similar story about Cady's hit and gave their thoughts as the ball left Cady's bat. Neither believed Devore could make the catch. One of the headlines leading Marquard's article used a quote from what Marquard wrote: "Gives Credit to Devore for Saving Game with Greatest Catch Ever Made on a Ball Field."'

Chief Meyers's column was subtitled "I Would Have Bet My Life He Couldn't Get It—Marquard Never So Good." After making the case why he thought his Giants would win the series, Meyers gave more information about what Devore had done.

Boston's last chance in my opinion flickered out to-day when we stopped up even with the Red Sox. I believe it was the most exciting finish ever seen in the world's series. Little Josh Devore kept us in the race. I never saw such a wonderful catch as that of his which ended the game in our favor. I did not think he had even one chance in ten million to shut off the winning run.

Devore's catch was all the more remarkable because he was playing a short field and had to run way out for the vicious line drive. Captain Doyle knew that Cady, a left-field hitter, was not liable to drive into right. He wished, in case of the worst happening, to be able to shut off Wagner from scoring, as this would have been the winning run. If Hendrikson [*sic*] only scored, the game would be no worse than a tie. Devore was in close to have the advantage of a shorter throw to the plate in case of a hit into his territory.

"Rube" was in the hole, for he had curved two at Cady to the inside for called balls. The count was two and nothing, so I signaled for a fast one. It came like a bullet and Cady swung blindly. I knew it was half an accident, for the ball would have been two feet outside. Cady's bat got just about halfway round when it connected with the leather, square as any hit you ever saw.

Josh was away with the swing, running as he never ran before. He never once faltered nor looked back. If he had we would have lost. It was the most excellent piece of judgment I ever saw. But I would have bet my life on the ball.

My heart stopped beating. I held my breath, but looked on fascinated. I saw the little fellow leap high and turned away. I thought he missed. I turned away in chagrin, heavy hearted. The thundering applause of Boston's baseball mad rooters hushed in that tense moment.

A glance at the bench substantiated my worst fears. There strained my comrades like so many graven images, the set gray of their faces standing out of the semi-gloom of the bench like so many masks of stone. And then, as if some magician had touched a hidden spring, this tableau broke into life and joy. I knew we had won.

Yet I couldn't believe it. I turned back to look just as old Boston Town thundered its applause for what must have been a heart-breaking play. Devore still carried on and on in his career back toward the fence. But even as I looked he swooped round to the right as gracefully as a gull on wing and came dancing back toward us, his hard-earned trophy held aloft. I half envied him the glory of that supreme moment.

Damon Runyon led his *New York American* article with information other papers did not mention.

Listen, my children and you shall hear the story of how Josh Devore, the little ducklegged outfielder on the Giants, who has been taunted by the big town fans this season until his boyish heart was almost broken, came leaping up to grave emergency to-day rescuing his roommate, the sensational Rube Marquard, from the peril of impending defeat, and giving the New York team the third game in the world's series with the Red Sox by a score of 2 to 1.

References to Devore's height were many. He was five feet, six inches tall.

After playing for the Giants from 1908 through the 1912 World Series and in sixteen games in 1913, Devore was traded to Cincinnati. He played in the major leagues from 1908 to 1914 and was a .277 career hitter.

October 16, 1912—Harry Hooper

Harry Hooper was a superlative outfielder. With Tris Speaker in center field and Duffy Lewis in left field, Hooper formed one of the greatest defensive outfields in baseball history. Their talents were well known by the time Hooper made his great catch in the 1912 World Series.

In the 1912 Series, as great as Devore's catch was, the one by Harry Hooper in the eighth and deciding game may have been better. James C. O'Leary, one of the *Boston Daily Globe*'s sportswriters, described the catch in his synopsis of the Giants half of the fifth inning:

> Devore rapped out a hot one which hit Bedient in the shin and bounded back to the plate. Devore was out trying to steal second, Cady to Wagner. Larry Doyle put one up against the low fence in front of the old centerfield bleachers and Harry Hooper made the greatest catch, after a long run, ever seen on these grounds. Had he failed to make the catch the ball would have hopped over the fence on the first bound. The crowd went wild, and well it might for it is doubtful if ever a better catch was seen.
>
> Snodgrass singled to left. Murray fouled out to Cady. No runs, two hits, no errors, none left.
>
> Hooper was given an ovation as he came in from the field for Boston's half at bat.

T.H. Murnane, the *Globe*'s chief writer for the game, wrote of Hooper's catch:

> There was some fine individual fielding, with Hooper the headliner, Harry making the finest catch of his baseball career. Doyle hit the ball and Hooper turned and went down to the field on the dead run. Turning completely around as he went close to the short fence, he hooked in the ball with his back to the field, only a few feet from the fence, cutting off a sure home run.

The *Boston Herald*'s Sporting Editor, R.E. McMillin, wrote in the next day's paper:

> Many sensational grabs have been made in the series, but all paled into insignificance when compared with that which Harry Hooper collared yesterday. Harry, in speaking of the play, said that it struck his bare hand and turned him into the fence.

Later in the article McMillin wrote:

> Harry Hooper, with the greatest catch of the series, saved the battle early in the afternoon. There was one out in the fifth when Larry Doyle planked a drive straight toward the crowd behind the short right field bleachers. Hoop streaked across the sward, finally reaching up with his back to the ball and jumped. Doyle, roosting on second, would not believe that the drive had been clutched until Umpire Evans came across country with the details of the wonderful bare-handed grab.

Walter Johnson, the Washington Senators' fireballing right-hander, in writing about the last game of the 1912 series for the *Boston Herald*, said of Hooper's catch:

The greatest catch ever seen on a ball field was made by Harry Hooper, the speedy right fielder of the Red Sox. Larry Doyle caught one of Bedient's fast ones on the nose, and it set sail for the right field bleachers. Harry was away at the crack of the bat, but it did not look as though he had the slightest chance of getting anywhere near the ball.

Hooper judged the ball perfectly, for just before he reached the fence he turned, and seeing that the ball was sailing over his head, stuck out his bare hand and grabbed the ball. This hit would have been good for three bases and possibly a home run, and in all probability would have broken up the game.

In his 1923 book *My Thirty Years in Baseball*, Giants manager John Mc-Graw called Harry Hooper's catch a "great" one.

For his 1966 book *The Glory of Their Times*, Lawrence Ritter interviewed Joe Wood, the second, and the winning, pitcher the day Hooper made his catch. Wood told Ritter:

Larry Doyle hit a terrific drive to deep right center, and Harry ran back at full speed and *dove* over the railing and into the crowd and in some way, I'll never figure out quite how, he caught the ball—I think with his bare hand. It was almost impossible to believe even when you saw it [157].

Harry Hooper, shown here in his Chicago White Sox uniform around 1921, was for six years (1910–1915) the right fielder in one of the most superb sets of outfielders ever, along with Tris Speaker in center field and Duffy Lewis in left field.

In his book *Harry Hooper: An American Baseball Life*, Paul Zingg wrote that Hooper himself felt the catch was at the top of his accomplishments in the majors. It certainly was the defensive highlight of the series for Boston fans. For Giants fans Fred Snodgrass's drop was the defensive low point. After the Giants had taken the lead in the top half of the tenth inning, Snodgrass dropped an easy fly ball in the bottom half of the tenth.

After his drop, Snodgrass made a terrific catch on the next batter, Harry Hooper. He chased Hooper's long drive into right center and made a lunge at the end to pull the drive in. Many years later Hooper told Lawrence Ritter, as reported in *The Glory of Their Times*, he didn't know how Snodgrass could get to the ball. Frank P. Sibley, a *Boston Daily Globe* sportswriter, called Snodgrass's catch on Hooper's drive "a miracle catch."

However, the error Snodgrass made on the first batter in the tenth contributed to a loss that was painful for the New York fans to take. Unfortunately for the Giants and their fans, Snodgrass' "miracle catch" could not erase the base runner aboard due to his error. The Giants' Christy Mathewson was in command of the Red Sox hitters through the first nine innings. The first batter up in the Red Sox tenth was Clyde Engle, who lofted a hard-hit but catchable ball into left center field. Even though the ball seemed to be more in Red Murray's area than Snodgrass's, Fred ran over for the ball, called for it, and readied to catch it. This easy chance turned into an error as the ball popped out of his glove.

Hooper hit a ball to deep left center on which Snodgrass made the remarkable catch. Mathewson walked Yerkes. Speaker sent up a foul fly which first baseman Merkle, catcher Meyers, and Mathewson all could have caught, but no one called for it, and the ball dropped between them. Speaker then followed with a single that scored Engle. On the throw to the plate, Yerkes and Speaker moved over to third and second respectively. Mathewson walked Duffy Lewis, and Gardner hit a fly to deep right scoring the winning run.

T. H. Murnane of the *Boston Daily Globe* caught Mathewson's sadness in defeat:

> Christy Mathewson, the greatest pitcher of all time had lost after pitching a remarkable game. It was no fault of his. It was the one game in his twelve years on the ballfield that he had set his heart on winning, for it meant the championship of the world and one more thrill before passing out of the limelight as a remarkable performer. Mathewson, the baseball genius, was heartbroken and tears rolled down his sun-burned cheeks as he was consoled by his fellow players.

In his column on the game for the *Boston Herald*, Walter Johnson, the great, hard-throwing pitcher of the Washington Senators, made it clear that shoddy fielding by Snodgrass cost Mathewson a shutout and the game. He noted that Snodgrass misplayed a routine fly ball into a hit that led to a run in the seventh, and dropped another routine fly ball in the tenth that led to another run.

The unidentified *New York Times* writer of the lead story on the last game went beyond Walter Johnson's analysis of the shoddy fielding behind Mathewson. The *Times* writer, clearly a diehard Giants fan with a heavy emotional investment in the team, was incensed and unforgiving. Snodgrass was his target. The writer had to put Snodgrass's error in the "proper" perspective. The titles on the front page of the *Times* read:

GIANTS LOSE
ON MUFFED FLY
Snodgrass Drops Easy Ball,
Costing Teammates $29,514,
Boston Winning 3–2

The *Times*' writer began the article with:

> Write in the pages of world's series baseball history the name of Snodgrass. Write it large and black. Not as a hero, truly not. Put him rather with [Fred] Merkle who was in such a hurry that he gave away a National League championship. Snodgrass was in such a hurry that he gave away a world championship. It was because of Snodgrass's generous muff of an easy fly in the tenth inning that the decisive game in the world's series went to the Boston Red Sox this afternoon by a score of 3 to 2, instead of to the New York Giants by a score of 2 to 1.

On September 23, 1908, with Moose McCormick on third, Fred Merkle on first, and two out, the Giants' Al Bridwell hit a single to center which scored McCormick and gave the Giants an apparent 2–1 victory over their close rival, the Chicago Cubs. Unfortunately, Merkle didn't advance to second to complete his play. Seeing that the winning run would score, Merkle simply began his trot to the clubhouse before he reached second base.

Cubs players recognized Merkle's lapse in his attention to details, and scrambled to throw the ball to second base to get a force out on the missing Merkle. The Giants' winning run was negated, and the umpire called the game a 1–1 tie. When it was determined that the Giants and the Cubs were tied for first place at the end of the season, the two teams played another game. The Cubs won that last game, giving them the National League championship. Merkle's place as a goat for all time thus was assured.

The *New York Times'* writer then told about how much in command of the Red Sox hitters Mathewson was, and about Red Murray's double in the top of the tenth, followed by Merkle's single that scored Murray and a broke the 1 to 1 tie. He continues:

All that Engle can do with the elusive drop served up is to hoist it high between centre and right fields. Snodgrass and Murray are both within reach of it, with time to spare. Snodgrass yells, "I've got it," and sets himself to take it with ease, as he has taken hundreds of the sort. Murray stops, waiting for the play that will enable him to line the ball joyfully to the infield just to show that his formidable right wing is still in working order.

When the ball is soaring its leisurely way let us pause for a moment to think what hangs upon that fly.

It is not the 2,000 Giant rooters who are gayly waving their blue and red flags and yelling exultantly over the certain downfall of the foe. It is not the 15,000 Boston fans who have groaned and sat silent, as though at a funeral. A President is forgetting the bitter assaults that have been made upon him. A former President is being eased of his pain by his interest in it. A campaign which may mean a change in the whole structure of the Nation's Government has been put into the background. What happens will be flashed by telegraph the length and breadth of the land, and thereby carried over and under the sea, and millions will be uplifted or downcast.

And now the ball settles. It is full and fair in the pouch of the padded glove of Snodgrass. But he is too eager to toss it to Murray and it dribbles to the ground. Before Snodgrass can hurl the ball to second Engle is perching there.

Manager McGraw was gracious in defeat. At the end of the game he rushed across the diamond to congratulate Jake Stahl, the manager of the Red Sox. In mentioning McGraw's meeting with Stahl, Frank P. Sibley of the *Boston Globe* added that "an over-enthusiastic fan literally shoved McGraw down the steps of the Red Sox dugout. The fan knew he had been over-enthusiastic a moment afterwards for McGraw bounced out again and let go a straight left that crumpled up Mr. Fan completely."

In his article for the *New York Times* the next day, McGraw's sportsmanship was apparent. He began:

Well, the Red Sox won, and we are not handing out any alibis....

I am not blaming anybody. All the boys did their best and worked their hardest. Errors and tough luck are everyday affairs in baseball, and we merely regard them as part of the game....

...Snodgrass had a little hard-luck to-day, but this is a game a man has an opportunity to make a misplay on every ball hit in his direction, and it must be remembered that Snodgrass has done some nice fielding for us during the series. He was a little over-anxious to-day, but that was all....

The muff by Fred Snodgrass was tough on his mother. A brief article in the *New York Times* the day after the last series game read as follows:

Snodgrass's Error Makes Mother Ill

Los Angeles, Oct. 17—Overcome by emotion when the electrical score board at the local theatre showed Fred Snodgrass's muff of the fly which cost the New York Giants the world's championship, Mrs. Snodgrass, mother of the New York outfielder, fainted. Mrs. Snodgrass is an ardent "fan."

The 1912 World Series may have produced the most great catches ever made by three players in a Series, those by Devore, Snodgrass, and Hooper. Of those, Hooper's has been the one most people remembered years later.

May 16, 1914 — Ty Cobb

Ty Cobb was well known for many things, among which were being a fierce competitor, a great hitter, and one the greatest base runners in the history of baseball. His fielding was at a high level, but rarely got the attention that his intense competitiveness and his other accomplishments on the field have received.

In discussions of great fielding outfielders in the history of baseball, his name usually is not mentioned along with Tris Speaker, Joe DiMaggio, Terry Moore, Willie Mays, and Duke Snider, among others. However, just as he was a great expert on how to hit, Cobb was a stickler for details on how to play in the field. Due to this desire to play his position expertly, he made some extraordinary catches. What might have been his best catch was made at Fenway Park on May 16, 1914.

In a 3–0 Tiger loss to the Red Sox, which featured stellar fielding work by other players, including Harry Hooper, Cobb made the great catch. The unidentified writer for the *Boston Herald* said, "Cobb made one of the best catches of his career," and then described it.

> Larry Gardner sent one far out into centerfield. It didn't seem as though Cobb had a chance to get it. But he turned on his heel, sprinted toward centerfield bleachers and half turning reached the ball, juggled it in his hand for a minute and then—held it safe. It was the fielding feature of the afternoon.

Later in the article, the same author wrote that "Cobb has rarely made a better catch."

The *Boston Post*'s Paul H. Shannon was direct in his appraisal of how outstanding the catch was:

> Cobb failed to make a hit, chiefly because he was twice passed to first, but he made one of the most superb catches ever seen on any park when he went away back to the centre field bleachers in the eighth and pulled down a fly off Gardner's bat which should have earned three bases. It was a magnificent play.

Even more enthusiastic about Cobb's effort was the *Boston Globe*'s T.H. Murnane.

> Ty Cobb made one of the most sensational catches ever seen at Fenway Park, and perhaps for that matter, at any other park. It was in the eighth inning that Larry Gardner smashed a savage drive to the right of center. It looked like a 10-to-1 shot that the ball would go to the fence, but Cobb shot across the field and as the ball was passing over his head, he leaped for the ball, managing to block it with his gloved hand and protect it with his right hand before he reached the ground.
>
> Taking into consideration the wonderful speed that Cobb displayed covering the ground, and the supreme effort he made to reach the ball, the catch was nothing less than marvelous, and he received well-deserved applause until he went out of sight into the dugout.
>
> It was a catch that one is not likely to see in a lifetime, for there are few outfielders who have the speed of Cobb and the agility to control the ball after they cover the distance.

The *Detroit Free Press*'s E.A. Batchelor mentioned the Cobb catch three times on the sports page, once calling it "wonderful," and another time writing that the "one-handed running catch of a line drive from Gardner's bat was the most sensational defensive play pulled by a Tiger this year." He went on to say that Cobb got "the ball while on the run with his back to the plate...."

Well-known illustrator Wallace Goldsmith drew cartoon stories about baseball games for a number of years for the *Boston Globe*. On May 17, 1914, he told of several events from the Detroit Tigers–Boston Red Sox game of the day before, the most prominent being the great catch by Ty Cobb on a ball hit by the Red Sox' Larry Gardner.

In another column, Batchelor told of the Boston's fans' reaction to Cobb's catch.

Cobb was given a wonderful ovation by the Boston crowd after his catch in the eighth. The fans stood up and cheered for several minutes and burst out again when he came to the bench. The applause was deserved because it was a magnificent fielding stunt, one of the best of his career.

October 7, 1916—Harry Hooper

Harry Hooper's accomplishments as a player were considerable. One of his accomplishments was his development of the "sliding catch." Hooper described the catch in a letter to George W. Poultney, a copy of which is now in Hooper's file at the Baseball Hall of Fame:

The sliding catch I hit upon by accident. For some unexplained reason I made one, and found it so much more effective than the usual procedure of sliding on one's elbows, that I perfected it and thereafter employed it instinctively, so to speak, during the greater part of my career.

The advantages are: 1) One's hands and arms do not hit the turf, lessening the chance of losing the ball; 2) One does not skin his elbows; 3) Most important, one can come to his feet immediately after the catch.

One of the most outstanding catches I ever made was in an early game of the 1916 series, against Brooklyn. Zach Wheat, a fast man, was on third, with one or no out, when a line drive was hit my way. I made a "sliding catch," and threw him out at home-plate by a good six feet. This play probably saved that game, and, I believe, took a lot of "heart" out of the Brooklyn team. Casey Stengel will recall it. He was a member of that team. I believe no one could have made that catch in the usual diving manner and have completed the play at the plate.

Hooper's catch and throw to nail Wheat at the plate in the 1916 World Series occurred in the first game. Boston won that home game 6–5 and went on to win the Series four games to one. The *Boston Globe*'s Edward F. Martin described Hooper's actions as he made the catch and the throw.

The fourth frame was some inning. The big play of the game, Hooper's sensational catch and throw, was pulled off in this inning and the Robins also tied the score, the spectacular performance by Hooper choking off another run.

Stengel was first up and breezed a single to left and counted when Wheat poked a triple over the lid of Harry Hooper, the ball hitting the right field bleachers. With the count knotted, Wheat prancing around third base line, nobody out and Cutshaw up, it looked promising for the boys of Rotund Robby.

Cutshaw ripped a low liner to right. Hooper was playing fairly deep, but judged the slam cleverly. In real Hooperesque style he tore in, but just as he was approaching the ball he slipped and while all other parts of him were down, his head was up and sitting on the old green he gathered the ball.

Getting to his feet quickly and by a perfect throw to the plate, he snared Zachariah, who was trying to score from third. Both the catch and throw were wonderful. Had Hooper failed to get the ball, Wheat would have scored easily and Cutshaw might have made at least two hassocks. Making the superb throw under the conditions after the catch, just brought everybody to their toes.

The sliding catch Hooper made in the 1916 Series was then a novel way to make a catch. Evidently Hooper was still perfecting it and writers were not familiar enough with it to credit Hooper with a purposeful slide to make the catch. In the *Boston Herald*'s "Notes of the Game" section, an unidentified writer commented on Hooper's catch.

Harry Hooper's marvelous play in the fourth will long be remembered by the crowd. It was even better than his great catch off Larry Doyle in the 1912 Giant-Sox series, and that was thought to be the last thing in outfielding. In Harry's play yesterday he not only made a catch of a half-liner as he was slipping to the ground after a hard run, but regained his feet and threw directly into Cady's hands, doubling up the speedy Zach Wheat, who was attempting to score from third.

One of the *Boston Herald*'s subtitles over N.J. Flatley's article on the game was "Hooper's Catch and Heave Home in the Fourth Inning One of Greatest Plays of Its Kind." Flatley also did not fully credit Hooper with intending to make the catch the way it happened.

Harry Hooper was the big hero of the big afternoon.... Harry, Hero Harry, as somebody calls him, perpetrated the most brilliant play ever seen in a world's series. He did it in the fourth frame after the Dodgers had scored one run and there was a man on third and nobody out. Cutshaw hit one of those half-fly, half-liner affairs over Janvrin's head. Hooper tore in like Mercury on the last five yards of a century dash. Almost to the infield he sped and lunged forward for the ball. His cleats slipped in the soft turf and he fell. But his hands surrounded the ball, nor would they let go.

Zach Wheat, who happened to be the man on third, saw Harry fall, saw him catch the ball. He thought he could score and he dashed for the plate. With wondrous agility Hooper got to his feet and threw. The ball zipped into Cady's big mitt with the resounding thud of a bomb explosion. Wheat, fleet as the wind, was doubled up yards from the saucer. The first big cheer of the day shattered the silence and the pennant-won confidence of the Dodgers ebbed with almost apparent suddenness. It was a play of plays, one of the kind that not even fiction writers dare to imagine.

The *Herald*'s front page had a picture of Hooper. Above the picture the caption was "Hooper's Play in Fourth Inning Never Equalled."

Grantland Rice, writing in the *New York Tribune*, called Hooper's grab as "a highly spectacular catch, falling as he gripped the ball. Wheat tore in from third, but Hooper regained his balance in time to wipe his man off at the plate with a low line throw into Cady's mitt."

It wasn't only writers who did not seem aware of Hooper's purposeful effort. One of the reporters for the *Boston Globe* was Christy Matthewson, the great pitcher, who had recently completed his last year in the major leagues. Matthewson's comments were transcribed in the *Globe* by John Wheeler. About the Hooper catch Mathewson said:

> With Wheat on third base and no one out, Cutshaw pushed a short fly to right field and Hooper made a play for the book. He came in on the ball and fell down making the catch. John Coombs, a wily worker, was coaching on third base, and he had to make up one of those snap decisions that come up and mean so much.
>
> He took a glance at Hooper lying flat and made up his mind that he could never get up in time to make the throw. Wheat broke for the plate and Hooper came up with a perfect toss....

Wilbert Robinson, Brooklyn's manager, was quoted in the Boston and New York papers. The *New York Tribune*'s Frank O'Neil quoted Robinson and Jack Coombs, the Brooklyn third base coach Matthewson mentioned, about Hooper's catch. Robinson called Hooper's catch "the greatest play I have ever seen," and went on to tell more about the play.

> It was the luckiest, also. To begin with, Hooper had to make a hard run to get near Cutshaw's drive, which was away in close, and over near the foul line. Then, after making the catch, he fell, but staggered to his feet in time to shoot the ball to the plate and nip Buck Wheat. He was off his balance when he made the throw, but the ball never varies an inch to the plate, and Buck lost the race by an eyelash.

Coombs said, "Hooper may never make another play like his classic in the fourth inning. It pulled Boston out of a yawning chasm. It was the greatest play I have ever seen."

Jack Coombs was a Brooklyn pitcher doubling as a third base coach in the game Hooper made his sliding catch on George Cutshaw. Coombs began his career with the Philadelphia A's in 1906, had several outstanding years pitching for the A's, and was traded to Brooklyn before the start of the 1915 season. He was the winning pitcher in the third game of the 1916 Series, the only game Brooklyn was to win.

An Associated Press writer gave the most succinct description of what Hooper did.

> Harry Hooper, right fielder of the Boston Red Sox, uncovered the star individual play of the first game in the world's series on Saturday when in the fourth inning he made a great running catch of Cutshaw's twisting fly and nipped Wheat trying to score from third. The ball left Cutshaw's bat as if undecided where it was going and Hooper had to sprint well over toward the foul line just back of first base before he could get his hands on it. The effort caused him to slip to the turf in a sitting position, but he was up like a flash and while still rising hurled the ball straight as a bullet to Cady. The latter slammed it on Wheat's ankle as he reached for the plate with his foot, at the end of a perfect hook slide. The thrilling catch and throw was the outstanding feature of the first game.

The *Boston Post*'s Paul Shannon told how unlikely it was that Hooper could make the play.

> Cutshaw, a dangerous batter, one of the men whom rival pitcher prefer to walk in a pinch, went to bat with instructions to hit out.
>
> He did. Meeting the first ball, he drove it on a line to right field, and a groan arose as Wheat started home with what looked like a sure and easy run. There didn't seem to be a chance in the world for Hooper to get near the ball, yet, by a wonderful piece of sprinting, he finally got under it, held on, but slipped and fell as a result of his sudden stoppage of speed. Wheat, surprised at the catch, dashed back to the bag and touched it, then headed for home with not even the ghost of an idea that the throw would be made. But Hooper, jumping to his feet, made one his most beautiful and accurate pegs, the ball just beating the runner to the plate, and out to the field with the score still tied went the crestfallen Dodgers, while the overjoyed grandstand occupants and bleacherites howled at the wonderful achievement until they were out of breath and voice.

Among a list of quotes about Harry Hooper, and compiled by his son John to help make the case for Hooper to be elected to the Hall of Fame, were those by his Boston teammates Babe Ruth, Ray Collins, and Tris Speaker. The documents from which the following quotes come are in Hooper's file at the Hall of Fame.

Ruth, who considered Hooper the greatest fielding outfielder, said:

> He could do anything any other outfielder could and on top of that he was a great position player. His instinct for knowing where the ball was going to be hit was uncanny. I'm sure too that he made more diving catches than any other outfielder in history. With most outfielders the diving catch is half luck; with Hooper it was a masterpiece of business.

Comparing Hooper and Speaker, Ray Collins said:

> Speaker sometimes would range into left and catch a ball that might perhaps have been in Duffy Lewis' territory. But he never did the same thing toward Hooper in right. Hooper played the sunfield. In Fenway Park, he had far more ground to cover. Racing in and sort of sliding—with one leg tucked under him—he made catches you'd think nobody could make.... Hooper had a more accurate arm. As far as outfielding is concerned, I wouldn't put Speaker over Hooper. I'd place them together—two great outfielders—on a par.

Tris Speaker, evidently commenting after the Boston Red Sox's Jimmy Piersall made two outstanding catches in Cleveland on July 19, 1953, said:

> I saw Piersall make those two game-saving catches in the last series here. Yet they'll never stand up with the one Harry made off Doyle in the 1912 series with the Giants. That brought home the bacon. Harry was not only a great fielder, but he had the best arm of the three of us. He actually threw strikes from the outfield. And those running-in catches he made, sliding on his left knee, thrilled the fans whenever we played.

Speaker was a Cleveland resident in 1953, and thus the "here" he mentions most likely refers to the series being played in Cleveland.

Harry Hooper played for the Red Sox from 1909 to 1920, and spent the 1921 to 1925 seasons as a productive player for the Chicago White Sox. In 1971, he was elected to the Hall of Fame, in major part for the high level of his defensive work.

October 2, 1919—Edd Roush

Now almost lost in the 1919 World Series stories is the fielding excellence of Cincinnati's Edd Roush. The obviously clumsy play by some Chicago White Sox players, the ensuing investigations about the fixed World Series, and the continuing debate about keeping Joe Jackson out of the Hall of Fame because of his role in throwing games, have kept the catches of Edd Roush in that series less well known than they should be.

Edd Roush, a strong left-handed thrower, was one of the finest defensive centerfielders in the game, especially from 1917 to 1926 with the Reds. He was a lifetime .323 hitter and twice led the National League in batting average.

In Lawrence Ritter's *The Glory of Their Times*, Heinie Groh, who was a teammate of Roush's with the Reds, said, "Why Eddie used to take care of the whole outfield, not just center field. He was far and away the best outfielder I ever saw" (273). Groh's major league career, all of it in the National League, spanned from 1912 to 1927, and was mostly with the Reds.

Although Roush made three outstanding catches in the 1919 Series, the one in the second game in Cincinnati was a great one. I.E. Sanborn, writing for the *Chicago Tribune* after the October 2 game, gets right to the quality of the play Roush made.

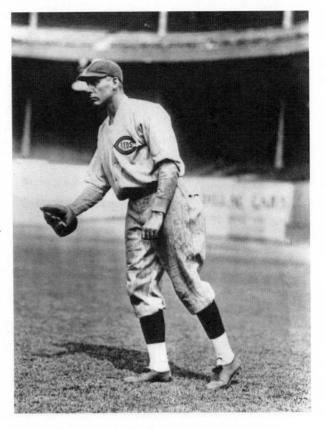

The Cincinnati Reds' centerfielder Edd Roush was an outstanding all-around player who made several wonderful catches in the 1919 World Series against the soon-to-be-tainted Chicago White Sox.

> But the play that decided the game ... was a miraculous pinch by Roush in the sixth chapter. Hap Felsch hit a ball several miles over center field and it would have been good for a home run if he had hit it in any other direction on account of the geography of Redland park.
>
> Here it was possible for Roush to tear back to within a few feet of Western avenue and pick the pill out of the sun over his shoulders while running at top speed. It was a catch of a lifetime and it squelched one of the most likely looking rallies the White Sox made.

James Crusinberry, Sanborn's colleague at the *Tribune*, quoted White Sox manager Kid Gleason on Roush's catch:

> Then there was that wonderful catch by Roush of Felsch's long drive clear over his head in the sixth with Weaver on third base and two out. It was one of the greatest catches ever made in a world's series. If they hadn't already scored three runs and held a commanding lead, Roush never would have been playing back far enough to have caught that ball. With three runs to the good, they weren't worried about our runner at third base. He laid back there and was able to go and get that one.

In the *New York Times*, the uncredited front-page story of the game featured an account of Roush's catch.

> The most illuminating play of today's game was a glittering grab by Eddie Roush when he pulled down Hap Felsch's life-sized smash in the eighth inning. Weaver had doubled at the

momentous occasion and was presented with a free ticket to third when the veteran Sallee forgot himself and unraveled a balk, which is a rare thing in a big game. With Weaver straining at the leash at third and two gone Felsch, who had twice laid down sacrifice hits, welcomed this occasion to take a healthy swing at the ball.

Hap hit it squarely on the nose and the ball sailed high and far in the general direction of the centre field battlement. Roush took one peek at the ball, then turned and ran for the fence. As he galloped along with his back to the ball it seemed as if the little white object was going to crash against the green painted center field fence.

When Weaver had crossed the plate and Felsch was rounding second base on his hilarious gallop, Roush turned suddenly. He did this by intuition, for it was impossible for him to see where the ball was, as there are no eyes in the back of his head. As he twisted quickly about, both hands reached skyward and he corralled the ball just as it was about to whistle over his roof. Up to this time the fans were settled back comfortably in their seats and had come to the conclusion that nothing more could happen in this series to flicker the magnetic spark of their jagged nerves.

A hair-raising catch of this kind, however, was too much to allow to pass unnoticed, so once more the human caldron began to seethe and boil. Cheers and shouts rose from tired throats, cow bells, rattlers, fish horns, and whistles rent the air. The deafening noise bounded against the hill sides of Clifton and came echoing back again.

Twice more in the October 3 *New York Times* writers told about Roush's catch. One account read:

Then came Happy Felsch.... He whaled a terrific drive to centre which would have cashed in if anybody but the shadowy Eddie Roush had been in centre field. You would have mortgaged the farm that Eddie would never get on speaking terms with the ball. Eddie dashed back several yards at high speed and made an unbelievable catch, which ended that dangerous session for Sallee.

And in the inning by inning account in the *Times*:

Then Felsch tried to murder the ball and forced Eddie Roush into the greatest play of the game. Felsch's bat crashed against the horsehide, and it went sailing rapidly to the permanent fence in centre field. Roush, with the crack of the bat, was off like a deer, with nothing more than a passing look at the swift-moving sphere. Once he looked over his shoulder as he sought the ball in its flight and, ascertaining the direction of the hit, increased his speed. Just when the ball seemed about to fly past him the Red outfielder gave one jump and snared the pill in his gloved hand with his back turned to the roaring stands. The momentum of his chase after the ball carried Roush bang up against the fence, and he caromed off and raced toward the bench amid ear-splitting cheers sent up by a gratified baseball populace gone crazy with the joy at the sight of a wonderful play.

In an inning-by-inning account of the game, the *Cincinnati Enquirer* writer called Roush's catch a "startling, leaping catch, one of the greatest ever seen on Redland Field."

The *Cincinnati Times-Star*'s praise of Roush's plays in the field was a heavy dose of hometown pride. The chief cheerleader was the *Times-Star*'s W.A. Phelon. The day after Roush's catch Felsch, Phelon wrote:

GREATEST OF ALL CENTERFIELDERS. It was Roush who saved the second game, in all human probability. Sixth inning, one out. Weaver smashed a double to left. The terrible Joe Jackson stood like a statue while the third strike was called, and the crowd roared its boisterous joy. Weaver took third on a balk, and Hap Felsch, a tough man in a pinch, came up. There was a blinding crash as the ball went up and on and over. Roush went back, and farther back. He neared the great green wall at the extremity of center field. He sprang, and came down with the ball, and with the barrier only a few feet away—one of the most splendid catches ever seen on any field, and a saver to a certainty.

The Reds won that second game by a 4–2 score.

After the sixth game in Cincinnati, which the Reds lost in the tenth inning by a 5–4 score, Phelon of the *Times-Star* had a box at the top middle of the page with the title:

KING ROUSH
ROAMS THE CENTER GARDEN
UNMATCHABLE

Below this title W. A. Phelon wrote:

> In this series Edd Roush has conclusively shown himself king of all centerfielders. American league critics had all asserted that Felsch was the best in the world; that neither Roush or any other fielder could surpass him, and that nobody could hit a fly ball over his head—he would get anything inside the boundaries of the park. And Roush has absolutely outclassed him all the way! Roush has made catch after catch that Felsch couldn't have approached; ball after ball has gone over Felsch that Roush would have taken down. There has been nothing to the comparison, nothing whatever.

In an article just below the one praising Roush, Phelon reacted indignantly to comments from unnamed sources claiming that the Reds, who had just lost by one run, had thrown the game. Phelon gives a few of the comments: "Aw, that game was thrown." "The Reds laid down." "They just wanted to spin out the series and get more money for Herrman and Comiskey." Phelon went on to tell of things Reds players did during the game that would refute those claims, including as an example: "Roush's desperate catch, which temporarily saved the game in the eighth, need not have been even attempted. Not a fan in the park would have accused him of throwing the game had he let Risberg's grass-cutting liner get away."

At the time Phelon wrote these two articles, he evidently did not know that some Sox players were in fact throwing games. One of the players in on the scam was Happy Felsch. Part of Felsch's contribution to the Sox's downfall was to "misjudge" a few fly balls, to misposition himself, and to make off-target throws.

The *New York Times'* baseball writers covering the games included many of the odd plays by some White Sox players. For example, Felsch's strange behavior was apparent in the fifth game that the Reds won 5–0 in Chicago on October 6, 1919.

> When Eller came to the bat in the beginning of the inning, Happy Felsch moved over toward right field. There was a hole between Felsch and Jackson wide enough to send a regiment through. It is difficult to understand why the White Sox thought that Eller was a right field hitter. Their scouting report must have been bad. If they only remembered how Eller beat the Giants in New York last Summer by plastering the ball into the left field bleachers for a home run, they would never been under the impression that he was a right field hitter. This is only one of many instances where the Reds have shown themselves a smarter lot of ball players than the American Leaguers.

Knowing what we know now, the *Times-Star's* Phelon, in comparing Roush and Felsch, was comparing an apple with a rotten apple, one tainted by gamblers.

To baseball people, the poor defensive play by Felsch and Joe Jackson had to have been suspicious. Both were considered outstanding fielders and may have been the two best throwers in the game at that time. In an October 11, 1946, article, the *New York World-Telegram's* Joe King praised the throwing of the St. Louis Cardinals' Enos Slaughter in the World Series game against the Boston Red Sox a day earlier. In the article, King quotes Duffy Lewis, who noted the throwing arms of Jackson and Felsch:

> Duffy Lewis, one of the greatest outfielders, says Slaughter does it the way his outfield used to do it for the Sox. "He takes the ball low which is the secret of throwing to a base, because you

always have to come low from high before you can throw," Lewis insists. Duffy only sees two rivals, Dom DiMaggio of the Red Sox and Ron Northey of the Phillies, as contenders of Slaughter's.

Throwing is a lost art and not so important as it was in Lewis' day. Ruth was a great thrower, but Lewis esteems Joe Jackson first and Happy Felsch second as the best throwers of a chucking era.

Though he was performing at less than his capability at times during the 1919 Series, it was clear that in the second game Felsch was putting maximum effort into the swing that eventuated in Edd Roush's making one of the best catches in any game. For that moment Felsch was on the up and up, and Roush bested him.

SIX

1920–1929

April 28, 1920—Tris Speaker

Tris Speaker was considered to be without peer as an outfielder during his long prime. As good as other outfielders were during his day, even outfielders like Harry Hooper, Ty Cobb, and Clyde Milan said that Speaker was the best

In a July 1914 article about Speaker in *The Baseball Magazine* there was a section called "Comments from Able Critics." Six baseball men were the commentators. Among them were Ty Cobb and Joe Jackson, both very good outfielders themselves, and Clark Griffith, a former pitcher and, in 1914, the manager of the Washington Senators. Cobb said, "If I were asked to express an opinion on the greatest all-around outfielder in the game, I would choose Tris Speaker." Jackson said, "In batting he doesn't lead, though he is a close runner up. But Speaker is the best outfielder in the business." Speaker was the greatest hitter for average of all the "great" centerfielders except Ty Cobb. Speaker's .344 lifetime batting average is the seventh best of all time. Finally, Clark Griffith said: "Tris Speaker is the best outfielder I ever saw. He has a style all his own. No outfielder is in his class." It should be remembered that Griffith played with Bill Lange, who, as was mentioned earlier, Griffith later called equal to, or better than, all the outfielders he had seen through 1950.

In his prime it was Speaker's fielding which was not equaled among the major league players of his time. He is well known for playing a very shallow center field. He was supremely confident of his speed to go back to get balls hit behind him, and knew that most balls would be in play in front of him. This enabled him to make plays close to the infield, acting almost as another infielder, and contributed to him having the highest major league assists total of all-time for an outfielder. He also had a strong, accurate arm.

Speaker had been perhaps the major league's top fielding outfielder for over a decade by 1920, the year he made the catch he considered his greatest. Ten years earlier, during a game on July 18, 1910, a 9–4 victory over the Detroit Tigers, Speaker had made another outstanding catch. Paul H. Shannon of the *Boston Post* wrote that "Speaker robbed Davy Jones of a hit with one of his wonderful running catches...."

The unnamed writer for the *Boston Globe* told more about the catch.

> Speaker turned in one of his superb fielding games. He made hard catches look easy, and then pulled off one play that went for the headliner of the piece. With a man on second in the seventh, Davy Jones cut a low liner to short left center that Tris came across like a flash and seeming to double his speed for the last few yards, hooked the ball falling to his full length. It was a wonderful catch, after a remarkable start and a great sprint.

Later in the article, the writer came back to Speaker's catch on Jones: "Then Speaker brought the house down with a remarkable running catch off Davy Jones, a catch that could only have been made by a great outfielder."

Tris Speaker's greatest catch was made on April 28, 1920, not long after his 32nd birthday. At that time he was the manager of the Cleveland Indians. Speaker would lead the Indians to the American League Championship, and then to the 1920 World Series title over the Brooklyn Dodgers.

The game against the White Sox was played in Cleveland's League Park, which had a center field fence at 420 feet from home plate. Just to the left of center field the distance was 450 feet. In right center the distance was 400 feet. The Indians played the Chicago White Sox.

As the 1920 season began, the baseball world, including the White Sox fans, had yet to be fully informed that some White Sox players had thrown World Series games in 1919. In fact, for White Sox fans, 1920 brought the promise of another outstanding season from Chicago's players. The White Sox stayed in close contention until the final week of the 1920 season, which was just about the time the stories began to surface about action to be taken against some of the White Sox players.

In April 1920, White Sox players again were playing to win. Among those playing well for the White Sox was the great Joe Jackson, a former Cleveland Indian. It was on a ball Jackson hit on April 28, 1920, that Speaker made his greatest catch. Larry Woltz of the *Chicago Herald and Examiner* wrote:

Old Tristram Speaker of Hubbard City, Tex., is a robber and a thief. He would not hold you up in a dark alley and relieve you of your watch and dough. Neither would he sneak into your home and lift the hidden treasures, but he would take a baseball game away from you any time the opportunity enters. He did it today, the White Sox losing the second game of the series to the Cleveland Indians, 5 to 4. The ball game should be written around Speaker's catch of Joe Jackson's liner in the seventh inning.

Two White Sox were on the paths when Mister Joe Jackson went to bat in the seventh. Two were out. Jackson already had busted a single and a home run, driving in three of Chicago's four scores.

Generally considered the greatest centerfielder of his time, first for the Boston Red Sox and then for the Cleveland Indians, Tris Speaker made many superlative catches, his greatest while he was with Cleveland in 1920.

Jackson likes to hit against Bagby. He proved it today.

The count was two balls and one strike. Then Joe leaned against the ball. It was apparently good for a triple, and the Cleveland fans moaned. Jackson's drive sailed to deep right centerfield. It was the hardest hit ball of the afternoon. Speaker ran like a scared man. He headed straight for the concrete wall, leaped into the air and stabbed the ball. He almost knocked the stone wall down, but he held the old baseball.

Tris has made many brilliant catches, but nothing to equal this one.

Irving Vaughn of the *Chicago Daily Tribune* characterized Speaker's catch in a similar way.

Because Tris Speaker charged against the concrete wall in right center and caught a terrific drive off Joe Jackson's bat, the White Sox were given another bump by the Indians today, 5 to 4. Speaker staged his burglary of a legitimate triple when two gents were on base in the seventh, and took all the starch out of Kid Gleason's men. They didn't rally after that.

As might be expected, the Cleveland writers were more expansive about what Tris Speaker had done. The unidentified reporter for the *Cleveland News* wrote about Speaker's catch:

Tuesday's 3 to 2 triumph was thrilling, but it paled into insignificance compared with Wednesday's 5 to 4 achievement. There were great plays and greater plays inning after inning. Both teams sparkled offensively and defensively.

But it remained for the seventh inning to furnish the real wonder sensational play of the day— THE GREATEST CATCH IN THE HISTORY OF BASEBALL. Wilkinson was safe on Chapman's low throw and after Leibold flied out, Weaver singled. Collins also flied out and then it happened. Jackson connected for a terrific smash to deep right center. It wasn't a flyball but one of Joe's copyrighted high line drives. Speaker cut across the lot at breakneck speed, but there didn't appear to be a chance for him to catch up with the ball. When he was ten feet away, Spoke realized he could catch the ball, but it occurred to him he might pay the penalty by crashing into the wall. He covered a few additional feet, decided he could take one more step and possibly reach the ball and take a chance on the result. He took the step up on the embankment, the ball stuck. Speaker's hand went kerplump against the wall, but his glove was closest to the cement and he was not injured and the greatest catch any of the players or spectators ever saw any time or place was consummated. Jackson was robbed of a triple and the game was saved.

The *Cleveland Plain Dealer*'s Henry P. Edwards wrote:

Tris Speaker's catch of Joe Jackson's tremendous drive in the seventh inning of yesterday's ball game at League Park allowed Cleveland to defeat Chicago 5 to 4, sent the White Sox into third place and the Indians into a tie with Boston for first place. It was the greatest catch in the history of League Park and admitted by Speaker to be his greatest endeavor. That means it was the best ever as Speaker is the last word in outfielders. There were two on with two out when Jackson came to bat. He had made a single that drove in two runs and a home run over the right field wall. This time Pitcher Jim Bagby sought to prevent Jackson from duplicating his four-sacker. He pitched two outside the further corner. Jackson made no effort at either. Bagby sought to get the next on the outside but failed. It was a fast ball and Jackson met it squarely and sent it on a line to deep right center.

Speaker gave it one look and then tore for the wall beyond the second exit gate with all his speed. With one more step to go, he gave a glance over his shoulder, grabbed the ball which was traveling at rifle-ball speed, threw out both hands, hit the wall, bounded back and still gripped the ball. Forty-five hundred spectators arose to express their enthusiasm for the most phenomenal catch they ever witnessed and to applaud the player who made it.

It was a catch that robbed Jackson of a triple and Chicago of at least two runs if not more and possibly of the victory.

It was the proximity to the wall that made Speaker's catch so remarkable. Tris probably has gone further to make brilliant catches but never when he had to consider the danger of colliding with the concrete as well as figure on making the catch, a catch that meant victory or defeat.

There was not a single person, even Speaker, who thought there was a chance to make the catch. The Chicago base runners certainly didn't, for both sped for home while Jackson had passed first and was well on his way to second when Spoke grabbed the ball. "I did not think it possible," murmured Kid Gleason of the White Sox. "I did not think any man could get that ball. And there was only one and he was on the job."

It was fortunate that the Cleveland manager was not injured for straight ahead of him, only one step away, was an upright column of concrete. That the redskin pilot was not hurt was because of his own quick thinking. He had one foot in the air as he made the catch. When he brought it down he braced himself with all his strength and broke the force of the collision.

Ross Tenney of the *Cleveland Press* began his article by comparing Speaker's catch to the great catch Edd Roush of the Cincinnati Reds had made in the 1919 World Series. Tenney wrote:

> When Tris Speaker sat in the press boxes at Cincinnati and Chicago during the last world series he gathered a lot of pointers on how to beat the Chicago White Sox.
>
> He saw the Cincinnati Reds' outfielders playing so deep for Kid Gleason's sluggers that the peppery Kid, game after game, let out the wail that the "Reds weren't playing in the ballpark—they were playing clear out in the suburbs."
>
> But the system of planting themselves way out, as mapped out for the Reds by Scout Johnny Evers, one of baseball's brainiest players, enabled those Reds to upset the dope pot all over the White Sox and win a world championship.
>
> For weeks after the world series the praises were sung of a wonderful catch by which Eddie Roush of the Reds robbed Happy Felsch of a home run and saved the day for Cincinnati.
>
> Well, Speaker saw that catch from the pressbox and he went one better in the Indians' 5 to 4 victory Tuesday at League Park by which they yanked the White Sox from the lead in the American League. Spoke made two catches in the same game, both of which rank with Roush's.
>
> In the fifth round after Joe Jackson had pasted a four-bagger over the fence, Spoke ran nearly to the flag pole and pulled down a drive of Felsch's that was every bit as long as the one that gave Roush a chance to earn undying fame in the big series.
>
> But this catch wasn't in it with the one by which Spoke saved the day at Joe Jackson's expense in the seventh.
>
> ### THE CATCH OF CATCHES
> A low throw of Chapman's and Weaver's line single to center had put two on for the Sox in the seventh and there were two down when Dixie Joe stepped up and Spoke moved out.
>
> He never hit a ball more solidly than he did the liner he pasted over Spoke's head to deep center, but Spoke turned and chased for all he was worth. But nobody dreamed he had a chance to get it.
>
> It looked like madness to try anything but to head the ball off on the rebound and keep Jackson from making a home run. But Spoke figured otherwise.
>
> "I knew I could make that catch," he said afterward. "But I didn't know whether I could keep from crashing into the fence full force and putting myself down and out."
>
> Just as he got within reach of the ball, he took a momentary glance at the fence, then grabbed the flying sphere out of the air overhead, held it with one hand and braced himself off the fence with the other as he ran into the wall on the very next step.
>
> "I've never seen a greater catch in all my baseball days," says Billy Evans. "It was one chance in a thousand to save the day and Spoke did it." The Indians were one run to the good at the time and the Sox never threatened after that.

Umpire Billy Evans had been in major league baseball since 1906.

Frank Gibbons of the *Cleveland Press*, in his January 7, 1955, "Anecdote Alley" column, wrote about Tris Speaker's greatest catch. The memory of the catch was triggered by a conversation about Willie Mays' then recent catch on Vic Wertz's drive in the 1954 World Series. Gibbons wrote about the catch on Joe Jackson, and then quoted Speaker.

Speaker still had no doubt about the greatest catch of his career. It was at League Park in 1920 against the White Sox. Joe Jackson hit a line drive to right center with the bases filled and Spoke caught it before crashing into the fence.

"What makes a great catch is how important it is," says Speaker. "Mays made his in a World Series and mine helped win a pennant.

"After I bounced off that wall I was stunned for a moment. When I regained my wits, I remember looking down to find the ball was still in my glove. That was more amazing than the catch.

"I remember thinking, 'Baby, it's sure good to see you!'"

May 11, 1922—Johnny Mostil

The Chicago White Sox's Johnny Mostil was one of the best outfielders during the years he played in the 1920s. He had outstanding speed; in 1925 and 1926 he led the American League in steals. In *The Sporting News'* obituary article of Mostil's death on December 10, 1970, a catch he made in a pre-season game in 1925 in Nashville was noted.

> It was in a minor league park in 1925 that he made one of the most unusual plays in baseball history—a centerfielder catching a foul ball.
> During an exhibition in Nashville, [Bib] Falk was playing left field and he never won a foot race with anything or anybody. A long, high fly drifted over to the left field foul area and Mostil took after it. Falk just watched and Mostil kept running until he caught it.

In the *Nashville Tennessean* of April 8, 1925, Blinkey Horn wrote the article on the Chicago-Nashville game of the day before. He did not mention where Johnny Mostil made his three putouts, but he did note one of Mostil's catches: "Johnny Mostil had to rob Mahlon Higbee, by a fine running catch, however, to prevent a home marker in the fifth." Writers from the *Nashville Banner* and the *Chicago Tribune* did not mention a catch by Mostil.

In *A Donald Honig Reader*, Ted Lyons, the Hall of Fame pitcher who spent his early years in the major leagues as Mostil's teammate, called Mostil "a great centerfielder, one of the greatest." Lyons continued, "He could go get 'em. It was like turning a rabbit loose when the ball was hit out to center field" (91).

On May 11, 1922, in a 4–1 victory by the Yankees over the White Sox, Mostil came up with a wonderful effort. Arthur Robinson of the *New York American* described it this way:

> The Yankee half of the sixth was emblazoned by a startling catch by Mostil. Miller drove the ball hard and low on a line to right center. Mostil raced in, and unable to reach the ball while on his feet, dived for it with his gloved hand just as it was about to hit the ground.

An uncredited writer for the *New York Times* saw the catch as a colorful one.

> Despite all the errors, it was a Chicago player, Mostil, who was the fielding star of the game. He handled seven flies without a quaver, and in the sixth he ran into short right centre and caught Miller's liner with one hand while reclining on his left ear. It was quite a catch and earned a rousing ovation from the assembled fans.

Frederick G. Lieb of the *New York Evening Telegram* went further in his tribute to Johnny Mostil's catch.

> However, to atone for the fielding sins of his compatriots, Johnny Mostil made as fancy a catch as it ever was our good fortune to see. He ran across country for Miller's liner in right

centre as long as he dared, and slid the rest of the way on his stomach. While sliding along he stuck out one hand and grasped the ball. How he did it we can't say, but he did. After the inning in which Mostil made the catch, he got one of the greatest hands any visiting player was ever tendered on the Polo Grounds.

The *New York Herald*'s W.O. McGeehan described Mostil's catch somewhat differently.

Perhaps the star performance of the afternoon was a catch by Mostil, the Sox fielder. Elmer Miller lashed out what looked like a sure triple. It was just nosing the tops of the grass when Mostil dived for it, skimmed the outfield with his nose used as fulcrum, rolled over and came up with the pill clutched in his digits. The customers gave him considerable applause.

Among the other things written after Johnny Mostil died was Hall of Fame second baseman Eddie Collins's comment in Mostil's obituary notice in *The Sporting News*: "Eddie Collins, his former Manager and teammate, once called Mostil the 'greatest' centerfielder. 'He could go farther for a ball than Tris Speaker,' Collins said. 'For covering ground, Mostil was in a class by himself. I never saw his equal.'"

October 7, 1922—Bill Cunningham

In *My Thirty Years in Baseball*, John McGraw wrote about Bill Cuningham's catch on a ball Babe Ruth hit in the 1922 World Series at the Polo Grounds. He called the catch "great," and added:

We sort of suspected that Ruth would pull one of those long range shots of his. At any rate we took no chances on not being ready. Cunningham played just as far back as possible. At that he had to run as far as he could and then fall against the fence to make the catch.
 That catch may not have had much effect on the final outcome of the series but it certainly had great effect on lowering Ruth's morale. Incidentally, that is the longest fly ball I ever have seen caught [168].

Thomas S. Rice of the *Brooklyn Eagle* complained of the Yankees' poor decisions after Cunningham's catch off the Ruth drive. He wrote:

In the first inning, when the Yanks scored two runs, it was only the stupid work of the runners, or else the coaches, that prevented them from making it three or more. After Witt and Dugan singled, Ruth came to bat with none out and smashed a ball with a terrific wallop close to the center-field fence. Cunningham got the ball, making one of the most sensational catches ever seen under Coogan's Bluff, but in so doing he turned a complete somersault and lay on the ground for a moment before he got his throw off. When the smoke cleared there stood Witt on third and Dugan on first!
 There was no reason in the world, it seemed to us, why Witt could not have made home on the throw from deep center after the delay, and certainly inexcusable that Dugan should not have gone to second.

The Yankees went on to lose this game by a 4 to 3 score on other poor base running decisions.

As was the case when Red Murray made his famous 1909 catch under adverse conditions, the fourth game of the 1922 World Series was played in poor weather. The unnamed writer for the *New York Times* commented on those conditions, and made comments about the failure of some Yankee players to play smart baseball.

The game was staged under miserable conditions—infinitely worse than the ninth inning of Thursday, when the game was called on account of darkness. If the umpires were anxious then that the game be decided only under the best conditions, they should have been doubly anxious yesterday. Both fans and players would have been better served if the contest had been postponed.

When the game started a misty rain was falling, compelling the fans in exposed sections to put up umbrellas and newspapers or get thoroughly drenched. A haze rising from the Harlem River enveloped the field, and it was so dark in the first inning that it was almost impossible to see Cunningham, away out in the shadow of the centre field bleachers, make a sensational tumbling catch of Babe Ruth's long fly.

In describing Cunningham's catch in more detail, the writer also put it into the context of poor base running, which, incidentally, did not cause the Yankees to lose runs. Subsequent hits brought the first two base runners in to score:

Right at the start the Yanks played uninspired baseball. They jumped on McQuillan with gleeful shouts in the first inning. Witt, the first batter, slammed the ball back at McQuillan and grazed his head with a liner that continued on out to centre field. Dugan singled sharply to left, sending Witt to second and bringing Ruth up.

Let it be said that the Babe emphatically got hold of the ball. He blasted a terrific fly ball to centre field. Cunningham ran far back until he was almost at the bleacher fence. There he got his hands on the ball and then rolled like an acrobatic tumbler, coming up with the pellet still in his glove.

A runner as fast as Witt should have scored easily, even from second base. He was at third before Frisch had received Cunningham's throw, but Miller Huggins, coaching there, put up the red semaphore and stopped him. What Dugan was thinking of in the meantime can never be accurately gauged. In any event, he did not get even to second.

In another article on the game, a *Times* writer said, "As Ruth came to bat the Giants' outfielders moved deeper into the field. Cunningham, in centre, was playing away back. Yet he had to run almost to the bleacher fence to gather in Ruth's long smash. As Cunningham caught the ball he turned a complete somersault." Ruth's drive through the misty rain to the center field fence went about 483 feet, the longest distance in the field, justifying John McGraw's comment about its being the longest fair ball he ever saw caught.

In a notes section of the *Times'* sport pages on October 8, 1922, another reference to Cunningham's catch appeared.

Cunningham, racing like the wind and his back to the ball, speared Ruth's terrific drive near the centre field bleacher wall in the first, and under his own momentum the ... fly-chaser was thrown heavily to the ground. He held onto the ball for dear life, though thoroughly shaken up. The game was halted for a brief minute until Smiling Bill regained his equilibrium. It was a wicked drive strangely reminiscent of Battering Babe at his best. And it was a glittering catch.

Heywood Broun of the *New York World* gave another view of the proceedings.

Most vital of all the defensive deeds of the Giants was a miraculous catch by Cunningham in the first inning when it seemed as if the Yankees were going to decide the issue then and there. Cunningham lived up to the tradition that World's Series glory is won by substitutes. The little redheaded outfielder would now be on the bench if Casey Stengel's "charley horse" had not afforded him an opportunity to ride into action.

Later on in the article Broun describes the catch.

McQuillan tried slow ones on Ruth and couldn't control the wet ball very well, so he ventured a fast one. For the first time in this series Babe actually got hold of the ball. His drive was high but also mighty. It headed into dead centre.

Cunningham was playing deep, but he had to turn and run. Every now and then he would look back over his shoulder despairingly as if he did not believe the ball could go so far. He and that drive seemed like parallel lines destined to meet only in infinity. Cunningham was not to be jilted after so long a chase. He stretched out as far as he could go and made the catch. The business of slowing up was even harder. Falling on his face, Cunningham's feet and legs kept on going. He spun around on his neck like [circus performer] Fred Stone in an acrobatic act. Finally he came down again, slap against the wall of the centre field bleachers.

It was impossible to hear the thud because of the cheering but even the cheering of the 37,000 came to Cunningham like a whisper because he was so badly shaken up. They had to help him to his feet and induce him to give up the ball.

In the second game of the 1923 World Series Babe Ruth hit two home runs. However, he also hit a longer ball that was caught by Casey Stengel. As was noted earlier, Stengel had learned to play Ruth deep when Babe, as a minor league player with the Baltimore Orioles, hit balls over his head, so he was already playing very deep in center field. Stengel caught the ball near where Bill Cunningham had finally flagged Ruth's ball down in 1922.

Bill Cunningham played as a part-time starter for the Giants from 1921 through the 1923 season. He played in the most games of his major league career, 114, with the Boston Braves in 1924. He was a .286 hitter during his years in the majors.

July 8, 1924—Bib Falk

The subtitle of Charles A. Taylor's July 9, 1924, *New York American* article on the New York Yankees–Chicago White Sox doubleheader was "Falk Makes Astounding Catch." Taylor's first three paragraphs were:

> "Bib" Falk and Wally Pipp were the only two outstanding personalities in the doubleheader between the Yankees and the White Sox at the Ruppert ball lot yesterday afternoon, which resulted in an even split. The visitors walloped their way to an easy victory at 10 to 2 in the opener, and the home boys retaliated with an 8 to 5 triumph in the closing clash.
>
> "Bib" Falk is put right to the front of the minutes because of his hair-raising catch of Joe Bush's drive to left in the fourth inning. "Bib" realized it would take a super effort to nab the ball and he made it. He slid for some ten or twenty feet and then stuck up his gloved hand while lying prone to make the catch.
>
> According to Sam Jones, who was sadly watching the proceedings from the stands with an extra large boil protruding from his chin, this play of "Bib's" was the best he had ever seen in his long span as a baseballer.

Sam Jones at the time was a pitcher for the Yankees, and had been a major leaguer since 1914.

The unidentified writer for the *New York Times* was more glowing in his praise of Falk's catch: "Battling Bib turned a circus catch in the initial engagement that for sheer daring and brilliance had never been bettered on any diamond. Major league baseball abounds with great plays and the players come to take them as a matter of course, but not the catch of Falk's."

Fred Lieb of the *New York Telegram and Evening Mail* in his July 9, 1924, column not only described the catch, but before doing so told of Falk's transition from pitcher to outfielder.

> Then consider the changes that a few months have made in the life of Bib Falk. I had quite a chat with this player in Florida early in the spring, when the Giants and the White Sox were on their "Seeing Dixie First" tour.

Falk broke in with the White Sox in 1921 as a Texas college sensation, and had a splendid year in 1922. Last season he had an off year, and was not used regularly. He had been a college pitcher and outfielder, and a decree went out from the Sox board of strategy that Bib should do nothing but pitch in the future.

That didn't suit the young Texan at all and he was disgruntled and dissatisfied at the Sox training camp.

"Why they won't even let me hit in batting practice," was his sad comment. Falk got little chance in the first six weeks of the championship season. He sat on the bench, occasionally breaking into a game as a pinch-hitter.

While Chicago was on its last visit to New York, Evers shook up his team and placed Falk in left. He hit two homers that afternoon to celebrate his return to regular duty. Bib has been clouting the ball ever since, and now leads the American League in hitting. In yesterday's doubleheader he cracked out five hits in nine official times at bat.

"Bib is satisfied and happy this year," one of the Chicago players told me. "And he sure is a hitting fool."

Falk can do more than hit. He proved that to a 20,000 crowd when he made the greatest catch seen in New York this season on Joe Bush in the fourth inning on the first day.

Defensively, the Chicago White Sox left fielder Bib Falk often played in the shadow of the fleet centerfielder Johnny Mostil, except for a catch that stunned the fans and the press at Yankee Stadium on July 8, 1924.

Thurston had just had some rough going. Pipp and Schang, successive hitters, slammed homers into the right field bleachers. Ward followed with a single and Scott fouled out. Then Bush banged one to left, a clout which was a strong bid for another homer, or at least a triple.

Falk dove across that cinder track in left field for the ball, and as he was gliding along that cinder path on his elbows, he caught the ball. Such a catch is almost uncanny. Falk skinned both elbows, but he held the ball. I don't recall a greater catch since Dode Paskert made his historic catch on Merkle in 1911.

Lieb evidently forgot that the player who hit the ball Paskert caught in 1911 was Fred Snodgrass.

Under a section heading "Falk Does the Impossible," Harry Cross of the *New York Post* wrote:

In addition to this hitting ability Falk made a fielding play yesterday which some day may be perpetuated in bronze. Joe Bush plugged a long drive to left field close to the field boxes with all the confidence in the world of delivering at least a two-bagger. Falk came from nowhere, took a long running dive, and while he was mixed up on the cinder track stuck out one hand and grabbed the ball. Many who saw it do not believe it yet.

John Kieran of the *New York Tribune* gave the Falk catch the highest acclaim.

At last it has arrived! Fans have been talking about it for years, and the 20,000 who were at the stadium are ready to swear it came yesterday. "The greatest catch ever seen on the local diamond" is the play in question. It was made by Bib Falk, who slid across Phil Schenck's running track on his right elbow and at the end of his skid caught a wicked wallop by Joe Bush in the hand which was attached to the elbow on which he was sliding.

In telling about the first game of the doubleheader, Irving Vaughn of the *Chicago Tribune* praised pitcher Hollis Thurston's effort and described Falk's catch in terms similar to those noted above. He said it would be a long time before Falk or anyone else made a catch like the one he had made. Later in the article, Vaughn said the catch was "startling."

In the October 28, 1924, *New York Evening Journal*, under the title "Greatest Play I Ever Saw," Falk's teammate, third baseman Willie Kamm, told *Evening Journal* writer Ford Frick about Falk's catch.

I think the greatest individual play I ever saw was pulled right in the Yankee Stadium—and the boy who made it was Bib Falk.

It was last Summer, and we were playing the Yankees. There were two men on bases, and Bob Meusel was up. Bob, as you know is a line-ball hitter, and when he takes a real cut at the ball he hits it with terrific force.

He did it that day. Thurston was pitching, and Bob swung viciously. The ball sailed on a dead line over third and down the left field foul line. It looked like a sure double at the least.

But Bib was away at the crack of the bat, and he came in fast. No one thought he could possibly get there. I don't think he thought so himself. But he kept coming. And when it seemed the ball would surely hit the ground he left his feet in an old-fashioned football dive.

Watching him from third, it seemed to me he slid full twenty feet, and then he stretched out his hand and took the ball. His head and shoulders were on the ground, his feet in the air, and he was only inches from the concrete stand. But he held on—and came up with the ball.

The stands rocked with applause as he walked to the bench. Even the Yankees rushed out of their dugout to pat him on the back.

I've seen a lot of great plays, but that one, to my mind, was the greatest I ever saw.

It appears that Willie Kamm misidentified the batter. The other reports note that the batter was Joe Bush.

October 10, 1925—Sam Rice

Sam Rice's catch for Washington in the third game of the World Series caused a sensation, in part because he got to the ball, but also because, after making the catch, he fell into the crowd, where he stayed for several seconds before emerging with the ball.

Rice's catch in right center field at Griffith Stadium in Washington was a difficult one. A man with lesser speed than Rice, still swift at age 35, might not have made it to the ball. For defensive purposes in the eighth inning, Washington Senators manager Bucky Harris had just switched Rice to right from center, and put Earl McNeely in center in place of Joe Harris, who had been playing right field.

Damon Runyon's report of the game was the lead article in the *Washington Herald*, and also was a lead article in the *Pittsburgh Gazette Times*. His account told of Rice's feat.

It was a defensive move, because Bucky Harris figured that a single fielding mishap late in the game might destroy that one-run lead, and Joe Harris was the one man in the Washington lineup that was most apt to sustain a mishap of that nature.

A few minutes later, Sam Rice, called "Man 'O War" because of his speed, made an astounding one-handed catch of a ball driven by "Oil" Smith, the talky Arkansas man who catches for the Pirates, that would have been a home run, and then destroyed the Washington lead.

Rice reached into the bleachers in center field and apparently grabbed the ball right out of the lap of a man sitting in the front row.

Joe Harris, racing with all his might and main, could not possibly have driven his bulky body over from right field in time to get that ball. It took a man with sprinter speed, such as Rice possessed, and an unerring clutch. Rice had that, too

His back was turned to field and the crowd as he grabbed at the ball.

The chief talk of conversation among the visiting baseball experts was whether Sammy had made the catch. There was some talk to the effect that Manager Bill McKechnie, of the Pirates, was going to protest the game, backing his protest with affidavits from fans in center field.

This McKechnie denied, saying he accepted the ruling of Umpire Rigler on the play. Rice himself characterized as ridiculous any talk to the effect that he "juggled" or "trapped" the ball. He asserted:

"I caught the ball firmly in my glove and had it there when I went into the bleachers. Neither did it leave my glove after the crash. It was a clean catch."

Personally, I thought Rice made the catch all right, but no man in the press section, or in the grand stands can pass on that play, because they couldn't see him actually grasping the ball. Only a few hundred of the bleacherites saw that. But the next few days undoubtedly will produce at least ten thousand claimants to that visual distinction.

N.W. Baxter, sports editor of the *Washington Post*, wrote about Sam Rice's delay getting out of the stands after going into the crowd: "Sam Rice says he caught the ball and that momentary delay which was apparent between the time he caught it and his emergence from the crowd was because his Adam's apple hit the head of a spectator and he was choking."

The lead *New York Times* writer for the game, Harry Cross, put Rice's catch at the highest level.

In all the future years that world's series will be played, to all the games that have been played under high nervous tension in the past, one will never see a more thrilling catch than that grand grab by Sam Rice. The Pittsburgh players protested. They wouldn't and couldn't believe that it was humanly possible for any fielder to make such a catch.

To pull a ball out of the azure, with one's back turned to it, as Rice's was, is not so much skill as it is baseball intuition.

The *Washington Star* reported that Clark Griffith, who earlier had played for and managed the Senators and who owned the team after those stints, also had the highest praise for Rice's catch: "Clark Griffith, who played baseball when the game was in short trousers, declared that he had never seen any catch to approach it. 'It was a catch you are lucky to witness in a lifetime.'"

Predictably, the *Pittsburgh Press*'s sporting editor, Ralph S. Davis, told about dubious Pittsburgh fans seated near where Rice made his play. He told of two men who said they saw a boy handing the ball to Rice. He went on to claim that other fans in the vicinity said that Rice did not make the catch.

The *Pittsburgh Gazette Times*' sporting editor, Chester L. Smith, clearly had doubts about whether Rice caught the ball. The large title about the game expressed Smith's doubts: "DISPUTED CATCH DEFEATS PIRATES, 4–3 AS HIT INTO BLEACHERS BECOMES 'OUT.'" Smith led his article with:

How did Sam Rice get the ball Earl Smith hit into the bleachers in the third game of the World Series? This threatens, tonight, to become one of the historic puzzles of sportdom. For upon the answer depends the authenticity of the 4-to-3 score by which the Senators of Washington defeated the Pittsburgh Pirates.

...Rice and the ball reached the bleachers rail at the same instant, and Sam leaned far into the crowd, with his back to the infield, and almost hidden from the view of the grandstand.

There was a tense second during which the crowd did not know if Rice had made the catch. The second became two, then three, four and five. Finally Rice straightened up, the ball in his hand, and Umpire Rigler of the National League waved out Smith who was rounding the bases.

The umpires were immediately surrounded by irate Pirates who insisted that Rice did not get his hands on the ball, but the decision could not be changed and the arguments were in vain.

May 3 and May 4, 1927 — Arnold "Jigger" Statz

The name of Jigger Statz is almost unknown by baseball fans today. He last played a major league game in 1928, and by that time had played for four different major league teams and had two stints in the Pacific Coast League. In 1929, Statz went back to the Pacific Coast League and was a star player there for another decade.

Statz, like Edd Roush, originally signed with the New York Giants, but John McGraw parted with them before either man could show off his impressive skills. Both Statz and Roush were outstanding fielders. However, Roush was a more consistent hitter, and he became a star and a Hall of Famer. Statz was a less consistent hitter at the major league level, and was a singles and doubles hitter during the twenties when many managers were looking for long-ball hitters, not the punch hitters of the earlier decades. Jigger Statz's best offensive year in the major leagues was in 1923 when he was with the Chicago Cubs. He hit .319, had 209 hits and stole 29 bases.

After the Chicago Cubs purchased Statz's contract from the Los Angeles Angels in 1921, an unidentified writer for the *Brooklyn Eagle* in December 1921 predicted that he would be another Ty Cobb, based on his performance in the Pacific Coast League. The article's author, among other things, wrote:

> If Statz turns out to be half as good as experts predict he is destined to rank among the truly greats of the pastime. Jack Doyle, Cub scout, who watched the youngster during the coast league season, says that Tris Speaker in his palmiest days never covered as much ground in centerfield.
>
> Statz not only gets all around the outfield but has a bullet-like throwing arm.

Statz played four years for the Cubs, and demonstrated his peerless defensive ability. However, his trouble generating consistent offense up to the .300 level his coaches wanted led him to return to the Los Angeles Angels for the 1926 season.

As had been the case with the Angels in 1921, Statz was a dominant player in the Pacific Coast League in 1926. Tommy Holmes, writing in the *Brooklyn Eagle* after Statz was acquired by Brooklyn in mid–September 1926, said:

> Mercury had nothing on Statz when he set himself after a long fly ball. "Jigger" can go in any direction, including up, for a hard drive. He committed so many bits of stark brigandage in the course of the past season that one rival owner wanted him "handicapped" by sewing 10 or 15 pounds of lead in his uniform.
>
> Statz always did act that way. During a previous three-year term in the National League,

Max Carey, then at his best, was the only other athlete in the business who could spot Statz six inches and beat him to any given spot.

With Los Angeles, Statz, the defensive wonder, became Statz, the offensive threat. "Jigger" shagged flies in his accustomed flashy style and supplemented his superb fielding with "apple knocking" of a high order.

Statz led off the Los Angeles attack—the position to which his keen eye and his great speed entitled him. "Jigger" didn't bombard the fences. Lack of a convincing drive to his wallops was his main difficulty when he was up with the Cubs. But he did loop enough hits over, under and through the infield to finish fourth in the league batting averages.

Holmes's reference to handicapping Statz was the subject of a September 18, 1926, *Brooklyn Eagle* article:

Jigger Statz, shown here in about 1924 when he was a member of the Chicago Cubs, was considered by some to be on a par with, if not better than, any centerfielder in the history of baseball.

Handicapping horses by weight is an old tradition of the track to equalize competition, but to use the same system on a mere outfielder to keep his club on an equal basis with the league seems to be a brand new one in the national pastime.

Officials of the Los Angeles club that is playing here tell an amazing story along these lines in connection with Arnold Statz, who has just been sold to Brooklyn. Statz has been burning up the Pacific Coast League and through his great work has the Los Angeles club breezing to an easy pennant. He has been rated as a one-man outfield, as his flanks only catch the ball hit to where they are standing—Statz gets the rest.

Five double plays have been pulled this season by him on short drives over the middle bag. With men on first and second they hold their bases, figuring the "Jigger" is going to glove the drive, but he scoops up the ball from the ground and doubles up the boys at second.

Opposing magnates and managers have wept all season over the manner in which he has been wrecking and killing their chances. Recently, after Statz had given a single-handed exhibition of taking a series from a certain club, officials of the Los Angeles team were asked to attend a conference held by the defeated owner.

"We cannot stand the killing of the game out there by that fellow Statz," said the magnate when the conference got under way. "He is taking the competition out of our league. I have a suggestion that I wish you would consider seriously. For the benefit of the pastime in general would it be possible for you to make him carry 20 pounds of lead in his uniform when playing second division clubs? With contenders it is all well and good to let him run free, but for the love of Pete give us low clubs a chance."

Statz's ability to catch balls already conceded to be hits was evident from some accounts of games he played at the major league level. On May 12, 1923, the unidentified *New York Times* reporter for the Chicago Cubs–New York Giants game wrote about a low liner Irish Meusel hit over the second baseman's head and Statz's seemingly fruitless rush in to catch the ball: "When man and ball met, Statz was going at top speed, his body bent over, his glove extended down to his ankles, and there the ball stuck. How it was done will have to be explained by Mr. Statz himself."

John Kieran of the *New York Herald-Tribune*, in his "Briefs" section written after a Cubs-Giants game of June 7, 1924, tried to capture the essence of Statz's speed to get to a ball hit by the Giants' catcher Frank "Pancho" Snyder: "Jigger Statz went back to the wall for Snyder's smash in the third and came in just back of second for Pep Young's short hoist in the fourth. Statz doesn't run; he flies. If he had one small feather he would be a bird."

May 3, 1927

What may have been Statz's greatest catch occurred on May 3, 1927, when the Brooklyn Robins played the New York Giants. About the catch, Richards Vidmer of the *New York Times* wrote: "Bentley did what he could with a homer in the last of the eighth, and after Mueller had singled with one out in the ninth, Tyson hit one that looked like a triple, and no bargain at that, but somehow Statz got one hand on it and held it. How he got it nobody knows."

About the same catch, W.B. Hanna of the *New York Herald Tribune* wrote: "Statz saved the game for Jess Barnes. He raced for the right field compartment of the bleachers to which stand the ball was drilled, and caught it in his glove as he raced."

Frank F. O'Neill of the *New York Telegram*, under the title "Classic Catch by Statz Robs Giants of Victory," wrote about Statz's catch of Tyson's drive:

> The greatest catch of the year in metropolitan circles turned back the Giants at the Polo Grounds yesterday. Jigger Statz, centerfielder of the Robins, made that catch. Al Tyson was the victim of Statz's spectacular burglary pulled off at the wall of the center field bleachers in the sight of ten thousand fans.
>
> The score at the time was 7 to 6, with Brooklyn leading. Heinie Mueller was half way to third with the tying run when the grab was made. Tyson was just a few strides off second on the first half of a certain home run that would have won the game.
>
> Statz's catch was a fitting climax to one of the most sensational games seen here or there in many a moon.

To reach the wall O'Neill mentions took a drive of about 460 feet.

The subtitle in the May 4, 1927, *New York Evening Post* account of the Giants-Brooklyn game of the day before included "Statz Makes Wonder Catch." The author of the article on the game, Frederick G. Lieb, just the day before had written about the three most memorable catches he had seen. Under the section heading "This Catch Belonged in the Circus," Lieb wrote:

> Uncle Robby would scarcely have been in such an amiable frame of mind last night but for a catch made by "Jigger" Statz on Al Tyson in the ninth inning at the Polo Grounds yesterday. Boys, that was a catch!
>
> Yesterday I discussed the three greatest catches that I have seen in covering some 3,000 games. I placed Hooper's catch on Doyle in the 1912 world series first, a catch by Dode Paskert on Merkle in 1911 second, and Elmer Miller's catch on Speaker in 1921 third.

Well, this thing by Statz yesterday was on a par with that historic grab by Paskert sixteen years ago. In fact, it was the same kind of catch.

One run behind, one out and Heinie Mueller on first base in the ninth inning, Tyson caught one of Jesse Barnes's fast ones on the end of his bat and the ball sailed on a bee line to deep right center. It looked like a sure triple and possible homer. Certainly it would have sent over the tying run and put the winning run on third with one out.

But Statz never gave up. He rode out with the ball and at the last moment he thrust out his trusty gloved hand and the leather-coated sphere stuck snugly in his glove. It was a wonder catch, and snuffed out New York's dying rally.

Statz may not be living up to his .354 Coast League batting average, but he sure can go back and get 'em.

"Daniel" (Dan Daniel) of the *New York Telegram* added something about Statz's catch on Al Tyson that no other writer did. He wrote:

The smashing attack of the Giants would have triumphed in spite of that bad pitching but for an astounding catch by "Jigger" Statz in the ninth inning. With Mel Ott gone Heinie Mueller batted for Cheeves and singled to right.

Al Tyson, who had not hit safely all afternoon, then took hold of one of Jess Barnes' fast ones and cracked it to right centre.

It was triple, perhaps a home run. But the ball never hit the ground. Statz, who had started with the ball, made a great sprint and lunged for the leather with his bare hand. He got it on his finger tips and somehow held it there.

Daniel was saying that Statz caught the ball with his bare hand. If true, this would make Statz's grab even more remarkable. However, other writers, like George E. Phair of the *New York American*, said Statz caught the ball with his left hand, which was his gloved hand.

May 4, 1927

Statz may have made an even better catch the next day, May 4. Frank O'Neill of the *Telegram* wrote:

In the ninth inning the Giants tied the score, but more than that they tried with courage of heroes to win it out, and only a marvelous catch by Jigger Statz prevented it. Statz went back to the Grant memorial for Jack Cummings line drive and caught it.

Earlier in the ninth Statz caught Hornsby's liner which McGraw says was the hardest hit ball that sped off Hornsby's bat this season.

Richards Vidmer of the *New York Times* described the Statz catch on the ball Cummings hit. He said:

Cummings made one of Ehrhardt's fast ones faster with a drive that looked like it would reach the exit gate in centre field and score enough runs to end the game, but there was that little pest, Jigger Statz, to contend with.

Statz turned almost before the ball was hit, touched a few of the high spots on the way and finally grabbed the ball with one hand as it fell over his shoulder.

Vidmer felt that the catch on Cummings was better than the one the day before on Tyson. The ball Cummings hit would have traveled about 480 feet.

After the May 4 game Thomas Holmes of the *Brooklyn Eagle* couldn't decide which of Jigger Statz's catches in the last three Brooklyn games was the best, so he described the best one in each game. In addition, he used his space to lobby for Statz to play even if he was not hitting up to the level he was expected to reach.

Somebody.—it was the immortal and imperious Tyrus Raymond Cobb if memory serves— once remarked that a .250 hitter and great outfielder was more valuable than a .325 slugger of pitched balls apt to be skulled by a fly at any odd moment.

Wilbert Robinson was asked his opinion on the subject last night. He bit right away.

"Statz isn't a .250 hitter," he objected strenuously. "His batting is improving right along. He hit .300 when he was with the Cubs and he'll hit .300 for us."

"But if 'Jigger' were a .250 hitter he'd be worth a .325 hitting outfielder who was mediocre defensively, wouldn't he?" the inquirer persisted.

"Uh-huh," replied your Uncle Wilbert. And there you have it—a flat contradiction that a weak-hitting outfielder need necessarily pay his own admission to the ballpark.

Oh! The Comfort of a Fast Outfield

The theory isn't amazing when you think about what a comfort a good, fast outfield can be to a toiling pitcher liable to slip one in some hitter's groove at a moment when a long hit can raise merry hob with the score.

It must ease a pitcher's mind to know that his centerfielder will grab anything hit out there, if grabbing is humanly possible, that a fly ball has to sprout real wings to get by a steady ball hawk and a line drive has to get down fast to hit in front of him.

When these spots arrive the pitcher lays one in there and prays; a Brooklyn flinger has a fair chance of his prayer being answered with a chap like Arnold Statz out on the grass behind him.

The little outfielder can and probably will hit better than he has been hitting. But if Statz never makes a hit his necromancy out in center will cut off more runs than the average slugger drives in.

Statz Right at Home With "Trouble"

Those long line drives he's pulled down in the last few days were labeled "trouble," every one of them would have passed through for long extra-base hits with an ordinary centerfielder. "Jigger" pulls those kind in with a nonchalance impossible to describe. A great outfielder!

Two ball games in the Brooklyn winning streak of five straight, checked by the New York Giants, were won through Statz's ability to fly here and there, hither and yon, and also hence and thither in quest of the elusive line drive. Picture the ninth inning of Saturday's game. The tying run on the bases—two out—Petty weakening fast—a Philadelphia pinch hitter and a Texas Leaguer over second—a race between "Jigger's" flying feet and a swiftly falling ball—the fans giving up hope—then one desperate lunge and a shoestring catch for the final out.

A Picture No Artist Could Paint

Or picture the last half of the ninth at the Polo Grounds Tuesday. The Robins a run ahead—one out and a man on first—Tyson reaches out and pickles one into right center—the Robin fans moan. "Three bases sure"—it looks through the alley—the fans aren't watching the fielders—their eyes are glued to the ball—it will reach the fence—out of the southwest corner of nowhere, his back to the stands and racing like mad, comes Statz—he's fast, may hold Tyson to three—then suddenly, an upraised arm—his glove thrown in front of his right shoulder attracts the ball like a magnet—it socks in there and it sticks.

Incidentally, a ball always sticks when it gets into that glove.

"Jigger" might have saved yesterday's game also, but the situation got beyond his control in the ninth, and later in the tenth inning. The socking Hornsby hit a terrific line drive to center to start the ninth. Statz set himself in front of the drive and grabbed it with two eager talons.

They kept hitting Big Jim Elliott. Finally, two runs were in, the tying run on first. Cummings, McGraw's young catcher, laid the wood solidly against a fast ball.

Try This One On Your Piano

Out into center field the ball sailed, headed straight for the Eddie Grant monument on the fly. "Jigger," his back to the plate as he raced, was out there right with it. Running with the ball and a little to one side, Statz' glove darted out to make a backhand catch as the "Jigger's" nimble legs were churning over the turf at top speed.

The tying run scored on that sacrifice fly, but had the ball got past there would have been no tenth inning.

Edward T. Murphy of the *New York Sun* devoted almost his entire May 5, 1927, column to Statz's fielding deeds of the previous two days. His entire column, titled "Statz Stars in Outfield," follows.

Offensively, the Arnold Statz, who patrols center field for the Brooklyn Dodgers, today is not an improvement over the same Arnold Statz who had a trial with the Giants a few years ago and who later drifted to the Cubs to play as a regular in the outfield. Arnold, who is better known as Jigger, comes close to being a perfect outfielder as far as judging and pulling down flies are concerned. He can, to borrow a ball player's phrase in describing a good outfielder, go and get 'em.

With every team he has played Statz always was a dependable flychaser, but it is doubtful if he ever gave as brilliant an exhibition of outfield work as he did in the last two games at the Polo Grounds. In each contest he amazed onlookers by making what appeared to be impossible running catches on terrific drives and each catch came to a crisis and prevented the Giants from scoring their winning tally.

In the ninth inning of yesterday's contest Cummings was the victim of Statz's second sensational catch. Cummings batted for Kent Greenfield, and when he stepped to the plate there was one out, two runs in, Farrell on third and Mueller on first. The Dodgers were battling to hold a one-run advantage. Statz evidently figured that if Cummings raised a fly it would be directly over second base, so he played the batsman accordingly.

Cummings leaned against one of Rube Ehrhardt's offerings and the ball sailed high in the air and over second base. As soon as it was hit Statz realized he would have to go back quite a distance in order to make the catch, if one could be made. He turned his back and ran. When he was a few yards from the exit gate he turned his head and got a glimpse of the ball, now almost about to fly over his shoulder. Jigger threw his gloved hand into the air to make an almost impossible backhand catch. Once the ball struck his hand he clutched it tightly and then went about the business of returning the sphere to the infield. After the putout Farrell scored from third with the tying run. Had Statz failed to make the catch two Giants would have crossed the plate and Cummings would have received credit for breaking up the game with a triple.

Hard Blow for Dodgers

The Giants were unable to get another run in that frame, but in the tenth they managed to push over the deciding tally.

As in yesterday's combat Statz's remarkable catch of the day before came in the ninth inning and it was the only thing which saved the Dodgers from a defeat. With the score 7 to 6 in favor of the Dodgers, one out and Mueller on first base, Al Tyson hit what appeared to be nothing less than a triple and probably a home run.

The ball went high over the heads of the Dodger infielders and seemed to be bound for the Giants' bullpen. Statz tore over in right center and while racing at breakneck speed stuck out his gloved hand and speared the flying pellet. When the catch was made Mueller had slowed up at second base and had to hustle back to first. If Statz failed in his attempt Mueller would have scored easily and Tyson might have had a home run. If Tyson had been held to a triple he would have scored when Lindstrom followed with a sacrifice fly to Gus Felix.

Gives Pitchers Trouble

As a batsman Statz may be unable to hit over the .250 mark, but his ability to pull down terrific drives offsets whatever weakness he has as a batter. Jigger, however, gives opposing pitchers more trouble than his batting average would indicate.

"Statz," said Bob McGraw, while the Dodgers were in training, "is a difficult fellow to pitch to. He may not get many hits, but he is always trying to get on the basepaths and it would be foolish to underestimate his ability. He's a good bunter and he is always liable to drag the ball along the first base line. His great speed will enable him to beat out a lot of taps."

The catch on Al Tyson on May 3 was one that Roscoe McGowen, the long-time Brooklyn Dodgers writer for the *New York Times*, referred to in 1954 after Duke Snider made a breathtaking catch in Philadelphia. In his article in *The Sporting News* of June 9, 1954, McGowen wrote that the only other catch that the had seen which could be compared to Snider's was Statz's catch on the ball Al Tyson hit. He wrote: "Jigger Statz, a great ball hawk for the Dodgers, once caught a ball hit by Al Tyson at the Polo Grounds that your correspondent and all other press box observers that day thought could not possibly be caught. But Jigger was in the open field when he made his extraordinary catch." Roscoe McGowen was comparing Statz's catch to all the other catches he had seen since 1927.

John Drebinger wrote an article on Babe Herman that was included in the *Best Sports Stories of 1945*. Herman was the great hitter and sometimes unpredictable fielder for the Dodgers in the late 1920s and early 1930s. Drebinger, who covered the Brooklyn team in the late 1920s and later covered the New York Giants, seemed to be referring to the ball Statz caught on the May 4 drive off the bat of Cummings when he wrote:

> To every veteran baseball scribe who has beaten the trails in the major leagues for twenty years and more, most plays fade out in a general blur. Only a few of the truly great ones leave a lasting impression.
>
> In our book there remain three, made by outfielders, that time we doubt can ever erase. One was a catch Jigger Statz made at the Polo Grounds when, tearing clear to the center-field clubhouse at top speed and with his back to the diamond, he let the ball drop in his gloved hand which he held low behind him like a major domo in a hotel dining room reaching for a tip that will assure a better seat [52].

Since he covered Brooklyn during the two years Statz was there, Drebinger had many opportunities to see brilliant defensive work by Jigger. In mid–June 1927, a rainout of a Brooklyn game at Pittsburgh led Drebinger to write in the *New York Times* about the upturn in the fortunes of the Robins.

> The replacing of Hendrick by Statz has really strengthened the outfield defensively, and while it was wrench for Uncle Robbie to bench so fine a hitter as Hendrick, the fact that Jigger also is beginning to sock the ball hard has been a welcome surprise.
>
> Afield, Statz has been one of the high lights of nearly all the games the Robins have played recently, and even in this city the sport writers, accustomed to seeing such stars as the Waner brothers and Cuyler doing their daily stunts, have sat back astounded at Jigger's amazing work in cutting down line drives and making trick catches.

Statz's struggle to win a regular place due to manager Robinson's having other hitters than Statz in the lineup continued throughout the 1927 season.

After the end of the 1927 season Statz's talent as a golfer was on display. Despite playing little or no golf during the long baseball season and having limited practice from early October until December, Statz carded a 66 in a pro-am tournament in California. His score was lower than that of top professionals, including Tommy Armour, and of the top amateur, Bobby Jones. In a December 31, 1927, article in the *Brooklyn Eagle*, Ralph Trost wrote about Statz's extraordinary abilities as a baseball player and as a golfer. He told of the different physical demands of each sport, and how few people had accomplished what Statz had in both sports. Trost said Statz "can be classed as the best of all outfielders in the game." Later in the article Trost tried to indicate what made Statz such a wonderful fielder.

> He has the eye. Any one visiting Ebbets Field during the summer can learn that much by watching him catch flies. Statz can play his centerfield position closer to the infield than any one else, yet catch balls hit into deep center. That, in itself, bespeaks extraordinary co-ordination

between mind and muscle; the ability to start with the sound of the hit besides the instinct which tells him where the ball is going.

Trost also attributed Statz's success in two different sports to Statz's being "cool, calm and decided," and to having a "directness of purpose which makes champions...."

The problem around Statz's hitting continued when spring training began in 1928. Drebinger in early March 1928 wrote an article in the *Times* about the efforts to help Statz become a better, more free-swinging hitter, including the suggestion to change his batting stance to be like some other hitters. Drebinger's article says this was something that had been suggested in 1927. From the much-decreased playing time he was to get in 1928, it is apparent that he was not able to effectively use the suggestions he was given in spring training.

Drebinger could not pass on the chance to include more about Statz's fielding ability:

> Gifted with great swiftness afoot, a keen eye that almost instantly seems to gauge the depth and direction of a line drive or soaring fly, and a remarkable pair of hands, the little Jigger astounded fans last year with his daily stunts.
>
> John McGraw doubtless still remembers that afternoon at the Polo Grounds when the Jigger robbed the Giants of a hard-earned victory by tearing out to the Eddie Grant tablet and hauling down a certain home run by merely sticking his gloved hand behind him.

In mid–May 1928, Statz was beginning to hit well. At the end of his *New York Times* column on the Brooklyn-Cincinnati game of May 17, Drebinger noted: "But the hitting of Jigger Statz is the thing that is giving Robbie his biggest kick out of life these days. When hitting, the Jigger at once becomes one of the game's greatest outfielders, for there is none who can run even close to him as a fielder."

Unfortunately for Statz, his hitting was not consistent enough for his manager, and his playing time was to diminish to almost nothing by the end of the year. He still made great catches when he played, as was evident from Drebinger's description of a catch in Chicago on August 17, a catch Drebinger felt sure the fans in attendance would remember for a long time. "It was a mighty fly to dead centre which the Jigger got under after great sprint. With his back to the diamond he made one of those vestpocket catches in the manner of Rabbit Maranville on an infield pop." Rabbit Maranville, a Hall of Famer, was a shortstop in the National League from 1912 through 1935, and caught fly balls using what later became known, when Willie Mays routinely caught balls with his hands cupped under the ball, as a "basket catch."

Brooklyn finished sixth out of the eight National League teams in 1927 and 1928. Statz hit .274 in 507 official at-bats in 1927, and .234 in only 171 plate appearances in 1928. His .274 average in 1927 was higher than either of the other two outfielders who played alongside of him. The player who played the most center field for Brooklyn in 1928 had a batting average of .247. In the four major league seasons in which he played more than 100 games, Statz averaged .293. How seldom the spectacular-fielding Statz was given a chance to play in 1928 suggests not only that the management was looking for more power, but that Statz fell out of favor with manager Robinson, whose team lost games because of the inferior play of his other outfielders.

Jigger Statz left the major leagues after the 1928 season and returned to the Los Angeles Angels in the Pacific Coast League, where his fielding continued to dazzle fans. Altogether he spent 18 years with the Los Angeles Angels, a record for playing with one club in the minor leagues. With the Angels he had a career batting average of .315. He holds the Pacific Coast League records for games (2,790), hits (3,356), doubles (595), and triples (137), and led the league in stolen bases three times.

That Statz would be welcomed back by fans in Los Angeles was noted after he suited up for the first time in spring training. In his February 2, 1929, article on the Los Angeles Angels, the *Los Angeles Examiner*'s John Connolly wrote:

Arnold Statz, probably the niftiest fly chaser who ever put foot on Coast League soil, donned a monkey suit yesterday for the first time. Statz is still the same looking, tricky fly hawk of a few years ago. While he never raced from one end of the outfield to the other, what fly balls he did field were shagged in such a manner as to betray the old master's polish.

Two months later, John Connolly, in writing about the Los Angeles wins in both games of a doubleheader on March 31, wrote about Statz's play in the field: "Arnold Statz was the fielding sensation of the two games. His work in running down high flies and the ease with which he does it made a decided hit with the 12,000 cash customers in the stands."

Edward J. Montagne saw Statz play many times, and wrote a letter to the *Los Angeles Times* just after Statz passed away at the age of 91 in 1988. He wrote:

The passing of Jigger Statz brings many fond memories to mind for I was a charter member of the Statz fan club. I remember the first time I saw him at the old Washington park. He had been sent down to the Angels from, I think, the Chicago Cubs. I saw him play many, many times and consider him the best centerfielder I ever saw. And I saw DiMaggio and Mays in their primes. With that little glove, the middle cut out, he could handle anything that stayed in the ballpark.

It's ironic that he didn't play longer in the majors because he could hit around .275 up there, although he was a .300 hitter in the Coast league. Can you imagine what he would command today? A .275 hitter who could field like Tris Speaker. The line would go around the block.

Rest in peace, Jigger, and thanks for the memories.

In a conversation I had with him in 2002, Mr. Montagne, who played ten years of semi-pro baseball, said he saw Statz play at least once a week when Statz played for the Angels. Mr. Montagne also worked in New York from 1947 to 1960, and saw Joe DiMaggio and Willie Mays play. He also saw Vince, Joe, and Dom DiMaggio play in the Pacific Coast League. He still contended that Statz, who played a shallow center field and who could go back for a ball as well as anyone he ever saw, was the best fielder.

Edward Montagne's point about Statz's having a chance to continue a major league career even though he was a .275 hitter is well taken. Statz's career batting average in the major leagues was .285, the same as Max Carey, a great fielding outfielder for the Pirates 1910 to 1926. Carey is in the Hall of Fame, and Statz, for all his greatness as a fielder, was relegated to spot duty as a player for Brooklyn over his last year and a half in the major leagues. In 1927 and 1928 Carey and Statz were teammates in Brooklyn. In both years the aging Carey played in more games than Statz and hit for a lower average than Statz did.

In 1929 Statz returned to the Pacific Coast League, where his hitting was routinely above .300, and where for over a decade he amazed fans with fielding and base running. Upon Statz's leaving Brooklyn and signing with the Los Angeles Angels, Harold Burr of the *Brooklyn Eagle* wrote:

"Jigger" Statz has gone into the sunset with his impossible catches and his not quite good enough hitting. He has returned to his old manager at Los Angeles, Marty Krug, who is glad to get him back.

"I'm tickled the Jigger's returning to the Angels," declared Marty. "He's a great boy and very popular on the Coast. I don't mean just among our own fans. I mean with the crowds around the whole circuit."

His hitting couldn't keep pace with his fielding—that is the epitaph of so many ball players.

It was Statz's swan song, too. Robbie says he never saw a better fielder, and he's seen a lot in his day, coming and going out for the ball.

Wilbert Robinson played in the major leagues from 1886 until 1902. He managed the Brooklyn team from 1914 through 1931. He had seen all of the National League's best outfielders over his years in Brooklyn, and had seen great fielders, including his teammate in Baltimore Willie Keeler, from the time his playing days began in 1886. Yet he never saw a better outfielder than Statz, whom he chose to play infrequently over the last year and a half Statz was in Brooklyn.

In a February 1966 *Baseball Digest* article titled "Statz, 'Best' Center Fielder, Played in Record 3,373 Tilts," Al Wolf wrote, "Jigger is regarded by old-timers as the greatest defensive centerfielder of all time. They rate him over Tris Speaker, Joe DiMaggio and even Willie Mays in catching the ball."

The St. Louis Cardinals' Terry Moore was regarded as one of the best centerfielders of all time, mostly based on his defensive skills. Moore was a highly valued member of the Cardinals during his time on the field from 1935 to 1948. Moore was a .280 lifetime hitter. It seems that Statz was in the wrong decade to be a highly valued major league player.

June 8, 1928—Taylor Douthit

Taylor Douthit played sparingly for the St. Louis Cardinals from 1923 through 1925. However, he did make an impression on several writers in a September 14, 1924, game against the Giants in New York. The New York Giants defeated the St. Louis Cardinals 8 to 2 at the Polo Grounds. In that loss the Cardinals' Taylor Douthit made a particularly outstanding catch. The *New York Herald Tribune*'s W.B. Hanna wrote: "Douthit, who had been gathering them in all over the moor, ran to the Hotel Commodore in the second and absorbed one of Jackson's characteristically long belts. He acknowledged the applause with a Babe Ruth grin."

The *New York World*'s "Monitor" (the pen name of George Daley) called the catch "a supergorgeous catch of a far-flung drive by Jackson...."

About a ball the New York Giants' shortstop Travis Jackson hit and Douthit caught, Charles A. Taylor of the *New York American* wrote: "Douthit's catch of Jackson's long smash to right centre in the second was one of those for the encyclopedia."

In 1928, Taylor Douthit established the major league record for putouts in a season by catching 547 balls. Nicknamed the "Ballhawk," he was a .291 lifetime hitter. Perhaps his greatest catch was a long running grab of a ball the Giants' Fred Lindstrom hit at the Polo Grounds on June 8, 1928. In the *New York Times*' "Pickups and Putouts" section of brief comments about the day's doings with the Giants, an unnamed writer included: "Douthit went so far back to catch Lindstrom's long drive in the first inning that they had to declare a recess while he returned to his position."

Not long after that catch, in an uncredited July 1, 1928, article in the *New York World*, Douthit's career to that point was discussed. The author led the article with Douthit's fielding ability and his catch on Fred Lindstrom.

> It has not been so long ago that the Cardinals were at the Polo Grounds and played four games against the Giants. It was in that series that Douthit showed his greatness as an outfielder and as a hitter. He made one catch off Fred Lindstrom in the third contest that was one of the most remarkable ever made under the shadows of Coogan's Bluff.

Lindstrom is a real hard hitter, and on this particular day he slammed a long drive into left centre field. The crowd was sure, and so was Lindstrom, that it was an extra base hit. Freddy started down the first base and tore for second while the crowd cheered. In the mean time a gray streak was heading for the distant bleacher wall. Suddenly the gray streak was seen to stretch its arm into the air and catch the ball.

It was a marvelous catch—a catch that every one, even the other St. Louis players, thought was impossible for Douthit to make. But the young outfielder travels fast when he gets started, and few line drives get beyond his reach.

The *St. Louis Globe-Democrat's* Martin J. Haley wrote of Douthit's catch on Lindstrom in the Cardinals' victory over the Giants.

Taylor Douthit was the only Cardinal to go hitless, but Douthit had glory enough. He centered it all in one play, in the first inning, when he made one of the most beautiful running glove hand catches ever seen at the Polo Grounds. In turn Douthit received one of the heartiest showers of applause that ever drenched an alien player in the shadow of Coogan's Bluff. It seemed as if everyone was in on the hand, save the Giants and Lindstrom, the victims.

That catch, which Douthit enacted while running at full speed, with his back to the plate and with his glove stretched high in the air was, of course, the only one of its kind during the easy victory. Sherdel did not require any further support of that iridescent stripe.

October 9, 1928—Babe Ruth

Babe Ruth was a very capable fielder. In addition to his strong throwing arm, Ruth had good running speed. While playing right field, he made a catch on May 11, 1928, that led to the following uncredited note in the "Pickups and Putouts" box in the *New York Times*, about the Cleveland Indians-Yankees game: "If anyone ever made a more spectacular catch than Ruth of Summa's curving liner in the eighth we were some place else at the time."

On October 9, 1928, in the final game of the World Series, the thirty-three-year-old Ruth made another catch that was much commended in New York. Ruth's performance across the four-game sweep of the St. Louis Cardinals was one of the most outstanding in World Series history. He hit .625 on ten hits in sixteen at-bats, including three doubles and three home runs. The three home runs were hit in the last game. Ruth made a long running catch under adverse conditions to end the game in St. Louis.

The next day, the *New York Times'* James R. Harrison could not contain his admiration for what the Yankees had accomplished and for Ruth's transcendent talents. After writers had used the existing superlatives again and again for Ruth's achievements, what words were left to describe what he did? A number of times in his article Harrison sought to capture a higher level of appreciation for Ruth's uncommon abilities. For example, he wrote:

It was thus that the world's series of 1928 passed into history—with Ruth triumphant, with Ruth rampant on a field of green, with Ruth again stranger than fiction and mightier than even his most fervent admirers had dreamed he would be.
"The king is not dead, long live the king!" they might have shouted as this amazing play boy, this boisterous soul, in the great hour of his career, added new records to a list already stretching ten years back into baseball history.

Before the 1928 World Series the Yankees were thought to be at a disadvantage because of injuries. Their centerfielder Earle Combs had a broken wrist and would not play in the field in the series, though he did pinch-hit in the fourth game. Harrison said that Combs "admits no rivals in the centre-field business." In addition, the Yankees' great second baseman Tony Lazzeri and Ruth had leg injuries.

After the Yankees demolished the Cardinals, several writers humorously noted that the Yankees had been made underdogs in the series because of the injuries. One of those writers was Westbrook Pegler, whose account that appeared in the *Buffalo Courier-Express*.

That pale and trembling invalid, Mr. Babe Ruth, achieved something startling in the way of a convalescence out in the open air and summery sun glow this afternoon. Three times he laid his crutch in the way and knocked the baseball out of the St. Louis baseball park and finally in the last half of the ninth inning shook his groaning chassis into a wild loose-legged run to the rail of the temporary seats in left field, where he leaned over and plucked a foul ball from the feathers of a lady customer's millinery for the final putout of the world series of 1928.

In his *New York Telegram* column on October 10, Joe Williams emphasized the good nature of Ruth. Williams finished his column by noting his catch.

To Babe the game of yesterday and the whole series, in fact, was a lark. He exchanged snappy repartee with the customers all through the games, and out in left field, where he played in the West, he joshed the bleacherites constantly.

After each home run yesterday he trotted out to the bleachers and led the cheering for himself. In between times he paused to describe the manner of the pitch he hit and the flight of the ball. He was the soul of amiability and cheerfulness. It must be nice to be knocked stiff by such a jovial conqueror.

And, as if the fates were in perfect sympathy with the drama of the day, the last play of the game was a high foul down near the left field boxes, which the Babe caught on the run with his gloved hand, apparently catching the ball right out of the whiskers of a startled native. It was one of the great plays of the series.

The writers for the *St. Louis Post-Dispatch* and the *St. Louis Globe-Democrat* did not mention the assorted papers and other objects the fans along the left field seats were tossing at Ruth as he was trying to make the catch on Frisch's foul fly ball. The *Boston Herald*'s Burt Whitman did not miss the behavior of the fans. He wrote:

In the eighth inning Babe went to left field to the thunder of the acclaim of those who had been hollering for his heart's blood and who had been booing him earlier in the game. This was immediately after Bam's third homer. There is nothing but unalloyed praise and appreciation from your real baseball fan for such deeds as Ruth performed today.

The very last play of the game had on it the trade mark of the Bambino's greatness. Frank Frisch sent up a foul fly toward the nearer grandstand in the left field. Ruth came tearing in, his long, thin legs pumping and carrying him along at a speed which only those who know can appreciate.

Fans in the field boxes tossed out papers before his very eyes to bewilder him and to make him take his eyes off the ball. The sun was very bright in a cloudless sky, what the craft calls a "high sky," but nothing seems to bother this one-track genius of modern baseball.

He raced through a veritable blizzard of newspapers and with his right hand, the gloved hand, far extended, caught the ball not more than a stride from the field boxes in front of the grand stand and raced on with the ball triumphantly raised, as Spartan warriors proudly held up their shields when returning from the first campaigns.

BEST CATCH IN MODERN SERIES HISTORY

This was undoubtedly the most spectacular and, in many ways, the best catch of modern world series story. It was made by a sore-legged athlete, who had already made three homers, tying his own record for one game. It was made in the face of a flurry of thrown papers, the like of which has not been seen in world series annals. It is the tip-off, if any big-league city fan needs additional tip-offs on the subject, of why the world of baseball loves Babe Ruth.

SEVEN

1930–1939

August 30, 1930—Babe Herman

Babe Herman was known as a terrific hitter, but had a reputation as a mediocre fielder. As Tot Holmes tells in his book *Brooklyn's Babe*, through hard work and with the help of the coaching staff of the Brooklyn Dodgers, Herman became a respectable fielder who more than once made spectacular catches and throws. Even at 6' 4" tall and 190 pounds, he was one of the fastest runners in the league and could get to balls others might not track down. He also had a strong throwing arm.

On May 12, 1928, Herman made an outstanding catch in Pittsburgh. John Drebinger of the *New York Times* told of the catch Herman made on the Pirates' Earl Smith: "In the sixth Hendrick fumbled a grounder by Scott and Earl Smith followed with a smashing blow that headed straight for the concrete wall in right. Herman, making a great leap, got his glove in the way and froze the ball for an amazing catch."

The unidentified writer for the *New York World* was even more impressed with Herman's effort: "One of the greatest catches that has ever been made in the right field territory of Forbes Field was performed in the sixth with a Pirate on base. The Babe risked a bad injury in leaping high against the concrete wall to pull down a long smash by Earl Smith. Herman was given a great round of applause when he trotted to the bench."

What may have been Herman's greatest catch was one he made in New York against the Giants on August 30, 1930. The batter was Fred Lindstrom. G.W. Daley wrote about the catch in the *New York World*: "Herman made a stunning catch of Lindstrom's long one to right...." Joe Villa of the New York Sun called Herman's catch on the Lindstrom ball "miraculous." Westbrook Pegler of the *New York Evening Post* wrote: "Babe Herman ... galloped quite a long piece and to the amazement of the assemblage, stretched out and took the ball in a backhand reach."

Fifteen years later, in the *Best Sports Stories of 1945* (originally in the September 1945 *Baseball Digest*), John Drebinger described the three most memorable catches he'd seen. A catch by Jigger Statz in 1927 and a catch by Terry Moore in 1936 were the first two. The third was Herman's catch on Lindstrom.

And, believe it or not, the third was made by none other than Herman himself at the Polo Grounds as he dashed along the right-field wall for a drive that was screaming down the foul line. For a moment it looked as though the ball had shot by the Babe. But in some miraculous fashion he managed to spin around and by reaching out with his gloved hand seemed to snare the white pill just as it threatened to bang into the concrete wall [52].

June 20, 1931—
Fred Lindstrom

Fred Lindstrom spent most of his career with the New York Giants as a third baseman. He played one game in the outfield in 1926 and 51 in 1927. The remainder of his play from 1924 through the 1930 season was spent in the infield, mostly at third base. In 1931 he became the Giants' right fielder, a position at which he quickly excelled and mostly played until his retirement in 1936.

It was in 1931, not long after he became the Giants' right fielder, that Lindstrom made a catch at the Polo Grounds that had the writers looking for ways to describe it. On June 20, the Giants played a doubleheader against the Pittsburgh Pirates, with the Giants winning both games. It was in the first game that Lindstrom made his great catch. The *New York American*'s George E. Phair wrote about the catch under the subheading: "GREATEST CATCH EVER."

Better known for his hitting, the Dodgers' Babe Herman was a tall, long-striding and fast runner who worked hard to become a fielder with good skills.

In this crucial period there were Pirates on first and third and one man out when Gus Suhr smacked a tremendous drive toward the underwear sign in the right field corner. Sprinting with his back toward the plate, Lindstrom made a stab with his left hand, turned a couple of somersaults and came up with the ball. Old timers in the press coop swore it was the greatest catch they had ever seen.

The *New York Times*' John Drebinger was equally enthusiastic.

Walker here fanned Comorosky, but Suhr crashed a terrific liner in the direction of right centre that looked good for any number of bases and the ball game as well. Then followed one of the game's most dramatic episodes as Lindstrom, McGraw's transplanted third baseman, tore across the turf and with a headlong plunge snatched the ball out of the air with his gloved hand for one of the most remarkable outfield catches seen at the Polo Grounds in years.

Harry Cross of the *New York Herald Tribune* wrote:

Freddy Lindstrom dominated the opening pitchers' battle between Walker and Spencer. Afield and at the bat he was marvelously efficient. Lindstrom made a superlative catch of Suhr's drive in the sixth inning which reached the peak of fielding acrobatics. There were two runners aboard and one out when Suhr, the Pirate first baseman, buzzed a speedy drive between right and center.

Running at a right angle with the flight of the ball, Lindstrom sped and his task looked hopeless. The smash was ticketed for a homer, or a triple, if ever one was. He glanced over his left shoulder and hurled himself horizontally at the ball.

His gloved hand met the horsehide as Lindstrom plunged forward on his head. Thoroughly shaken, he held the ball. Even old-timers who have been going to the Polo Grounds since the days of horse cars got excited about this catch and called it the greatest they had ever seen.

The *New York Daily News'* Jimmy Powers called Lindstrom's catch "spectacular" and "great." The sportswriters for New York papers that did not have Sunday editions recounted Lindstrom's grab of Suhr's long belt in their editions for Monday, June 22, 1931. The *New York Evening Journal's* Frank O'Neill noted Lindstrom's transition from third base to right field.

Lindy was the best third baseman in the National League, with a deferential bow to Pie Traynor of Pittsburgh. He promises to win high honors as an outfield star before many months have elapsed.

...

The Polo Grounds delegation insists that Lindstrom's catch of Suhr's drive in Saturday's game was the greatest ever made on the Polo Grounds. That perhaps is a large order, for there have been many spectacular plays made in the home of the Giants. It certainly was great; had to be great to be a live topic of baseball gossip for two days.

There were many critical eyebrows arched when John J. McGraw moved Lindstrom from his station at third base where he had starred since 1924 and entrusted the difficult assignment to Johnny Vergez, fresh from the Pacific Coast League. Lindy looked pretty raw out there for awhile and there were times when he wanted to go back to third base.

In the *New York Post*, Fred Lieb, never one to shy away from giving his estimation of the greatest catches he'd seen, put the Lindstrom catch at a high level, just as he had done with Jigger Statz's catch in 1927.

"Lindy" ... contributed a catch on Gus Suhr, Pirate first baseman, Saturday that ranks with the greatest catches ever seen in the Harlem yard. It ranks with the historic catch Dode Paskert, former Philly outfielder, made on Fred Merkle in 1911 and Elmer Miller's memorable catch on Tris Speaker in the final week of the 1921 American League

An outstanding third baseman for the New York Giants, Fred Lindstrom, here shown early in his career, seamlessly made the transition to right field and soon made outstanding plays there.

season. The Yanks at the time still were tenants at the Polo Grounds. Lindstrom would make a catch like that on a .190 hitter.

It should be noted that Lieb had mentioned Yankee centerfielder Elmer Miller's catch in other places when he listed the top catches he had seen. Miller's catch occurred in a critical September 26, 1921, game between the New York Yankees and the Cleveland Indians, a game the Yankees won 8 to 7 to increase their lead over the Indians to two games. Miller's catch came in the eighth inning when there were two out and runners on second and third. Carl Mays had just relieved Waite Hoyt to pitch to the Indians' Tris Speaker. Speaker hit what looked to be a sure single into short right center. Elmer Miller raced in on the ball, which looked like it would drop in for a hit, and at the last second reached down to catch the ball just off the grass. Thus, Miller helped save the Yankees' win. At the time, writing for the *New York Evening Telegram*, Lieb called Miller's catch "remarkable." Frank O'Neill of the *New York Herald* said, "It was a classic in captures...." The *New York World*'s sportswriter Monitor called Miller's effort "a wonderful shoestring catch."

Back to Fred Lindstrom. In the *Pittsburgh Press* sports page of June 21, 1931, an unidentified author included a mention of Lindstrom's catch on June 20: "Lindstrom, who previously had saved the game for the Polo Grounders by a dazzling catch of Suhr's bid for a triple with two on, slashed one against the wall in right for a three-bagger, scoring Allen, and made victory sure by counting himself on Terry's single."

Frank Graham, in the June 22, 1931, *New York Sun*, noted how accomplished Lindstrom had become in right field by including him among the best in the league. Graham also quoted Lindstrom on the things he had to consider in moving from third base to the outfield. The title of Graham's article was "Lindy First-Rate Outfielder."

No longer will Freddy Lindstrom be able to pretend, even for purposes of wise cracking, that he is just an old third baseman doing the best he can in the out field. The other ball players—always quick to recognize the worth of one of their number—are beginning to claim for him the distinction of being the best right fielder in the National League. This claim may be regarded as premature, considering that among the other National League right fielders are Hazen Cuyler of the Cubs and Paul Waner of the Pirates, but Lindstrom is pressing these young men and conceivably is destined to pass them.

The highest point which Lindstrom has achieved thus far, came in the course of last Saturday's doubleheader, when he made that almost impossible catch of Gus Suhr's smash to right center and twice raced into the right field corner to make spectacular catches of foul flies. Into making these catches went all that a first rate outfielder must have: Judgment, speed afoot, baseball sense, and deftness of action.

That catch of Suhr's drive may not have been the greatest that ever was made. That, admittedly, is taking a lot of territory. But it was the greatest catch that many who saw it ever have seen. Every one who saw it still is trying to describe it adequately, either in speech or in print, but succeeding only partially. It was the sort of catch that had to be seen to be grasped.

For the record here is Lindstrom's own description of it, although even he cannot do justice to it.

"When the ball was hit I didn't think I would catch it," he said.

"I figured it would hit the wall, and I wanted to get as close to it as I could to play it on the rebound and maybe hold it to a double. But in the last stride or two I saw I could catch it by lunging at it, so I did. I hit my head pretty hard on the ground and the muscles on that side of my face and neck are still sore."

Lindstrom likes the idea of playing the outfield—has always liked the idea of playing out there some day. That's why it was no hardship for him to abandon third base, where he had established himself as second only to Pie Traynor, greatest of modern era of third basemen, to start all over again in right field.

"The biggest problem I had to contend with in the beginning was my throwing," he said. "At third base I used to do most of my throwing under hand or side arm, but moving to the outfield, I first had to accustom myself to the longer range and then develop an overhand throw to get distance.

"And of course I had to learn how to combat the lights and shadows of the different right fields around the league. The one I'm still wrestling with is the one in St. Louis. When we got there Ott told me I'd have more trouble there than anywhere else, and since he was speaking from experience he knew. The grand stand there is cut out at the back and this produces a set of lights and shadows that are very confusing. Sometimes it actually is impossible to see the ball as it is pitched, and this naturally imposes a terrific handicap on the right fielder, because he doesn't see the ball when it is hit, but suddenly sees it coming at him out of the air...."

The next day, on June 21, Lindstrom proved his catch on Gus Suhr was no fluke. He again robbed Suhr with a catch the *New York Times'* John Drebinger called "another startling catch" when Lindstrom "leaped high in the air" just as the ball "was about to crash into the right field wall."

Frank O'Neill of the *New York Evening Journal* commented on the second catch Lindstrom made on Suhr.

One way or another Lindy picked on Suhr during the series. He made a slashing catch on Gussie's belt that was turning in toward the wall yesterday. Lindy had to leap and climb the concrete out there but he did the climbing and held fast to the leather. A nifty bit of outfielding.

October 7, 1934—Jo Jo White

There has been a long line of outstanding catches in World Series competition. The Detroit Tigers' Jo-Jo White's catch in the 1934 Series against the St. Louis Cardinals was one of those outstanding catches.

The *New York Times'* John Drebinger, making his comparison with other World Series catches, at least with those he had seen by this time in his career, felt White's catch was not surpassed by any other. Drebinger told about White's effort on the long drive by the Cardinals' Pepper Martin to deep left center field.

But simultaneously with that ball moved Jo-Jo White. He moved over the ground like a man with all the demons in creation at his heels and just as it looked as though ball and runner would end their mad chase in a grand crash against the bleacher wall Jo-Jo caught the ball.

The *Detroit Free Press's* Charles P. Ward mentioned White's catch three different times. The most detailed description follows:

Martin came up then. With the count two strikes and one ball, he drove a terrific liner to deep left center. It looked like the ball game. But Mr. White, who plays center field for Detroit, is fast. Besides, he wants to win this Series. So he set out after that ball. Feet flying like those of a greyhound, he raced back. He must have run 100 yards. The wall in center worries Jo Jo. It is the wall Earl Combs ran into, almost knocking his brains out. But Jo Jo kept pounding toward it. A step or two away, he raised his hands gracefully and pulled down the drive. The stands groaned and then cheered. It was the best catch of the Series.

One of the writers covering the World Series for the *Detroit News* was Billy Evans, the former umpire and manager. Evans called White's catch better than Harry Hooper's in the 1912 World Series and better than Babe Ruth's Series-ending play in the 1928 World Series.

The *St. Louis Globe-Democrat*'s contributing writers included Grantland Rice, who commented on White's catch. Rice had just finished saying that the St. Louis fans had seen that Detroit's pitcher, Tennessee-born Tommy Bridges, would be difficult to beat on that day.

> They proved this with a stirring tribute to Bridges when he came up to bat—the tribute sportsmen pay to a game, smart and gallant competitor who has done his stuff. Along the banks of Old Man River they know their baseball, and they held nothing back in slipping the Tennessee Shad everything he had coming for a big day in a tight spot.
>
> The great Dean fell in his second start. If you only knew all the story you could understand the heavy pall that hangs over the Southwest—crepe on the cottonwood trail—the cypress and the weeping willow that catch the soft autumn breezes of Oklahoma.
>
> Dean turned in a good day's job, but Bridges had the call—too much stuff for the Cardinal bats. So the Tigers return to Tigertown to face one of the greatest welcomes a ball club ever drew, needing one lone game to take over the main crown, with Schoolboy Rowe all set to deliver the fatal thrust—which still rests with the gods of chance.
>
> The great defensive feature of this fifth game was provided by Jo-Jo White of Red Oak, Ga., in the eighth inning. With Whitehead—running for Davis, a pinch hitter, who had singled—on first, Pepper Martin, the Wild Horse of the Osage, hammered a terrific wallop to deep left center. It looked to be good for three bases.
>
> The series apparently might have hung on that mighty blow, but the deer-footed White raced at least 50 yards against the fence for the greatest single catch of the series to save the day on a miracle performance. It was the most vital play of the big show up to date.

The *St. Louis Post-Dispatch* had Babe Ruth among its correspondents. Ruth called White's catch "a gem" and mentioned his worry that White was going to collide with the concrete wall as his teammate Earle Combs had in July of that year.

After telling about the pitching of the Cardinals' Dizzy Dean and the Tigers' Tommy Bridges, the *St. Louis Post-Dispatch*'s Herman Wecke called White's catch "one of the greatest catches in world series history."

June 6, 1936—Terry Moore

Terry Moore was widely regarded as the National League's best defensive centerfielder from the mid–1930s until the mid–1940s. In his instructional book for young players, *Covering the Outfield*, Moore mentions three catches he made which qualify as great catches. Other writers also wrote about them as extraordinary catches, which were made on Mel Ott, Morrie Arnovich in 1941, and Joe DiMaggio in the 1942 World Series.

The first was in St. Louis against the New York Giants on June 6, 1936. In his book, Moore wrote:

> ... there was the day ... when the Cardinals were playing the Giants and Mel Ott came to bat with the bases loaded. I was playing him as a right-field hitter, which he was on most occasions.
>
> However, this time Mel cracked a sizzling line drive into left center field. I started after it and discovered I had made a mistake of trying to take the ball on the fly. If it got past me, it meant extra bases; so I decided to try at least to knock it down, so that I could hold him to a single.
>
> I made one frantic leap for the ball. Luckily, it hit my bare hand and stuck there. I skidded across what seemed half the outfield on my elbow, but the ball stuck in my hand [8].

J. Roy Stockton of the *St. Louis Post-Dispatch* described the catch this way:

In the third Parmelee hit Smith with a pitched ball and Joe Moore, Whitehead and Leslie singled to score one run. Ott then hit a low liner to center and Terry Moore made a catch that ended all talk of all other catches that he ever made. Moore ran in for the ball and just as he was diving for it, it took a dip to the right, after the fashion of a sliced golf ball. But Terry saw the dip, stuck out his right hand as he skidded over the turf and caught the ball. Before he could scramble to his feet and throw, Joe Moore had scored the second run of the inning.

The *St. Louis Globe-Democrat*'s Martin J. Haley had Moore diving even lower on the catch: "Ott lined low to center, Terry Moore sliding on his face for a remarkable barehand catch."

John Drebinger of the *New York Times* wrote of Ott's drive and Moore's catch: "It looked like a base clearing wallop until Terry Moore swooped down on the ball for one of the most amazing catches seen on a ball field in years. Diving headlong for the sphere the young Card snared it with his bare hand."

Terry Moore's fielding greatly impressed Rud Rennie of the *New York Herald Tribune*. On June 5, Rennie wrote about two catches Moore made that day:

> Words are inadequate to describe the back-hand running catch Terry Moore made in the second inning. There were two men on bases and two out. Bartell pounded a line drive into left center field. Moore ran like a racehorse. The speeding ball was getting ahead of him when he reached out and caught it.

The Cardinals' Terry Moore was the premier centerfielder in the National League and some contended in all of major league baseball.

Terry Moore made another good running catch of one Mayo hit in the fifth. He got both hands on this one.

On each of the next two days Moore's catches on balls Mel Ott hit caused Rennie to write about the quality of Moore's fielding. On Moore's June 6 catch, Rennie wrote:

> Then Terry Moore, the Cardinal centerfielder, made a catch that veteran writers agreed was one of the greatest fielding plays they ever saw. Ott hit a low line drive. To make it tougher, the ball was curving as it descended. Moore, racing in, hurled himself head-foremost and was flat on his stomach when he reached out and caught the ball in his bare hand.

Despite Moore's catch, the Giants won both games in the doubleheader on June 6, 1936.

On June 8, Rennie wrote: "This Terry Moore is incredible. He was backed up against the center-field wall waiting for a long one Ott hit in the eighth. It takes speed to go that far that fast. He is the best defensive centerfielder either league has seen in a long time."

Rennie wrote about Moore's being the best in a long time less than two months into Joe DiMaggio's rookie season. DiMaggio soon would be compared to Tris Speaker as a fielder, while Terry Moore, despite his tremendous ability in the field, usually was not. Rennie's evaluation of Moore indicates that it had been years since a centerfielder in either league had fielded noticeably better than others.

In Terry Moore's clipping file at the Baseball Hall of Fame is part of a column, from an early spring 1935 paper, which includes brief sketches of St. Louis Cardinal players. Included in the sketch of rookie Terry Moore was: "Perhaps the fastest man in the major leagues."

After Terry Moore became the manager of the Philadelphia Phillies in 1954, the *New York Times'* Arthur Daley wrote a July 19 column about the Phillies' managerial situation and about Moore's fielding ability. Daley wrote about two of Moore's best catches, one being on the left-handed, pull-hitting Ott's ball in 1936, the one Moore caught with his bare hand. About the ball Ott hit, Daley wrote: "It was so low that Leo Durocher, the Cardinal shortstop, leaped vainly in the air, only to have the ball shoot over his outstretched glove. It was so obvious a hit that no centerfielder would have attempted to catch it."

Eight years after the June 6, 1936, catch was made, John Drebinger, in the *Best Sports Stories of 1945*, included Moore's catch of Ott's ball as one of the three catches he remembered after reporting on almost twenty years of years of catches. The May 4, 1927 catch by Jigger Statz, mentioned earlier, was one of the three. After telling of the Statz catch, Drebinger followed with: "Another was a low line drive off Mel Ott's bat in St. Louis that Terry Moore caught with his bare hand and at the end of a headlong plunge (52)." As noted earlier, Babe Herman's catch on Fred Lindstrom's drive in Pittsburgh was the third.

And what did Ott think of Moore's effort on him? In his book *Mel Ott: The Little Giant of Baseball*, Fred Stein quotes Ott about Moore's catch on the ball Ott hit.

> Terry Moore ... made the greatest outfield play I have ever saw back in 1936. He was playing right center where he should have been, and the ball was hit on a line over the shortstop's head. It was a sure triple if I ever saw one, but Moore comes tearing over. He throws himself at the ball, hits the ground, skids along for about five yards, and sticks out his bare hand, and catches the ball [74].

Years later, Rich Wescott interviewed Moore for an article that appeared in the May 1990 *Baseball Hobby News*. Moore told Wescott about his most memorable catch, the bare-hand catch of the Mel Ott hit. After Moore described the catch, Wescott quoted Moore's follow-up comment: "'Later,' Moore adds, 'I caught a lot of others in my bare hand. I have very big hands, and I would just reach out when I couldn't get the ball with my glove. In fact, I used to practice catching bare-handed.'"

October 2, 1936 — Joe DiMaggio

In his rookie year of 1936, Joe DiMaggio quickly had established himself as the best centerfielder in the American League. He made catches which veteran Yankee observers had not seen other Yankee centerfielders make. Among DiMaggio's Yankee predecessors in center field was Earle Combs, one of baseball's best outfielders in the late twenties and early thirties.

One of DiMaggio's best catches occurred in the 1936 World Series the Yankees played against the New York Giants. DiMaggio caught a long ball hit by Hank Leiber of the Giants in the second game of the Series. Michael F. Gaven of the *Newark Star-Eagle* wrote:

Afield Joe aided the southpaw [Lefty Gomez] more than any man in the Yankee cast. His catch at the clubhouse steps on Leiber to end the game was one of the best ever seen in any game, and there were two neat stabs of hard-hit balls off [Joe] Moore's bat and a couple of throws that turned fearful Giants back to third base.

Murray Robinson, the sports editor of the *Newark Star-Eagle*, began his October 3 column with:

Above all else, the final out of the second game of the 1936 World Series at the Polo Grounds will stand out in our memory for a long time. There was a crack from the bat of powerful Hank Leiber of the Giants and Joe DiMaggio, racing back to the foot of the stairs leading into the Yankees dressing-room, dragging the ball down within ten feet of the Grant monument, which is 473 feet from home. For that magnificent catch was a fitting exclamation point at the end of the story headed, "Frisco Boy Makes Good." He was the hero of the day, beyond any doubt.

When this photograph was taken, probably during his rookie season of 1936, Joe DiMaggio already was one of the best all-around players in the majors, and was an especially outstanding fielder (*N.Y. Daily News*).

James P. Dawson of the *New York Times* wrote:

Then, as a fitting climax, DiMaggio, twisting, turning and running like a deer, raced to the cinders beyond the bleacher line in distant center to make a marvelous catch of Leiber's fly with his back half turned to the plate.

Dawson's colleague at the *Times*, John Drebinger, like Murray Robinson of the *Star Eagle*, gave a good approximation of the distance Leiber hit the ball, and Leiber's reaction to DiMaggio's catch.

DiMaggio brought the uneven struggle to a dramatic close by making a spectacular catch of a towering shot directly in front of the Eddie Grant Memorial tablet in center field.

Hank Leiber had stroked that blow with an effort born of despair and wound up standing on second base in utter bewilderment, unable to comprehend why all the other players were rushing past him to the clubhouse.

Joe Williams of the *New York World-Telegram* gave more details in his column about the game. He singled out DiMaggio's catch on Leiber for praise.

The three hits the Yankee freshman got were incidental, but his fielding was sensational. I doubt if Tris Speaker in his most inspired mood ever played a finer defensive game. He made two catches that would have defied the most expert efforts of any G-man, one on a low liner from Joe Moore's bat in the sixth, and the other on a terrific smash by Hank Leiber in the ninth.

They were both difficult catches but of the two the one victimizing Leiber was the more thrilling. The ball was hit with such speed that it was almost over Mr. DiMaggio's head before he started to give chase. In center field at the Polo Grounds the bleachers, cut into two blocks, extend out on the field, leaving an open square in the middle. Leiber's drive was to the left center near the angle of the bleachers at that point.

To make the catch Mr. DiMaggio had to judge not only the flight of the ball but make up his mind whether the ball might carry him into the concrete angle. To do this he had to turn, take a quick look at the angle, turn again, get his eye back on the ball and make a catch that would have been phenomenal under the most ordinary circumstances. It was the greatest catch I ever saw in any series, and it was made by an instinctive ball-hawk who knew what he was doing every second.

Shortly after the 1936 World Series, on October 8, 1936, the *World-Telegram*'s Joe Williams again wrote about DiMaggio's catch on Leiber, and quoted Clark Griffith, whose major league career began in 1891 and ended in 1914. Griffith later became the owner of the Washington Senators, a position he held until his death at age 85 in 1955.

It will be a long time before a world series gathering sees a more thrilling catch than he made of Leiber's titanic drive out near the center-field bleachers at the Polo Grounds. Already baseball men accept the loose-limbed Italian as the best centerfielder in baseball, and he has been in the league only one year. "I think he's as good as Speaker ever was right now," said Clark Griffith, of the Washington club.

Griffith's comment about DiMaggio's being as good as Tris Speaker is a significant one. Twenty-two years earlier, in the July 1914 *Baseball Magazine* article about Tris Speaker, Clark Griffith had said: "Tris Speaker is the best outfielder I ever saw. He has a style all his own. No other outfielder is in his class."

Not only did DiMaggio impress Griffith, he also impressed the Giants' Bill Terry, then in his last year in the dual role of first baseman and manager. Terry began his career with the Giants in 1923 and hit .341 over his career. In his "Daniel's Dope" column in the *World-Telegram*, Dan Daniel quoted Terry as saying, "That DiMaggio is the greatest ball player on the Yankees!"

Daniel continued:

Of course, there is one Lou Gehrig to be considered over a season of play. But, judging the Yankees entirely on their two days of play against the Giants, Terry is quite correct.

DiMaggio not only got two singles and a double, he not only delivered a grand bunt in the first and a corker in the third, but he gave one of the most amazing outfield performances yet seen in a world series.

Joe really put on the heat in three clutches—on Joe Moore's line drive in the sixth, Jo-jo's liner in the ninth, and Hank Leiber's fly ball to the clubhouse stairs for the last out of the game.

The catch which DiMaggio made on Leiber was the longest in the history of the World Series. Joe said it was the best of his young life. You may have noticed that after DiMaggio had grabbed Hank's bid for a homer, he remained standing in the outfield. He had heard the announcer ask everybody to remain until President Roosevelt had left. Orders were orders. So Joe remained.

In saying that DiMaggio's catch on Leiber was the longest in Series history, Daniel may have forgotten the ball Babe Ruth hit in the 1922 Series that Bill Cunningham caught, and the ball Ruth hit in 1923, the one Casey Stengel caught. Ruth hit both balls close to the fence in dead center field, or about 483 feet from home plate. DiMaggio was not quite as far out, but he probably was nearly 475 feet away.

Over at the *New York Post*, Stanley Frank added more information about what DiMaggio did in catching the ball:

> DiMaggio was tearing back toward the center field bleachers, kept on coming until it seemed he must wind up in the clubhouse. He veered away from the wall, dug his spikes into the cinders of the runway leading to the exit, and turned instinctively at the last split second to clutch Hank Lieber's line drive, the longest and hardest hit ball of the series.

Frank went on to describe the Giants' reaction to what DiMaggio had just done in ending the 18–4 victory by the Yankees.

> The group reaction was typical of men released from a shocking experience. Some were grinning bravely, although they looked a little foolishly, as they went about their business briskly. Others were frightened and dazed. The facial expression of a few individuals indicated that they were trying—and failing—to make logic discredit that which their eyes had seen.

Frank also quoted Bill Terry, who said DiMaggio was the Yankees' best player and "the best rookie I've ever seen."

Will Wedge of the *New York Sun* noted how DiMaggio ran: "But DiMaggio did make it, with easy, long legged grace, going far, far back, almost to the edge of the steps leading to the visiting players clubhouse."

Later in his article Wedge gave more of Terry's comments: "'They beat our brains out, but we had bad pitching,' said Bill. 'Those Yanks are the toughest club I've seen in a long time, and that DiMaggio is a wonder. He's the best ball player they got. He can hit anything, fast, slow, curves. He's the kid for my money.'"

Writing in *DiMaggio: An Illustrated Life*, Glenn Stout, after describing the catch on Leiber's ball, pointed out that DiMaggio had to run about forty feet farther than Mays ran to make his famous catch on the ball Vic Wertz hit in the 1954 World Series, and that Mays' catch, thanks in large part to the photo of Mays making the over-the-shoulder grab, is renowned while DiMaggio's catch on Leiber, not having been photographed, is almost unknown.

On October 8, 1936, the *New York Sun*'s James M. Kahn tried to explain what made DiMaggio such a success in the Series and how it was that people in the National League appreciated his play. One of Kahn's sources was Joe Devine, a west coast scout for the Yankees. Devine knew DiMaggio well from watching him when he was with the San Francisco Seals. During the 1936 World Series, National League people were interested in learning more about DiMaggio from Devine. Kahn wrote:

> One of the things Devine pointed out to his National League inquirers was to watch DiMaggio's speed. It is deceptive, but he has it, and it comes from his long stride. Devine revealed for the first time during the series that he had taken DiMaggio down to the University of Southern California for a few test runs after his injured heel healed. They measured Joe's stride and found it to be seven and half feet when he is in full flight. It is a coincidence that this is the exact stride of Jesse Owens.

Fourteen years later, in the April 19, 1950, *New York Times*, John Drebinger wrote about DiMaggio's speed.

> It is almost uncanny the way DiMaggio, J., runs the bases. His sharp drive to the center-field wall in the second was an accepted two-bagger in anybody's book, yet so accurately did the Clipper calculate the time it would take brother Dom to retrieve the ball that he never slackened his pace for an instant as he rounded second, and kept right on going until he slid safely into third.

Dom DiMaggio was one of the quickest men in the majors, knew how to play caroms off Fenway Park's centerfield wall better than anyone at the time, and had one of the strongest throwing arms in the majors.

In this game Joe DiMaggio also had a double and stopped a Boston scoring opportunity by making what John Drebinger called "an electrifying glove-hand catch" of a ball Matt Batts drove deep into right center field. The Yankees won the game 15–10. These examples of the thirty-five-year-old DiMaggio's speed and know-how early in the 1950 season occurred only three days after he made one of the greatest catches of his career, one that rivaled his 1936 catch on Leiber and the catch he made in 1939.

August 2, 1939—Joe DiMaggio

As good as DiMaggio's catch of Hank Leiber's ball was, it was his catch of a ball Hank Greenberg hit in 1939 which people have recalled as his greatest catch

In a game the Tigers essentially had won, Arthur E. Patterson of the *New York Herald Tribune* called DiMaggio's catch in the ninth inning "truly worth the price of admission." He wrote: "At the crack of the bat DiMaggio turned and sped away from the plate. A few feet in front of a sign which reads "461 Ft." he stuck out his glove and the ball came down over his left shoulder and fell into the webbing. (Tris Speaker, please note.)"

Jack Smith of the *New York Daily News* gave more details.

Although Joe's twelve game hitting streak was stopped dead, he made one of the gol' darndest catches seen in the 100-year history of baseball.

It was in the ninth inning and Mrs. Greenberg's little boy Henry really connected with one. Traveling at least 450 feet, it was one of the longest balls ever hit at the stadium. DiMaggio took one peep, turned his back to the infield, put his head down and sprinted. A few strides away from the flag pole, without turning, he flung his gloved hand high in a desperate gesture. He didn't even look for the ball. But it dropped and stuck right in his mitt!

The fans and the players on both benches went wild and continued cheering until the inning was over and DiMag trotted to the dug out.

Ancient Arlie Latham, press box custodian and ex-major leaguer who says, "I'm 81 and never been vaccinated," called the catch the greatest he's seen in seventy years of watching ball games. DiMaggio absolutely made it blind. From the time he turned and ran, he didn't see the ball until it nested in his glove. Averill, who was on first when Hank hit it, had almost reached third when DiMag made the catch.

The *New York Sun*'s Edward T. Murphy didn't agree with Jack Smith's statement that DiMaggio did not see the ball until it was in his glove.

The catch made by Joe was a four-star feature, if there ever was one, and from now on it wouldn't be a surprise if DiMaggio dashed up the Interborough station which overlooks the Yankee Stadium and caught a ball.

With one down and Earl Averill on first base, Greenberg teed off of one of Spurgeon Chandler's fast pitches. The ball, smacked solidly and with all of the power the 200-pound Hank could muster, zoomed high over the heads of the Yankee infielders. It was bound directly toward the center field bleachers. When bat and ball met, DiMaggio turned and ran swiftly for the far-flung center field barrier. He glanced over his shoulder to catch sight of the flying pellet.

No one in the park expected Joe to make the catch. The cash customers, of whom there were 12,341, and all of the ball players looked for the pellet to sail over Joe's head. But it didn't. As DiMaggio later explained, he was about ten feet in front of the fence and a little to the center field side of the Miller Huggins monument when he snared the ball, much to the astonishment of all, in his gloved hand. He caught it with his back to the diamond and just as it went over his right shoulder.

When DiMaggio made the marvelous catch he was approximately 450 feet from the home plate. The play robbed the astonished Greenberg of at least a triple. Hank never hit a ball harder, and no outfielder ever made a more sensational catch at his expense.

... "When I was running after the ball, I took my eyes off it three times to see how close I was getting to the fence," said DiMaggio. "It was the best catch I ever made."

In the *New York Daily Mirror*, Charles Segar told of the excitement the catch generated among the fans who saw it. After listing several things which were discouraging in the Yankees' 7 to 2 loss, Segar wrote:

Despite all these discouraging events, there wasn't a rabid Yankee rooter who did not leave the Stadium satisfied.

For in the first half of the ninth inning, Joe DiMaggio electrified the crowd with the greatest catch seen in the Bronx ball orchard in years and one of the most spectacular that anyone will ever see. Hank Greenberg was the victim.

Hank, hitless up to this point, caught hold of one of Cracker Chandler's serves and slammed it deep into centre field, just to the right of where the Huggins monument is located.

DiMaggio, playing over toward left, started in pursuit. It didn't seem he had a chance to get the ball, but just as everyone had given up hope, Joe, after running about 100 feet, shot his glove up into the air and speared the ball.

He was still on the run and was only a few feet from the wall when he grabbed the drive with his back toward the stands. That ball traveled 450 feet.

Louis Effrat was covering the Yankees for the *New York Times* on August 2, 1939, and had the following to say about DiMaggio's catch:

Despite the one-sidedness of the score it was an exciting struggle, with the greatest thrill coming in the ninth as DiMaggio and Greenberg collaborated on what probably was the greatest catch ever made in the Stadium.

With Earl Averill on first, Hank drove a tremendous fly to deepest center. Turning with the crack of the bat, DiMaggio raced to within two feet of the 461-foot mark on the wall and, without looking backward clutched the ball in his gloved hand just as it appeared about to hit the fence. Averill, nearing third, had to retrace his steps, and a double play was averted only because Frankie Crosetti's relay from DiMaggio hit Averill in the back.

The fans, forgetting about [Atley] Donald's setback, cheered DiMaggio for several minutes and the Yankees swarmed all over him when he returned to the dugout. It will be a long time before DiMaggio's catch will be forgotten, especially by Greenberg, who stood with his hands on his hips muttering, "Just what does a fellow have to do to get a hit in this league?"

Atley Donald was a rookie pitcher who had won his first twelve straight games.

Praise for Joe DiMaggio's catch was given in Detroit too. The uncredited writer for the *Detroit Free Press* wrote:

But while DiMaggio was stopped at bat, the Italian star who yesterday had 10 putouts, today contributed one of the greatest catches ever seen on a diamond when he pulled down Hank Greenberg's long drive in the ninth inning.

With one out and Earl Averill on first base, Greenberg, hitless up to this time, caught hold of one of Chandler's pitches and sent it like a cannon shot out to deep center. DiMaggio, playing over toward left, started in pursuit. He ran about 100 feet. Then, with his back toward the stands and although he was dangerously close to the wall, he shot up his gloved hand and pulled down the drive which had traveled about 450 feet from the plate.

Under the "Editorial Comment" section of the January 1940 issue of *Baseball Magazine*, Joe DiMaggio's catch of the Greenberg liner was discussed. The comment was:

Anyone who saw Joe DiMaggio's catch of Hank Greenberg's terrific drive at the Yankee Stadium on August second will fan about it ten, fifteen, twenty years from now if he is still alive. He may even assert without fear of contradiction that it was the greatest catch ever made.

Spectacular catches are fairly numerous on the major league ball fields. So much so that the players rarely pay attention to them. But when Joe nabbed that liner of Hank's the entire Detroit dugout rose to its feet, salaamed and doffed their caps in ironic salute.

Up in the press box sat Arlie Latham, who started playing ball back in '82 with Al Reach and hasn't missed a trick since. He gasped in astonishment and sputtered, "In all my looking at ballgames, I've never seen a catch the like of it."

Beside him was a veteran Associated Press man who had been watching major league baseball for more than fifty years. He said, "I'd pay the $1.10 admission fee any day of the year just to see the catch over again."

The ball was hit slightly to the right of the Miller Huggins Memorial where the mark on the fence registers 461 feet (from home plate) with DiMaggio playing a shallow field.

"I knew I hit the ball hard," sadly recalled Greenberg. "I saw at first that DiMaggio was playing short and thought the ball was a cinch to go over his head. Watching him as I went from first to second, I still didn't think he had a chance. It looked as if he was giving the old college try and intended merely to get as close as he could to the ball to take it off the fence on the rebound. I was within a few feet of second base when he caught it and was stunned with surprise."

Joe DiMaggio frankly admits it was the best catch he ever made. It was as difficult as it looked. Said Joe, "The unusual part of it was that the sun glasses I was wearing were a handicap. I took my eyes off the ball three times in its flight to watch that fence. I didn't want to crash. The fence is painted dark green and after looking at it through those glasses it was hard to turn and pick up the ball out of the light blue sky. I wasn't looking over my shoulder when I caught the ball 455 feet from the plate. I got a flash of it as it passed into the darkness of the glasses. I quickly stuck out my glove."

Arlie Latham actually began his major league career in 1880.

In an uncredited article in the August 3, 1939, *New York World-Telegram* titled "Joe's Catch Rated Tops In Stadium," Joe DiMaggio's catch was lauded this way:

> Joe made what was undoubtedly the greatest catch in the history of Yankee Stadium, a gloved-hand stab of a long drive by Hank Greenberg, which traveled 450 feet on a line with the flag pole in left center.... Joe caught the ball within four or five yards of the fence, after taking his eyes off the drive three times to be sure he wouldn't crack up against the parapet.... He was slowing up to avoid a collision when he stuck out his gloved hand, with his back to the plate and clutched the ball.
>
> Joe McCarthy stated afterward he never had seen a catch to equal it.... Nobody on the Yankees remembered a catch comparable with Joe's effort and Joe himself, grinning, said: "I couldn't make a better one, because this is the only park I could catch such a ball in."

In his 1992 book *Five O'Clock Lightning*, Tommy Henrich, the Yankee right fielder the day DiMaggio made the catch, recalled the catch against Greenberg. Henrich wrote that DiMaggio's catch on the ball Greenberg hit was the greatest catch he ever saw. He also went on to say:

> You can talk about Willie Mays and the catch he made off Vic Wertz in the 1954 World Series, or name any other you like, but the one Joe made off Hank Greenberg at Yankee Stadium in 1939 was the greatest anyone who was there ever saw, including home plate umpire, Bill McGowan [63].

A few weeks after Joe DiMaggio made his catch of Hank Greenberg's ball, *The Sporting News* quoted Bucky Harris, then the manager of the Washington Senators, about Joe DiMaggio. Harris said Joe DiMaggio was "the greatest ball player I ever saw." He went on to say, "I'm honest enough to admit I don't know how he does it. He just materializes out of thin air. I don't care where the ball is hit, he is in the line of flight." Bucky Harris began his major league career in 1919.

In his book 1994 book *All My Octobers*, written with Mickey Herskowitz, Mickey Mantle conveys the same sense of DiMaggio's appearing out of nowhere when he describes a play in the 1951 Series against the New York Giants that also contributed to the pain Mantle would play under for the rest of his career. He wrote that, because centerfielder DiMaggio had chronic pain in his Achilles tendon, Casey Stengel told Mantle to take any ball he could reach from his position in right field. In the third game the Yankees were leading 2–0 when the Giants came to bat:

> In the fifth inning, Willie Mays led off for the Giants and popped a fly ball into short right-center. I knew there was no way DiMaggio could get to it so I hauled ass. Just as I arrived, I heard Joe say, "I got it!" I looked over and he was *camped* under the ball. I put on the brakes and the spikes on my right shoe caught on the rubber cover of a sprinkler head. There was a sound like a tire blowing out and my right knee collapsed. I fell to the ground and stayed there, motionless. A bone was sticking out the side of my leg. DiMaggio leaned over me and said, "Don't move. They're bringing the stretcher."
>
> I guess that was about as close as Joe and I had come to a conversation. I don't know what impressed me more, the injury or the sight of an aging DiMaggio still able to make a difficult catch look easy [7].

Another example of Joe DiMaggio's making a difficult catch look easy occurred on July 6, 1941, during his 56-game hitting streak. He made a catch on the Philadelphia A's Bob Johnson in Yankee Stadium. The *New York Herald Tribune*'s Rud Rennie told about DiMaggio's effort: "DiMaggio made Johnson's long fly in the fifth inning of the first game look easy. He ran back almost to the center-field fence and caught it with one hand as it came over his shoulder, just as easy as if it were nothing." Elsewhere in the article Rennie called DiMaggio's catch on Johnson in the first game "spectacular."

In his book *They Too Wore Pinstripes*, Brent P. Kelley asked Duane Pillette, who pitched for the Yankees in 1949 and 1950, about Joe DiMaggio. Pillette called DiMaggio "the greatest player he ever saw." He went on to say, "He made everything look so easy." Duane Pillette added:

> I saw him do things in 1949 I've never seen any ballplayer do. Line drive over second base and he comes in and catches it off his shoetops and the next ball's hit 450 or 460 feet to center field and he turns around and waits for the ball. You wonder, "What the hell is this guy?!" [159].

When he couldn't make the catches look easy, writers for the *New York Times* used words like "eye-filling" (a catch on the Detroit Tigers' Pinky Higgins, 6-25-42), "electrifying" (a catch on Dave Philley of the Chicago White Sox, 6-20-47), and "miraculous" (a catch on Lou Boudreau of the Cleveland Indians, 5-13-48).

In the 1949 edition of his book *I'm Lucky to Be a Yankee*, Joe DiMaggio said his catch on Greenberg "was the best outfield play I ever made, before or since" (124).

EIGHT

1940–1949

July 23, 1941—Terry Moore

In Sportsman's Park in St. Louis the Cardinals were playing a tight game with the New York Giants. Terry Moore made a catch in the twelfth inning that enabled the Cards to hold the Giants scoreless. The Cards won the game with a run in the bottom half of the twelfth. The Giants had scoring opportunities in the tenth and eleventh innings, but good fielding by the Cardinal players prevented a run from scoring in either inning.

About Moore's catch in the twelfth, James P. Dawson of the *New York Times* said: "And to top it all, with Burgess Whitehead on second after a pass and a wild pitch by the left-handed Ernie White with two out in the twelfth, Terry Moore raced to the fence in left center to pull down pinch-hitter Morrie Arnovich's towering drive."

J. Roy Stockton of the *St. Louis Post-Dispatch* wrote of Moore's catch: "Terry Moore saved the game with a spectacular catch of Arnovich's fly near the wall in left-center. Terry slipped as he reached the ball, but held it as he slid against the concrete wall."

In the *New York World-Telegram*, Joe King mentioned a second catch that distinguished Terry Moore's game against the Giants on July 23.

> Terry Moore was at his sparkling best.... The Card star snared a terrific two-out blast by Moe Arnovich in the twelfth, with Burgess Whitehead on second, which he had to catch while on the dead run. Moore had plucked a tremendous drive by Mel Ott off the fence with a running, leaping play in the second.

Will Wedge, in the *New York Sun*, told how Moore's catch on the Arnovich ball allowed the pitcher Ernie White to get the victory after pitching just one inning.

> White owes thanks to Terry Moore for saving his hide defensively, and thanks to Creepy Crespi and Estel Crabtree, who delivered for him offensively.
> With two out and Burgess Whitehead on second base in the twelfth, as a result of a walk and a wild pitch, Moore ran to the brink of the left-center bleachers to make an unbelievable diving, sliding catch of Pinch Hitter Moe Arnovich's long liner, cutting off a sure Giant run.

Arthur E. Patterson, in the *New York Herald Tribune*, agreed that Moore's catch was "unbelievable."

> At the full count Morrie mauled one toward the left-field bleachers. A strong tail wind added to its flight, but Moore raced back and then in a half-sitting, half-crouching position, he caught the ball over his left shoulder within inches of the cement wall 380 feet from the plate.

Under the title "Moore's Sliding Catch Thrills Card Fans," an unidentified writer for the *New York Journal-American* noted how Terry Moore's catch was the highlight of the game from the night before.

Terry Moore's great exhibition of fielding is still the talk of the town today.... Moore saved yesterday's game for the Cardinals in the twelfth inning by racing to the wall and making a sliding catch of Arnovich's drive with the winning run on base.... Joe DiMaggio is the only other outfielder in baseball who could have made the catch.... And it was Moore's first day back in the lineup after injuring his shoulder in Boston.

This New York writer must have felt obligated to say that the Yankee's Joe DiMaggio could have made the catch Moore made on Arnovich's blast. DiMaggio might have played Arnovich closer to the wall than Moore was and thus would have already been at the wall to make the catch. However, since there is no great catch attributed to DiMaggio which had the inventive, diving, sliding qualities of Moore's catch, all things being equal, it is unlikely DiMaggio would have done what Moore did to make that great catch.

Martin J. Haley of the *St. Louis Globe-Democrat* called the catch "hair-raising."

In his column just after Terry Moore was named the Manager of the Philadelphia Phillies in 1954, Arthur Daley of the *New York Times* recounted Moore's catch on Arnovich. He credited Moore with inventing the catch so as to avoid running into the concrete wall and to be sure that he did not allow the winning runs to score. Daley pointed out that none of the then premier modern centerfielders, Willie Mays, Duke Snider or Mickey Mantle, had tried to do the kind of catch Moore made on Arnovich: "He slid into the wall like a man sliding feet first into second base. He cupped his hands at his waist and caught the ball as it whisked over his shoulder."

In his book *Covering the Outfield*, Terry Moore mentioned the Arnovich catch. Moore was discussing making the overhead catch and pointing out the need to be aware of where the outfield wall is while moving at top speed for a ball. He then wrote:

> I remember a game we were playing against the Giants in 1939. Morrie Arnovich came up in the eleventh inning with the winning run in scoring position and two men out. Morrie laid into one and knocked the ball all the way out to the wall. The year before I had crashed into that same wall and ended up in the hospital with a concussion of the brain which sidelined me for about six weeks.
>
> This time I knew exactly where the wall was and I kept an eye on it all the time as I hustled back to get Arnovich's long-hit ball. The ball carried so far I had no chance to turn back and catch it facing the infield. So I slid into the wall, hitting it with my feet, and caught the ball over my shoulder [52].

Moore had the wrong year for his catch on Arnovich. The catch was made in 1941.

When he wrote his book Terry Moore was aware of two outstanding outfielders who had their careers altered for the worse by full-force collisions with the concrete wall in St. Louis: Earle Combs in 1934 and Pete Reiser in 1942.

June 24, 1942 — Dom DiMaggio

By 1942 Dominic DiMaggio was widely known as a speedy defensive standout. Even before he had played a major league game, he was touted as a superior ball catcher and thrower. People who had seen him in the Pacific Coast League knew how good a player he was. Charles P. Ward included quotes about Dom DiMaggio in a January 14, 1940, column in the *Detroit Free Press*. Ward quoted Jo Jo White, who made the outstanding catch of the 1934 World Series for the Tigers, and who played against Dom DiMaggio in the Pacific Coast League in 1939.

"I think this DiMaggio is the greatest ball player I ever saw," White told Bing Miller, Tiger coach, the other day. "He can do everything, and do most things faster than his brother Joe.

"He can run like a deer. He can hit. He is not as big as Joe and consequently cannot hit the ball quite as far. But he can hit it through the infield fast enough to knock down the infielders. And he will hit an occasional ball out of the park. He has power.

"And throw—Mister, you ain't seen no thrower yet! Wait till you get a look at this guy. The American League thinks Joe DiMaggio's pretty hot, and he really is, for I've seen him make some dandy throws. But this kid is not only a stronger thrower but more accurate. Besides, he gets the ball away faster."

White remembered DiMaggio's throwing accuracy because of a painful incident last summer.

"I tried to take an extra base on a hit," he said, "and would have made it if any other outfielder had fielded the ball. But this kid threw me out by 10 feet. I called the umpire a liar just on general principles, but I never was more completely out in my life."

When Dom DiMaggio threw him out in 1939, White was only was 30 years old, in trim playing shape, and presumably still had good running speed.

In spring training 1940, John Drohan of the *Boston Traveler* wrote about the Boston Red Sox rookie Dom DiMaggio. Drohan's March 6 article featured quotes from the Boston Braves' pitcher Bill Posedel, who gave his and Lefty O'Doul's appraisals of Dom's chances to be successful in the major leagues. Lefty O'Doul was a two-time batting champion in National League, an astute judge of baseball talent, and had managed first Joe DiMaggio and then Dom DiMaggio on the San Francisco Seals of the Pacific Coast League.

"You needn't worry that the Red Sox made any mistake in letting Joe Vosmik go to make room for Dom," replied Bill. "I pitched against his brothers, Joe of the Yanks and Vince of the Reds and I think this kid has a better chance of becoming a better player than either. "For one thing he's faster," went on Bill....

... "While I was working out in Frisco I was talking to O'Doul about him.

... "Lefty, without any hesitation, told me this kid was the best of the three and he had the three of them from the time they decided not to become fishermen until they broke into the big time."

Lefty O'Doul went on to say Dom DiMaggio was a better hitter than his brother Joe. Although Dom was a good hitter, as his .298 lifetime average shows, Joe's lifetime average of .325 indicates he was the better hitter.

Dom DiMaggio was called the "Little Professor" because he looked scholarly in the glasses he wore during his playing career. In his 1966 book *Cowboy at the Mike*, long-time Red Sox broadcaster Curt Gowdy wrote that, other than Ted Williams, Dom was the greatest student of baseball he ever saw. DiMaggio watched opposing players during pre-game batting practice to see if their swinging was unusual, and especially was vigilant watching the swings of players he hadn't seen hit before.

In his book *Fenway*, Peter Golenbock quotes Tony Lupien about his former teammate Dom DiMaggio. Lupien said DiMaggio "was a great student of the game" (142). One example Lupien gave was that Dom DiMaggio practiced with the infielders so he made sure he would not make errors on ground balls coming to the outfield.

In 1946, Hugh Duffy, the outstanding outfielder for the Boston Beaneaters in the 1890s, praised Dom DiMaggio's play on ground balls to the outfield. First Duffy and then DiMaggio are quoted in Ed Rumill's article on DiMaggio in the September 1946 *Baseball Digest*.

"You can't show me an outfielder today who can go and get a ball better than Dom," remarked the man who hit .438 in the majors....

"I've seen them all, including Tris Speaker, and I'll tell you the Little Professor is right up there with the greatest," resumed Duffy. "In fact, I'll tell you something he does even better than Speaker. Charge a ground ball."

Rumill quotes DiMaggio's reason he charged ground balls so well.

"When I was playing sandlot and high school ball around San Francisco, I was an infielder," explains the young brother of Joe and Vince. "I used to stand at second base and watch runners race past me on their way to third, while our center fielder just stood there and waited for ground balls to come to him. Going from first to third on a single to the outfield was routine. We'd lose a lot of games that way, too. So I vowed that if I ever got the chance to play center field, I'd charge ground balls as they'd never been charged before."

On July 4, 1942, the Red Sox played a doubleheader against the Yankees with each team winning a game. The *Boston Herald* headline writer for the Red Sox-Yankees games wrote: "Williams' Slugging, Epic Catch By Dom DiMag Save Final." Burt Whitman wrote the article on the games. He had a lot to say about Dom DiMaggio's great catch.

Last play of the day was an epic. It was Dom at his brilliant best. There were two Yanks out in the ninth, two on base, one Yank already had crossed, and Pitcher Johnny Lindell, a slugging hurler, was fingered by Acting Manager Art Fletcher to pinch hit for Pitcher Murphy.

Lindell smashed one of the most wicked liners on record to straight center field. It was ticketed to carom off the dead centerfield bleacher wall on the fly. It was that lethal type of liner which seems to keep rising, so great its velocity that it seemingly laughs at the laws of gravity.

Dom naturally plays in closer than most center-fielders. However, he reads papers and knew that only the other day Lindell won a game for the Yanks with his hard hitting.

The Little Professor played Lindell somewhat deeper than usual, and well he did. At the crack of the bat, back-pedalled Dominic. Fan hearts forgot to beat. Back coasted the Professor, up he flung his gloved hand. The ball met the glove aloft, seemed to bubble up into the air and on toward the near concrete wall. But Dom kept his eye on that ball, didn't stop, caught it with both hands in the air before it had a chance to fall, and halted just inches shy of the sinister and dark barrier—as glorious a last play of a holiday doubleheader as you'll ever see, and one for your book of baseball memories.

It may be that Brother Joe, the Jolter, might have made this catch. We know of no other centerfielder around capable of making the clutch.

The first game had seen Jolting Joe catch 10 fly balls in centerfield, some of them very good, too.

The Little Professor made only one putout in the opener, but it was another catch of sheerest artistry. It was at the expense of Brother Joe. It came in the sixth, with two out and after a Tommy Henrich double. Joe lashed a ball to remote left center. Dom gave chase, never daunted by the wall, and with a leap, one-handed the ball up on the wall, not far from the flag pole, a mitt-hand catch which left the big coterie of N.Y. writers agog and the crowd wildly appreciative.

After seeing catches which Dom made in the west recently, and after singing his praises loudly and repeatedly, we admit these two at-home clutches of his gave us a tremendous belt.

The *Boston Sunday Globe*'s Gerry Moore singled out the catch on Lindell for praise.

Lindell showed his nomination was no mistake. He powdered a well-tagged drive that appeared headed for the centre field bleacher wall near the flagpole.

Dom turned his back to the plate and sped in pursuit of the soaring sphere. Just at the last instant, while going at full speed, the Little Professor took the ball over his shoulder, juggled it for what seemed hours on the tips of his gloved fingers while still running at full tilt, then finally nested the precious sphere back into the hole of his mitt.

The subtitle of the *Boston Sunday Post*'s coverage of the doubleheader was: "Great Catch by Dom DiMaggio in Ninth Saves Nightcap, 6–4—Champs Win First, 6–3." The *Post*'s writer for the games, Jack Malaney, called the catch on Lindell "miraculous." The *New York Herald Tribune*'s Rud Rennie called Dom DiMaggio's catch on the Lindell drive "wonderful" and "a thrilling finale." John Drebinger of the *New York Times* called DiMaggio's catch "glittering," and noted that Dom had bobbled the ball: "For one fleet second the ball almost got away from the youthful DiMaggio's glove." Later in his article, Drebinger commented on the fielding plays of the DiMaggio brothers in the Yankee–Red Sox games: "Baseball perhaps has never seen such an unbroken performance of flawless center fielding as the two DiMaggios put on whenever the Yanks and the Sox clash."

The play of the DiMaggios in the Boston–New York games was mentioned again in 1946. After a May 11, 1946, Yankees 2–0 win over the Red Sox, Louis Effrat of the *New York Times* commented on the

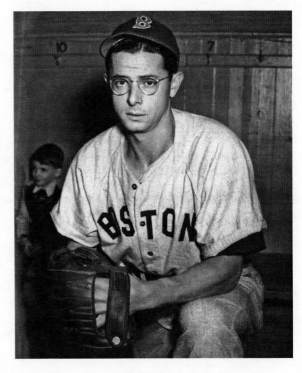

The Boston Red Sox' Dominic DiMaggio was a superlative player whose skills and abilities as a fielder rivaled those of any centerfielder.

two DiMaggio brothers' work against each other: "The two DiMaggios have been robbing each other of hits ever since they have been playing against each other. Yesterday was no exception, Joe taking one away from brother Dom in the seventh."

Before July 4, 1942, Dom DiMaggio already had made a number of great catches. On May 30 he made two extraordinary grabs in a doubleheader in Philadelphia against the A's. He also had seven hits in the twin bill. The *Boston Sunday Globe*'s Melville Webb commented on both catches: "Dom also brought the crowd to its feet with two magnificent running catches—one of a low 'sinking liner' from Larry Davis and the other a one-hand leaping clutch of a 415-foot drive by Elmer Valo right to the middle field wall."

The *Boston Herald*'s Arthur Sampson told more of DiMaggio's exploits that day.

It wasn't Dom DiMaggio's fault that the Sox lost the second game. The little professor gave one of the best exhibitions of his colorful career. He drove out three singles and a double in five trips to the plate and it took a larcenous play by shortstop Jack Wallaesa to stop him from going five for five.

In addition, DiMag kept Terry from being shelled from the mound early in the game by making two of the most sensational fielding plays ever made in historic Shibe Park.

He robbed Davis of a double by racing far into left center and stabbing the drive with his back hand at his shoe tops while traveling at top speed. This phenomenal bit saved a run in the second, and Dom robbed the A's of another in the third when he went back a country mile for Valo's long poke and took it with his back hand, more than 400 feet from the plate.

Dom lost his balance just as he made this miraculous catch and turned a double somersault out by the distant flag pole. But he held the ball. And the 17,166 partisan rooters rose to their feet and applauded for several minutes.

A visiting player has seldom been given a louder or more wholehearted applause than Dom received after these two thrilling catches.

Less than a month later, Dom DiMaggio, on June 24, 1942, took an unconventional journey to rob a hitter of extra bases to preserve a 1 to 0 three-hit victory in Detroit by Boston's Charley Wagner. After praising Wagner, Charles P. Ward of the *Detroit Free Press* told of Dom's catch.

After two men were out in the fourth Preston Rudolph York hit a long drive to left center. For a time it looked as if the ball would go into the stands to give York his fifteenth home run of the season. But just as it was about to cross the barrier, Dom DiMaggio backed up against the screen and made a leaping catch with his glove hand. And that was that.

In another section, Ward called DiMaggio's catch "one of the best catches made at Briggs Stadium this season."

One of Ward's uncredited colleagues at the *Detroit Press* felt more strongly about Dom DiMaggio's catch:

Best outfield catch of 1942 was made by Dominic DiMaggio in the fourth inning, when he pulled himself up the screen in left-center and caught Rudy York's 400-foot drive with his glove hand.... It looked like a certain home run for Rudolph until bespectacled Dominic crawled up screen and shoved his glove up.

Boston writers told more about what DiMaggio had done to make the catch. Jack Malaney of the *Boston Post* wrote:

Wagner's pitching and Ted's homer were the big features of the game, but Detroit's fandom as represented by the 13,193 who turned out will talk for some time of a catch they saw Dom DiMaggio make in the game.

It came in the fourth after Cramer had hit into the second double play. Rudy York crashed a mighty drive to centre field bordering on left. At first it seemed the ball would get into the stands for a homer, and then the wind or wind currents, which prevail in this park, held the ball back.

Dom DiMaggio never gave up on the ball, but he appeared stymied as the ball was destined to come down against the screening which rises about 15 feet in front of the stands out there. But Dom, with a last second desperate try, leaped and grabbed the railing which holds the screening and then stuck up his glove.

After describing the catch in terms similar to Jack Malaney's, the *Boston Globe*'s Melville Webb added: "It was one corking bit of work."

The *Boston Herald*'s Burt Whitman gave more description about how Dom DiMaggio made the catch.

Dom DiMaggio—and no game these days seems complete without something about the Little Professor—made one of his most brilliant catches in the fourth. Two were out when Rudy York blasted a ball to far left-centerfield. It looked as if it would clear the screen and go into the lower stands. But it was held up a bit by heavy, dark, damp atmosphere. Dom gave it the Old 'Frisco try, as Cronin calls it. He went aflying to the barrier, saw he'd have to jump, and jump high; so he grabbed the net in his bare hand, leaped and pulled with the hand, managed to go up four or five feet, then caught and held the ball securely. The crowd roared its acclaim for a catch the like of which few had ever seen. The Little Professor has made some miraculous grabs, but this was downright larcenous and you can't blame York for feeling frustrated.

Under the subtitle "SNATCHES THE BALL OUT OF THE GRANDSTAND," John Drohan of the *Boston Traveler* gave another expert's opinion of the catch.

Dom DiMaggio brought the crowd to its feet with one of the greatest catches ever seen on this historic park, where the Georgia Peach flourished for 21 years. It was off Rudy York, the big Injun slugger of the Tigers, in the fourth inning. The ball was headed for the bleachers at the 400-foot mark when Dom climbed up the wire fence and, while holding onto the fence, snatched the ball out of the stand with his gloved hand. They cheered Dom every time he came to the plate to bat thereafter. Harry Heilmann, who played alongside The Peach, declared it the best ever.

Hall of Famer Harry Heilmann and the Georgia Peach, Ty Cobb, were teammates on the Detroit Tigers from 1914 through 1926.

In a September 1946 *Baseball Digest*, Ed Rumill asked about Dom DiMaggio's greatest play.

> DiMaggio's greatest play? Was it the day he climbed the screen in front of the left-center stands at Briggs Stadium and made a glove-hand stab of Rudy York's bid for an extra base hit?
>
> "No," Dom replied when queried. "I'd have to pick the one I took off Crash Davis one time in Philadelphia. It was a line drive just over shortstop, in the hole between Ted (Williams) and myself. I couldn't see the ball very well as it came out. It became a blur along the edge of the stands. I honestly didn't think I could get it. But I ran over on the double, reached out backhand with my glove where I thought the ball ought to be and it stuck in just a few inches off the ground. And you should have heard Ted!"

October 3, 1942—Terry Moore

The third catch Terry Moore briefly discusses in his book *Covering the Outfield* is one he made in the third game of the 1942 World Series against the Yankees, which the Cards won. The Cards went on to win the Series that year.

Moore had an outstanding series in the field, making two catches on Joe DiMaggio which drew raves. One catch came in the fourth game at Yankee Stadium when DiMaggio hit a towering ball out to about 457 feet in center field. The other, in the third game, was a catch on a ball to deep left center, which was more in Stan Musial's territory in left field than Moore's territory in center.

John Drebinger of the *New York Times* called Moore's catch of October 3, 1942, on Joe DiMaggio's long clout "sensational," and recalled DiMaggio's fielding against the Cardinals earlier in the Series: "In St. Louis the other day DiMaggio had given the Mound City fans a rare exhibition of his flawless defensive play. This time Joe was to be the victim while right in New York the National League's foremost ball hawk was to put his own brilliance on display."

In the *New York Herald Tribune*, Rud Rennie wrote about Moore's near collision with Stan Musial: "Moore, racing from center field regardless of Musial hustling from the opposite direction, caught the ball. Just as he did so Musial swerved out of the way and went tumbling head over heels to avoid a collision."

J. Roy Stockton of the *St. Louis Post-Dispatch* praised the New York fans for their reaction to Moore's catch.

> ... with two out in the sixth Cullenbine singled to center and DiMaggio hit an old fashion country wallop to left center. It looked like a triple, sure, with empty terrain extending far out to the wall, more than 450 feet from home plate. But Terry Moore was off with the bat's crack. Racing at full speed, he made a final desperate lunge, reached out his glove hand and made the catch.

The stands roared with applause. This is a New York crowd, but it is a baseball crowd too, if you get out of the radio booths, and this was baseball worth while.

The *St. Louis Globe-Democrat*'s Martin J. Haley told of the New York fans' reaction to Moore's catch on their hero DiMaggio.

Terry Moore sprinted far into left center to snatch DiMaggio's long drive out of the censored air just as Musial, going at top speed in the other direction, dropped to the turf. That play cost DiMaggio at least a triple and the Yanks a run. The fans kept applauding the catch for many seconds.

And later in the article:

After Moore made his sensational stab of DiMaggio's drive to left center, Joe kept staring at Terry as the Cardinal captain raced in and the Yankee outfielder started out to his position. Joe apparently couldn't believe that anyone could have snared that ball, perhaps even DiMaggio.

After the next day's fourth game, which the Cardinals won 9–6, the *Globe-Democrat*'s Robert J. Burnes also took up the comparison between DiMaggio and Moore.

Before this series started most New Yorkers refused to put Terry Moore in the same fielding class as Joe DiMaggio, but now these same critics are undecided whether to put Terry ahead or just bring him up on even terms. To add insult to injury, his two greatest catches have come on long wallops by DiMaggio.

Writing in the *Globe-Democrat* on October 5, John Lardner had already praised Terry Moore's long run to catch a DiMaggio drive in the fourth inning of the game on the day before. He went on to recap what Moore had done.

Reviewing the series to date. Terrence has been in it right along. It was he who wrecked Rufus Ruffing's no-hit game last Wednesday. He aided the cause of John Beazley Thursday with a bunt that set up the second and last run of the day, and he made another circus catch that had a sidelight to it—the ball, a deep drive to left and legitimately Stan Musial's, was caught in a lateral sprint by Moore because he saw Musial had lost it in the sun. All told, this Moore is quite a specimen.

In *Covering the Outfield*, Terry Moore described what happened on the play.

In the 1942 World Series, we were playing in Yankee Stadium. It was the eighth inning of the third game and the tying run was on second, with two men out. Joe DiMaggio blasted a line drive to left center.
Stan Musial, our left fielder, lost the ball in the sun. I was practically sure I couldn't get to the ball from center field, but I headed for it anyhow. At the last second, I made a dive for the ball in an effort to catch it.
My arm extended as far as possible, and I barely caught the ball. I went tumbling and rolling all the way to the left-field foul line, but I was able to hold the ball for the third out in the inning [8].

J. Ed Wray titled his "Wray's Column" in the October 5, 1942, *St. Louis Post-Dispatch* "He's in a Class All by Himself." The first entry in the column of various bits of information about the series was about Moore's ranking as a fielder.

Every day in every way, you get the idea that Terry Moore is not merely the No. 1 player in the world series, but one of the all-time great fielders of history.... There is no better fly catcher today than Moore—a Terrible Terry, to long ball hitters. Defensively, he rates with Tris Speaker, No. 1 center fielder of all time.
And this is not to disparage the great play of DiMaggio, Keller and Slaughter.... These fielders all have earned the glad hand during this hectic series.

Twenty-seven years later, Bob Broeg, the long-time *St. Louis Post-Dispatch* writer, wrote an article in *The Sporting News* (April 12, 1969) comparing the speed of the then Cardinal outfielders Lou Brock, Curt Flood, and Vada Pinson with the speed of outfield trios of the past. One of the past threesomes was the early 1940s group of Stan Musial, Moore and Enos Slaughter. In that comparison, Broeg quoted Casey Stengel about Moore.

"That Moore," he said, "was the most amazin' I ever saw at divin' for a ball in the outfield. Now, most outfielders, they look like that Annette Kellerman, the swimmer, the way they dive straight down, but Moore could lunge far out, make the catch and not kick the ball away from himself. And when had to, he could reach out with that big bare hand."

April 16, 1946—Bob Lemon

Bob Lemon began as a third baseman, shifted to the outfield, then shifted to pitcher. After spending the rest of his career on the mound, he ended up in the Hall of Fame. As an outfielder, he possessed outstanding running speed and a powerful right arm. On opening day of 1946, he made a catch that his teammate Bob Feller, in his book (with Bill Gilbert) *Now Pitching: Bob Feller*, said "ranks up there with some of the greatest I've seen" (199).

The catch Feller wrote of occurred in a game Feller pitched and won, 1–0, against the Chicago White Sox in Chicago. In a story which began on the front page of the April 17, 1946, *Cleveland Plain Dealer*, Alex Zirin praised Feller's superlative effort. In the midst of the praise for Feller, he noted Lemon's catch.

Right now, however, it must be told of the thrilling climax on one of the outfield drives. Bob Lemon, using all of his vaunted speed, made a diving, glove-hand catch of Pinch Hitter Murrell Jones' short looper, then threw to Lou Boudreau, doubling Bob Kennedy, another sub batter, who had drawn the lone walk, ending the game.

In the *Cleveland Press*, Frank Gibbons put Lemon's catch into a prophetic perspective.

Bob Feller's pitching job against the Sox here yesterday was a work of art, but Bob Lemon's game-saving catch in the ninth inning was a masterpiece. Feller, no doubt, will pitch other games as good or better, but Lemon never will make another play like that.

Starting at the beginning, until a big guy named Murrell Jones awkwardly hit a curved ball off Feller in the ninth and popped a sickly fly into the wind in right center, it hadn't been a great day for Lemon. He had looked bad at the plate, nervously striking out twice and he handled his work in center in a somewhat uncertain way. Everybody said: "Well, it is his first major league opener and the position is still new and you have to forgive a man for that."

Lemon did lay down a perfect bunt in the sixth to advance George Case to second base, from where the ace Case scored the winning run on Hank Edwards' hot single to right. Among baseball people, a good bunt in the right place is as difficult as a home run.

Feller started the ninth by issuing his first walk in the game. After a really masterful exhibition it seemed that he was getting a trifle tired. Bob Kennedy batted for Pitcher Bill Dietrich and drew the walk and Kennedy sprinted to second on a careful bunt by Wally Moses. Jones, a big, right-handed hitter, came up swinging for Floyd Baker, the rookie third-sacker.

Feller fired a fast ball ... that Jones missed. Then he broke off a curve and Jones missed even more foolishly. The Indians said after the game that they thought another fast ball was in order, but Feller gave him the curve again. It was outside and Jones hit at it in desperation, apparently. Certainly not with any malice aforethought.

The ball looped toward right field, caught by the treacherous winds of Comiskey Park. It looked more like Edwards' ball than Lemon's, but Lemon decided to be around. Kennedy set sail for home with the tying run and Taft Wright ... started toward the plate as the next hitter.

But Lemon never stopped. The ball drifted and drifted toward right field and Lemon ran and ran. At the last possible moment he dived and stretched out his gloved hand. The ball landed squarely in the pocket of the glove, six inches above the turf and just before his arm struck the ground with jarring impact.

Had the ball hit his mitt a fraction of an inch in any direction it is doubtful that he could have held it. He had enough presence of mind left to go to his feet after the skid of four or five feet and throw to Lou Boudreau at second for the double play that ended the game.

... Lemon is our premier performer for opening day, 1946. The rookie who looked so bad on third base in spring training, looked like Tristram Speaker in center yesterday. He may not hit well enough to stay there, but for one glorious instant he was everything any ball player has been.

The *Cleveland News'* Ed McAuley lauded Lemon's effort, and gave another long-time baseball man's opinion on the catch.

Robert Granville Lemon, the rookie third baseman was signed to center field in one of the most surprising managerial moves of the spring, may or may not justify Boudreau's lofty appraisal of his prospects, but for one breath-taking instant yesterday, the 25 year-old ex-sailor from Long Beach, Cal. made 20,160 fans forget that Feller had fashioned a three-hit masterpiece and struck out 10 to start the season with a 1–0 victory.

"That," said Vice President Roger Peckinpaugh, "was as fine a catch as I've ever seen an outfielder make. Lemon not only had to run at top speed, then dive along on his stomach. He had to worry about the danger of a collision with Hank Edwards. That thought didn't slow him up for a fraction of a second. He simply took charge of the situation."

Peckinpaugh referred to the play which ended the game—Lemon's miracle catch of a wind-blown blooper from the bat of Pinch-hitter Murrell Jones with one out and the tying run on second base.

On second base, did I say? That tying run, represented by the fast-moving person of Bob Kennedy, was practically crossing the plate. There was no question in anyone's mind that Jones' Texas leaguer would fall safe in short right-center.

In anyone's mind, that is, except Lemon's. The young man from the Coast simply refused to quit. He had struck out twice in his first appearance of the year. He had been so anxious at the plate that he had started his swing almost before Bill Dietrich threw the ball. In three official times at bat, he hadn't come close to hitting safely, though he had laid down a neat bunt to move the only run of the game into scoring position.

But at the critical spot of the airtight battle, he showed the stuff of champions.

After making the incredible catch, Lemon had merely to find his feet and lob the ball to second base, where Boudreau was waiting to double Kennedy, who had no chance to retrace his steps. The Indians' big bullpen squad charged across the outfield to pummel the new outfielder with congratulations. It was the day of days for Robert Granville Lemon.

Roger Peckinpaugh began his major league career in 1910 and finished it in 1927. As a long-time American League shortstop, he had seen many of the greatest centerfielders of all time, including Tris Speaker, Johnny Mostil, and Earle Combs.

The Chicago papers had little to say about Lemon's catch other than giving it a mention as part of the game. However, the day after the game, John Carmichael of the *Chicago Daily News* did have a note about Lemon in his "The Barber Shop" column.

Manager Lou Boudreau of the Tribesmen is rather optimistic concerning the future of Bob Lemon, his rookie centerfielder. At spring training Bob was an infielder and stationed at third base pending the return of Ken Keltner from service. Gene Woodling was in the middle.

But Woodling's hitting fell off about the time Keltner arrived and Lemon was given a crack out yonder.

He's turned out to be a slick fielder with a throwing arm which can be mentioned in the same breath as Dom DiMaggio, Ron Northey and Andy Pafko. Now, if he'll only hit...!

If Lemon had been only an average hitter on a day-to-day basis, he may not have not made the leap to being a full-time pitcher, one of the best of his era, and a Hall of Famer. He became a good left-handed hitting pitcher who cracked 37 home runs in his career.

June 10, 1947—Willard Marshall

Before Willie Mays joined the Giants in 1951, the Giants had a number of fine fielding outfielders, especially Red Murray from 1909 until the mid-teens, Hall of Famer Ross Youngs in the late teens into the mid–1920s, and Bobby Thomson of the late 1940s and early 1950s.

Willard Marshall was another good outfielder for the Giants in the mid- to late 1940s. What may have been his best catch occurred on June 10, 1947, in a game at the Polo Grounds against the Pittsburgh Pirates, a game the Giants won 3–2 in twelve innings. Writers in Pittsburgh and in New York praised his catch on a ball that the Pirates' Frank Gustine hit. Vince Johnson of the *Pittsburgh Post-Gazette* wrote:

Willard Marshall saved the game for the Giants with a sensational catch of Frank Gustine's 400-foot smash to deep right-center with the bases full, two out and the score tied 2–2 in the eleventh.

Twisting frantically backward, Marshall flung out his gloved hand and snared the ball high over his head. He fell on his back, rolled over and came up with the ball. After that catch, which robbed Gustine of a triple, the Pirates seemed to lose heart and it was only a matter of time until the Giants would take matters into their hands and end the game.

The *Pittsburgh Press*'s Les Biederman gave Marshall a much longer run to get to the ball.

The toughest blow of all came in the 11th, when the Pirates loaded the bases on Thompson with two out. Gustine ran the count to three and two, then belted a drive, headed for the Giants' bullpen in deep right, 450 feet away.

Bill Marshall traveled back, and while on the dead run, grabbed the ball over his shoulder, then tumbled to the ground. But he held tight onto the ball, saving the game then and there.

Marshall's catch on Gustine's drive gave the *New York World-Telegram*'s Joe King a chance to praise Marshall as a fielder.

The great defensive strength the Giants have shown in close games again was the

In the late 1940s the New York Giants' Willard Marshall was long-ball threat at the plate and a very capable fielder.

lifesaver. The club has won all three extra-inning tests this season, and in each a gent named Willard Marshall was the No. 1 man. Marshall does his job so smoothly and competently that he seldom is in the spotlight as he was last night when he made his great running, jumping, tumbling catch of Gustine's 360-foot drive with three Bucs aboard with two down in the 11th. That was the ball game for sure....

In the 11-frame victory in Chicago Marshall's spectacular throw to home averted a Cub victory. In the 11-inning job on the Cards Will played a different role, with his three-run homer to win. A handy chap to have on the lot.

The *New York Times*' Louis Effrat went further in appraising the relative merit of Willard Marshall's catch: "Marshall, after a long run and a desperate leap, snared the ball, fell flat on his back and held it for the third out. This was one of the greatest defensive plays ever seen here."

August 17, 1947—Ted Williams

Like Babe Ruth, the name Ted Williams does not often go with great fielding. However, Ted Williams, like Ruth, was a highly skilled outfielder. He became expert at playing balls off the Green Monster in left field at Fenway Park, had a strong arm, and, as a young player, was a fast runner. With his long strides he could get to balls quickly. However, two other factors made his fielding seem less noteworthy. One was the fact that he played for many years next to Dom DiMaggio, a superlative centerfielder, who routinely made difficult catches look easy. The second factor was Dom's brother Joe, with whom Williams regularly was vying for the American League's most valuable player award. The graceful fielder Joe DiMaggio was a fan favorite and was widely regarded as the American League's premier outfielder. Williams was not a particularly graceful runner and did not get nearly the fan support which Joe DiMaggio was given.

For his 1995 book *In the Shadow of the Babe: Interviews with Baseball Players Who Played With or Against Babe Ruth*, Brent Kelley talked with Eldon Auker, who pitched in the major leagues from 1933 to 1942 with the Detroit Tigers, the Boston Red Sox, and the St. Louis Browns. Kelley asked Auker about who was the best pure hitter. Auker said Williams was the best hitter and mentioned Joe DiMaggio as a "great hitter," and then drifted into commenting on the fielding of DiMaggio and Williams.

Joe was a hell of a hitter and a great ballplayer—one of the greatest arms I ever saw. The thing about Ted Williams, also he really didn't get the credit for being an outfielder, but he was a hell of an outfielder. He was a guy a little bit like Charley Gehringer—he seemed to sense where to play. When the ball was hit to left field he wasn't too far to the left or too far over to center. It seemed like he was always near the ball. He studied those hitters as much as he did the pitchers and he had a great sense for being close to the right place most of the time.

On top of that, he took long strides and he got a break on the ball and he was always in the ballgame. He didn't have his head up in the stands looking around [136].

Another former standout Red Sox pitcher, Mel Parnell, echoed Eldon Auker's view of Williams as a talented fielder. In *The Early All-Stars: Conversations with Standout Baseball players of the 1930s and 1940s*, author Brent Kelley asked Parnell about Williams as a hitter, and Parnell, like Auker, wound up talking about Williams as a fielder.

Who was the one best hitter you saw?
Ted Williams, without a doubt. Williams was the best by far, and DiMaggio was a better outfielder than Ted, but not that much. Ted was a very underrated outfielder. He was a big, gangly type of guy that didn't look good going after the ball, but he got there and got it.

He played that left field wall better than anybody I've ever seen, Yastremski included. Carl played it very well, but I think Williams played it even better. It seems like he knew where every rib in that fence was and knew what kind of bounce you'd get off that wall.

The guy was amazing. He was the most perfect self-made man I've ever seen. Everything encountered he did it to perfection [122].

In his 2001 book (with Tom Keegan) *Sleeper Cars and Flannel Uniforms*, Eldon Auker twice more talked about Williams in the field.

Ted didn't only know every pitcher in the league; he made damn sure he knew every hitter in the league too. I never saw a coach move him around in the outfield. He moved himself around. He knew the hitters as well as anybody, even when he was only a rookie. He knew where they were going to hit the ball. When I pitched he knew that Luke Appling would hit me a certain way, Lou Gehrig would hit me a certain way, Red Rolfe would hit me a certain way. He would come in or back up, move to left-center or toward the line. They didn't have to move Ted. He studied those hitters better than they did [137].

And later Auker tells of Williams' speed.

As time passes, baseball historians seem to want to label Ted as little more than a bat, a great bat at that, but not a versatile baseball player. He could run. Ted was fast. He took those long strides, like DiMaggio did. They were deceptively fast. DiMaggio could run like a damn deer. Ted wasn't as fast as DiMaggio, but he was fast. You saw some of those outfielders, they could run all day in a half-gallon bucket, they had such short strides. Ted turned a lot of base hits into fly-outs with those long strides that covered so much ground in such a short time [143].

The New York Yankees hosted the Red Sox on August 17, 1947, and lost an exciting game 3–0 in eleven innings. The game featured terrific fielding plays by both DiMaggio brothers, Joe and Dom, by Yankees third baseman Billy Johnson, and by Ted Williams. Williams' catch on a ball hit by Joe DiMaggio was the most outstanding. The *New York Times'* James P. Dawson wrote: "Williams robbed Joe DiMaggio of a triple with a hair-rising, one-handed catch over his shoulder on the run in the fourth, going almost to the bleacher screen."

Joe Trimble of the *New York Daily News* was more emphatic in his praise of Williams' catch.

Williams made the best catch seen at the Stadium this year when he took a triple away from DiMaggio in the fourth. Joe lined toward the 415-foot mark on the wall of the left field bleachers and Ted went within two steps of the barrier for a thrilling one-hand grab with his back to the plate. Yankee fans applauded wildly. Ted should remember that. He complains too much about how he is booed here. He didn't doff his cap in appreciation.

Ted Williams' complaints about how the New York fans usually booed him was in sharp contrast with the legions of fans who adored Joe DiMaggio. Before the August 17 game, a group of people from Hartford, Connecticut, presented DiMaggio with a new maroon Cadillac. After commenting on the Hartford fans' gift to their hero, the *Daily News'* Trimble, evidently unmoved by the lengths taken by those fans to get close to DiMaggio, added: "He already has one [i.e., a car]—a 1941 job."

The *Boston Globe's* Roger Birtwell was even less impressed by the Hartford fans' gift to Joe DiMaggio.

And before the game some Hartford, Conn., baseball fans—the extent of whose paychecks we do not know—presented a sleek and expensive convertible sedan to Joe DiMaggio, who earns $47,500 per Summer.... Next thing you know, the straphangers in the subway will get together and present a limousine to the president of General Motors.

Birtwell was one of two *Globe* reporters to write about Williams' catch. In so doing, Birtwell praised the DiMaggio brothers and Williams.

[Vic] Raschi had faced only 29 batters in nine innings when—with one down in the tenth—Williams doubled to center. Bobby Doerr banged a harsh ground single to center to provide what looked like the tie-breaking run. But Joe DiMaggio, charging the ball like an infielder, grabbed it and cut loose a dazzling throw to the plate that cut down Williams and prevented a Boston run.

It was in the eighth that the Yanks had their chance. With one down, Lindell doubled down the left field line. With two down, Stirnweiss hit a fly to short left center that seemed like a certain hit. Williams and Dom DiMaggio both raced toward the ball, then DiMaggio, flying at top speed, reached low and captured the ball off his toe-tops. Even Yankee fans arose and applauded as he came to the Boston dugout.

Williams, making perhaps the best catch of his entire career, raced deep and to his own left to make a one-handed stab off Joe DiMaggio's bid for a triple in the fourth. Williams caught it 405 feet from the plate.... Prior to his 10-inning double, Williams was robbed of hits three times by the Yankee shift.

The *Boston Herald*'s Ed Cunningham gave highest marks to both catches.

The fans were treated to two of the most amazing catches ever seen in this historic park by Dom DiMaggio and Williams. Dom prevented at least one Yankee run scoring in the eighth by an off-balance gloved-hand catch of Stirnweiss' looping drive for the third out, with Lindell, who was on second, and Robinson, on first, tearing around the bases. The ball drifted half way between Ted and Dom. Ted saw he couldn't reach it and pulled up, but Dom kept racing across country and just barely nabbed the ball only inches from the ground.

Williams showed the customers that he is every bit as a good a fielder as he is a batter by robbing Thumping Joe of a triple in the fourth. When Ted started after the ball, it didn't seem that he would even come close to it. Joe had given that authoritative ring to the drive which was directly over Ted's head.

Ted had to back-pedal straight for the Sox bullpen, and his long reach just intercepted the ball when apparently it had gone over his head. He pulled up right in front of the bullpen with the ball securely in his glove. The sign there reads 415 feet from home plate.

Despite having a cracked rib, Ted Williams made an outstanding catch in the 1949 All Star game in Brooklyn. In his July 13, 1949, column, the *New York Times'* Arthur Daley wrote about the rib and the catch: "Wonder of wonders, though, he bobbed up with the fielding gem, a stabbing backhand spear of Don Newcombe's liner off the wall with the bases full and none out in the second. It saved the Americans from utter disaster."

In his book *My Turn at Bat: The Story of My Life* (as told to John Underwood), Williams proudly recalled his All Star game catch on Don Newcombe and the comment someone made the next day about his being the best defensive left fielder in the American League.

October 5, 1947—Al Gionfriddo

In an exciting sixth game of the 1947 World Series between the New York Yankees and the Brooklyn Dodgers, left fielder Al Gionfriddo made a catch on the Yankees' Joe DiMaggio which has been rated with the greatest catches. The Dodgers had scored four runs in the top half of the sixth inning. John Drebinger of the *New York Times* continues the story after DiMaggio hit the ball.

Dashing almost blindly to the spot where he thought the ball would land and turning around at the last moment, the 25 year old gardener, who had been merely tossed as an "extra" into the deal that shipped Kirby Higbe to the Pirates earlier this year, leaned far over the bullpen railing and, with his gloved hand, collared the ball.

Al Gionfriddo has just made the catch on Joe DiMaggio's bid for a home run in the sixth game of the 1947 World Series.

It was a breathtaking catch for the third out of the inning. It stunned the proud Bombers and jarred even the usually imperturbable DiMaggio. Taking his position in center field with the start of the next inning, he was still walking inconsolably in circles, doubtless wondering whether he could believe his senses.

Immediately after he saw Gionfriddo make the catch, DiMaggio gave a little kick at the infield dirt to express his disappointment.

In the October 5, 1947, *Brooklyn Eagle*, Jack Cuddy quoted Gionfriddo about whether DiMaggio's drive would have cleared the four-foot fence separating the visitors' bullpen from the playing field, and thus been a home run had it cleared the fence and Gionfriddo's glove.

"I'm pretty sure it would have gone into the bullpen," Al said. "It seems to me I caught it about a foot and a half higher than the fence top. Then I banged into the fence sideways. No, I didn't get hurt."

The 5-foot-6 Italian, who wore a religious medal on a gold neck-chain, estimated that he ran more than 100 feet from short left-field back to the bullpen gate, where he whirled and grabbed the ball with his right hand. He throws left-handed.

"I wasn't sure I had the ball until it landed in my glove," he explained. "It was an awful close race—me and that ball. When DiMaggio smacked it I knew it was goin' for a long ride, and I whirled and ran for the fence as fast as I could. Runnin' that way, it was hard for me to follow the ball because it was up in the sun and then it came down through the shadows. You got to be lucky to make a catch like that."

...

Several baseball writers who had covered the Dodgers during the season agreed that if Gionfriddo hadn't gone into left field in the sixth inning—following Miksis and Gene Hermanski into that garden—the catch never would have been made and the game would have been lost. Gionfriddo was much faster than either of his predecessors.

Ben Epstein of the *New York Daily Mirror* also quoted Gionfriddo, whose comments were similar to those of Jack Cuddy. He also quoted Joe DiMaggio and the Dodgers' manager, Burt Shotton. First DiMaggio:

Later, DiMag one of the most disappointed of 'em all confessed: "I figured it was going into the bullpen. I guess I hit a few harder in my career but, right now, I can't remember when."

Then Shotton in the dressing room:

When someone hollered at Burt and pointed at Gionfriddo—"There's the hero!"—Mr. Shotton really ranted a stream of hyperbole:

"Was it the greatest catch I ever saw? It had to be. They just can't make any better ones. What do you birds expect? After all, all Al did was to run 900 miles and catch the ball with one finger!"

Dan Parker, also of the *New York Daily Mirror*, put the crowd in the action.

With two Yankees on base, two out in the sixth and Brooklyn leading, 8–5, Joe DiMaggio lashed out viciously at one of Joe Hatten's pitches and Yankee fans leaped to their feet shouting deliriously as they followed the flight of the ball toward the Dodger bullpen in left. Taking off with the crack of the bat, Gionfriddo was after it like the wind but it looked like a fool's errand to everyone in that tense crowd. The ball seemed headed for a souvenir hunter in the bleachers, or a Brooklyn pitcher in the bullpen, when Gionfriddo, backed up against the fence at the 415-foot mark, stuck his glove into the air and clutched it.

The biggest crowd that ever saw a World's Series game was left so speechless over the amazing catch that it was several moments before a hysterical non-partisan roar rent the tense atmosphere of the Stadium in spontaneous acknowledgement of one of the great catches of all time in World Series play.

After calling Gionfriddo's catch "one of the most unbelievable catches of all time" in his October 6, 1947, *New York Times* column, Arthur Daley gave an idea of how hopeless the chase for DiMaggio's blast was.

But while the ball soared through the air with the greatest of ease, a tiny figure was seen scooting over the Stadium turf in a pursuit that seemed as fruitless as a greyhound chasing a mechanical rabbit. But up reached a strong little arm above the bullpen fence and Gionfriddo had his rabbit.

Though DiMaggio later called Gionfriddo's catch a great one and more difficult than Willie Mays' catch on Vic Wertz in the 1954 World Series, he also had other thoughts about it. DiMaggio felt that because Gionfriddo was not positioned correctly, he had to make a frantic dash rather than being able to make an easier, less hurried grab. (David Halberstam wrote of this in his book *Summer of '49.*)

DiMaggio was one of the most expert practitioners of knowing precisely what he had to do and when he had to do it to be at the spot where he had could most economically catch a ball. In his book *Covering the Bases*, Bill Starr wrote about nuances in baseball that may be difficult for some fans to discern.

> For example, fans may be impressed with what appears to be a great catch by an outfielder. Yet the professional may see in that particular play an outfielder who was out of position in the first place or who got a slow jump on the ball, making a difficult catch out of what should have been a routine play. Joe DiMaggio spent his entire career making routine catches of fly balls that many other outfielders wouldn't have reached. That may be one reason why Bucky Harris stated that Joe DiMaggio was the greatest player he ever saw [104].

The day after Gionfriddo's catch on DiMaggio, Joe Williams, in his *New York World-Telegram* column, called the catch "the most remarkable catch I ever saw, world series or no." In his next paragraph, Williams couldn't praise DiMaggio enough, but knocked DiMaggio's teammates.

> A few words about DiMaggio. These other fellows who pose as Yankees ought to bow deep as they can as they pass this man today. He is so much the best. The best in all baseball. The supreme artist. You'll never hear of him making a great catch for the simple reason that he doesn't know how to make a catch look great. Or even difficult. The ball is in close. DiMaggio is there to take it. It's hit nine miles away. Somehow DiMaggio is there to get it. So easy. So effortless. This is an okay series from the fans' point of view. Excitement, drama, fight, hustle, all that sort of thing and mostly on the part of the Brooklyns. But the big guy, the top guy, the pro guy ... that's the DiMag. I think even the Brooklyn addicts hated to see him robbed of that home run.

In the next section, Williams asked a ten-year-old who was at the game whether he hated to see DiMaggio robbed. The youngster, a Dodger fan, asked Williams: "Mr. DiMaggio has robbed plenty of people, too, hasn't he?" It is likely that no rabid Dodger fans would have agreed with Williams' idea that even they didn't want to see the great DiMaggio robbed by Al Gionfriddo.

Although today Al Gionfriddo's catch is among the best known of all World Series catches, it should be noted that two days before, on October 3, 1947, all three Yankee outfielders made stirring catches to keep Bill Bevens's bid for a no-hitter alive until the last out in the ninth inning. That was when Cookie Lavagetto doubled in the winning run to cap a thrilling 3–2 Dodgers victory. In the third inning, New York's Johnny Lindell dove for and caught Jackie Robinson's fly ball heading toward foul territory past the left field line. The *New York Herald Tribune*'s Al Laney described Joe DiMaggio's main fielding contribution to the game: "DiMaggio's catch of Jorgensen's tremendous drive at the base of the centerfield wall in the seventh was done with such expertness and nonchalance that its greatness was concealed. He took one look, ran, turned and was there when the ball came within reach." Earlier in the game, in the fourth inning, according to the *New York Daily Mirror*'s Dan Parker, DiMaggio "ran back with the speed and grace of Mercury to make a one hand leaping catch" of a ball off the bat of Gene Hermanski.

The most praised catch was one by Tommy Henrich in the eighth inning on a ball hit by Gene Hermanski. Ben Epstein and Dan Parker of the *New York Daily Mirror* both wrote that Henrich leaped at least four feet off the ground to catch the ball Hermanski hit hard to the scoreboard. In his column of October 4, the *New York Herald Tribune*'s Red Smith wrote: "Henrich backed against the board and leaped either four or fourteen feet into the air. He stayed aloft so long he looked like an empty uniform hanging in its locker."

In his column in the *New York World-Telegram*, Joe Williams told how Hermanski's ball was headed for extra bases. Williams continues his tale of the catch.

> But wait. Tommy Henrich has his eye on the ball out there. He is crouched, ready to leap but he will have to have springs in his heels if he is going to catch this ball. There he goes. Up! up! up! In some indescribable manner this highly talented player, timing his jump split-second like, gets up there and spears the ball for the third out and Bevens' no-hitter is still alive.
>
> For the moment all the talk is about Henrich's catch. Old-timers in the press box say it compares with the one Hooper made against the Giants in the 1912 series. These comparisons are always loose and casual. To most of us this is the greatest catch we ever saw in any series game. If Hooper's was better somebody ought to write a book about it.

Two days later Joe Williams and many other people saw Al Gionfriddo's catch on Joe DiMaggio's and saw it as superior to the one Henrich made on Gene Hermanski in Game Four.

August 24, 1949 — Luis Olmo

Luis Olmo was a talented Puerto Rican player who had a good year at the plate for the Brooklyn Dodgers in 1945, hitting .313 and leading the National League in triples with 13. After the 1945 season he and some other major league players decided to make more money by jumping to the Mexican League. That league, backed by money contributed by Jorge Pasquel, was offering many major league players much more money to play in Mexico. Olmo returned to the Dodgers in 1949, played sparingly, and then went to the Boston Braves in 1950. He was with the Braves for two more years, during which he played very little.

On August 24, Olmo was in the lineup only because two other outfielders, Duke Snider and Tommy Brown, were not healthy that day. His catch against the St. Louis Cardinals' Stan Musial in the fifth inning at Ebbets Field preserved Don Newcombe's 6–0 shutout. The *Brooklyn Eagle*'s Harold C. Burr wrote that Olmo's grab was "a gorgeous leaping catch."

The *New York Daily Mirror*'s Gus Steiger described the importance of Olmo's catch in the game.

> ... the turning point of the game came in the fifth when Luis Olmo made a circus catch that took Newcombe right out of trouble.
>
> With two out, Red Schoendienst got one of

Puerto Rican–born outfielder Luis Olmo parlayed a good year with the Dodgers in 1945 into a more lucrative contract to play baseball in Mexico for the next three years. When he returned to the major leagues in 1949, he played infrequently but showed flashes of his talents on the field.

Don's two passes and made third on Marty Marion's double to left. Here the wonderful Stanley Musial rapped a screamer headed for the 351-foot marker on the left field wall. Olmo raced over, leaped and with two hands brought down the smash that, had it been a foot or two higher, would have been a homer.

Olmo profited by an unusual break here, for there is a recession in the wall under the stands where ground implements are kept. This gave Luis an extra foot or so leeway, otherwise he might have cracked up on the wall. As it was he came down off the roll top door as he fell to the ground with the ball.

Martin J. Haley of the *St. Louis Globe-Democrat* called Olmo's catch "glittering," and went on to write:

Dodger fielding kept the Cards from scoring in the fifth. Cox made a glove stop and threw out Glaviano, and he also caught Brazle's liner. Schoendienst walked and Marion put him on third with a double to left. Then Olmo raced to the exit gate in left center, 351-feet from the plate, for his jumping catch of Musial's blistering drive. Olmo dropped to his knees after coming down, but held the ball. A couple of feet higher and Musial would have had a homer.

In his column in the *New York Herald Tribune*, Red Smith told about Olmo's jumping.

In the fifth inning with Brooklyn leading, 2 to 0, and two Cardinals on base, Stan Musial aimed a monstrous drive at the top of the wall in left center, 351 feet from the plate. Olmo leaped, just failing to reach the mezzanine, and hauled the ball down, saving the game.

It was the second biggest jump Luis has made. He made his biggest, of course, in 1946. Jumped to Mexico.

The *New York Daily News'* Dick Young had more to say about Olmo's catch.

But the Cards soon were threatening to wipe out the edge. With two down in the fifth, Schoendienst had strolled on four serves and buzzed to third on Marion's double down the left line. There, with the menacing Musial up, and first base open, the Brooks decided to take a chance on pitching to Stan. After all, Slaughter was due to bat next, so what's the difference what type of truck you're going to be hit by?

In an instant, it seemed that the Brooks had made the wrong choice. Musial whaled the ball high and far toward the left-center wall. Olmo ... streaked back frantically—as far as he could.

Then, timing his leap perfectly, Luis climbed a cloud to grab the ball high overhead with both hands, and squeeze it tight for the impending impact of his back slamming against the corrugated exit gate on his descent. The fortunate quirk of the catch is that Olmo might not have been physically able to make it except that the ball was hit exactly at the point of the exit, which is indented about a foot beyond the regular wall—giving him that extra room to brace himself and secure the ball before banging into the barrier.

One of the subheadings above the *New York Times'* article on the game was "BRILLIANT CATCH BY OLMO." Louis Effrat's article had high praise for Olmo's effort.

Musial caught hold of an outside pitch and drilled a screaming liner toward the leftcenter stands. It looked like curtains until Olmo, racing across the slippery grass, literally climbed the wall and made the catch, bouncing high against the exit-gate 351 feet away. This was one of the most spectacular catches ever witnessed at Ebbets Field.

NINE

1950–1964

As the decade of the 1950s began in the American League, the Yankees' Joe DiMaggio and the Boston Red Sox' Dom DiMaggio still were making catches that dazzled fans. In the National League, Duke Snider and Carl Furillo of the Dodgers, Chuck Diering of the Cardinals, Richie Ashburn of the Phillies, and Bobby Thomson of the Giants were among those outfielders whose spectacular putouts were thrilling fans.

The arrival of Willie Mays to the National League in 1951 was a revelation. Mays was a fielder unlike what even veteran observers were used to. Even people partial to the graceful, efficient style of Joe DiMaggio, who many considered the best centerfielder of all time, were taken with the plays Mays could make. From 1951 through 1957, the year the Dodgers and the Giants moved to the West Coast, the outfield play by centerfielders in New York alone often was breathtaking. Not only was Mays routinely turning heads with his defense, but Brooklyn's Duke Snider regularly was making acrobatic catches, and Mickey Mantle was making lightning-fast sprints to track down balls in the far reaches of Yankee Stadium.

Jimmy Piersall's emergence in 1953 as a fielding wonder in the American League put him among the greatest outfielders in the history of baseball. Experts had not seen the likes of the fielding gems Piersall regularly made in his first full year in the outfield. Like Mays, Piersall had been a great fielder before he got to the major leagues, but like Mays again, he left the experts grasping to find comparisons to the stunning plays he could make.

Appropriately enough, Joe DiMaggio made the first great catch of the 1950s.

April 15, 1950—Joe DiMaggio

Although it may not have been as great as the 1939 catch he made on Greenberg's ball, Joe DiMaggio's catch of a Roy Campanella drive in an April pre-season game in Yankee Stadium was compared to the earlier catch nonetheless. Bert Gumpert of the *New York Post* wrote:

> DiMag went at least 100 feet to deep left center in the fifth inning for a magnificent haul of Campanella's 440 footer that was marked three bases. Joe snared the ball going away and had it been made during the regular season would have ranked with his historic catch at the expense of Hank Greenberg a decade ago.

The *New York Daily Mirror*'s Ben Epstein referred to the nagging injuries DiMaggio had had off and on for several years: "Forget all those DiMaggio infirmities after robbing Campanella of a certain triple for the second out in the fifth with an over the shoulder catch to the left of the centerfield flagpole to climax a 100 foot dash."

Writing in the *New York Herald Tribune*, Al Laney felt that for all the things which went on the game, which the Yankees won 6 to 4, the most important was what Joe DiMaggio did in making "one of his greatest catches." One of the titles for Laney's story was "12,632 Electrified By Clipper's Catch." Laney wrote: "DiMaggio's catch, for which he had to run a very long way, almost to the wall in left center-field, showed beyond any possible doubt that this great player is in shape. For, to pull this one down in the old DiMaggio way requires perfect judgment."

One of the *New York Times'* titles read "Clipper Robs Campanella of Triple by Amazing Catch." Louis Effrat, who was the *Times'* writer the day of DiMaggio's catch on Greenberg in 1939, again was at the typewriter for the *Times* on April 15, 1950. As might be expected, Effrat recalled the earlier catch.

> For while the ballpark had a new scoreboard, a new press box, a new visiting team dressing room and a couple of new Yankee faces, it was the old centerfielder of the Bombers who paced his club to victory. DiMaggio, 36 come November, was the DiMaggio of 1936, as he drew two thunderous ovations from the 12,632 fans on hand for the first local game of 1950.
>
> There's life—and plenty of it—in the old Yankee Clipper. In the fifth inning he raced some 100 feet and robbed Brooklyn's Roy Campanella of a triple and possibly an inside-the-park homer with the most amazing catch witnessed at the Stadium since DiMaggio's job on a drive by Hank Greenberg a decade ago. Then, leading off in the home half of the same frame, Joltin' Joe smashed an electrifying homer off Preacher Roe.
>
> Vic Raschi was on the hill for the Yankees when Campanella strode to the plate after one out in the fifth. DiMaggio, stationed in dead center, broke to his right when Campanella's bat contacted the ball. It was 100 to 1 and no takers that the blow would be for extra bases.
>
> But DiMaggio never gave up. With characteristic grace he headed for the bleacher fence in left-center, some thirty or forty feet short of the 457-foot sign. DiMaggio, going like the wind, his back to home plate, stuck out his gloved-hand and executed the catch.

Notice that Louis Effrat referred to DiMaggio as "old." Some people told DiMaggio it was a good catch for someone his age. This kind of comment caused DiMaggio to bristle.

In his book *My Life In and Out of Baseball*, Willie Mays wrote:

> DiMaggio told one of his greatest catches was off Campanella in an exhibition game, yet it hurt him—what they said about it, I mean.
>
> "It was just before my last season," Joe D. told me. "They wrote it was a hell of a catch for an old man. Let me tell you something, Will, it was a hell of a catch for anybody" [168].

Three days later, on opening day in Boston, Joe DiMaggio yet again showed his uncanny ability to get to balls. The *New York Times'* John Drebinger twice referred to a catch Joe made in the Yankees' 15 to 10 win. First: "An eye-dazzling Joe DiMaggio weighed in with a triple, a single and a double in the course of the three and-a-half-hour struggle, not to mention fetching up the crowd with a breath-taking catch in the seventh that prevented the Sox at that point from widening their lead by at least three runs." And later in the same article:

> To that Boston added one more in the seventh when Don Johnson forced in a tally on a single and three walks, DiMaggio, J. here saving further damage by racing clear to the distant bullpen in right center to make an electrifying, glove-handed catch of Matt Batts' clout with the bases full for the third out.

The *Boston Herald's* Arthur Sampson noted how good Joe DiMaggio's play was in the opening game. After calling DiMaggio's catch on the ball Batts' drive "miraculous" and "sensational," and telling how the Boston fans "applauded the Yanks center fielder for his exceptional display of fielding ability," Sampson gave other opinions of DiMaggio's play that day.

Big DiMag looks like the great center fielder of old this year.... He gave a wonderful defensive exhibition throughout the game and looked his same potent self at bat.... In addition to two or three sparkling catches, he nipped Zarilla with a beautiful throw to third base in the fourth.

The big fielding play of the day, however, was the clutch that Big DiMag made with the bases full and the Sox at bat in the seventh.... Joe ran a country mile for this drive by Batts, stuck out his glove, with his back to the plate, and just managed to spear the ball, a clear case of daylight larceny.

DiMaggio was not done with early season excellence in the field. In his May 7, 1950, report of the previous day's Yankees-Indians game, the *New York Times'* Effrat commented on another DiMaggio catch: "DiMaggio's catch of Mitchell's wrong-field drive in the third was a thing of beauty. The Jolter had to move into Gene Woodling's territory in left for a characteristically graceful over-the-shoulder DiMaggio putout."

On May 20, James P. Dawson of the *New York Times* wrote a report of the Yankees' sweep of their doubleheader with the Indians that included: "DiMaggio came up with a dazzling leaping catch on Luke Easter to rob the Negro star of a seventh-inning home run...." The catch on Easter's drive brought DiMaggio plaudits. His own reaction was reported in the *Cleveland Plain Dealer*: "'Just unconscious,' was Joe's reply to compliments on his great, leaping catch of Luke Easter's second-game home run bid. 'You just jump and hope on those.'"

June 20, 1951—Richie Ashburn

Statistically, Richie Ashburn was the greatest defensive centerfielder of all time. There is no one close to him in the number of putouts he achieved across the 1949 through 1958 seasons with the Phillies. He was everywhere tracking down fly balls. Four times in those ten years he had over 500 putouts, which only four other outfielders in the history of baseball have achieved, and then only once apiece. He also had seasons of 483, 495, and 496 putouts. Many of those putouts were of the sensational variety, mostly due to Richie's speed and his outstanding anticipation and break on balls.

In his March 1955 *Baseball Digest* article on Ashburn, Michael Gaven called him "the woefully underrated center fielder of the Phillies." Gaven made the case that Ashburn's high putout totals indicate that he catches balls that the much more highly touted Willie Mays and Duke Snider don't reach. Gaven continues: "Definitely he plays the hitters better and pays more attention to where the pitcher is trying to make the batter hit the ball. Therein may lie one advantage because Robin Roberts is one pitcher who has some idea of where he is throwing the ball." Gaven concluded that Ashburn's fielding excellence and his solid credentials as a hitter made him among the greatest players of all time.

Michael Hoban developed a system for rating players' offensive and defensive performance. In his 2000 book *Baseball's Complete Players*, Hoban's system of rating defensive performance led to Richie Ashburn's having the highest rating of any defensive player ever, regardless of position. Ashburn's 1951 year, in which he had 538 putouts, 15 assists, 6 double plays, and just 6 errors, was the highest rated year any defensive player ever had.

It also was in 1951 that Ashburn might have made his greatest catch.

Hoban's scaling system set a defensive player's score for a "Great Year" at 400. Ashburn's score for 1951 was a 608, the highest score Hoban calculated, and the only score ever over 600. Ashburn had seven other seasons when his scores were over 500, and was the only defensive player rated who had a career average score of over 500. Ashburn's career average was 529. For comparison's sake, the next three highest rated outfielders' career defensive averages were: Max Carey, the speedy Pirate centerfielder from 1910 through most of the 1926 season, at 490; Tris Speaker at 484; and Willie Mays at 456.

In his 1995 book *Baseball Ratings: The All-Time Best Players at Each Position*, Charles F. Faber noted Ashburn's high ranking as a fielder. Faber had Ashburn as the highest rated defensive centerfielder of all time. Pete Palmer, as reported in *Total Baseball*, had Tris Speaker and Max Carey only slightly ahead of Ashburn as the best defensive centerfielders of all time.

Richie Ashburn was one of the fastest runners in the major leagues. In a July 13, 1948, *New York World-Telegram* article by Bill Roeder, Ashburn is quoted about being a sprinter in high school: "'I was a track man in high school,' he says, 'but nothing special. I mean I was never the state champion or anything like that. I did 10.2 for 100 yards.'"

Despite Ashburn's modest appraisal of his speed, in a time when sprinting often was not systematically coached,

Shown here in at spring training in the mid–1950s, the Philadelphia Phillies' swift centerfielder Richie Ashburn made more putouts over a 10-year period (1949 to 1958) than any other outfielder in the history of baseball.

when most outdoor tracks were made of cinders unlike the more uniform track surfaces of today which can lead to faster times, and when track was not a big sport in most small towns like Tilden, Nebraska, where Ashburn grew up, 10.2 seconds for 100 yards was a very good time.

Many experts noted Ashburn's baseball speed. Roeder quotes Leo Durocher, whose opinions seemed to waffle on who was the fastest player he'd seen. "He [Ashburn] goes down the line faster than Pete Reiser did in his prime,' Leo marveled." Durocher would later write in his book *Nice Guys Finish Last*, that Pete Reiser was the fastest he'd ever seen. Leo did not mention Ashburn at all.

In another 1948 newspaper article in the Hall of Fame's files on Ashburn, Durocher again attested to Ashburn's speed.

In a chinfest last night one of the coaches said he knew of a prospect who is faster than Richie Ashburn, the Phillie phenom.

"Faster than Ashburn!" Leo exclaimed. "I don't believe it. Ashburn is the fastest man I've ever seen getting down to first base, faster than Reiser in his prime. Anybody who's faster than Ashburn isn't running. He's flying."

Among a series of comments about Ashburn in the March 8, 1995, *Philadelphia Inquirer* after he was elected into the Hall of Fame was one about his speed. Sam Carchidi of the *Inquirer* wrote: "When he broke into the majors in 1948, *Time* magazine called him 'a wing-footed dervish.' During his early years with the Phillies, he was clocked in 3.1 seconds from home to first after a swing."

By July of 1948 Ashburn was proving to be an outstanding hitter and defender as a rookie. A clipping in the Hall of Fame file on Ashburn dated July 4 was about Ashburn's rise as a player, and was titled "Ashburn Fastest Player in Major Loops." Within the uncredited article was a summary of data attesting to his speed.

> Right now, Richie is one of the league's leading hitters, and his speed on the base paths has the fans blinded, the opposing pitchers and hitters jittery, and his manager singing his praises. For instance, Ashburn bunts and beats it out. He hits a "single" and gets two bases out of the blow. He hits an ordinary grounder to short and second base, as he did against the Giants recently, and instead of two outs, it's two singles.
>
> Babe Pinelli, who goes back 25 years as a player and an umpire, says, "I can't think of a player who runs from first to third as fast as Ashburn. And I can't recall any either."

Ashburn made many fine catches in a wide variety of ways. In the 1951 All Star game he made a sensational running, twisting, leaping catch to rob the American League's Vic Wertz. Just three weeks before the catch in the All Star game, Ashburn made a catch that was even more highly regarded. It was during a June 20, 1951, night game at Pittsburgh in which Ashburn dominated defensively, making four outstanding catches in a 1 to 0 Phillies victory.

The June 21, 1951, Pittsburgh papers gave Ashburn his due for the game he had played the night before. The unidentified *Pittsburgh Press* reporter covering the game, probably Les Biederman, devoted most of his column to Ashburn's feats.

> ... the Pirates were still talking about Richie Ashburn, Phil centerfielder who personally led the Phils to their second straight over the Bucs last night.
>
> Officially the score of the spine-tingling contest was Phils 1, Pirates 0, but actually it should have been Ashburn 1, Pirates 0.
>
> Ashburn made six catches, and four were so sensational that when the game ended, players on both teams shook their heads. It was hard to believe.
>
> The most daring bit of burglary Ashburn committed came in the most crucial moment of the battle.
>
> With two out and bases loaded in the seventh inning, Gus Bell tied into one of Bubba Church's pitches and sent it on a line close to the right-center stands. Ashburn was off the moment Bell connected and the runners were flying around the bases.
>
> Just as it seemed the ball would strike the wall, Ashburn got there and took the ball over his shoulder, a second before crashing into the wall. It saved the game and went down as the "greatest catch since Barbara Hutton."
>
> Not content with saving Church's hide in the field, Ashburn made it a perfect evening by scoring the only run of the game.

At the time of Ashburn's catch, Barbara Hutton was one of the country's wealthiest women. She had been married and divorced several times, and, when not married, was a target of men seeking to marry her for her fortune.

Jack Hernon of the *Pittsburgh Post-Gazette* led with Ashburn's part in the game.

> Bubba Church sent out a wartime distress call last night and it was answered by Richie Ashburn as the Bucs bowed, 1–0, to keep the Phillie streak intact through four games.
>
> ... The Phil right-hander was rescued by just about the best center field job seen here in many long years as Ashburn roamed from left to right and far back to grab three extra-base hits off Pirate bats.
>
> If there is such a thing as a great catch, then Ashburn made one in the seventh inning to deprive the Pirates of a victory. There were three Bucs on the pond in the seventh when Gus

Bell hit a terrific smash to the corner of the right field stands, near the right-center exit gate.

Not a person in the park—including his mates—gave the fleet Phillie outfielder a chance to get his hands on the ball. But he did and he held on to it as he crashed into the concrete. That was that, and the three runs which had crossed the plate didn't mean a thing.

Prior to that sensational catch, Ashburn went almost to the exit gate to nab Bill Howerton's healthy wallop. Then he turned right around on the next batter, Joe Garagiola, and went to deep left-center for another four-star catch on the dead run. Both catches came in the sixth frame.

But when he took the triple away from Bell, every person in the ballpark stood up and gave Ashburn a sporting ovation.

That was the way Church staggered to a shutout.

Grant Doherty of the *Philadelphia Daily News* devoted his whole article to Ashburn.

Richie Ashburn beat the Pittsburgh Pirates last night, 1–0.

Ashburn it was whose sensational catches, one in the third inning, two in the sixth, and one in the seventh inning, robbed the Pirates of at least four runs and Ashburn came streaking home on Bill Nicholson's sixth-inning infield out, sliding in a cloud of dust which cleared to show his spikes shining above the plate with the game's only run.

Funny part of it was that before the game Pirate Coach Milt Stock compared Richie and Brooklyn's Duke Snider and given Ashburn the short end of the bargain.

"Make no mistake," Stock had said, "Ashburn's a good fielder and is getting better all the time, but I'd still take Snider. I think he's a shade faster and certainly hits a longer ball and gets more total bases during a season. Some day Ashburn may catch him but at the moment Snider is the better of the two."

That was before the game.

After the game, in the Pirate dressing room, Stock wore a sheepish grin.

"You may say," he said, "that I still like Snider, but that Ashburn almost caught him tonight," and he walked off to the showers.

Not that this is the first time Stock has had to rue an association with the Phils' tow-headed centerfielder. The Pirates third-base coach acted in a similar capacity for the Dodgers last October 1 and it was he who waved Cal Abrams from second, around third and toward home on Snider's single in that fantastic ninth inning. Had Abrams scored, the Dodgers would have won, 2–1, but Ashburn threw Abrams out at the plate by 15 feet and next inning Dick Sisler hit his pennant-winning home run.

Ashburn's first catch last night drew little attention. It came with two out and none on: Gus Bell whacked one 400 feet which Richie took in full stride and with little accompanying fanfare.

In the bottom of the sixth, however, things were a little different. The Phils had just scored and the Pirates were threatening with Bell at first, via an error, and one out. Bill Howerton stepped into a curve ball and practically knocked the cover loose.

Ashburn, who had been playing the left-handed hitting Howerton more than a shade to right, took off on a course that would intercept the ball and hauled it in, 425 feet away, in left-center.

Next batter was Joe Garagiola and he blasted one to right center but before it could hit the ground it plumped into Richie's glove, 365 feet from home plate.

As he ran in from the outfield the fans gave Ashburn a rising ovation but that was only the prelude to what will go down as being among the greatest catches of all time, if not the greatest.

It was the seventh inning by this time. The Pirates had the bases full, on three singles, and two were out.

Bell swung his bat in a vicious arc, met the ball squarely and it took off on a line toward the truck driveway in right center field.

Everyone knew that even Ashburn couldn't get this one—George Strickland crossed the plate, then Pete Castiglione, then George Metkovich and Bell was digging for third when an awed hush went over Forbes Field—for Ashburn was there. He stuck out his glove and the ball dropped in for the third out; a second later he crashed into the wall beside the sign which reads "475 feet."

The 12,751 Pittsburghers in attendance were stunned for a second then raised their voices in a yell of appreciation which they must have heard down town.

In his "NOTES" section following the main article, Doherty had another comment about Ashburn's catch on the Gus Bell drive in the seventh inning: "Benny Bengough labeled Ashburn's seventh-inning catch the greatest he had seen in 33 years of baseball." Benny Bengough was a Phillies coach, who began his major league career in 1923 with the New York Yankees and was one of the catchers on the team until 1930. Earle Combs, the speedy and talented centerfielder, was his teammate, and he saw many outstanding outfielding plays during the twenties, including plays by Johnny Mostil, Bib Falk, and Tris Speaker.

Stan Baumgartner, who wrote for the *Philadelphia Inquirer*, also was mightily impressed by what Ashburn accomplished in the game against the Pirates in the 1–0 win.

The brilliant centerfielder, who is playing the best baseball in the National League, not only scored the only run in the sixth inning, after beating out a bunt, but made three of the finest game-saving catches ever seen at Forbes Field.

His catch of Gus Bell's drive in the seventh inning with the bases loaded, two out, and the Phils leading, was the best of the season and many seasons.

The Pirates' big right fielder caught a Church fast ball on the fat of his bat and gave it a tremendous sock to right-center. Pirate fans, sensing a victory, leaped to their feet as the ball soared toward the fence.

Ashburn started after it, turned his back to the plate and raced toward the wall. As he reached the cinder track, 430 feet from the plate, he stuck up his glove. The ball hit his mitt and he hit the wall. He rebounded groggily but still held the ball. Bill Nicholson grabbed him around the shoulders and helped him across the field.

The Pittsburgh fans gave him a rousing ovation as he trotted toward the bench and his teammates leaped out of the dugout to pat his shoulders and throw their arms around him.

This catch was preceded by two almost as skillful in the sixth. With Bell on first and one out, Richie ran almost to the fence in right center to pull down Bill Howerton's smash, and the next moment raced to left center to grab Joe Garagiola's terrific liner. Had any of the three smashes gone safe Church and the Phils would have been beaten.

To round out his great work he opened the sixth with a clever bunt along the first base line that caught Ralph Kiner flatfooted. Willie Jones sent him to second with a neat sacrifice and he went to third when Gran Hamner lined a single to right. Nicholson then hit a grounder to Kiner which the latter fielded with his toe instead of his glove and Richie scored.

The *Philadelphia Bulletin*'s Frank Yeutter put Ashburn's fielding feats in lofty company before going on to describe Richie's four catches.

For Ashburn made four catches that were never excelled by Tris Speaker, Joe DiMaggio, Terry Moore or any other centerfielder.

Richie's first catch robbed Gus Bell in the third inning. He roved back to the 400-foot mark to haul it down in full stride.

In the sixth, with Bell on first, he captured terrific drives by Bill Howerton and Joe Garagiola. Either of these snatches would have been enough for one game.

The Howerton shot carried directly toward the extreme center field corner. Richie hauled it down at the 436-foot mark on the wall. That started a thunderous ovation. But when he reversed his field and romped to left-center to grab Garagiola's drive against the screen in front of the bullpen, the crowd went wild.

But his finest catch was the game saver in the seventh inning.

Church had allowed only four hits until that time. He seemed to run into a little trouble with his fast ball and his curve had lost its early snap.

George Strickland cracked a single to right field. Pete Castiglione rammed one into left and George Metkovich got a base hit on a ball just out of Eddie Waitkus' reach. That filled the bases with two out and the dangerous Bell at bat.

Bell hammered a line drive that was clearly labeled triple. It didn't seem possible that any human being could get near it.

But Richie, at top speed, outfooted the ball, leaped in the air, nabbed it one-handed and then crashed into the driveway gate at the extreme right-center field corner of Forbes Field —a drive easily 450 feet from the plate. When Richie grabbed the ball he had his back to the playing field and made the catch over his shoulder.

After the stunned silence, every voice in the park was raised in a mighty roar. There were only 12,751 persons present but they all let go with top caliber vocal power.

After the series between the Phillies and the Pirates was concluded and while waiting for the Phillies' first game against the Cincinnati Reds, Yeutter reflected on Ashburn and the catch he made on Gus Bell.

But with Richie Ashburn in center field, the Phils have just about the best player in the major leagues at that position.

Manager Billy Meyer, of the Pirates, said the catch Richie made on Gus Bell was the greatest he ever saw anywhere. And George Sisler, a Hall of Fame immortal, declared that Tris Speaker was never better than Richie was in that game.

In the 1952 *Baseball Stars* magazine, Frank Yeutter referred to the Bell catch and the catch Ashburn made in the 1951 All Star game, saying "that they will live forever in the memory of those who saw them." He also quoted George Sisler, one of the greatest players ever, who saw Ashburn's catch on Bell. Sisler said, "In 30 years of big league baseball I never saw better."

Three years later, in the June 1, 1954, *Inquirer*, the day after Duke Snider made a great catch in Philadelphia, Stan Baumgartner recalled Richie Ashburn's catch on Gus Bell in Pittsburgh: "Richie Ashburn's catch a few years ago in Pittsburgh with the bases full and the Phillies leading by one run was the closest thing to Duke Snider's clutch catch the writer has seen in the regular season."

In the August 14, 1951 *Philadelphia Bulletin*, Frank Yeutter wrote about Ashburn after the Phillies lost three straight games to the New York Giants, who then were beginning their charge to overtake the Brooklyn Dodgers for the National League title.

No game is complete without a brilliant catch by Richie Ashburn.... Leo Durocher says Richie is the best defensive outfielder in the league.... Duffy Lewis, traveling secretary of the Boston Braves, a member of the famed Hooper-Lewis-Speaker outfield, agrees with Leo.

Leo Durocher's appraisal of Ashburn as the best defensive outfielder in the league would be challenged the next day. On August 15, Durocher's own centerfielder, Willie Mays, was to make a play that amazed many veteran observers.

July 25, 1951—Willie Mays

Willie Mays already had dazzled fans in Trenton in 1950 and in Minneapolis in 1951 with his fielding. In the book *Say Hey* that he wrote in 1988 with Lou Sahadi, Mays discussed some of the catches he made which he remembered as outstanding. After writing about his famous catch against Vic Wertz in the 1954 World Series, which he didn't believe to be one of his greatest catches, he continues:

But I always thought the catch I made in Ebbets Field when I knocked myself out after diving for the ball was even more difficult. I also made one in Trenton in 1950 that was even more fun to watch. Lou Haymen of Wilmington hit a shot to dead center, right at the 405-foot sign. I ran back, jumped, and caught it bare-handed just as it was going over. I bounced off the fence and threw the ball on the fly all the way to home plate. Nobody knew about it because it was just another game in a small town [118].

Although I did not find a newspaper account of Mays' catch on Lou Haymen, several of his Trenton teammates remembered a bare-hand catch Willie Mays made in a game against York on June 27, 1950. Bill Klink, in *The Ol' Ball Game*, first quotes Eric Rodin, Trenton's right fielder that day. Rodin describes York's Bill Biddle hitting a ball to deep center field, a ball that would have carried over the fence. He assumed that Mays would not catch the ball. However, Mays did get to the ball, but, as he reached up with his gloved hand, the ball went by his glove. Rodin continues, "but his reflexes were such that he went up with his bare hand against the fence, caught the ball and came down" (131). As was to be the case a year later in Pittsburgh, his teammates did not know how to respond to Mays' athletic ability. Len Matte, a catcher for Trenton, told Bill Klink, "Everybody, including us, didn't know what to say. It's like this guy dropped out of the sky from somewhere!" (131).

Len Matte also told Bill Klink about the time after Willie Mays first joined the team for a game in Hagerstown, Maryland. Before the game Matte was working with Trenton manager Chick Genovese, who was hitting fly balls to the new player Mays. Chick Genovese was hitting fly balls all over the outfield forcing Mays to run hither and yon to catch the balls. After watching Mays catch balls in far-flung parts of the outfield, Genovese turned to Matte and said, "This guy has the kind of reflexes no one else has" (129).

In 1950, Trenton's Willie Mays was the first black player in the Inter-State League.

The next year, in Minneapolis, Willie Mays continued the kind of fielding which many onlookers there had not seen before. On May 7, just a couple weeks before he was called up by the New York Giants, Mays made a spectacular catch in Minneapolis's Nicollet Park in a 10–9 Minneapolis victory over Louisville. Bob Beebe of the *Minneapolis Star* wrote, "Mays in the third inning made the greatest catch anyone can recall at Nicollet Park. He literally climbed the right center field wall to pick off Taft Wright's jet drive."

Halsey Hall of the *Minneapolis Tribune* was equally enthusiastic when he wrote:

Willie Mays turned scoreboard boy. Off Taft Wright, in the third inning, the young genius looked like he was hanging up numbers as he leaped almost to the level of the big league board for a fly ball, banged into the wall and doubled a runner at second base. It will rank as one of the greatest catches you will ever see.

In the May 9, 1951, *Minneapolis Tribune*, Halsey Hall's colleague in the sports room, Joe Hendrickson, had more information about Mays' catch.

Willie Mays tells how he made Nicollet Park's most sensational catch in years off right field boards to ruin Taft Wright's cinch double. "I thought from the beginning that I could catch it because the ball didn't appear to be hard hit. I just kept running toward the fence and when I got there I used my foot for a vaulting pole. That's the way to catch them off the fence.
"I took off after hitting my foot about three feet from the bottom. I didn't catch the ball with my glove against the fence. My glove was at least a foot out. I had lots of room to snatch for the ball."

One day during a spring training game in 1951, Halsey Hall sat next to Jack Buck, then at the beginning of his long and distinguished sports broadcasting career. Buck was in his second year doing play-by-play for the Columbus Redbirds, a rival of the Minneapolis

Millers. In his 1997 book, *Jack Buck: "That's a Winner!"* (written with Rob Rains and Bob Broeg), Buck recounts his meeting with Hall, and Mays' subsequent play.

> He told me before the game, "Jack, you're going to see one of the greatest players who has ever come along in the game of baseball, that kid out there in centerfield, Mays." During the game somebody hit a ball into left center. Mays ran over, planted his foot in the middle of the wooden fence, caught the ball over his left shoulder, did a somersault off the fence and threw a strike to second base. I turned to Halsey and said, "I believe you" [61–62].

Elsewhere in his book, Jack Buck wrote that Willie Mays was the best baseball player he ever saw.

Jack Buck's assessment is the same as the one Ernie Harwell, the long-time voice of the Detroit Tigers, has made in several books. Harwell was one of the New York Giants' announcers when Mays first came to the Giants in 1951. In a 2002 book he collaborated on with Ernie Harwell, *Ernie Harwell: My 60 Years in Baseball*, Tom Keegan writes, "Ask Ernie Harwell to name the greatest player he ever saw, and he answers before the question has finished. Willie Mays, Harwell says" [112].

The Giants brought Mays up from Minneapolis and started him for the first time on May 25, 1951. Almost immediately he began to impress the New York fans with his fielding.

On July 25, the Giants were playing the Pirates in Pittsburgh. The teams first completed a game which had been suspended from June 17. The Giants won the suspended game. In the full game, Giants manager Leo Durocher gave rookie pitcher Al Corwin his first start in the majors. Corwin had a 4–0 lead through six innings, but the Pirates scored five runs in the seventh and eighth innings and won the game 5 to 4.

Mays' great catch in the game Corwin pitched received no mention in most New York papers, and no mention in the *Pittsburgh Press*, the *Pittsburgh Sun-Telegraph*, or the *Pittsburgh Post-Gazette*. Only Rud Rennie of the *New York Herald Tribune* mentioned the catch, and then only briefly. He wrote, "Until the seventh, everything looked good for the Giants and Corwin. Mays made a wonderful bare-handed catch to help him." It should be noted that an uncredited writer in the August 15, 1951, *Sporting News* did mention Mays' bare-hand catch, but said it took place in a night game on July 24.

Even though most writers seemed to miss Mays' catch, his teammates and others did not. Ernie Harwell was a young announcer for the Giants in 1951. In his 1986 book *Tuned to Baseball*, he wrote:

> To me, Willie's fielding was even more spectacular than his hitting. Great speed and a strong arm enabled him to make catches I have never seen by any other player. For instance, in Mays' rookie season of 1951 the Giants were playing the Pirates in Pittsburgh. Left-handed-hitting Rocky Nelson sliced a hard line drive to left-center. Mays, as usual, got a quick jump but as he ran toward left field, he realized he could not reach the line drive with his glove hand. So, he simply reached out with his bare hand and, while racing at full speed, grabbed the line drive. It was the greatest catch I have ever seen [191–192].

The long-time "voice" of the Detroit Tigers, Ernie Harwell broadcast major league baseball games from 1948 until 2002. After announcing for the Brooklyn Dodgers from late 1948 and through the 1949 season, Harwell joined Russ Hodges to broadcast for the New York Giants for four years. In 1951 he saw this catch by Mays, and after all his years in baseball still declared it the greatest he ever saw.

Monte Irvin, in his 1996 book *Nice Guys Finish First*, writes about his teammate's bare-hand grab of the Rocky Nelson drive and said he thought that that catch was Willie's best. Being the Giants' left fielder that day gave Irvin the best place in Forbes Field to view the catch Mays made. Irvin mentioned that Mays was playing the left-handed, pull-hitting Nelson straight away in center field and Nelson hit the ball directly over Mays' head in spacious Forbes Field.

Irvin also gave Leo Durocher's and Branch Rickey's comments after the catch: "Durocher immediately said, 'Fellows, I've seen great catches in my life, but this is the first time I've seen anything like this'" (182). Later Irvin writes, "To show how great that catch was, Branch Rickey was watching the game from his office upstairs by the broadcasting booth, and he sent a note down to Leo that described the catch as, 'the greatest catch I've ever seen anywhere, anytime'" (183). In a career that began in 1905, Branch Rickey had been a major league player, manager, general manager, and part-owner, and this was the greatest catch he had seen.

A decade before writing his own book, Irvin told Donald Honig, as reported in *Mays, Mantle, Snider*, about the catch on Rocky Nelson's drive. Irvin said Mays "was playing in close." He went on to say: "Leo was flabbergasted. We all were. Nobody had ever seen anything like it" (107). Monte Irvin told how Leo decided to pretend he hadn't seen Mays make the catch. He enlisted the other players to act silently as if Willie had made an ordinary catch. After Willie asked Leo if he had seen the catch he made, Leo said he hadn't, and told Willie to go out there and do it again before he would believe it.

On July 20, 1951, five days before he made the bare-hand catch on Rocky Nelson, Willie had tried another bare-hand catch in a game at the Polo Grounds in a Giants victory over the Cincinnati Reds. Louis Effrat of the *New York Times* wrote:

> Willie also made a number of fine catches in the outfield, but the one he did not get almost became the most sensational play in the game. Merriman drove the ball to deep right center in the eighth and Willie attempted a leaping barehanded catch. For an instant, it appeared that Mays had succeeded, but he dropped the ball, which was scored as a run-scoring double.

August 15, 1951—Willie Mays

Less than a month after the barehanded catch in Pittsburgh, Willie Mays made a play that deserves to be listed here even though it is more than a catch. It shows Mays' rare athleticism, and his giftedness for making a play.

The play occurred in a game at the Polo Grounds as the Giants were making their run at the league-leading Dodgers. Before that game the Giants trailed the Dodgers by eleven and a half games. The Giants went on to tie the Dodgers at the end of the regular season, and then to defeat the Dodgers in the playoffs on Bobby Thomson's dramatic homer to win the National League crown.

Prior to this series, the Dodgers had beaten the Giants in twelve of fifteen games, and appeared ready to win the National League title easily. The Giants won the first game of the series on August 14.

In the second game of the series, the teams were tied 1 to 1 as the Dodgers batted in the top of the eighth. The Giants went on to score two runs in the bottom of the eighth to win the game 3 to 1. Jim McCulley of the *New York Daily News* described the Dodgers' top half of the eighth. He wrote:

> Cox opened the eighth by rapping a single off Thomson's glove. Robby was sent up to swing for Terwilliger and flied to Mueller in right. Branca tried vainly to move Cox along, fouling off two strikes in an attempt to bunt. Then Brooklyn got a break. Hearn committed a balk and Cox trotted to second. Then Branca dumped a single into short right, sending his third baseman to the far corner.

That left things up to Furillo, who had singled in the first inning. Carl sent a fly to right centerfield, not too long, not too short. Mays had to run quite a ways for it and it looked as though Cox would easily make the plate after the catch. But Mays, after making the nab, made a complete turn like a discus heaver, and fired a strike to [Wes] Westrum. The ball and Cox arrived in a dead-heat. Wes made a nice tag and Cox, who came sliding in on the back top side of the plate, was out. He missed the dish by inches, but he may have been out anyway, it was that close.

That heave of Willie's was one of the best anybody will ever see, and it no doubt crippled Branca's spirit.

Willie Mays was the first one up in the bottom of the eighth. He singled, and later scored when Westrum hit a homer that won the game.

After describing the scene and noting that Carl Furillo sent a fly ball to right center field, Joseph M. Sheehan of the *New York Times* wrote, "It looked plenty deep enough to bring in Cox, especially since Mays had to run a long way to get the ball. But Willie, making a complete whirling pivot on the dead run, cut loose with a tremendous peg that boomed into Westrum's mitt in perfect position for the catcher to tag the sliding Cox."

Ken Smith of the *New York Daily Mirror* put the extraordinary quality of the play into perspective. He wrote:

The big excitement of the day, a play that will no doubt be long remembered in Mays' career, broke the Dodgers' hearts in the eighth. Cox, the only Dodger to hit twice in both games of the series, led off with a single. After Jackie Robinson flied out batting for Terwilliger, Cox took second on a balk. Branca singled to right and Chuck Dressen held Cox at third, a wise move as Don Mueller flung home hard and true.

Furillo raised a fly to Mays in normal centerfield territory. It looked like an automatic run but Mays, making a characteristic complete turn of his body, threw home to Westrum on the fly.

Cox, whose slide was slightly wide, was a surprised gent as Westrum tagged him out. He was no more amazed than everyone else in the park. Secretary Eddie Brannick, who has been around the Polo Grounds since 1908, described it as one of the most striking plays he had ever seen.

The amazement that other sportswriters had for Willie's play was apparent in their columns on August 16. The *New York World-Telegram and Sun* article by an uncredited writer left no doubt that others were in awe of what Mays had done. The part of this first article devoted to Willie's throw was:

Eddie Brannick, secretary, who has been with the Giants more than 40 years, seldom is moved to comment on a game or a play but he came dashing into the clubhouse to congratulate Willie Mays on the throw yesterday.

"I've seen Speaker, DiMaggio, Moore, all of them," Brannick said, "but I've never seen anything like that throw. This kid made the greatest play I ever looked at."

Kidding about the throw, Whitey Lockman got a rise out of Leo Durocher. Lockman was at the cutoff station, just in front of the plate, when the ball came in.

"What would you have done if I'd a cut it off?" he asked Leo.

"Cut it off! Well, you might just as well of headed straight for the clubhouse. And on the run, because I'd have been right after you with a bat in my hands."

Not everyone thought the throw was a stroke of genius. Asked what he thought of it, Carl Furillo said: "Luck. That was the luckiest throw I ever saw in my life. He can try that 50 times and he won't come close again. I make that turning throw once in a while, mostly to second base, and I get within five feet of the base about once every 10 tries. It has to be luck when you when you throw that way because you can't see where you're throwing."

Cal Abrams said it was the greatest throw he'd ever seen, and Jackie Robinson gave Mays credit for a perfect play. But some of the Dodgers took Furillo's stand and insisted they'd have to see it again to be convinced it wasn't an accident.

"It's the first time I ever saw an outfielder make that play," Charlie Dressen said. "I'd like to see him do it again. If he does it again I'll say he's great."

Durocher was unusually cautious with his superlatives. He just said that nobody has a better arm than Willie, that he has never seen a better throw, and that nobody will ever see a better throw.

Durocher's caution was in part because he knew very well that Furillo, whom he had managed, was considered to have the best arm in baseball, and that Furillo's arm was the most feared around the National League.

It should be noted that Leo Durocher came to the majors in 1925, and had played with two of the great centerfielders of all time, Earle Combs of the Yankees and Terry Moore of the Cardinals, and had managed the outfield phenom Pete Reiser when Reiser first came into the majors in 1940. Charlie Dressen began his major league career in 1925 with the Cincinnati Redlegs, and saw many outstanding outfield plays over his long career as a player and a coach or manager.

Bill Roeder of the *New York World-Telegram and Sun* called Willie's play "fantastic," and then described it. Among other things, he noted the trajectory of the throw.

Zooming along on a low line, the ball carried all the way to the plate, where Wes Westrum had Billy Cox blocked off for the out.

It was such a staggering play that the winning rally was an anticlimax.

Charley Feeney of the *Long Island Press*, who also was in the locker room after the game, quoted a few of Leo Durocher's comments and gave Willie's view of what he did.

Leo Durocher was beaming in his dressing room. "It was the greatest throw I ever saw," Leo chimed. "Don't let anyone tell you this kid can't throw, he can throw as good as anyone in the league." A reporter tried to pin down Durocher about the throwing ability of Furillo and Mays and Leo repeated: "He can throw as good as anyone in the league."

Feeney continued:

Here's Mays' version of the play: "I was going toward right field and I knew if I stopped to get set after catching the ball that I would lose time." A reporter asked Mays if he was thinking of throwing home before he caught the ball and Willie said: "Heck, you got to be thinking all the time out there and I know that Dressen is the kind of manager that always sends a runner home when he has any kind of chance. Leo told me that." Mays went on to say that he didn't see Westrum at home plate, but he saw Whitey Lockman who was in the "cutoff spot." I always aim my throws at Whitey's chest," Willie continued, "and today I just made a perfect throw. It sure makes a fellow feel good."

Barney Kremenko wrote in the *New York Journal-American*, "It was as spectacular and as perfect a play as the Polo Grounds has ever witnessed." Kremenko noted:

The pivot was what gave Mays' play the novel and eye-opening touch. It's a commonplace stunt for infielders, but few among the Giants or Dodgers had ever seen an outfielder do it before.
Let Willie explain:
"I had the thing figured out before I caught it," said the amazin' Mr. Mays. "In the first place, remember I am under instructions from Leo Durocher to catch flies hit between me and Don Mueller whenever a throw is necessary. So I have to be ready.
"Well, while I was racing for the ball I knew that if I tried to throw facing the right field foul line, I'd be off balance. If I stopped and took a windup, it would be too late. The runner would be across by the time I let go. The only thing to do was to pivot and heave. I had done it once before in Trenton last year.

"At the same time I was able to take aim. You see, I don't aim for the plate; I go for the letters on Whitey Lockman's shirt. Whitey, playing first base, always stands on a line between me and home plate. It's not very often that I can throw the ball on a line with Whitey's letters. But this time I happened to get it just where it should be."

What Willie did not explain, and maybe could not explain, was how he could pick up the exact line for the throw as his body and head and eyes were spinning so rapidly, and coordinate all this with his throwing motion.

How good was this play?

In his September 21, 1973, *New York Times* column (reproduced in his book *Sports of Our Times*), Dave Anderson wrote of his conversation with Willie Mays, then nearing the end of his career. "My best play," Mays reflected, "was the Billy Cox play" (12). Twenty-two years and thousands of plays later, he considered the play on Billy Cox his best.

In the minutes before the last game ever played at the Polo Grounds between the New York Giants and the Brooklyn Dodgers on September 8, 1957, some of the players were recalling things they remembered about playing in the Polo Grounds. Among the players quoted in Arthur Daley's column in the *New York Times* the next day was Carl Furillo, the Dodgers' right fielder: "'I saw the impossible happen here,' said Carl Furillo, 'that was when Willie Mays made that catch on me, whirled in a complete circle and threw out Billy Cox at home plate. It was a play that couldn't happen. But it did.'"

So, six years later a catch and throw made by Willie to cut down a speedy runner remained vivid in another outstanding outfielder's memory as an "impossible" play.

April 17, 1952—Del Ennis

Del Ennis was a very good player for the Philadelphia Phillies and later for the St. Louis Cardinals. He was a key member of the Phillies "Whiz Kids" team of 1950 that won the National League Championship. Ennis was known as a powerful hitter but not as an outstanding fielder. However, as quoted in Robin Roberts' book (with C. Paul Rogers III) titled *The Whiz Kids and the 1950 Pennant*, Eddie Sawyer, the Phillies' manager from 1948 to 1952, said Del Ennis was a good fielder who had good speed and a good arm.

Richie Ashburn was the Phillies' centerfielder during Del's time with the Phils. Ashburn covered a wide range from his center field spot, including into some of Ennis' territory more than occasionally. Ashburn's outstanding ball hawking usually overshadowed his mates in the outfield, including Del Ennis.

By the time of the April 17, 1952, catch Del already had made two amazing catches. On May 30, 1949, in a game at Shibe Park in Philadelphia against the Boston Braves, Phil Masi drove a ball at the left field wall. Frank Yeutter of the *Philadelphia Bulletin* described the catch.

Russ Meyer pitched the 10th and kept things even but it took Del's unbelievable catch against the left field wall to save the game. With Jim Russell on second base, two out, Masi cracked a liner that sailed over Del's head. Del raced to the wall, crashed into it with his shoulder and hip, yet jumped at least two feet and caught the smash in the webbing of his glove. It was one of the greatest catches ever seen in Shibe Park.

Stan Baumgartner of the *Philadelphia Inquirer* added more to Ennis' catch.

Ennis saved the game in the first half of the 10th with one of the greatest catches ever seen here.

... Ennis' catch is one that will long be remembered. Jim Russell was on second with two out when Phil Masi drove a Russ Meyer pitch on a line toward the left field fence. Ennis turned, raced to the stands, turned as he leaped in the air and caught the ball with his gloved hand. As he did so he hit the wood and the ball left his glove. But while still in the air he twisted, caught the ball again and fell to the grass. The fans gave him one of the greatest ovations he has ever received.

The cheers were still ringing in his ears as he came to bat with one out and sent a long drive to right for three bases. It was a magnificent hit.

Andy Seminick drove Ennis in with the winning run on a long fly ball.

Allen Lewis, a sportswriter for the *Philadelphia Inquirer*, submitted this Ennis catch for the "Greatest Catch" section in the September 1949 edition of the *Baseball Digest*. Part of what he wrote follows:

With two out in the tenth the Braves' Jim Russell was on second base when Catcher Phil Masi came to bat. Relief Pitcher Russ Meyer threw and Masi swung. The catch that followed was the greatest catch I ever saw in a major league game.

The ball traveled on a line toward the bleacher wall. The Phils' left fielder, Del Ennis, turned to his right and raced back. None of the 21,933 fans thought he had a chance to make the catch. It seemed the ball would surely hit the fence ten or 12 feet above the ground for a double.

Russell was speeding around third toward the plate with the leading run when Ennis neared the barrier. Del knew he must hit the wall if he were to have any chance to snare the ball—but he kept going. In his last stride he leaped with his right foot outstretched as if to climb the fence. Reaching as far and as high as he could he extended his hands in front of him and, a split second before crashing into the wall, the ball landed in his glove.

The right side of Ennis' body hit the fence with a dull thud and the ball popped out of his hands for a split second. He twisted, caught the ball again and came to earth as pandemonium broke loose in the stands.

Complete strangers shook each other by hand, pounded each other on the back or just stared at each other in wide-eyed amazement. Meyer, the Phils' pitcher, ran half way out to left field to meet Ennis on his way to the dugout and threw his arms around him while other players slapped him on the back in high glee.

Veteran pressbox observers called it the greatest, or one of the greatest catches ever made in Shibe Park. The radio announcer, Byrum Saam, almost had hysterics trying to describe the play.

Allen Lewis went on to predict that "Ennis probably will never be remembered as one of baseball's better fielders."

Although Lewis' prediction was essentially true, at least three times Del Ennis made catches that were startling and great.

Ennis' second great catch was made at Ebbets Field on June 29, 1951, in a 3 to 2 loss to the Brooklyn Dodgers. This time Ennis was a right fielder. Roscoe McGowen of the *New York Times* commented on the Ennis catch: "Two bare-hand catches were made, Del Ennis barely getting Robinson's sixth-inning fly that way and Roy Campanella similarly snaring Hamner's foul pop bunt in the ninth."

The *New York Journal-American*'s Michael Gaven put Ennis' catch in the context of a game with a number of noteworthy defensive plays.

... the crowd of 24,566 was treated to some of the best fielding plays of the season.

Snider and Robinson kept Palica in the game with astounding saves in the fourth, the former leaping for Gran Hamner's long wallop with the bases loaded. Del Ennis took a triple away from Robinson with a barehanded catch and Roy Campanella used nothing but his lunch hook to snare a foul by Hamner. But the hardest hit ball of the night was Peewee Reese's liner, for which Jones leaped in the ninth. It was that kind of night.

Frank Yeutter of the *Philadelphia Evening Bulletin* was particularly taken by the Ennis catch.

> No. 1 among the defenders was Del Ennis, who made what players on both teams acclaimed as the greatest catch they had ever witnessed.
> ... They'll never stop talking about Ennis' catch. There were two out in the sixth. Robinson hit a high liner to right center. Ashburn couldn't get close to it. Nor did it appear that Ennis could.
> But Del ran to the deepest corner, leaped into the air, and made the catch bare handed. Robinson had turned second. When he saw Ennis romping toward the infield, Jack stopped. He couldn't believe the ball had been caught. Nor did many of the 24,556 persons who thronged Ebbets Field. Umpire Al Barlick, who had sprinted to the outfield, raced back with his right arm extended upward, indicating the out.

The *Philadelphia Inquirer*'s Stan Baumgartner called Ennis' catch the best in a game filled with "thrilling plays." The *Philadelphia Daily News*' Grant Doherty wrote: "In the bottom of the sixth, and with two out, Del Ennis came up with the best defensive play in an evening full of fine defensive plays and one that brought the 24,566 Flatbushers in attendance to their feet with mixed cheers and groans of disbelief."

Robin Roberts, the outstanding pitcher with the Phillies, in *The Whiz Kids and the 1950 Pennant*, wrote about this catch. Roberts puts the year at 1950, but the catch was made in 1951.

> During the 1950 season, Jackie Robinson hit a shot to right center like a two iron off me. Del ran over, but when he got to the ball he was off stride. So he reached up and caught the ball barehanded, as easy as could be. He just threw the ball in like it was a routine catch. Jackie couldn't believe it and ran right past first base to right field and yelled at Del, "How did you ever catch that ball?" [241].

But what may have been the greatest of Ennis' catches is the one he made at the Polo Grounds on April 16, 1952. This barehanded grab was made more difficult because the field included a hazard for outfielders that caused Del to instantaneously alter how he had to make the catch.

Jim McCulley of the *New York Daily News* wrote:

> Jansen was lifted for a pinch hitter in this rally, and Spencer mowed down the Phillies in the 10th. Then, with two outs in the home half of the first extra session, Ennis pulled a daylight robbery job on Willie Mays' bid for at least a triple and possibly an inside-the-park homer. When Ennis grabbed Willie's drive to the left field bullpen with his bare hand, Mays was already going into second base.

Joseph M. Sheehan of the *New York Times* told more about Del's catch.

> A spectacular catch by Ennis saved the game for Konstanty in the tenth. Racing full speed with his back to the plate, Del made a bare-handed grab of a 425 drive to the left-field bullpen by Willie Mays.

In the *Philadelphia Bulletin*, Frank Yeutter described the Ennis catch this way:

> Del Ennis made one of the most spectacular catches ever seen in the Polo Grounds to retire Mays in the last half of the tenth.
> Mays hit a ball that very likely would have been an inside-the-park home run, for he is in the same speed class as Richie Ashburn. The ball traveled 425 feet on the fly. Ennis, running all the way to the Phils' bullpen in deep left center, stuck his bare hand aloft at the last split second and nabbed the ball. Even manager Leo Durocher, of the Giants, along with the crowd of 13,697, applauded Ennis.

In *The Whiz Kids and the 1950 Pennant*, Roberts recalled the catch on Mays. Roberts wrote about two outstanding fielding plays Ennis made, one being the catch on Robinson in 1951, and the other on Mays in 1952. Roberts gives the best idea of the extra difficulty Ennis had to cope with to make the catch.

Over the years, Del made some of the greatest catches in the outfield that I have ever seen. In 1952 against the Giants in the Polo Grounds, with the score tied in the bottom of the 10th, Willie Mays clubbed a ball high and deep to left center. It looked like it was going to land close to the 455 foot sign and might be a game-ending inside-the-park home run for the fleet-footed Mays. Del was off at the crack of the bat and was about to reach the ball when he tripped over our bullpen mound, which in the Polo Grounds was on the field of play. As he was going down he reached up the last possible moment and snared the ball barehanded with his right hand [241].

Another teammate of Ennis' was Steve Ridzik, a young pitcher then. More than fifty years later, Ridzik (in an August 2, 2002, conversation with me) spontaneously recalled Ennis' bare-hand catch on Mays and the difficulty Ennis had with the bullpen mound:

SR: They had a bullpen in the old Polo Grounds that was wide open. They had the pitching mounds for the relievers right there on the playing field in left center for the visiting team. The play was ten feet in front of us.

 Del Ennis came back on a dead run and ran right over the top of a pitching mound. This made the catch very tough. The pitching mound was high. As he went down the mound, he almost took a header. As he was heading down the mound he just reached up over his head and grabbed it bare-handed.

JA: His speed coming down probably pushed him further down than he thought he would be.

SR: Absolutely. He was going to try to catch it with his glove. When he came right over the top of the mound, we all commented, "Holy..., he's going to take a header."

Arch Murray of the *New York Post* reported that the Giants' manager Leo Durocher had a comment about Ennis' catch. He wrote:

All the talk was about Del Ennis' circus bare-handed catch of Willie Mays' 400-plus drive in deepest left in the tenth. "He didn't even know where the ball was," snarled Durocher. "He just stuck out his bare hand unconsciously and it stuck there. Willie was past second when he got it and almost surely it would have been an inside-the-park homer. Then there'd never have been another inning."

The Phillies won in eleven innings. The next day the Giants then began a series with the Brooklyn Dodgers, and on that day Willie Mays made what he often considered the best catch he ever made.

April 18, 1952—Willie Mays

The Associated Press' Joe Reichler's article in the *Newark Star-Ledger* told of the catch:

A spectacular catch by centerfielder Willie Mays, one of the most amazing ever witnessed in this park, prevented the Brooks from winning in regulation time. The Dodgers were trailing, 6–5, and had runners on first and second with two out in the second when pinch-hitter Bobby Morgan smashed a whistling liner that appeared headed for the fence in left center. Mays, running at full speed to his right, dove for the ball and speared it while flying through the air. He landed hard and bounced twice before he hit the wall head on.

The inning was the seventh, not the second.

Barney Kremenko of the *New York-Journal American* praised Mays' effort. He wrote:

Willie Mays provided one of the truly great defensive plays when he robbed pinch-hitter Bobby Morgan of an extra base hit with two on and two out in the seventh. It was a sharply hit line drive that started to dip near the fence in left center. It looked impossible to catch. But the Say Hey Kid went after it at full speed, went diving through the air, shot his glove under the ball, tumbled and skidded into the wall. He was bruised on the arm and leg, but managed to hold onto the drive for the third out.

Dick Young of the *New York Daily News* described the catch and told of Willie's effort this way:

In the seventh, Pafko finally got a ball he could swing at—and deposited it in the left field seats. Koslo was petering out. Hodges singled, and Furillo strolled on four serves, and when Bobby Morgan, swinging for Erskine, drove deep to left center on a line, the ball game appeared blown.

But Willie Mays, racing madly toward the wall, grabbed Morgan's blast with a desperation lunge. As the ball hit Willie's glove Willie left his feet. He actually bounced, crashed into the wall on the first hop, and rolled over on his back. But he held the ball—and you should have heard the cheers when, after a full minute, he finally arose from the circle of players from both clubs and trotted in a limp to the dugout.

Gus Steiger of the *New York Daily Mirror* gave another angle.

Without ado, Bobby swung on Koslo's first serve to send a whistling liner to left-center that was curving away from Mays. It didn't appear as if Willie could catch up to the ball but by means of a last-minute dive he snared the flying pellet with body parallel to the ground.

Joe King of the *New York World-Telegram and Sun* recalled Mays' catch and throw of the previous year in his comments about Willie's catch.

Jackie Robinson, Dodgers second baseman, stated Mays had made the most amazing catch he had ever seen.

The Giants' centerfielder "did it again" for the Dodgers. After his fantastic whirling throw to home against Brooklyn in the Polo Grounds last summer, Chuck Dressen and others of the Flock insisted Willie couldn't "do it again."

But his catch of Bob Morgan's pinch-hit liner in Ebbets Field yesterday was a repeat order of extraordinary baseball. The drive was a whistler into the left-center alley, heading just to the right of the 351-foot marker.

It did not seem possible the racing Mays could get to it, until he threw himself in a dive tackle at the ball and held it. He lay there, and the Giants thought that another of their stars had been injured. Leo Durocher never ran faster, to reach Mays.

Willie had lost his breath and bruised his right side. He received an ovation when he got up and walked groggily to the dugout.

Durocher probably had thoughts of another truly great talent he managed, Dodger centerfielder Pete Reiser, lying at the base of the outfield wall after colliding with it while going at top speed. Leo knew that Reiser's runs into the concrete played a major role in undermining his prodigious gifts for baseball. Seeing Mays on the ground at the base of the wall in Ebbets Field must have caused a chill in Leo's mind and the thought, "Please, not again."

Elsewhere in the *Daily News'* sports section of April 19, 1952, Dana Mozley wrote about the catch Willie had made. Under the title "Mays' Catch Greatest, Dodgers, Giants Agree," Mozley wrote:

"The greatest catch I ever saw in my life," Pee Wee Reese said of the diving, sliding grab of the sinking liner near the left center wall. He came up with it, I know that. There's no argument. It was in his glove when he turned over, and Thompson went over and picked it out."

Brooklyn Coach Jake Pitler said: "I just couldn't see Mays reaching the ball. I've never seen a catch like it." Said Leo Durocher: "Great. Great. The greatest." Said Morgan: "I guess he must have caught it. You could have knocked me over with a feather when the ump waved me out. I was going for three for sure when I saw him on the ground."

It took Mays himself, to tell how unbelievable the catch was. "You know something," he said while swigging a Coke in the dressing room, "I didn't think I had a chance at all to get it. It was sinking fast and seemed to be curving away. But I stayed with it and got it on the dive with both hands together. Slid along the ground and got shaken up, that's all. Little bruise here on my right side."

The "Thompson" Pee Wee Reese referred to was Henry Thompson, who was playing left field for the Giants in the game.

The *New York Herald Tribune*'s Red Smith called Mays' catch "one of the finest catches ever made at Ebbets Field."

In the *Long Island Daily Press*, Jack Lang quoted Jackie Robinson.

Jackie Robinson hailed Willie Mays' catch of Bobby Morgan's drive in the seventh as "the greatest I ever saw. Never in my life did I see a greater one. I don't care what team he's with, that was the greatest I ever saw."

More than fifty years later, in a conversation with me, Bobby Morgan vividly recalled Willie's catch on him. Bobby Morgan said he hit a "blue darter, a screamer all the way to the fence" for which "Willie dove headlong, laid out flat to catch. Willie caught the ball as I was rounding second."

Because he made so many dazzling catches, Willie Mays has been asked over and over which was his best. When Mays played he often replied that he didn't compare the catches, he just caught them. Despite this statement, Willie has mentioned several catches that he recalls for different reasons, The one which he has most consistently rated as his best is the 1952 catch on Bobby Morgan's low, sinking liner in Ebbets Field. In his book *Nice Guys Finish First*, Monte Irvin says Mays has cited the catch on Bobby Morgan as his best.

So, in the span of his first 124 major league games, Willie Mays made three of the greatest defensive plays in the history of baseball, and did so before his twenty-first birthday. A month after the catch on Bobby Morgan, Willie Mays was inducted into the Army and would miss the rest of the 1952 baseball season and all of the 1953 season.

October 4, 1952—Duke Snider

By the time Duke Snider made his October 5, 1952, catch in the World Series against the Yankees, he already had established himself as an outstanding outfielder.

Although now a Hall of Famer, during the late '40s and early '50s Snider's star was often eclipsed by the other centerfielders in New York while he played for the Brooklyn Dodgers. When Snider began playing for the Dodgers in 1947, Joe DiMaggio, despite nagging foot and leg injuries, still was regarded as the premier centerfielder in baseball. DiMaggio retired after the 1951 season, which was the season in which rookies Mickey Mantle of the Yankees and Willie Mays of the Giants were beginning to capture the headlines in New York. Because of the spectacular nature of their abilities, both Mantle and Mays would go on to be more renowned across time than Duke.

Snider's star on defense also was often eclipsed by players on his own team. Catcher Roy Campanella, first baseman Gil Hodges, second baseman Jackie Robinson, shortstop Pee Wee Reese, third baseman Billy Cox, and right fielder Carl Furillo were all considered among the best ever to play at their positions.

When Duke was healthy and in his prime, his fielding was routinely explosive and exciting in ways which DiMaggio's was not, Mantle's was not, and Mays' was not. He was a swift runner. As a young player in the Dodger system, he was timed at 6.7 seconds in the 60-yard dash in his baseball uniform and on a cinder track. To give an idea of how quick that time is, consider that the world's record for the indoor 60-yard dash in 1944 was 6.1, a time set in 1938 by Columbia University sprinter Ben Johnson.

The 6-foot, one-half inch tall Snider was a superior leaper. One of the Dodgers' scouts, Tom Downey, wrote that the prospect Snider had "steel springs in his legs." In addition to his speed and leaping ability, Snider made difficult catches look easy.

Snider's arm was one of baseball's strongest. Cal McLish, later to become a solid pitcher for the Indians and the White Sox, was a young prospect in the Brooklyn Dodger system when Snider also was a young player. In 1994, almost fifty years after McLish began in the Dodger system, he was interviewed by Larry Moffi for the book *This Side of Cooperstown: An Oral History of Major League Baseball in the 1950s*. Among other things he talked about was watching pre-game throwing by his teammates: "Years ago we used to stay out and watch infield, because you didn't want to miss watching those guys throw, Snider, Furillo ... especially Furillo. Now nobody watches" (220).

Snider became skilled at making catches by vaulting up walls. He was not alone in doing this. Other players, including Willie Mays, also learned to use the walls in Ebbets Field to get airborne. Snider had more opportunities over the years than most other players, and was a frequent high flyer at Ebbets Field, which had smaller outfield dimensions than nearly all other major league parks.

Besides the frequency of his climbs at Ebbets Field, Snider leapt up almost any wall he could get his cleats into. He climbed up concrete, wood, and screens, and did so from early in his career. At Pittsburgh on June 25, 1949, Duke made a leaping, fence-climbing grab of a ball hit by Eddie Bockman of the Pirates. In the *New York Times* Roscoe McGowen wrote: "Snider made a spectacular leaping catch against the left-center barrier of Bockman's drive, crashed into the fence and dropped the ball, although almost catching it again in his bare hand before it hit the ground."

How high Snider got was indicated by Les Biederman's "The Scoreboard" column in the *Pittsburgh Press* the day after the game, which the Dodgers won 17 to 10.

> Eddie Bockman almost put across the 10th homer, which would have tied the record in the ninth inning. Duke Snider made a miraculous leaping catch of his drive on top of the left-center screen, but the ball dropped back for a double. It appeared that Snider knocked the ball out of the bullpen and when he fell, his glove was suspended on top of the fence.

At the time Snider made his leap, the screen fence was twelve feet high at that point in left center. Snider's glove was over the top of the screen, which means that the top of Duke's glove probably was 150 inches above the ground. This further means that his feet were about 50 inches off the ground.

Snider's fondness for the screen in Pittsburgh led to a little humor during an August 1, 1951, game. The *New York Times*' Roscoe McGowen described it this way: "Duke Snider added a comedy touch to Kiner's home run by climbing the screen as if to catch the ball as it went over—and then getting his spikes caught and requiring help from Pafko to get down again."

Snider's great anticipation and his speed made him particularly adept at going back for long balls and coming in to make shoestring or diving and rolling plays. An example of how well he could come in occurred on August 18, 1948, when the Dodgers' Rex Barney threw a one-hitter against the Philadelphia Phillies. Early in the game, before there was a hit off Barney, Snider made a catch Roscoe McGowen of the *New York Times* described this way:

> [The early innings] saw gilt-edged support for Rex, the Brooks not only playing errorless ball but coming up with some brilliant plays, notably Snider's great diving catch of Granny Hamner's fly to short center when the potential tying run was on second with two out. Duke dived and caught the ball just off the grass, rolling over and coming up with it still in his glove.

Rex Barney, in Peter Golenbock's *Bums*, called Snider's catch the "damnedest catch I've ever seen in my life, sliding on his belly and coming up with the ball" (217).

In the seventh inning, Snider barely missed catching another looping ball, this time off the bat of Ralph Caballero. It was the first and only hit off Barney that day. Despite Snider's failed attempt to catch the ball Caballero hit, Barney bested the Phillies' young pitcher, Robin Roberts, in a 1 to 0 game.

On May 18, 1949, Snider made another diving, rolling catch the *New York Times'* Dodgers writer, Roscoe McGowen, called "remarkable." Over his career Snider was to make many of these sprinting in, and sometimes diving and rolling, catches that McGowen called "Snider Specials." These remarkable gymnastics on the baseball field were crowd-pleasers.

In 1949 Snider went on to make two outstanding catches to rob Joe DiMaggio of hits in the last game of the World Series, which the New York Yankees won. On DiMaggio, Snider made a shoestring catch, and a leaping catch at the center field wall at Ebbets Field. Photographers at the game caught both catches. Duke's leaping catch shows him in the air and in descent after catching the ball.

Arthur Daley, writing in the *New York Times* the day after the Yankees won the 1949 World Series, said of Duke's fielding:

> DiMadge would have had another hit yesterday if Duke Snider hadn't made a circus catch of his screaming liner in the third, stabbing the ball at the grass top level and snaring it in the webbing of his glove. A few innings later the Duke performed an even more outrageous bit of grand larceny on Tommy Henrich with a somersaulting capture of a rifle shot to right center. It was robbery in broad daylight, too.
>
> Make no mistake about the fact that the Duke will become one of the game's greatest stars some day.

Snider's spectacular fielding continued through the 1950s. In the next-to-last game of the 1950 season against Philadelphia at Ebbets Field, Snider made another clutch catch. The Dodgers had to win this game to be in position to play the Phillies in the last game of the season to force a playoff with the Phils for the National League crown. Roscoe McGowen of the *Times* described Snider's catch of a scorching liner hit by Willie Jones to the wall in right center field, a catch he called Duke's greatest of the year: "But Snider, getting a great jump on the ball, raced across from left-center, leaped in the air at the last split second and caught it. Duke's momentum carried him to the right-center concrete, which he half climbed before he could stop."

The *New York Daily Mirror*'s Gus Steiger said, "Snider brought the crowd to its feet by a spectacular one-hand catch at full speed of Jones' long smash almost to the centerfield wall to start the ninth."

The *Philadelphia Inquirer*'s John Webster, after writing about Roy Campanella's 400-plus-foot, three-run homer into the center field seats in the bottom of the eighth inning, also wrote of Snider's catch.

> With the lights flashing on as the ninth began, Willie Jones started the last stand. Willie, called Puddin' Head, chose a Palica fast ball—and drove it to right-center, almost the distance

of Campanella's wallop. But Snider, streaking to his left, robbed Jones with a madcap, one-hand catch, right at the boards.

Brooklyn rooters rocked the stands in appreciation. One young Flatbush citizen climbed out of a right-field box, ran all the way out to Snider's beat to congratulate him. A bluecoat, right out of a Keystone comedy, shooed the stripling off the playing field.

The Dodgers defeated the Phillies 7 to 3. The next day in Philadelphia, they lost a thrilling game, which gave the Phils the National League title.

Snider's greatest catch of the 1952 season was the one he made in the World Series against the Yankees in a fourth-game 2 to 0 loss. This catch was somewhat unusual in that Snider ran to the ball and went skyward before he got to the fence, almost like an infielder going up for a liner over his head. Bill Corum of the *New York Journal-American* best described the catch.

> Even though he could not hit Reynolds, either, as few could on a glorious Autumn afternoon that was made for sport, Duke Snider became the Duke of Flatbush in a losing cause when he made one of the most amazing catches ever seen over his head and in his gloved hand with a terrific despairing leap of a high drive off Yogi Berra's bat that followed Mize's game-winning blast.

Later in the article Corum returned to Snider's catch.

> Berra followed with a blast that looked like a sure triple. It didn't look humanly possible that Snider could overtake the high and terrific blast.
>
> But the Duke thought otherwise. At approximately the 407 mark Snider leaped, it looked like five feet in the air, stuck up his gloved hand just as the ball was about to sail over his head and came down with it.
>
> Amazing and sensational and easily the fielding play of the series to date it was.

Roscoe McGowen of the *New York Times* noted:

> The Duke was getting compliments from all sides on the extraordinary leaping catch he made on Yogi Berra's fifth inning blast. Snider caught the ball in front of the auxiliary score board just beneath the right center field bleachers, going down and making a back somersault before coming up with the ball.

McGowen's colleague at the *Times*, Arthur Daley, called Snider's effort "an unbelievable circus catch."

Tommy Holmes of the *Brooklyn Eagle* wrote:

> And let's not forget Edwin, the Duke of Snider. On Saturday, Snider sailed into the wide blue yonder to rob Yogi Berra after Mize's ruinous blast against Black. On Sunday, Berra hit one again after Mize's homer and Snider caught it after a long, hard gallop. Because of Saturday's catch, Snider's Sunday effort went practically unnoticed, yet it would have been the stick-out play of many a ball game. That Dodger infield was pretty slick too and left the Yankees grumbling about examining Billy Cox's glove for concealed magnets.

After earlier in his column calling Snider's catch on Berra's ball "an outrageously implausible catch," Red Smith of the *New York Herald Tribune* told of Mize's home run, and of Snider's catch.

> Snider ran a somewhat lesser distance, turned his back to the bleachers, shot skyward like a Roman candle. Timing his jump with incomparable precision, he got his glove on the ball at the very peak of his leap, hung up there breathing deeply of the rarified ozone, then crashed to earth, clutching the ball.

Three years later, in the first game of the 1955 World Series, the Yankees' Joe Collins hit a long home run that Snider pursued to the right center field fence. Snider showed his leaping ability in his attempt to make the catch. In his September 30, 1955, *New York Herald Tribune* column, Red Smith again gave an idea of Snider's vertical jump: "Duke Snider chased it, leaped and hung himself high on the auxiliary scoreboard—where the number on his shirt looked like four runs for the Dodgers—but caught only vertigo at that height."

Incidentally, in game four of the 1955 World Series, Snider and several other Dodger fielders made defensive plays that that enabled reliever Clem Labine to finish out a Brooklyn win to tie the series at two games apiece. Snider's contribution in the eighth inning led Bob Considine, whose article was in the *Buffalo Courier-Express*, to write:

> Snider was especially something to behold in the eighth. He sped like a deer across the grass in left center to pull in Martin's baleful liner with one paw, for the second out in the inning. And he ended the chapter by coming in like a bolt of lightning to make a stooping "as well as stupefying" catch off Bill Skowron's low poke.

As great as Snider's 1952 catch on Yogi Berra was, it was overshadowed by Yankee second baseman Billy Martin's dramatic, Series-saving catch on Jackie Robinson's infield pop fly in the seventh inning of the seventh game, which was played at Brooklyn's Ebbets Field. Left-hander Bob Kuzava of the Yankees came into the game with one out in the seventh, the bases full of Dodgers, and the Yankees holding a 4 to 2 lead. Kuzava got Duke Snider to hit a pop fly for the second out. The dangerous, clutch-hitting Jackie Robinson then hit a towering fly ball on the first-base side of the infield, about sixty-five feet off home plate. The Yankee players who ordinarily would have easily camped under the ball to make the catch, catcher Yogi Berra and first baseman Joe Collins, or even Kuzava the pitcher, seemed to have feet of lead and their mental faculties clouded to the fact that no one was going to go after Robinson's pop. Billy Martin, from his second-base position, recognized that his teammates were inert and were not going to make the catch. As the ball was sinking ever closer to the ground, he raced madly in, and at the last instant caught the ball just before it could hit the turf. It was a great catch, one which second basemen rarely make, and it saved the game.

Snider's performance in the 1952

Duke Snider descends after snaring Yogi Berra's bid for extra bases in the fourth game of the 1952 World Series (© Bettmann/CORBIS).

World Series was outstanding. In addition to the fielding gems, he batted .345 and had four homers and eight runs batted in. Snider's 1952 Series was recalled by the *New York Daily News'* Dick Young almost a year later after Duke had a wonderful catch in a September 20, 1953, game against the Phillies. By this time in the season the Dodgers were waiting to play the Yankees again in the World Series. Young wrote:

> Casey Stengel's espionage corps, which already has a high regard for Duke Snider's talents, must be growing to think of him as the world's greatest ball player— greater even than Mickey Mantle, perish the thought. He beat their brains out in the last Series. Then, when they came a-scouting Saturday, he banged two homers. Now, in yesterday's opener, they saw the other side of his brilliant ability—a game-saving circus stab in the final frame.
> Ben Wade, trying to wrap up his fine five-frame relief job, had issued a walk to start the ninth. One out later, Earl Torgeson, who had blasted Bob Milliken for a thee-run homer in the third, drove deep toward the left-center corner. It seemed certain that Kazanski would score the knotting run on the blast and that Torgy would wind up on third, with the possible winning marker. But Snider, who had been fading the south-swinger toward right, streaked back obliquely, shot into the clouds and one-handed the drive while running on air.

In the seventh game of the 1952 World Series, Billy Martin's dramatic last-second grab of Jackie Robinson's high pop fly that other, closer and better-positioned Yankee fielders inexplicably had not moved to catch, saved the game for the Yankees.

1953—Jimmy Piersall

In 1953 Jimmy Piersall had a fielding year which was brilliant from start to finish. He had a number of catches which veteran observers called the greatest they had ever seen.

Piersall's talent as an outfielder was apparent in the minors, but was not fully utilized by the Red Sox until 1953. His relatively slow ascent up the Red Sox ladder was addressed by Roger Birtwell of the *Boston Daily Globe* in a July 21, 1953, article.

> Why has it taken so long for Piersall's talent to be recognized? After all, this is his sixth year in the Red Sox organization.
>
> Answer: Our society seems to team up on anyone—particularly a very young person—whose talent borders on genius. It happens in all fields of endeavor, and it is mediocrity's protective device.
>
> There were those who, from the first time they saw him, appreciated Piersall. His first manager, Mike Ryba—at Scranton in 1948—tells me he had to battle with the Red Sox front office to be allowed to use him. The office wanted to ship him down to the deep bushes. Ryba used him—and the 18-year-old boy starred.
>
> The next year, around Memorial Day, Ryba was promoted to the managership of Louisville. Mike reports he found Piersall as bench-warmer there. Again Mike used him and again he starred.
>
> When Piersall was up with the Red Sox last year, Bobo Newsome, who'd played on the same team with Piersall at Birmingham, said Piersall was a better fielder than Joe DiMaggio or anybody Bobo had ever seen. But everyone seemed to think, "O, that's just Bobo." This reporter almost immediately tabbed Piersall as an outfielding genius, and thought he was the best thing which happened to baseball in a long time. But folks apparently thought this reporter was daffy—or else just creating a story.

In 1953, Jimmy Piersall was the Boston Red Sox' right fielder. The year before, in 1952, he played 30 games at shortstop, one game at third base, and twenty-two games in the outfield. For Piersall, playing in the infield was a very trying experience. He had been a highly successful outfielder since he was a kid, and his struggle to adapt to a new set of defensive demands played a role in the nervous breakdown he had in the 1952 season.

Jimmy Piersall's struggles to keep his sanity during 1952 was the subject of his book *Fear Strikes Out*. After successfully overcoming that struggle, Piersall emerged in 1953 to be the fielding talent Roger Birtwell thought he was. In 1953 Piersall had to endure a particularly high level of verbal abuse because of his psychological troubles of the year before. Two days after Piersall had had a particularly good game in Cleveland on July 19, 1953, Gerry Hern of the *Boston Post* had seen and heard enough of the abuse directed at Piersall. Under the title "Frick Should Halt Inhuman Attacks On Jimmy Piersall," Hern blasted the tormentors, especially the players in the opposing teams' bullpen near where Piersall played in the outfield. As the title of his article indicates, Gerry Hern wanted Commissioner Ford Frick to take action to halt the cruel taunting.

The taunting, as bad as it was, did not stop Piersall from having a sensational season as a fielder.

May 9, 1953

On Friday night, May 8, Jimmy Piersall made a terrific catch on a ball hit by Yankees pitcher Johnny Sain. Arthur Sampson of the *Boston Herald* described it this way:

> Jimmy Piersall treated the crowd to one of his spectacular going back one handers when he raced to the right field fence to rob Sain of an extra base hit in the eighth.... This spectacular effort, a patented Piersall maneuver, sent the crowd wild with joy.... Jimmy was cheered all the way back to the dugout at the end of the inning.

Elsewhere in the *Herald*, Will Cloney quoted Boston manager Lou Boudreau on Piersall's catch on Sain.

"...And that catch by Piersall on Sain in the eighth. I've never seen a ball hit harder in that direction by a right-hander.

"I never thought Piersall had a chance on that one. He has the wonderful faculty of being able to run back full speed and still keep his eye on the ball all the time."

Piersall joked, "My wife was watching on television so I had to make it look good for her."

The *Boston Daily Globe*'s Hy Hurwitz quoted Piersall about the catch on Sain: "That's one I didn't know if I had all the way. I had my doubts when I started."

The *Boston Evening Globe*'s Bob Holbrook quoted Boston's winning pitcher Skinny Brown's comments on Piersall.

When the name Piersall was mentioned he practically glowed.

"Piersall's a sweetheart out there," he declared. "You never have to worry about anything with Jim playing. Listen, I first played with Piersall at Scranton when I originally was with the Red Sox organization. He was playing centerfield for Scranton and I've seen him go to the right and left field lines to take fly balls the other fielders couldn't handle. He's great, that's all."

Piersall, of course electrified the 33,055 present last night with a brilliant running catch off the bat of Johnny Sain, the losing pitcher.

On the next day, May 9, 1953, Piersall made an even better catch on a ball hit by Mickey Mantle. In describing the Red Sox' 6–4 loss to the Yankees at Fenway Park, Bob Holbrook of the *Boston Sunday Globe* included a description of Piersall's catch.

Jim Piersall thrilled the crowd with his second tremendous catch in as many games.

Friday night he brought the crowd to its feet with a pulsating grab off Johnny Sain. Yesterday, he equaled it with an over-the-shoulder catch on Mickey Mantle's tremendous drive into center field.

There were two out and two on base when Mantle hit one of his patented high skiers. Piersall broke at the crack of the bat and sped diagonally to the left edge of the bullpen where it says 420 feet.

He reached up and snared it back-handed.

The Yankees were stunned. They couldn't believe it and manager Casey Stengel kept pointing to the spot where the larceny was committed.

Elsewhere on that *Globe* sports page Roger Birtwell presented "A few comments on Piersall's catch":

SPORTSWRITER, right after catch: "That wasn't in right field. That was in center."

SECOND SPORTSWRITER: "Center, your grandmother. It was BACK of center."

LOU BOUDREAU: "I never thought he had a chance."

CASEY STENGEL: "That wasn't no catch where a fellow runs along the fence and sticks out his hands and stabs it. It was BY him.... He turns his tail to the plate and outruns the ball. He catches up with it."

PIERSALL: "Tom Umphlett helped me. He yelled to me that I had room. That helped a lot. It relaxes you."

UMPHLETT: "I saw I couldn't get it. So I yelled 'Take it.' Then I yelled 'Plenty of room.'"

PIERSALL: "It's no good when you don't win."

More on Piersall:

STENGEL, making out his lineup: "M-m-m-m, let's see.... I don't need anybody to hit to right. Nobody's goin' to third on that guy anyway."

SAM LEVY, *Milwaukee Journal* baseball writer for 30-odd years: "The best catch I ever saw was made in a game between the Milwaukee Brewers and Louisville. Taft Wright was playing left field for Louisville and Piersall was playing center. One of our fellows hit one to the left field corner. Piersall ran right by Wright and caught it."

The *Boston Sunday Herald* again had its two writers covering the game and both reported on Piersall's catch on the Mantle ball. Arthur Sampson reported on the game, and Will Cloney gave quotes and other thoughts about the game. Sampson's column included:

Jimmy Piersall, who seldom goes through a game without making a hair-raising catch or throw, came up with one of his best grabs when he robbed Mickey Mantle of a triple and two Yank runs in the fifth inning.

With two out and two runners on base, the powerful Mantle, who had smashed his fifth home run of the season over the left-field wall in the third, cracked a soaring drive to right-center off a Bill Werle pitch. It seemed headed for the corner of the Red Sox bullpen.

It didn't seem possible Piersall could come close to this one, even though he had been grabbing drives all over the spacious right-field territory all day.

But it appears that no drive inside the park escapes Piersall these days. He turned his back on this wallop and raced for the deepest corner of the field, and just as the flying ball passed over his head he snared it back handed.

The startled fans could hardly believe their eyes. When they realized what had happened they stood and cheered Piersall to the echo as he raced to the dugout, a broad smile on his face. It was the same kind of sustained cheer that used to greet grandslam homers by Ted Williams, Vern Stephens, and Bobby Doerr.

"Yes, I guess we're going to have to thrill the fans with our fielding plays rather than our home runs," said Lou Boudreau after the game.

Under the main title "Piersall's Robbery on Mantle's Drive Biggest Thrill," Will Cloney began his column with:

The biggest thrill for the 26,065 spectators at Fenway Park yesterday was Jimmy "Catch-a-Game" Piersall's cinder-path robbery against Mickey Mantle in the fifth inning. But while the crowd was still filing out, Piersall himself was muttering in the dressing room, "Gee, I wish we could have beat those guys. I'd rather beat this club than any other team in the league."

Manager Lou Boudreau, too, was disappointed at the loss, but he thought Piersall's catch was tremendous. "That was even better than the one he made Friday night," said Lou. "It's unbelievable that he can make catches like that."

Piersall wasn't particularly impressed with his own fielding. "I kind of thought the one Friday night was better," said Jim. "I wasn't sure I had that one. What do I think about when I'm trying to make a catch? Just about how close the fence is, that's all. When Tom Umphlett told me I was clear of the wall, I didn't worry.

"You can't catch a ball unless you're relaxed. We protect each other when the ball gets close to the fence. I ran past the center-field corner, didn't I? The ball would have been in the stands if it had been a little more to right field."

In the Yankee locker-room, Mantle slowly unwrapped the Ace bandage he wears around his gimpy right knee. Somebody asked him about Piersall's theft and Mickey answered, "Shucks, Bauer would have been camped under the ball."

Bauer didn't think so, though. "That boy really goes and gets them," said Hank. "He comes up with some awfully good plays."

The *Boston Post*'s Gerry Moore gave a verbal picture of where the Mantle drive went.

Mickey Mantle, who had blasted his fifth homer of the year half way up the left field light tower his previous time at bat, again laid his right-handed power to a Lefty Bill Werle fast ball and sent it sailing towards the 420-foot marker on the centre field wall where the dirt triangular corner is formed by the centre field bleacher wall and Red Sox bullpen barrier.

Piersall, playing a medium right field for Mantle swinging right-handed, was off and running again only as he can. He never stopped until he sped up the slight incline in the aforementioned dirt corner, stuck his glove back handed again, and securely nestled the ball, more than 400 feet from its starting point.

While Stengel and the entire Yankee bench gave gestures of their disbelief, Mantle watched Piersall transfixed all the while he was trotting to his own centre field position and Jimmy went on in to receive five different ovations.

The first was a standing salvo that lasted the whole time Piersall ran into the dugout. Next came when he moved out to the on-deck circle. Another burst accompanied his going to bat. They even cheered when he flied out and the final one came when he resumed his right field position for the next inning.

Long-time Red Sox radio and television play-by play man Curt Gowdy, in his 1993 book (with John Powers) *Seasons to Remember*, wrote about the catch on Mantle. Piersall made three of the five greatest catches Gowdy saw during his long career as a broadcaster, and the one on Mantle was the best. He quoted Casey Stengel as saying it was the greatest catch he ever saw.

In the *New York Daily Mirror*, Ben Epstein called Piersall "a sensational outfielder by any standard," went on to describe the catch on Mantle: "With two away, and two on, Mickey smashed to deep center. Right fielder Jim, who roams all over the outfield and parts of the infield, just—well, sprinted away and caught it—touchdown fashion."

In his 1964 book *The Quality of Courage*, Mickey Mantle wrote a chapter on Piersall having overcome serious, and public, mental problems in 1952. Mantle gave his assessment of Piersall as a fielder and told about the great catch Piersall made on him.

> ... he made some of the greatest catches any outfielder ever made anywhere. I remember one he made off me. The day before he had robbed the Yankees of a victory by turning a home run into an out with a great catch. This day I was batting right-handed and I pushed a ball deep to right center in Fenway Park, way back toward the bullpen. I thought it was a homer or, if it didn't reach the fence, a sure triple. But Piersall went over and back to the bullpen, jumped, balanced himself on his right hand and at the same time reached up with his glove hand and caught the ball. I kicked about a ton of dirt out of the infield, and up in the press box one of the New York sportswriters wrote, "In 27 years of covering baseball, I never saw a catch like that."
>
> He made plays like that all year long—and all through his career. I haven't seen Willie Mays in too many ball games because he's in the other league, but if Willie is a better outfielder than Piersall he must be just about the greatest ever [120–121].

In the May 11, 1953, *New York Times*, Louis Effrat wrote of the catch on Mantle: "Boudreau said Piersall's catch of Mantle's drive in front of the bullpen yesterday was the greatest he had ever seen. 'I still get goose pimples when I think about it,'" Lou said.

In his May 20, 1953, article in *The Sporting News* about Piersall, Al Hirshberg stated his high opinion of the catch on Mantle's long ball and quoted Phil Rizzuto.

> Piersall ... continues to be the talk of the club and the league. He makes at least one sensational catch a game, and about every three days he makes an "impossible" one. The great granddaddy of all great catches, however, was made by the young right fielder, May 9, and it robbed Mickey Mantle of a triple in the second game of the Yankees series.
>
> In the fifth inning, Mantle hit a screaming liner towards right-center field. Piersall took only one look at the ball and then turned and, back to the plate, ran over to where he figured it would come down. At one point in his chase, the ball appeared actually to be ahead of him.
>
> It headed for one corner of the bullpen, which turns on a sharp angle in towards the bleacher fence. When he arrived at that point, Piersall, his bare hand apparently on the rail of the bullpen, practically slid along, frantically reaching up with his gloved hand at the same time. When the ball landed in his glove, everyone in the place went wild.
>
> Phil Rizzuto, who watched Joe DiMaggio at close quarters for years, later called it "the greatest catch I've ever seen in my life." Both Boudreau and Manager Casey Stengel of the Yanks raved about the play and one of the veteran New York writers soberly remarked, "That Piersall is the greatest outfielder who ever lived."

July 19, 1953

In the ninth inning of the second game of a doubleheader between the Red Sox and the Cleveland Indians the Indians were mounting a comeback. Jimmy Piersall made two outstanding plays in a tense game. After listing six "exploits" of other Red Sox players, Bob Holbrook of the *Boston Daily Globe* went on about Piersall.

> But none of these things compares with the defensive show Piersall put on in the ninth inning of the nightcap when the Indians continued to threaten and easily could have won the game except for Sunny Jim.
> Piersall accomplished all three outs, turning a loft by Al Rosen into a double play and finally snatching a rifle shot off pinch-hitter Bob Lemon to end the game.
> The 34,796 who witnessed this show were transfixed by the kid from Waterbury. So good was he in the ninth that as soon as the game ended manager Lou Boudreau and every member of the team rushed to shake his hand.
> His feats led former umpire Red Jones to say—"Piersall could play on my team even if he hit into a triple play every time at bat."

Later, in another column, Holbrook quoted Lou Boudreau about the ninth inning Piersall had: "Boudreau paid high tribute to Piersall.... He went to the kid and said, 'That's the greatest inning I've ever seen in baseball from one player.'"

Arthur Sampson of the *Boston Herald* described the catches this way:

> Rosen, instead of pulling a fly toward the distant left field barrier, smashed a sinking liner to right. This drive seemed like a sure base hit when it left the bat. But Piersall, rushing in like a roaring tiger, snared the ball off the top of the grass and without breaking stride, fired a bullet-like strike to Dick Gernert at first which doubled up Westlake by an eyelash.
> ...
> The first batter to face him [Kinder] was Bob Lemon, a pinch hitter. Lemon pulled the second pitch on a line toward the low right field wall near the foul line. The drive seemed certain to either hit the wall for a double or scale it for a homer. Piersall again charged over the sod like a wild bull on a rampage, however, disregarding a sign on the wall where the ball was about to hit which read, "Cleveland values your life, be careful," Jim leaped and snared this drive in his extended glove.

Sampson quoted Cleveland manager Al Lopez: "After the game, a sad Al Lopez said, 'I've never seen a right fielder influence the result of a game as much as Piersall did today. He played the greatest game of short right field I've ever seen.'"

The Cleveland papers of July 20 also paid tribute to Piersall's fielding of the day before. The *Cleveland Plain Dealer's* Chuck Heaton wrote a column basically about Piersall.

> While vaulting into third place in the American League with yesterday's stadium sweep, the Red Sox got some sharp pitching and several timely home runs, but a bubbling Lou Boudreau could only think of Jim Piersall's game-saving outfielding in the ninth inning of the second game.
> "You really saw something today didn't you?" the Red Sox manager exclaimed in the dressing room. "That guy is the best, absolutely the best.
> "He can come in or go back and grab the ball anywhere. That Billy Goodman can move around, but he's chasing him off those pop flies half the time."

Under a section titled "Indian Items" in the *Cleveland Press*, an uncredited writer gave another slant on Piersall's achievements on the 19th.

> Old Indians and new Indians agreed unanimously that Jim Piersall of the Red Sox gave the greatest outfielding performance in yesterday's second game that they have ever seen.

"No wonder Casey Stengel says he plays second base and right field at the same time," observed Bob Lemon, who was robbed of a hit by Piersall in the ninth.

The spirited Piersall, fighting back from a nervous breakdown last year, had seven putouts. Not one of them was easy, and the two most valuable and difficult he saved until the ninth when the Indians threatened to rally and win.

"How can you get a base hit off him?" asks Bobby Avila. "He play close and catch line drives. He go back so fast he catch long flies. I never see such a man."

Under the title "Piersall Gets Tribe's Vote for 'Greatest,'" the uncredited writer for the *Cleveland News* added quotes from others seconding the superlative defensive play by Piersall.

Before Sunday's doubleheader between the Indians and the Red Sox Jim Piersall ran past the Tribe bench and hollered: "Dig them crazy Indians."

There were several retorts including, "Come over here Jimmy and let us take the birdie off your head."

But, after the doubleheader the Indians had a different slant of the Red Sox right fielder. Their unanimous opinion, from the rawest rookie to Manager Al Lopez was:

"The greatest outfielder in the game."

Several of them even went further. They insisted, "He's the greatest outfielder who ever lived."

Said Joe Tipton, for one, "They talk about Joe DiMaggio having been so great. This kid Piersall is better. He's the best I ever saw."

Larry Doby, himself considered tops as an outfielder, said, "He's the greatest. Never saw anybody better. He may be crazy but not in the outfield."

Here's what Piersall did, Sunday. He made two fine plays in the first game, which the Indians lost 2–0. He stole the second game from the Tribe all by himself, 7–5. He made a couple of tough catches early in the game but in the late innings he made several "impossible" ones almost seem routine.

Bill McKechnie, the gray-haired Red Sox coach who has been around the majors longer than he cares to disclose, said, "Maybe now folks will believe me when I tell them there never was a better fielder than this boy. Today's performance wasn't just a spasmodic thing. He makes these catches game after game. I don't know what it is, probably a special instinct.

"You say to yourself, 'Now I've seen everything.' Tomorrow he'll show you something greater."

Reporters have been asked by the Red Sox brass "to take it easy" on Piersall because of questions at the mental breakdown he suffered last season, after which he had to be institutionalized for a short period.

But after Sunday's show an interview was necessary. Said the irrepressible outfielder, "See, they take pictures of the guy who hits the home run (George Kell, in this instance). But they don't take pictures of the guys who catch the ball." It was true. The photographers were ignoring Piersall.

When some of the Boston writers asked Lopez about Piersall he said, "You don't have to tell me about him. I saw him as a center fielder in the American Association. I told you last year he was great. Remember, I told you that if the Red Sox ever wanted to give up on him, we'd take him?"

Lopez had one consolation. The Yankees, who come to town Tuesday night, have no Piersall.

Neither do the Indians.

In his July 21, 1953, column about the Red Sox getting ready to begin a series in Chicago with the White Sox, Gerry Moore of the *Boston Post* also told of pitcher Hal "Skinny" Brown's view on Piersall's fielding prowess.

"Every pitcher on our club should be grateful to Jimmy Piersall," observed Skinny Brown. "He is a positive marvel, the best I ever saw and just possibly the greatest of all times. I played with him at Scranton his first year out of high school in 1948 and we called him "Bucket." Playing center field, he used to go behind the right and left fielders to catch balls they couldn't reach."

August 15 and 16, 1953

Jim Piersall's fielding feats in August were against the Washington Senators in Boston. On consecutive days he robbed Mickey Vernon, at the time the leading hitter in the American League. The Senators won both games of the doubleheader on August 15, and split a doubleheader the next day.

After August 15's game, both the *Washington Star* and the *Washington Post* writers commented on Piersall's catch on Vernon. The *Star*'s Burton Hawkins wrote: "Piersall made a fine running catch of Coan's deep drive in the fourth inning of the second game, but topped it in the fifth when he reached into the right-field stands to shoulder-high level after a long run to deprive Vernon of a home run." The *Washington Post*'s Herb Heft said: "Mickey Vernon, the Nats' first baseman, had his worst day of the season, going 0-for-9 with the Red Sox right fielder robbing him of a home run by leaning over the fence and pulling down his long drive in the second game."

As might be expected, the Boston reporters had more to say about Piersall's fielding on August 15. Jack Barry in the *Boston Evening Globe* wrote:

Piersall's initial coup in the night cap came at the expense of Gil Coan in the fourth. The Nats' leftfielder sent a rising line drive to Piersall's right, the ball being headed for the 380-foot mark on the short wall in front of the visitors' bullpen.

Piersall, off at the crack of the bat, running at full speed, extended his gloved hand to reach the ball, reaching as far up as he could. On the dead run, Jim just turned to brace himself against the wall and his momentum then forced him back toward the diamond, but he held the ball.

The great right-fielder had hardly tipped his hat to the applause of the fans when he even bettered this spectacular catch, by taking a "sure thing homer" Vernon home run right out of the lower pavilion stands, where the grandstand curves past the foul pole. Piersall backed up to the wall and timed his leap to glove the ball just as it was dropping into the seats.

The *Boston Herald* had two reporters commenting on the catches by Piersall. In his account of the game Henry McKenna wrote:

Piersall's "impossible" catches are becoming almost routine and his going-away, one-hand grab of Gil Coan's wallop in the fourth of the second tilt was typical of the pattern. He speared it, took one stride, and then crashed off the gate that leads into the Sox bullpen.

But his catch off Mickey Vernon was one you'll rarely see repeated. It came an inning after the grab off Coan and the crowd kept applauding him repeatedly thereafter, even when he fanned in the seventh. Eddie Yost was on first when the American League's top batter stroked what appeared to be a home run into the right field stands. Piersall, playing Vernon toward center, took off at the crack of the bat. His tremendous speed and jump usually are sufficient to make these catches but yesterday they were only contributing factors. He never broke speed as he raced into the flight of the ball down in the right corner of the field. He lunged over the wall, speared the ball, bounced sideways into the very corner of the field with his back to the plate.

For a split second, the crowd didn't realize he had made the catch. It appeared that he reached, caromed off the wall and missed. But, when he wheeled and fired back to the infield to prevent Yost from advancing, the roar of applause was almost deafening. Truly, it must rate as one of the all-time great catches in baseball. For sheer ability and courage, the catch hardly could be surpassed.

McKenna's colleague Arthur Sampson quoted Piersall about the catch.

"That catch of Vernon's drive was one I didn't think I was going to make," said Piersall. "I figured I'd get the other one if the wind didn't carry it into the bullpen, but I thought Vernon's drive was gone. In fact, it was. It was in the stands, but I flipped the glove in after it and there it was, right in the webbing."

After August 16's games, the Washington writers, particularly the *Star*'s Burton Hawkins, were more animated in their accounts of Piersall's catches. Hawkins made Piersall's catch the leading part of his report. He began:

If Mickey Vernon misses his second American League batting crown by a narrow margin he'll know where to place the blame. It will be directly on two incredibly superb catches by Jim Piersall, Red Sox right fielder who is making astonishing fielding plays seem routine.

"I've never seen a better defensive rightfielder. Piersall is simply fantastic," Bucky Harris said yesterday after the Nats split a double-header with the Red Sox, losing the first game, 4–1, and capturing the second, 7–4.

"Those two catches were by far the best ever made off me," Vernon said, "but I'm not exactly surprised. I've seen him in action for a couple of years and he's made some fine stabs against us. I had dinner with Sid Hudson [Red Sox pitcher] the other night and he told me Piersall is making great catches every day."

Piersall robbed Vernon of a two-run homer in the second game of the double-header Saturday, when he smacked into the chest-high rightfield wall, reached in and plucked the ball from the seats.

The Nats won that game anyway, but in the first game yesterday, with two on in the eighth and the Nats trailing by three runs, Vernon smashed a seemingly certain home run toward the rightfield seats. Again Piersall took off and again, with a thrilling split-second leap that carried him two rows into the grandstand, Jim came up with the ball. It preserved the game for Mel Parnell, who carried on to register his 17th victory, although requiring relief from Ellis Kinder in the ninth. It also meant Vernon's average dipped a bit. Those two Piersall grabs meant four points to Mickey's average.

The 25,564 customers surged to their feet, roaring at Piersall's accomplishment. His two unbelievable catches cost Vernon two home runs, five runs batted in and kept the Nats from creating a tie in the first game.

"What can you say?" asks Lou Boudreau, Red Sox manager. "The catches Piersall makes simply defy description. They have to be seen to be believed and he keeps making them."

Will Cloney of the *Boston Herald* indicated where Piersall was at the stands when he made the catch on Vernon on August 16.

Mickey walloped a high blast to right, a drive ticketed for a score-tying homer. But Piersall, who won't give up on a ball unless it lands in Kenmore Sq., raced to the low wall, timed his oblique jump perfectly, and gloved the ball out of a fan's hair over the third row of seats.

Although Jim hit the wall hard and scraped his right side and back, he recovered in time to throw to first, just missing a great double play as the crowd went positively hysterical.

Earlier in the article Cloney wrote: "Jimmy Piersall, floating through the air like a space-cadet ... to steal a three-run homer from Mickey Vernon...."

The *Boston Daily Globe*'s Hy Hurwitz wrote:

Parnell escaped in the eighth on Piersall's marvelous catch. Mel Holderlein and Eddie Yost had singled. Terwilliger took a third strike. Vernon drove one into the right field grandstand, with Jim racing full speed and leaping as high as he could to make the superman catch and prevent a tie.

"This was the greatest catch I ever made," said Piersall about his spectacular grab.... The ball was in the same part of the park as the one Mickey stroked on Saturday.... But the one yesterday was higher and farther into the stands.... "I'll say it was tougher," quipped Piersall, "look at the bruise on my back and you'll see for yourself." ... Jim rammed the wall after catching the ball and had a three-inch red welt halfway down his back for a souvenir.

Arthur Sampson of the *Herald* told more about the catch and Piersall's and Vernon's reactions.

Carrying a long red welt on the left side of his back where he had crashed against the fence making his game-saving catch in the first game, Piersall gave the fans in the right field stands credit for the grab.

"Those fans made a little cup for me," said Jimmy. "They got out of the way so that I could reach several feet into the stands for the ball. Had we been playing on a rival field I couldn't have made that catch. The opposing fans would have knocked me out of the way. As it was, the fans not only moved away so I could reach after the ball, but actually shoved me back onto the field so that I wouldn't fall into the stands."

Piersall has made so many great catches he couldn't classify this one as the best. "You guys can tell better than I," he said. "But I think this one today was even better than the one I made off Vernon yesterday."

Vernon merely shook his head when asked what he thought of Piersall's robbery. "I think I hit the ball a little better than yesterday, but I never thought either of them would be caught."

Bill Cunningham divided his *Boston Herald* column into two topics: the return to the starting lineup of Ted Williams, who had completed his tour of duty with the Marine air corps in the Korean War; and the Red Sox' general manager Joe Cronin's comments about Piersall's catches on Vernon drives over the past two days. Cunningham was not at he game of the day before because he was watching women's tennis, but he did want to know Cronin's thoughts about Piersall's fielding. He begins by quoting Cronin.

"Well, I wouldn't know about tennis," said the Red Sox generalissimo, "but I do know this. If you missed those games yesterday, you missed the greatest fielding play in the history of baseball.

"I mean exactly that," he continued. "Piersall made two catches down there yesterday that were absolutely unbelievable, but I'm talking about the second one—the one in the fifth inning of the second game, when the score was 1–1. Mickey Vernon hit the ball, and it was a certain home run until Piersall did this thing.

"I don't say it was the greatest catch I ever saw," he said. "I say it was the greatest catch ever made. It would be impossible to beat it. I'd be willing to bet you can wait all your life and never see another like it. That was the limit—the only one of its kind...."

Mr. Cronin eventually went his way over to the presidential box in the adjoining section, the park filled, the scribes arrived and the day's performance began. Mr. Parnell seemed to be both good and bad, but that first game rocked along to the eighth inning with nothing exactly historic happening, and then this same Mr. Vernon suddenly did it again.

To approximately the same spot, again he smote the same sort of ball. It looked a certain home run from the crack of the bat. Again Piersall came tearing from well out in the pasture, to charge the wall and throw himself upward in a high, twisting gainer that seemed to corkscrew him inward over the heads of the pewholders. Again the arm went up and in, with split second timing, and again he caught the ball, and fell in a sort of halfspin back onto the playing field with the missile safely held in his glove.

The park went crazy. So did I and all around me. Shortly, Larry Woodall was pulling my sleeve. "Joe Cronin just called on the phone from Mr. Yawkey's box and told me to tell you he was wrong about Piersall's catch yesterday. He said he takes it all back after seeing this one just now. He said you'd know what he means."

Larry Woodall was a catcher for the Detroit Tigers during the 1920s, a coach for the Red Sox in the 1940s, and, in 1953, was the head of public relations for the Red Sox. "Mr. Yawkey" was Red Sox owner Tom Yawkey.

Joe Cronin, elected to the Hall of Fame in 1956, began his major league career in 1926 with Pittsburgh, and two years later joined the Washington Senators. He played shortstop seven years for the Senators, went to the Red Sox in 1935 and was with the Red Sox for the remainder of his career, which, as a player, ended in 1945.

After the second game in which Piersall had taken a home run from Mickey Vernon, Red Sox coach Bill McKechnie, who began his major league baseball career in 1907, told a writer for the *Boston Traveler*: "Piersall is the best I ever saw in right field. I've seen a lot in 50 years."

In his March 1954 *Baseball Digest* article about Piersall called "Mr. Centerfielder?" Fred Fichonne also quoted McKechnie, who was elected into the Hall of Fame in 1962: "He gets balls that Tris Speaker never would have reached. I've seen Terry Moore. I've seen his marvelous diving catches. And I think Piersall would have caught some of those STAND-ING UP!"

In the June 1993 *Baseball Digest*, George Vass wrote an article titled "Will There Ever Be Another Center Fielder Like Mays?" Vass compared centerfielders from days past to more contemporary fielders. George Vass quoted Casey Stengel as saying, "I thought Joe DiMaggio was the greatest defensive outfielder I ever saw, but I have to rate Piersall even better."

September 20 and 26, 1953

Jimmy Piersall's fielding feats continued on through the end of the 1953 season with a catch against the Yankees in Boston on September 20, and another catch in Yankee Stadium on September 26. Hy Hurwitz of the *Boston Daily Globe* told of Piersall's catch during the first game.

> Jim Piersall's latest larceny came in the ninth ... with Gil McDougal on first (he didn't dare to move too far off, either). Joe Collins conked one that went sailing out to the Sox bullpen.... Piersall was playing Joe to pull the ball.... He had to run a good 50 yards to catch up with it and while on the go, reached up and over the bullpen railing to make the catch.... His right elbow struck the railing and hit a nerve that caused him considerable pain but it didn't last long.... "I don't know how I caught it," Piersall said, "when you're running out there all you think about is catching it. How doesn't matter. But I have been practicing all year on making a catch in the bullpen. I usually have Sid Hudson throw me some balls every day and I've reached over to catch 'em. But this was the first one I caught in a game."

The *Globe* had two other writers who added more to the Piersall legend in the making. Harold Kaese's "UP FRONT" column was titled "Piersall Catch on Collins 'Most Larcenous' Yet," and had a robbery theme.

> The Yankees will be glad to stop playing the Red Sox and start playing the Dodgers in the World Series next week. The Dodgers only have Carl Furillo in right field.
>
> After Jim Piersall had reached frantically into the Red Sox bullpen to steal a home run from Joe Collins in the ninth inning at Fenway Park yesterday, one incredulous New Yorker muttered thinly, "Where was this guy during the Brink's robbery?"

When the game was over, Piersall was asked if by any chance he was wearing a visored cap, pea jacket, and Halloween mask in the vicinity of Prince st. at 7:10 the night of Jan. 17, 1950.

The outfielder laughed heartily, and replied, "No, but that reminds me of our first trip to Cleveland this season. I made a couple of good catches in one game, and the next day a Cleveland paper had a headline like this: '$40,000 Holdup (Piersall Didn't Do It).'

"That's the No. 1 item in my father's scrapbook for this year."

The *Globe*'s Bob Holbrook focused on comments Casey Stengel, who began his major league career in 1912, made about Piersall.

Casey Stengel said months ago that Jim Piersall is the greatest right fielder he's ever seen.

And he's more convinced than ever that he was right.

When Piersall raced to the bullpen wall in right field, leaped and grabbed Joe Collins' "home run" in the ninth inning Casey didn't believe it—nor did Collins.

"When a guy makes a catch like that," said Case, "the hitter should come back to home plate and holler up at the official scorer and say. 'Give me a home run on that smash. Say it wasn't a home run and you're a liar!'

"When I said Piersall was the best right fielder I ever saw I had to take into consideration that he's playing with the lively ball. It wasn't so hard to catch up with the dead ball, you know.

"Remember, that Piersall is taking home runs away from hitters—not just base hits. He's robbed us of four or five anyway. He's saved more runs than most people realize.

"We went into Cleveland one time after the Red Sox left there and they were telling me how Piersall robbed Lemon with a great catch. I said to them, 'Ain't that too bad. He's done that same thing to us, too.'"

...

Jim had to agree that the catch was pretty good, but he didn't get the thrill out of this one that went with his larceny off Mickey Vernon.

"I have to think about next year's contract," he said. "Gotta hustle.

"When I backed up for the ball the guys in the bullpen told me to lay off.... it was gone. Thought I'd give it a try anyway."

"Sure, the ball was in the bullpen," agreed Perfesser Stengel. "Ask the players—they'll tell you."

...

Casey was asked if he'd play Piersall in center field rather than right.

After consideration he said, "No. That's a mighty big right field you got there. The wall would handicap him. Where would he go in left center?"

...

Casey believes the more room you give Piersall, the better he'll be.

The *Boston Herald*'s Henry McKenna continued the praise for Piersall's catch on Collins's ball. He began:

The outfielding genius who plays right field for the Red Sox pulled another of his Houdini catches yesterday at Fenway Park and with it eased the bitter taste of a 10–8 loss to the New York Yankees, the uproar of three home runs, a spectacular catch by Tom Umphlett and still another thriller by the visitor's Hank Bauer.

Jim Piersall has made sensational catches all season long and arguments will rage all winter over his greatest play, but in the opinion of many yesterday's was the last word. It came off the Yanks' Joe Collins in the ninth inning with Ellis Kinder, fifth Sox hurler, on the mound.

Joe hoisted a deep fly slightly to the right of center. The wind was blowing out and the ball was well hit. Piersall, shading Collins toward the foul line, raced over to almost to the centerfield end of the Sox bullpen, leaped above the top railing, speared the ball in his glove several feet inside the warm-up area and then fell off the railing back onto the field.

Said Casey Stengel: "It's amazing what that boy can do. He's the best rightfielder I ever saw in Boston against the lively ball. He plays in, grabs those ground singles and makes runners

The *Boston Post*'s sports cartoonist Bob Coyne captured the sequence of things that Jimmy Piersall did to complete what some observers called his greatest catch during the 1953 season, on the Yankees' Joe Collins at Fenway Park on September 20 (copyright Globe Newspaper Company, republished with permission).

stop taking that extra base, and when you hit the ball over his head he has the speed to go back and get it.

"...He helps the pitchers, he kills rallies and I know he makes those catches against other clubs. How many runs do you think he's saved this year?"

The most far-reaching praise came from the *Boston Post*'s Gerry Moore, who began his column by putting Piersall in another realm defensively: "Fourth place was clinched for the Red Sox at 3:29 yesterday afternoon when Washington lost to the A's again and more than an hour later, nonstop Jim Piersall was removing any remaining doubt that he is the most spectacular defensive outfielder in baseball history." After calling the catch on Joe Collins "the greatest of all Piersall catches," Moore gave his description of the catch.

> In typical fashion, Piersall was off at the crack of the bat from the stand he had taken for the usually pull-hitting Collins.
> Going full speed, Jim leaped right into the bullpen barrier, stuck his glove arm backhanded over the wire fence into the bullpen up to his elbow, caught the ball with the glove only and was whirled completely around as he bounced off the iron and concrete obstruction by the force of his original crash.
> He landed on his feet, returned the ball to the infield in an unsuccessful attempt to double up the back-tracking McDougald and then trotted around right field swinging his right arm, that had been jammed between his body and the bullpen wall while he was making the unforgettable catch.

Piersall was asked to rate the catch on Collins's blast. The *Post*'s Moore quotes Piersall:

> "I can't really tell. It happens so fast that I miss a lot of the details. All I know is that I kept hearing cries of 'No! No!' from our bullpen, but I still kept going and there was the ball in my glove."
> Over in the Yankee clubhouse, Casey Stengel, who earlier had called Piersall's catch on Mantle in the dirt track beyond the Red Sox bullpen the greatest Casey had ever seen, provided some of his inimitable humor for this one.
> "Tell Boudreau the reason I wanted him for an All-Star coach is the expert way he places his outfielders," said Case with his famous wink.

The New York papers also wrote of Piersall's catch on Collins, but not in as much detail. For example, Joe Trimble of the *New York Daily News* wrote: "Folks got their biggest kick out of another of Piersall's great catches, the rapid rightfielder racing to the right-center bullpen for a slam-bang catch of Collins' drive. He actually took the ball with one hand as it passed beyond the bullpen railing in home run territory."

The *New York Times'* John Drebinger wrote that pitcher Ellis Kinder "was saved by a great catch by Jim Piersall who almost impaled himself on the right-field railing."

Six days later, on September 26, the Piersall defensive magic "struck" again, this time in Yankee Stadium. Since the Yankees already had clinched the American League crown, the game itself was inconsequential. Three New York writers led with Piersall's play, which they might have done even if the game had had an impact on the American League pennant.

Rud Rennie of the *New York Herald Tribune* began his September 27, 1953, article with:

> For a game that did not mean anything, both the Yankees and the Red Sox made a lot of work for themselves yesterday playing it, and it was a fine contest, won in the eleventh by the Sox, 2 to 1, after Jim Piersall, the Boston rightfielder, made another of his dare-devil, acrobatic catches, robbing Hank Bauer of what would have been a three-run homer in the tenth. And it was Piersall who drove in the winning run, batting a long fly to center with the bases loaded in the eleventh off Johnny Sain.

Later, Rennie called Piersall's catch on Bauer "magnificent."

Both Joe Trimble of the *New York Daily News* and Ben Epstein of the *New York Mirror* spent much of their accounts of the September 26 game on Piersall's fielding prowess. Trimble led with:

The folks in our town never really had a chance to appreciate the fielding genius of Boston's Jimmy Piersall until yesterday, at the Stadium. The acrobatic right fielder made another of his incredible catches to save an eleven-inning thriller, which the Sox took, 2–1, to bar the Yanks from their 100th victory.

Piersall was the whole show in the game, which was surprisingly exciting for a contest which meant so little. The hustling Socker scored the run that kept his side even in nine innings and, after the big grab in the 10th, made it a personal triumph by driving in the winning run in the 11th.

Later Trimble returned to Piersall's catch.

Then Hank Bauer came up and clouted a long drive to the Yanks' bullpen in right-center.

Piersall raced backwards, and turning, flung his mitt high as he reached the barrier. He leaped and gloved the ball, jack-knifing across the three-foot high metal railing. He held the ball while teetering there, then managed to wiggle back onto the playing field to make the catch legal. Had he fallen beyond the fence, Bauer would have had a homer.

It was the sixth spectacular fielding play he has made against the Yanks this year, and, according to Boston writers, he's made a dozen others against the rest of the league.

The *Mirror*'s Ben Epstein gave Piersall extremely high ratings as a defender. Epstein's lead also was about the Red Sox right fielder: "To whom it may concern: Why not exhibit Jim Piersall before each Series game? Sure, the Yankees and the Dodgers boast pretty good fielders but Piersall, a fly chaser and fly catcher, is in a class by himself."

The Boston writers, Hy Hurwitz of the *Boston Globe* and Henry McKenna of the *Boston Herald*, had yet another opportunity to rave about Jim Piersall near the end of the 1953 season. Hurwitz called Piersall "baseball's greatest home-run grabber," and called the catch on Bauer "another of his game-saving catches."

McKenna had could not disguise his pride in Piersall's accomplishments for the Red Sox.

If this keeps up, the New York Yankees will welcome the world series and the Brooklyn Dodgers instead of playing the Red Sox and Jim Piersall. Jim virtually beat the Yankees single-handed, 2–1, in 11 innings, with the crowd of 13,307 forgetting almost entirely that the world champions were in the game. Waterbury, Conn., Jim's native city, took over and swayed even rabid fans.

All the brilliant right fielder did was to get the first hit off Vic Raschi, steal his 11th base of the season, score the first run, drive in the winning run and make what must be one of the greatest catches ever seen in the Stadium.

...

Piersall's catch was another of those "out of this world" affairs. It came in the 10th with two out and two runners aboard. Bauer really hit a ball out of the park only to have Piersall make another "home run" catch.

The drive wasn't too high and it was deep, directly toward the Yank bullpen, in front of which is a chain fence waist high. Jim wasn't playing Hank deep because he's an accepted pull hitter and this ball appeared long gone. But Piersall turned his back and went flying after it.

He left the grass, crossed the gravel warning strip, leaped as high as he could, speared the ball in his glove several feet inside the bullpen, then jack-knifed over the top railing of the fence, barely preventing himself from going into the warm-up area. The crowd didn't realize he had made the catch until he recovered his balance, straightened up and held the ball aloft in his glove.

After the conclusion of the 1953 season, Hy Hurwitz, in an article in *The Sporting News*, also referred to Bobo Newsome's early assessment of Piersall's talents as a fielder.

"There is the greatest outfielder I've ever seen," remarked the much traveled Bobo Newsome, who has put in more time and played in more places during the past 25 years than anyone in Organized Ball.

Newsome pointed to a slick, swift, 22-year-old lad who was making his debut at shortstop for the Boston Red Sox in April 1952. "I don't know how he'll go as a shortstop, but as an outfielder, there ain't nobody who can reach him."

Now it is two seasons and scores of sensational catches later that proved Newsome, among others, as a great prophet. Piersall's shortstop career lasted about six weeks. After being shifted to the outer pastures, Jim became the greatest defensive outfielder of the day and is being hailed by such baseball authorities as Casey Stengel and Tris Speaker as the top right fielder of all time.

One of the subtitles of Hurwitz's article gave what manager Lou Boudreau found to be Piersall's defensive contribution to the team: "Fielding Which Saved 75–100 Runs and 15–20 Games in '53, Boudreau Estimates."

In a February 5, 1954, *Collier's* magazine article on Piersall, the veteran baseball writer Tom Meany tried to get an idea of what made Piersall's fielding so outstanding.

What makes Piersall such a great outfielder?

"Instinct, I guess," says Jim himself, somewhat uncertainly.

Piersall's greatest asset, of course, is his speed; but sheer speed wouldn't permit him to cover the ground he does. Del Baker, a Red Sox coach who has been around for 40 years, credits the terrific jump Jim gets on the ball.

Nobody gets more close-ups of Piersall's catches than Ellis Kinder, the veteran Boston relief pitcher. Kinder practically lives in the bullpen, which at Fenway Park, is the vantage point for watching Jim operate. "I've heard of outfielders starting with the crack of the bat," says Kinder, "but Jim actually starts before the crack of the bat." Piersall is in motion, he claims, when the ball meets the bat, before the sound of the impact has time to carry across the field to the bullpen.

In addition to his speed and quick jump, Piersall is a sure judge of a fly ball (his "instinct"), and exhibits reckless daring.

Such disregard for fences hasn't been seen since Brooklyn's Pete Reiser repeatedly fractured himself trying to prove flesh and blood stronger than steel and concrete.

In his March 14, 1954, column, Arthur Daley of the *New York Times*, writing from St. Petersburg, Florida, devoted one of his regular columns to Jim Piersall. Under the title "Too Good to Be True," Daley told of several of the catches Piersall made in 1953, told of Piersall's long dislike of the Yankees, and compared him with former Boston Red Sox and Cleveland Indian great Tris Speaker. As had the writers in Boston and New York who covered him in 1953, Daley also talked about the seemingly magical Piersall: "There is an airy quality about Piersall that almost borders on the ethereal, especially when he plays the outfield. Then he's a disembodied spirit who suddenly materializes in the most unexpected places and performs feats of ghostly magic."

Fred Fichonne's article "Mr. Center Fielder?" in the March 1954 *Baseball Digest* quoted Lou Boudreau as saying, "The best outfielder I ever saw. And I doubt if anybody before my time ever saw a better one, either...."

After the 1953 season, Jimmy Piersall played five more seasons with the Red Sox, then three with the Cleveland Indians, a single full season with the Senators, and then became a part-time player with the American League's Los Angeles franchise, which went to Anaheim to become the California Angels while Piersall was with that team.

Beginning in 1958, Gold Glove awards were given to the outstanding fielders at each position in each league. Jim Piersall won the American League awards in 1958 with the Red Sox and in 1961 with the Cleveland Indians. Both awards were for his work in center field. During the 1954 season, he became the Red Sox' centerfielder. Piersall continued to make outstanding catches for Boston and Cleveland as a centerfielder. For example, as an

On September 11, 1961, the Indians' Jimmy Piersall and Willie Kirkland raced to the Yankees' bullpen in Yankee Stadium, where Piersall (left) robbed John Blanchard of a two-run homer.

Indian, he made an outstanding catch on a ball that Hector Lopez hit in the sixth inning at Yankee Stadium on June 11, 1960. Harry Jones of the *Cleveland Plain Dealer* called the catch "a season highlight," "stunning," and "spectacular."

Much higher praise, and an estimate of the distance the ball traveled, came from Louis Effrat of the *New York Times*. Effrat called the catch on Lopez the greatest at Yankee Stadium since Joe DiMaggio's catch on Hank Greenberg in 1939. "Piersall turned and ran and didn't stop running until he caught up with the ball a step or two after reaching the cinder track. There he made the 'impossible' catch, clutching the ball and stumbling until he crashed into the wall near the 461-foot marker." For Effrat, DiMaggio's catch on Greenberg evidently was the standard for judging the greatest catches, and Piersall, at age 30, made a catch that reached that standard.

Over a year later, on September 11, 1961, Jimmy Piersall made a catch which an unidentified *New York Times* writer praised. The catch came shortly after two youths jumped on the field and tried to attack Piersall. Piersall knocked one to the ground with a well-aimed punch and chased the other while kicking at the youth's rear end. Both attackers were further subdued by Piersall's teammates and then arrested by the police.

With order restored, Yankees batter John Blanchard took his place at the plate. The *New York Times'* writer told what happened next: "When play resumed, Piersall drew cheers that welled into a mighty roar when Blanchard, completing his turn at bat, lifted a fly to the auxiliary scoreboard in right. Piersall, after colliding with Willie Kirkland, made a spectacular catch off the bleacher wall."

Clearly, his fielding continued to be at a very high level for years, but he did not receive the level of praise that he received as a right fielder for Boston during the 1953 season.

1954—Willie Mays

If any year can be said to have been a banner year for great outfielding from start to finish, it might be 1954. Much of this is attributable to the return of Willie Mays to the New York Giants during spring training, and to the Giants' having him for his first full season. Willie may have had his best all-around year in 1954. He led the league in batting (.344), slugging percentage (.648), and triples (13). He had the most putouts (448) and double plays (9) from his center field position in his career. He hit 41 home runs and knocked in 110 runs.

Brooklyn's centerfielder Duke Snider also had his best all-around year, which included a continuation of his sterling fielding. Snider hit .341, had 40 home runs, drove in 130 runs, and led the league in runs scored (120).

Much had been made of Willie Mays' catch on Vic Wertz in the 1954 World Series, but he and Snider both made catches during the 1954 season which could be considered better.

In addition to Mays, Snider, and Richie Ashburn and Mickey Mantle, who both were in their primes covering an enormous amount of ground, 1954 had the following outfielders patrolling major league outfields: Jimmy Piersall, Carl Furillo, Bill Tuttle, Al Kaline, Jim Delsing, Minnie Minoso, Chuck Diering, Wally Moon, Bill Bruton, Larry Doby, Jim Rivera, Jim Busby, Gil Coan, Monte Irvin, Henry Aaron, and Jackie Jensen.

After being away from major league baseball nearly twenty-two months, Willie Mays came back in a big way on March 2, 1954. The *New York Times'* Louis Effrat wrote of Mays' return.

> Twenty-seven hours after he had been discharged from Fort Eustis, Va., and one hour after he had alighted from a plane from Washington today, Willie Mays stepped up to the plate as a Giants pinch-hitter and smashed a 400-foot homer over the leftfield wall. That was in the fifth inning of a full-time contest in which the Regulars beat the Yannigans, 8–5. And it was only the beginning. For a man who had spent twenty-one months in the Army, the 22-year-old Mays was a revelation. He had played only one game of baseball since he fractured his left foot last August, but if today's exhibition means anything at all, Willie is ready to start the season tomorrow.
>
> His round-tripper against Pete Modica was an eye-opener. Then in the seventh, with Bill Gardner on first, Harvey Gentry blasted the ball close to the wall in right center. It looked like an extra baser, but the incredible Willie made a spectacular, one-handed catch, whirled and fired to first in time to complete the doubleplay. In the same stanza, Mays raced back fifty feet and made an over-the-shoulder catch that robbed Bill Taylor of a double.

In his March 26 article on the Giants as they were about to break spring training camp, Effrat wrote of others' views of how talented Mays was then. He wrote: "The centerfielder's return provided the 'lift' that Durocher believed was needed. Willie, called by Durocher and Scouts Tom Sheehan and Dutch Ruether the 'greatest defensive centerfielder I have ever seen,'" is leading the club in batting with a .426 mark.

Tom Sheehan began his major league career in 1915 as a pitcher for the Philadelphia A's, and ended his career with the Pittsburgh Pirates in 1936. Dutch Ruether, also a pitcher, began his major league career in 1917 with the Chicago Cubs, and ended his playing career in the big league with the mighty New York Yankees team of 1927. Both men saw many defensive outfielders who were outstanding throughout their many years in baseball. And Mays, just out of the Army and with only 155 games of major league experience behind him, was the "greatest" they'd ever seen up through spring training 1954.

Willie's throwing arm was a big feature of his defensive game, and many long-time baseball observers used superlatives to describe how good Mays' arm was. Even before he played his first regular season game with the Minneapolis Millers in 1951, spectators were wowed. Halsey Hall's April 10, 1951, *Minneapolis Tribune* column included comments about Mays' arm. He wrote that Mays' manager Thomas Heath said Mays was the best prospect "I ever had anything to do with." Heath also told Hall: "And he's got the best outfield arm I ever saw without an argument."

Hall himself weighed in with his own assessment of Mays' arm.

> Having seen Mays unfurl a few miracle heaves, this is a considered opinion. He has the strongest arm this observer has seen.
> The beauty of it is that he doesn't throw just for distance. He throws line drives. He will throw ground skimmers or balls that look like fast ball strikes pitched on some gargantuan diamond.

From early in the 1954 season until late in the season Willie's arm was noteworthy in ways that usually do not get mentioned in the press. Early in the season, in his account of the April 19 game against the Pirates, Joseph M. Sheehan of the *New York Times* remarked: "Willie accounted for his daily sensation with a rifle throw to third in the second inning. He lost his man when Thompson booted the toss but got credit for an assist."

In a game against the Phillies on May 24, Mays cracked two home runs, one a tape-measure shot. The *Philadelphia Bulletin*'s Frank Yeutter noted these blasts in his account of the game, but a throw of Willie's was highlighted in the article.

> They talk about how Tris Speaker and Bob Meusel could throw or how Duke Snider and Carl Furillo, of this generation, can throw, but there never was an outfielder in any generation who made a better and more timely throw than did Mays last night to cut down Earl Torgeson trying to score from third base after Del Ennis hit a long fly to Willie.
> Torgeson, one of the fastest men in the league, was in danger of being knocked off by another Mays throw just before that play. On his drive to deep right field, which was good for a double, he tried for a triple, then hesitated when he saw the toss from Mays to Hank Thompson would beat him to the bag. However, the ball went through Thompson and Earl made third on the error.
> Then came Del's long drive. Mays took it in running stride toward the plate. He let go with a low, whistling throw that hit Ray Katt's mitt like an arrow zipping into the bull's-eye. Torgeson was out by five feet.
> Veterans Bing Miller and John Lobert, in the press box, and members of the Boston Red Sox, taking a "busman's holiday," were aghast at the ease, speed and accuracy of Mays' mighty maneuver.

Bing Miller began his major league career as an outfielder with Washington in 1921, and finished in Boston in 1936. John Lobert, almost exclusively a third baseman during his major league career, began with Pittsburgh in 1903, and finished with the Giants in 1917.

The same Frank Yeutter of the *Bulletin* was again rhapsodic about a throw Mays made on July 5 against the Phillies. The Giants won both ends of the doubleheader at the Polo Grounds, and in each game Willie Mays did something spectacular in the field. In the first game it was a catch on a long drive by the Phillies' Mel Clark, and in the second game the throw Yeutter was to write about.

> However, the play that will live forever with everyone who sat through the two games was Mays' throw that nailed Richie Ashburn at third base in the fourth inning.
> There were two out. Richie Ashburn walked. Smoky Burgess lined a single to center. Ashburn had a good lead and headed for third like fanned wildfire. Willie came in fast, made a

low, running pickup of Smoky's shot and, as he fell on his face, cut loose a perfect high-speed throw that beat Richie by a couple of feet.

Experienced baseball writers and Johnny Mize and Frank Frisch, two former topflight big leaguers who were in the press box, unhesitatingly acclaimed it the greatest throw they ever saw.

The other two Philadelphia reporters on this game also mentioned the throw, but did not invoke higher authorities like Mize and Frisch. Stan Baumgartner of the *Philadelphia Inquirer* wrote: "In the second game, Mays ... made a sensational play that brought the crowd to its feet when he picked up Smokey Burgess' looping single to left with one hand and pegged on the button to third, getting the fleet Richie Ashburn." Joe Greenday of the *Philadelphia Daily News* commented on Richie Ashburn's speed which Willie Mays' throw negated.

> Willie's play in the second game came on Smoky Burgess's looping hit to center with Richie Ashburn on first. Richie's speed under ordinary circumstances would have carried him to third easily, but not with Mays in center. The 23-year-old Giants' flash came in fast on Burgess' hit, scooped up the ball and rifled it to Hank Thompson in time to nip Ashburn. It had the Phils talking.

Two New York writers mentioned Willie's throw. Ken Smith of the *New York Daily Mirror* wrote that Willie "cut down fleet Richie Ashburn with a gilt edge throw to third." Jim McCulley of the *New York Daily News* said "Mays pulled a dazzler" with his "off-balance throw to Thompson that caught Ashburn trying for third."

One of the throws that Willie Mays himself remembered years later was in an August 29 game in St. Louis, which the Giants lost in 11 innings, 5–4. In his book *Willie Mays*, Arnold Hano recalled Mays' ninth-inning throw on a ball that Solly Hemus had hit to the right-center field wall for a double. With Joe Cunningham running from first before Hemus hit the ball, Mays tracked the ball down at the fence and fired it to home plate to get Cunningham out. Hano called the throw one of Mays' great throws and added parenthetically, "(some say he never made a better one)" (113).

In his book *Born to Play Ball* (written in 1955 with Charles Einstein), Willie Mays pondered what might have been his best play. Although he remembered several plays, he didn't commit to one. However, among those he did mention was the throw he made to get Cunningham at the plate after Solly Hemus hit the double to the wall in St. Louis.

John Drebinger of the *New York Times* commented on Mays' throw to get Cunningham: "But Cunningham, on base at the time, seemed to be running backward. He was nailed at the plate on a beautiful peg by Mays."

In his September 12 *New York Times* column, Arthur Daley wrote about the St. Louis Cardinals rookie Wally Moon, an outfielder having a good season, and who later was voted the National League's Rookie of the Year. Daley talked about his swiftness afoot, his solid hitting, his "reasonable power," his fielding and his throwing arm.

> He's an excellent fielder and his lone weakness, if any, is that his throwing arm is good but not great.
> "If Wally could throw like Willie Mays," said Mike Ryba, the Cardinal coach, "he'd be as good as Willie Mays. But who else can throw like Willie? There's the best thrower I ever saw in my life and I've seen all of them. Let me tell you about that throw he made in St. Loo***." Some other time, Mike.

It appears certain that Mike Ryba was talking about the throw to get Cunningham at the plate. Ryba began his major league pitching career in 1935 with the St. Louis Cardinals, and was a teammate of the great fielding centerfielder Terry Moore, who also began his major league career with the Cards on 1935. Mike Ryba played for the Boston Red Sox from 1941 to 1946, before taking coaching and managing positions. He was Jimmy Piersall's manager at two minor league levels. Mike Ryba may not have "seen all of them" throw, but he had seen many outstanding outfield throwers during his years in baseball, including the DiMaggio brothers—Vince, Joe, and Dom.

During the 1954 season, and in the years to follow, there were other references to Mays' powerful throwing arm, but the throws in 1954 were among Willie's best.

It is the constancy of his outstanding fielding which distinguishes Willie Mays from most others. From his earliest days in pro baseball until well into his career, until at least 1964, he was making catches that observers in many places were calling the best they'd ever seen. The "greatest" catches were scattered across most of the ballparks in which he played, but especially in the Polo Grounds until the Giants left for San Francisco after the 1957 season.

During the 1954 season, Willie made at least five catches that rivaled or surpassed the catch on Vic Wertz, and for which he had to travel as far, if not farther, than he had to run to make the now storied World Series catch. Mays himself has said that he considers other catches and plays he made to be better than the catch on the Indians' Vic Wertz. Although there were some still photos of Willie either in the act of catching the ball, or just after he had grabbed the ball with his back to the plate, nothing like the film and sequence photography of the catch on Vic Wertz's drive is known to exist on those other catches. The pictures from the Wertz catch do give us an idea of the kind of thing Willie and a few of his contemporaries, especially Duke Snider, could do in the ballparks with long distances to run. Earlier players, like Bill Cunningham, Jigger Statz and Joe DiMaggio, also pulled off similar long-distance feats in the Polo Grounds.

April 25, 1954

In the April 25, 1954, game that the Giants won 5 to 0, Phillies catcher Stan Lopata blasted a Johnny Antonelli pitch. Joseph M. Sheehan of the *New York Times* wrote: "Mays contributed the fielding gem of the long afternoon by racing all the way back to the left center field fence to haul down Stan Lopata's 450-foot drive in the seventh inning of the second game."

Bob Cooke of the *New York Herald Tribune* agreed: "Willie Mays made the play of the game when he loped back near the left centerfield bleacher wall to take Stan Lopata's 430-foot fly."

Incidentally, on May 30, 1955, Lopata hit a ball inside the Polo Grounds which went even further, and which Mays could not track down. John Drebinger of the *New York Times* wrote: "Even the amazing Mays couldn't catch up with this one, the ball landing on the gravel patch between the bleachers. Traveling on the fly about 470 feet, it was one of the longest clouts ever hit inside the Polo Grounds arena."

May 26, 1954

On May 26, 1954, in a game the Giants won 2–1, Mays made a catch on a ball blasted by Bob Skinner of the Pittsburgh Pirates which a number of people think is among the greatest catches ever. William J. Briordy of the *New York Times* wrote: "Mays turned in the most spectacular play of the game in the first when he made a one-handed stab of Bob Skinner's long blast to the bleacher screen in center. Willie had his back to the diamond when he made the catch."

The *New York Herald Tribune*'s Rud Rennie told more about Mays' effort on Skinner.

> Mays added another remarkable catch to his collection in the first inning when Skinner stroked a tremendous fly which would have struck the green screen on the front of the right centerfield bleachers if it had continued on its way. Mays, running with his back to the plate, reached out with his gloved hand and caught the ball so close to the screen that he had to spin to avoid crashing into the corner of the bleachers.

Arch Murray of the *New York Post* was even more impressed with Willie's catch on Bob Skinner's drive.

> They got the big play, too—one by Willie Mays in the very first inning—that they had to have. Willie made probably his greatest catch of the season when he raced to within a foot or two of the screen in right center 460 feet away to haul down Bob Skinner's screaming drive with a man aboard. That looked like a sure triple. Not many balls have been hit harder at the Polo Grounds. But Mays got it and saved at least a run.

The *Pittsburgh Press*'s Les Biederman agreed with Arch Murray.

> Willie Mays made a startling over-the-shoulder catch on Bob Skinner in the first inning that must have been the play of the year on television screens.... Mays ran to the right-center bleacher wall, took the ball over his right shoulder and Skinner's 460-foot plus wallop was just a putout.... It might have gone over the deep right-center wall at Forbes Field but in the Polo Grounds Mays had just enough room to stab it.

The *Pittsburgh Post-Gazette*'s Jack Hernon, who later would write that this catch on Skinner was the best catch he had seen during 1954, including Mays' catch on Vic Wertz in the World Series, wrote: "Willie Mays made another sensational catch today.... In the first, with one on, Bob Skinner hit a long drive to deep center and the Amazin' Willie loped back for an over-the-shoulder catch with one hand as he used the other to avoid colliding with the wall.... The ball carried about 460 feet."

In his 1963 book *My Giants* (written with Al Hirshberg), Russ Hodges, the long-time "voice" of the New York Giants, compared Mays' catch on Cleveland's Vic Wertz in the 1954 World Series with the ball Mays caught on Skinner's long ball. Hodges wrote:

> The big Pirates rookie hit a vicious smash into the same place where Wertz's had gone, but on a much lower trajectory. Mays didn't have time to turn back and run. He had to race at an angle and spear it going away. I don't know how he caught up with that ball, and neither does he. I doubt that any outfielder alive, with the possible exception of Jimmy Piersall, could have made that play [129–130].

June 23, 1954

Almost a month later, on June 23, 1954, he did it again. This time the ball was hit by the Milwaukee Braves' centerfielder Bill Bruton in a 5–2 victory by the Braves at the Polo Grounds. The *New York Post*'s Arch Murray devoted most of his column to Willie's outstanding game at the plate and in the field. Of the catch on Bruton, Murray wrote:

> On the very first play of the game he made one of his superlative catches on a terrific drive unloaded by Bill Bruton, the Milwaukee leadoff hitter. He made it over his head just a step or two away from the gravel in front of the clubhouse in dead centerfield. "I'd say it was the second

best catch I've ever seen him make," said Wes Westrum. "I don't think anybody can ever match the one he made on Bobby Morgan at Ebbets Field early in '52. You remember he made that skidding along the ground and took a triple away from Bobby with two men on base. But this was to be the next best."

The Milwaukee writers were lavish in their praise of Mays. In his column on the game, the *Milwaukee Sentinel*'s Red Thisted mentioned Mays' catch on the Bruton ball. In another column he did on the same day he had more to say about Mays.

There may be a better ball player somewhere than Willie Mays, but it will demand a lot of proof. He has to be seen to be properly appreciated. Willie galloped almost to the distant centerfield bleachers for Bill Bruton's drive to open the game and scampered almost as far in right center in the eighth for Del Crandall's smash. Twenty-two homers and a .325 batting average tells you the rest.

The *Milwaukee Journal*'s Cleon Walfoort was expansive about Mays' abilities, and agreed with Red Thisted that Willie "has to be seen to be believed." He wrote: "With the exception of Edwin Snider, the Duke of Brooklyn, there is no other outfielder who can come close to him in the combined execution of hitting, fielding, throwing, and running. There is a breathtaking quality about the way the husky young Negro plays baseball." Walfoort went on to describe the catch on Bruton.

On the very play, Bill Bruton hit one of the longest balls of his career to dead center. Mays wheeled and raced back to the distant recesses of the spacious center field precinct, not once looking back until just before the ball dropped over his shoulder and into his glove. Bruton already had rounded second and would have been a cinch to score if Mays had not caught the drive.

Walfoort ended the piece by saying Mays "had not broken stride while making an all but impossible catch appear easy."

July 5, 1954

On July 5, the Giants played a doubleheader against the Phillies. It was in the second game that Willie Mays threw out Richie Ashburn with a great throw. In the first game he made a terrific catch on the Phils' Mel Clark, one of his best of the year. The *New York Times'* John Drebinger noted the catch: "In the seventh of the opener, Mays tore out to the left centerfield bleachers for Clark's towering clout. With his back to the infield, Willie the Wonder caught this one right off the boards."

In enumerating the high points of the Giants victory in the first game, Ken Smith of the *New York Daily Mirror* listed Mays' catch among them, describing it as "a great running catch by Mays with his back to the diamond clawing a 450-foot drive by Mel Clark at the edge of the left-center field bleachers...."

Jim McCulley of the *New York Daily News* called Willie's catch on the Clark ball "sensational," and Rud Rennie of the *New York Herald Tribune* said Mays "made another miracle catch a step from the left-centerfield bleacher wall in front of the green screen."

The *Philadelphia Inquirer*'s Stan Baumgartner gave his thoughts about Mays' catch on Mel Clark: "Willie Mays robbed Mel Clark of a possible homer with a spectacular back to the plate catch against the centerfield wall. He got a great hand."

Joe Greenday of the *Philadelphia Daily News* wrote: "Willie raced to deep centerfield to make an over-the-shoulder catch on Mel Clark's drive in the seventh inning. Mel's blast was a good 460 feet from the plate and a sure homer in most major league parks."

In discussing the first game between the Giants and the Phillies, Frank Yeutter of the *Philadelphia Evening Bulletin* paid tribute to Mays' catch on the ball hit by Mel Clark.

> Willie's most sensational contribution was a catch he made when Mel Clark hit a line drive that carried better than 450 feet to the wall in front of the centerfield bleachers.
>
> As great as was Duke Snider's catch at Connie Mack Stadium on Memorial Day, it would suffer by comparison with Willie's spectacular wrinkle yesterday. He sped at least 75 feet from his normal position, twice looked over his shoulder, then, when it seemed inevitable that he would crash into the wall, he leaped and snared the ball in his glove.

After almost 50 years, what did the victim of the Mays' July 5, 1954, catch think about what Willie did? In an August 2, 2002, conversation, I asked Mel Clark about the catch Willie Mays made on him.

> Mel Clark: The pitcher was Johnny Antonelli. When I played I was considered a line drive hitter, not a long ball hitter. Willie Mays usually played me pretty shallow on account of that. I hit a ball in the Polo Grounds to deep center. When I got to second base they held me up. I thought I hit a home run. He caught it just as he was about to hit the center field wall, which at that point was 462 feet.
>
> JA: He's got to run about 100 feet to get there.
>
> MC: Absolutely.
>
> JA: And you said you didn't have much arc on the ball.
>
> MC: It was a line drive. It wasn't the kind you hit up in the air and it comes down. It was the kind that keeps rising for a while. A line drive.
>
> JA: And if it hits off the wall, it cracks off the wall.
>
> MC: Right.
>
> JA: It was like the catch he made in the World Series against....
>
> MC: It was exactly like that. Of course, his hat was off, and he caught it over his shoulder.
>
> JA: The one he caught against Vic Wertz, he actually had a little room to run. But not against yours.
>
> MC: That's right. Our bullpen was out there, and the pitchers in the bullpen said just as he caught it, he put his foot up against the wall to keep from hitting the wall. It was the longest ball that I ever hit that was caught.
>
> JA: Was he playing you straight away?
>
> MC: He was playing me straight away. I tried to hit the ball through the middle all the time and they played me straight away.
>
> JA: Did Mays say anything to you about the catch?
>
> MC: I talked to him just passing by. I said, "Why were you playing me so deep?" He said, "I wasn't," or something like that. He was amazing how he got back to it. I had no idea he'd catch it when I hit it. I thought it'd be off the wall or maybe over it. I couldn't believe when they held me up and said the ball was caught [laughs].
>
> It wasn't a ball that was hit high. It was a line drive.
>
> Are you familiar with the Polo Grounds, how it was in dead center? There was an open place there. The one he caught off Vic Wertz was to the right of center, and mine was just to the left of the entrance to the open space.
>
> JA: Who's out there today who's as good as Willie Mays?
>
> MC: Best all around player I ever saw. He could do anything to beat you. He'd steal a base. He could hit a home run. He could bunt. He could field and throw. He was complete.
>
> JA: He had to be awfully fast to catch the ball he caught off you.
>
> MC: He had to be. We once stood around the batting cage before a game, and I talked a little bit about it. I told him, "You ought to play me a little deeper so you wouldn't have to run so far. Then I could hit the ball in front of you [laughs]."

JA: He was pretty good coming in on the ball. I read somewhere that he was considered one of the best ever, if not the best ever, at coming in to take a ball on the ground. He fielded like an infielder.

MC: He did. I remember one instance about him. Puddin' Head Jones was the runner on third. It was questionable whether Willie Mays was going to catch the ball or not. The outfield was slippery from the rain. As he was coming in fast, he had to stop and field the ball on one hop. As he fielded the ball with his bare hand, his feet were sliding out from under him. As he was falling backwards, he threw Willie Jones out at home....

There's something I got to mention to you. I've got to admire Robin Roberts. He'd have a clubhouse meeting and he'd tell us all about every hitter. He would go over every hitter on the opposing team, and he'd tell everybody how to play them. He said, "If they don't hit the ball there, it's my mistake."

JA: That's pretty good confidence in what you're going to throw and where you're going to throw it.

MC: It really is. And that's what you do, go over every hitter.

In his 1955 book *Born to Play Ball* (as told to Charles Einstein), Willie Mays also comments on the importance of the pitcher in helping the defense. He writes:

> As a general rule ... your batter is going to hit most of the time to a certain area of the field. If he doesn't, it's usually because of the way he's being pitched.
>
> ...
>
> The link between pitching and defense is far greater than most fans think.
> Again, the reason is that the defense sets against the hitter for *where he will hit where he is pitched.*
> Confidence in the pitcher, such as the Giants have in Sal Maglie, is a great defensive boost. We know Sal's in there to make them hit where we are [107].

In 1955, Sal Maglie had nine wins and five losses before being traded to the Cleveland Indians, where he was in ten games and had no wins and two losses. In the spring of 1956, the Indians gave up on him and he was picked up by the Dodgers. He performed superbly for his old foes and was a major reason the Dodgers repeated as National League champions.

In mid–June 1956 Sal Maglie won his first game in nearly a year with a three-hit shutout of the powerful Milwaukee Braves. In *Sports Illustrated*'s June 18, 1956, "Highlight" section, an unidentified writer quoted Pee Wee Reese, who, as Willie Mays did the year before, commented on Maglie's mastery: "Shortstop Pee Wee Reese, no rookie himself, dreamily paid his tribute: 'I stood out there and watched him pitch to each man exactly the way we discussed it in the clubhouse. Most guys talk about it in the meeting and then go out there and do something else. This is a pitcher.'"

The *New York Daily Mirror*'s Ken Smith did a five-chapter series on Willie Mays. Smith later turned the series into the book *Willie Mays*. The *Daily Mirror*'s Chapter 4 (in the July 7, 1954, paper) in part dealt with some of Mays' greatest plays: the 1951 catch on Furillo and the throw to get Billy Cox at the plate, the diving catch on Bobby Morgan's screamer in 1952, and four plays Willie made in 1954 before Smith wrote the series. The series evidently was written before the catch on Mel Clark.

After describing the catch on Furillo and the great throw to get Cox at the plate play in 1951, Smith commented on Mays' throw: "Old-timers went back to a peg by Myril Hoag, on the fly at Fenway Park in the early 30's, and the deeds of the three DiMaggio brothers were aired, but nobody could top Mays' accomplishment." Smith then presented the great 1954 plays up to the time of his column.

> One reporter prefers his miraculous journey to the edge of the Polo Grounds bleachers for a Herculean hoist by Bob Skinner of the Pirates this year. Frank Forbes, state boxing official

and former player, umpire and promotional director of the Negro League, votes for the ball caught on Bill Bruton last month when he sloshed through wet grass to the corner of the bleachers near the Giants' clubhouse steps.

"What made this one the prize in my book was the way he righted himself after misjudging it," Forbes pointed out. "His body was poised in one direction but instinct caused him to swerve for the grab. He took a tumble, he was so off balance when he clutched it."

Russ Hodges, who has seen them all, insists that his May 24 seizure of a fly by Del Ennis at Connie Mack Stadium and throw-out of Earl Torgeson at the plate eclipsed all other stunts.

Fred Lindstrom's eyes popped on June 12 when Mays tore in, capturing a short bid for a hit by Hank Sauer for the third out with a run streaking homeward. Usually they lay back for the Cubs' slugger and nobody knows where Willie came from. But Lindy was deeply impressed when, on the following afternoon, with Elvin Tappe on first, Bob Rush knocked a one to short center which Mays took at his kneecaps and without losing motion, doubled Tappe off first.

"He never could have made the throw if he didn't catch the ball with his hands pointing downward as he always does," the Northwestern University mentor commented.

July 8, 1954

On July 8, Willie Mays continued his amazing catches in 1954 with a catch at Ebbets Field on the Dodgers' Walt Moryn. John Drebinger of the *New York Times* wrote that the "Say-Hey Kid came up with one of his great catches when he went up against the left center-field wall to rob Moryn of an extra-base hit." Drebinger also noted a catch by Duke Snider in the same game: "In the sixth Snider gave the Mays admirers something to think about when he went into deep right center near the wall and leaped high to take a hit away from Thompson."

The catch on Walt Moryn caught the attention of Jack Lang of the *Long Island Press*.

And how about Mays' catch of Moryn's smash to center ... with a man on second at the time. Willie, back to the plate, made one of those impossible catches of his and caught the ball right in front of the wall. It was one of those "he can't get it" drives but Willie did just as the Dodgers have been hearing he can.

The day after the game, which the Giants won 10–2, Pee Wee Reese was quoted in the *Brooklyn Eagle* on the catch Mays made on Moryn.

As a fielder, Mays drew praise from Pee Wee Reese who said, "Maybe he catches the ball funny but he controls that outfield. That catch he made Wednesday night, the one where he caught it and bounced off the wall, that was just the ball my boy Pete [Reiser] would have crashed on.
"Pete would've caught it but he wouldn't have bounced."

Even before the World Series, Willie Mays had made catches on Stan Lopata in April, Bob Skinner in May, Bill Bruton in June, and Mel Clark and Walt Moryn in July which may have been as good or better than the catch on Vic Wertz in October. In addition, he had made throws to nail Earl Torgeson and Joe Cunningham at the plate and Richie Ashburn at third which were among the greatest throws he ever made.

September 29, 1954

Willie Mays' catch on Vic Wertz on September 29 was the last of the sensational catches he made in 1954. Beginning in spring training just hours after he was discharged from the Army, and ending six months later in the World Series, Mays' year in the field may have been the greatest year in the outfield anyone ever had, with the possible exception of the year Jimmy Piersall had in 1953.

Willie Mays' catch on the Wertz drive has been described in detail by Arnold Hano in several places, especially in his 1955 book *A Day in the Bleachers*. Hano, who was in the center field stands that day, believed that the speed of the ball and its low trajectory of the drive helped make Willie's catch so special. The immediate turn and throw Mays executed made the play even more remarkable.

Russ Hodges, the Giants' play-by-play man, who saw Mays' catches on Skinner and Wertz, found the trajectory of the Skinner ball to be lower, the catch more difficult, and the Skinner catch greater than the catch on the Wertz ball. The ball Mel Clark hit on July 5 also may have had a lower trajectory than the Wertz drive.

Leo Durocher, in his book *Nice Guys Finish Last* (with Ed Linn), discussed the reaction of others after Mays' catch on the Wertz drive, and his own view of the catch's difficulty. The writers were ecstatic about the catch and were calling it a great catch. Leo acknowledged that the catch was great, but told them that for Willie Mays the catch was routine and that he had made better catches. The Cleveland writers found it difficult to believe that the catch they had just witnessed was "routine."

After the game with the Indians, according to Jim McCulley of the *New York Daily News*, Willie told reporters:

> "I had the ball all the way. There was nothin' too hard about that one.... And I remember one catch I made this year which was better. One on Skinner of the Pirates. I had to go right to the wall for it and make the catch with one hand. But that catch today, you should never miss those kind."

McCulley continued: "Those reporters and fans who saw Willie make the catch on Skinner back in mid season know that yesterday's catch did not compare with it for sheer skill."

The *New York Times*' Louis Effrat wrote of the Indians' reaction to the catch.

> Unanimously the Indians agreed that the catch of Mays, robbing Vic Wertz in the eighth, was the turning point in the encounter.... "It was one of the greatest catches I have ever seen," Lopez averred. Doby, the centerfielder, echoed his manager's praise of Mays.

In Bob Cooke's article in the *New York Herald Tribune*, Al Lopez made a more definitive statement abut the Mays catch: "Best I ever saw," he said. Given that Lopez began in the major leagues in 1928 and was a catcher for nearly twenty years, mostly in the National League, his opinion carries considerable weight. Not having seen Mays as often as Russ Hodges and Leo Durocher had seen him, Lopez was not in a position to compare the greatness of the catch on Wertz to Willie's other catches.

Wertz, who now has become known as the victim of Mays' great catch, had a very powerful day: a triple, a double, two singles, and the ball that Mays caught 450 feet away from the plate. He had great leverage on every ball he hit. The *Buffalo Evening News*' Cy Critzer quoted both Sal Maglie, who started the game, and Giants manager Leo Durocher about Wertz's performance. Both Maglie and Wertz had played for the Buffalo Bisons.

> "Our scouting report said to pitch Vic high with lots on your fast ball," said Sal.
> "Next time I face him, I'm throwing the book away. He is going to have to hit the best pitch I can throw. I don't have the fast ball to overpower Wertz, but he may have a problem handling my curve ball down low."
> Wertz collected his four hits on a fast ball outside, a slider, a change-up inside and a fast ball down the middle. This is Sal's recollection.

And Durocher: "'He hit every one of those balls on the nose,' the Giant manager declared. 'That double in the tenth was hit like a ton of bricks. We're going to have to go over Mr. Wertz again. Obviously we gotta change our way of pitching to him.'"

In Roscoe McGowen's *New York Times* article on the game Sal Maglie was asked if Wertz was tough to pitch to. "'He was tough all right,' replied Maglie. Then he grinned and added: 'He was good enough to hit a 420-foot triple and a 450-foot out, but Vic should have done what Rhodes did—just hit a 270 foot home run.'" The "Rhodes" Sal Maglie was talking about was Jim "Dusty" Rhodes, whom Leo Durocher summoned to pinch hit in the tenth inning. Rhodes, a left-handed batter, popped up a ball off the Indians' Bob Lemon. The ball carried to the second level of the right field stands for a three-run homer to win the game. The right field stands at the Polo Grounds were just 257 feet away from home plate. The ball Rhodes hit, an out in any other stadium, just carried into the upper deck.

Of the ball he hit which Mays caught, Wertz, as quoted in Louis Effrat's article in the *New York Times*, said, "I never hit a ball so hard in my career as the one Willie caught."

Joe DiMaggio, as quoted by Geoffrey Fisher of the *Cleveland News*, indicated that he held a high opinion of the Mays catch on Wertz's blast. Joe, who was sitting directly behind Fisher, said "it was one of the greatest catches I ever saw." This is exactly what DiMaggio himself wrote in his article in the *Cleveland Press*. "As remarkable as the ground Willie had to cover to make the catch on Vic Wertz—and he just did get to the ball—was the judgment he showed in not letting the wall scare him off. One of the most difficult plays for an outfielder to make is to go at top speed to the fence for the ball."

The *Cleveland News'* Fisher went on to record his version of Willie's catch.

> Vic swung and the ball headed up and towards the Harlem River. Mays spun on his spikes and shot for the remotest edge of the center field pasture. As he churned up the turf on the edge of the field and the towering green wall loomed up directly in front, he reached up and took the ball, spun and shot a strike to the infield. It was a monstrous catch of a monstrous blow.

In his day-after appraisal of Mays' catch on the Wertz ball, Dan Daniel of the *New York World-Telegram and Sun* went back more than thirty years in making his comparisons with Willie's catch. Daniel thought the catch was better than Al Gionfiddo's on DiMaggio in the 1947 Series, better than DiMaggio's catch on Hank Lieber in 1936, better than Sam Rice's grab in the 1925 Series, and better than Bill Cunningham's catch on Babe Ruth in the 1922 Series. "Just how good was the catch of Willie's? Well, it was so good, it couldn't have been any better! How much farther could he have run? He had to make the wall before the ball got there, and the wall lost."

In the *Cleveland Press*, Frank Gibbons called Mays "the Jesse James of center field," and went on to discuss Willie Mays' grab on the ball Vic Wertz hit.

> It was only right that Mays was discussed more than Rhodes by the free loaders in the press room, the late watch at Toots Shor's and the counter men in the hamburger joints.
>
> Nobody was able to separate the catch he made of a transcontinental drive by Vic Wertz from others he has achieved just as spectacularly.
>
> "Don't ask me," Leo Durocher grinned. "This guy makes so many I can't separate them. I think the one he made on Bob Skinner of the Pirates that was further out, right smack against the wall."
>
> Mays didn't think much of it, or played it that way. "Any outfielder ought to catch one that high," he said.
>
> Maybe so. But any other outfielder might not have run as fast or on compass to where the ball came down, just a stride away from the right portion of the bleachers.

The *Cleveland Plain Dealer*'s sports editor, Gordon Cobbledick, credited Willie Mays as being the hero of the game, not Dusty Rhodes. Cobbledick began his article on the game this way: "This was a ball game that went strictly according to the scenario. The Indians had excellent pitching—the Giants had Willie Mays. Mays won." Cobbledick called the catch on Wertz "fantastic" and also wrote: "What they've been saying about Mays is true. What they've been saying he can do he did today."

Elsewhere in the *New York Times*, an unnamed writer cited Tom Sheehan about Willie's catch on Vic Wertz.

> Although Willie Mays had no answer when asked if his catch of Vic Wertz' terrific drive was his greatest of not, his chief admirer—and an expert observer—had one. Tom Sheehan, the chief scout for the Giants, said, "His greatest catch, and the greatest I ever saw anybody make, was in Ebbets Field. He caught a ball way down here (Sheehan indicated a point a few inches from the ground) on the cinder track in left center, rolled over against the wall and came up with the ball.

Tom Sheehan's ranking of the catch on what Dodger Bobby Morgan called his "blue darter" liner to left center in Ebbets Field on April 18, 1952, fits with what Willie has said several times was his greatest catch.

The *New York Daily News*' Dick Young wrote the most colorful description of the events around Mays' catch. After discussing the short fly ball Dusty Rhodes hit for a home run to win the game for the Giants in the 10th inning, and its effect on the Indians' pitcher Bob Lemon, who threw his glove high into the air in anger over the surreal ending to his long day on the mound, Young continued:

> It was the first time Lemon had pitched in the Polo Grounds. He had heard of this strange structure that pitchers regard as a haunted house, and now he knows—first hand. Not only does he know of Rhodes' ludicrous homer, but of another peculiarity of this most peculiar of all big league ballparks.
>
> Lemon would have won the game in regulation time, and Rhodes wouldn't have had the opportunity to become a ... hero if not for the fact that a ball hit 450 feet to center field can be caught in the Polo Grounds—and the added fact that the Giants have just the boy to catch it.
>
> That would be Willie Mays, the NL batting champion—and fielding champ. Willie didn't get a hit in three official swings against Lemon, but he did make one of his no-man-can-do-that grabs to preserve a 2–2 tie in the eighth.
>
> That frame had opened with a walk to Larry Doby and a scratch hit into the short hole by Al Rosen. Here, with south-swinger Vic Wertz coming up, manager Leo Durocher yanked Sal Maglie. It wasn't that Sal had lost his stuff, or was being hit hard, but rather that he was having trouble with his curve ball ... particularly against left-handed hitters, specifically against a left-handed hitter named Wertz.
>
> Vic had stroked a long triple and two singles in his three previous trips. He was to pole a double in the 10th inning for a fine four-hit day. But this time, in the critical eighth, the Giants got him out. They got him out, by bringing in Don Liddle, who fooled Wertz so badly that Vic hit the ball only 450 feet.
>
> In this park of strange dimensions, where a home run travels little more than half that distance, Wertz's straight-away drive was catchable. Willie Mays, back to the plate, took off after it. He ran for about five minutes, slowed down slightly to turn his head for another look, then, seeing he hadn't yet reached the estimated point of arrival, threw his legs into high again and ran for another couple of minutes.
>
> As Willie reached the cindered fringe of the outfield, just in front of the right segment of the bleacher seats, he shot up his hands over his head, the way a football player goes for a lead pass. Sure enough, there was the ball.

"I had it all the way," commented Mays in the clubhouse later. "You should never miss that kind."

Willie heaved this easy chance back to the infield so frantically that he wound up on his hands and knees. It is conceivable that, if he had delayed the return, even slightly, Doby could have scored from second. As it was, Larry pulled up easily at third, and Rosen, who approached second, returned to first.

In the winter after Mays' catch on Wertz, Mays' manager Leo Durocher gave Mays the most glowing accolade he could give. The first sentence in an article included in the January 19, 1955, *Cleveland Press* under the title "Mays Even Greater Star than Ruth, Musial—Leo," stated: "Leo Durocher declared flatly today that Willie Mays is "the greatest ballplayer I've ever seen," and that includes 'em all, from Babe Ruth to Stan Musial."

Leo went on to talk about Mays as a fielder of ground balls.

"Willie would be great at any position you put him. Third base, first base or shortstop. Why, a lot of times before games, he gets out there at shortstop and I hit grounders at him until I get blisters on my hands. He handles the hottest ones I hit at him as if they were nothing.

"'Is this where you used to play?' he needles me. "Why it's just like an old man's home.'"

After analyzing the catch on Wertz and saying that he did not think other great centerfielders could have made the catch because "no one else was as fast in getting to the ball," Arnold Hano, in *A Day in the Bleachers*, gave what he felt to be the defining characteristic that differentiated Mays from other players.

I wonder what will happen to Mays in the next few years. He may gain in finesse and batting wisdom, but he cannot really improve much because his finest talent lies in his reflex action. He is so swift in his reflexes, the way young Joe Louis was with his hands when, cobra-like, they would flash through the thinnest slit in a foe's defense, Louis, lashing Paulino Uzcudun with the first hard punch he threw, drilling into the tiniest opening and crushing the man who had never before been knocked out. That is Mays, too. Making a catch and whirling and throwing before another man would have been twenty feet from the ball.

And until those reflexes slow down, Mays must be regarded as off by himself, not merely *a* great ballplayer, but *the* great ballplayer of our time [124].

May 31, 1954—Duke Snider

As remarkable as Willie Mays' fielding year was, the title of the "greatest single catch of 1954," and perhaps of all time, might well go to Duke Snider's Memorial Day 1954 vault up the wall in Philadelphia.

The Memorial Day 1954 game was an exciting one, with the Dodgers prevailing in 12 innings with a 5–4 victory over the Phillies in Philadelphia. Though only a month and half into the season, the game was tense and hard-fought, almost like a World Series game, and had a number of thrilling events. The pitching was strong. Brooklyn's Preacher Roe had a no-hitter for five innings. Phillies right-hander Bob Miller pitched all 12 innings. The Dodgers' right fielder, Carl Furillo, made a spectacular catch. The Phillies' third baseman, Willie Jones, made two sensational fielding plays to take hits from Dodger batters. Five home runs were hit, one a pinch-hit three-run homer in the eighth by the Phillies' Smoky Burgess to give the Phils their first lead, one a shot of 500 feet plus by Duke Snider early in the game, and another being Gil Hodges' long drive to left in the 12th, which proved to be the winning margin.

But the exhilarating, magical end of this struggle in front of 22,386 fans was Duke Snider's last-out catch in the Phillies' half of the 12th.

Snider was no stranger to ascents up outfield walls. He had been going vertical for many years, mostly out of necessity given the cozy dimensions in his home park, Ebbets Field. He didn't have the opportunity to use his speed to make long runs to track down balls hit beyond 400 feet. Ebbets Field's longest distance from home plate was at 384 feet in center field in 1954. So Snider developed approaches to going up the walls in his territory. There are a number of photos showing him at various places and heights up on the walls.

Other outfielders in the National League also sprung up the walls at Ebbets Field, but it is likely no one was as vertically adventuresome as often as Duke Snider was. He had many opportunities, and he had the daring to use his outstanding physical gifts to challenge the walls often. The wall at Ebbets Field from the left field foul line to left center field was almost ten feet high. From center field to the left edge of the scoreboard the fence angled away from the field almost ten feet and then had another ten feet of concrete going straight up. A twenty-foot screen topped the concrete portion.

The left field to center field wall at Connie Mack Stadium, earlier known as Shibe Park, which Snider climbed on May

At Ebbets Field in July 1954, Duke Snider takes a practice leap up the angled right field wall. The bend in the fence just above Duke's right elbow is 9 feet, six inches above the field. It appears that Duke's head is about a foot higher than the bend, which indicates that his feet are about 55 inches off the ground (© Bettmann/CORBIS).

31, 1954, was made of concrete faced with wood. The wall was 12 feet high, and in 1954 had an additional wire fence rising to about four feet above the 12-foot wall.

The *New York Times*' Roscoe McGowen gave high praise for Duke Snider's catch in Philadelphia: "Duke Snider made one of the greatest catches of his career for the final out in the twelfth inning today and preserved a 5–4 victory for the Dodgers over the Phils at Connie Mack Stadium." The baseball writers for the other New York papers went further than McGowen's "one of the greatest catches of his career." Several of them referred to the catch as "the greatest" without any reservation.

Bill Roeder of the *New York World-Telegram and Sun* referred to the catch as "the catch of a lifetime." He went on to write:

It isn't often that you'll see teammates racing from the dugout all the way to center field to show their gratitude.

That was the spectacle with Russ Meyer outlegging the field, after Snider scrambled up the wall at the 405-foot point to clasp the ball which Willie Jones socked. Unclasped, it would surely have meant defeat because there were two runners tearing around ahead of Jones.

It was a daredevil catch, the kind Pete Reiser used to make with the pardonable difference that Snider neglected to fracture his skull. Bob Miller, the losing pitcher, no doubt might have been happy to attend to that oversight.

In the *New York Herald Tribune*, Harold Rosenthal called the Snider catch "miraculous." Rosenthal went on to describe the scene and the catch and added: "It was Duke's best defensive effort in a long time, a positive sparkler by a centerfielder to whom fine plays are routine."

Michael Gaven of the *New York Journal-American* called Snider's catch on Willie Jones's drive "the most sensational you ever saw." He went on to talk about the height of Snider's leap and the scene after the catch..

How many feet the Duke leaped he could even guess himself. But when he clutched the ball in the webbing of his outstretched glove, it didn't seem to be any more than a few inches from the top of the 13-foot fence. And clutch the ball he had to do because he couldn't get close enough to palm it.

If ever there was a miraculous catch that was it. The Dodgers leaped almost hysterically, with most of them running into the outfield to joyfully paddy whack him through the crowd which had already swarmed on the field.

"Incredible" was the word Dick Young of the *New York Daily News* had for Snider's catch.

It was as great a grab as any NL player made in his career and greater than any catch Joe DiMaggio ever made during, or after his career. What's more, it was the ball game. If Snider didn't get it, two runs would have scored for Philly, and Clem Labine would have blown another toughie.

Labine had come in from the pen in the ninth after Preacher Roe had wilted and Jim Hughes had been belted. Labine sweated through a couple of jams while waiting for a run. Then, after getting it from Hodges, he almost tossed it away. He had two down in the Phils' 12th when he walked pinch-hitters Dan Schell and Bob Micelotta.

It was then that Willie Jones sent his drive to deep left-center. Snider took off

In a 1954 game against the New York Giants, Duke Snider goes onto the Ebbets Field wall in an effort to catch a ball that evidently got there just before he did.

after it—but it looked like a futile gesture. To most of the 22,386 fans, it seemed that the drive would either go into the seats or bang against the wall to score two men and produce a sudden-death thrill.

They got their thrill, but in a different way. They got it from Snider. Duke, sprinting furiously, reached the wall and didn't stop.

He took off, dug his spikes into a fence that didn't seem possible to dig into, and went higher—just enough to throw his glove hand high above his head and across his body.

When he came down, he was waving the ball in his glove. Ump Jocko Conlan, working at second base, stood petrified for the briefest moment, then dramatically threw his fist into the air, signifying the game-ending out.

The Dodgers, a pretty blasé bunch as a rule, exploded emotionally. Those in the field ran out to meet Snider and smother him with hugs and backslaps. Those in the dugout raced to shake his hand.

Even many of the Philly fans swarmed onto the field to congratulate the hero. By the time he had reached the infield, he had to claw his way through the dugout underpass.

Snider's catch dwarfed his early-inning homer—which is quite a trick considering that the drive cleared the clock above the scoreboard in spacious Mack Stadium. You have to hit one close to 500 feet to leave the park at that point.

Three other papers used the word "Greatest" in the titles. The *New York Post*'s headline was: "It Was Just the Greatest." Sid Friedlander of the *Post* began by quoting Dodger coach Jake Pitler.

"In forty years of baseball, I never saw a catch like Snider made," said Jake Pitler.

"But I remember one catch back about 1909 when the Giants were playing in Pittsburgh," continued Jake. Christy Mathewson was pitching and Jack Miller was the hitter. Red Murray was playing right field for the Giants that day.

"Dark clouds were hanging low over the field and it seemed Miller hit the ball right up into them out of sight. But Murray ran over into center field and as he made a leaping barehanded catch there was terrible flash of lightning. I'll never forget it."

"But Snider's was a better catch," said Jake.

Greatest catch they ever saw, that's what all the Dodgers said.

Pitler's comments about the catch Red Murray made indicate that Pitler was there in Pittsburgh when Red and the lightning flashed across the Forbes Field turf. Pitler was born in 1894 in New York, and began in the majors in 1917 with the Pittsburgh Pirates. At the time of Murray's famous catch Pitler would have been fifteen years old. It is likely he read or heard vivid accounts about the catch in 1909, and heard more about it later when he was member of the Pirates.

Sid Friedlander then described the Phillies' inning up to Duke's catch, and continued with a quote from Dodgers manager Walter Alston.

"The thing that made it the greatest," said Manager Walt Alston, "was that he not only had to make a great catch of the ball but he had to fight the fence, too. It wasn't like diving for the ball in an open field. I don't know how he got so high on the wall. It looked as though he was climbing it with his spikes."

Snider didn't know how he got up either. "I caught the ball backhanded," he said, "and the force of it spun me around against the wall."

Duke was asked if he could remember any catches he made that could approach this one but he shook his head. "This was my best," he said.

Don Thompson, who was in left field, was the closest to Snider when he made the catch. "Duke ran straight for the wall. As he leaped, he turned his right side toward the wall but he spun after making the catch and his left knee hit it."

Veterans like Ted Lyons and Billy Herman couldn't remember a catch to match. "I saw

Jimmy Piersall make that catch last year everybody wrote about," said Herman. "But this catch of Snider's was better."

The Duke is having quite a year at that. He has already made more than a half-dozen sensational catches and he is up with the batting leaders with a cool .356.

The titles over Jack Lang's June 1, 1954, *Long Island Press* article on the Memorial Day game in Philadelphia were: "Better Than Piersall, Mays 'Specials'" above, and in bigger print below, "Duke's Game-Saver Tabbed 'Greatest Ever.'"

None of the Dodgers seemed to know how Duke Snider made it—least of all Snider himself—but they all agreed that the Duke's spectacular catch of Willie Jones' tremendous liner against the left center field wall in Connie Mack Stadium was the greatest they'd ever seen.

"The greatest, the greatest, the greatest!" that's all you could hear in the riotous dressing room for fully a half hour after the game as they milled around in groups sipping beers and soft drinks and shaking their heads in amazement.

And as they boarded a train an hour later to start their western trip, all they talked about were other great catches they've seen in the past but to all of them, none was greater.

"Was it the greatest catch I ever saw?" Manager Walter Alston beamed. "That was the greatest catch anyone ever saw."

"Never saw anything like it," chimed in Billy Herman and Ted Lyons, the two coaches who have been around a long time and undoubtedly saw many great catches during their careers.

"I was at Yankee Stadium last September when Jim Piersall made that catch out in front of the right field bullpen that they're still talking about but it couldn't compare to this," said Herman.

"I thought that the catch Willie Mays made on Bobby Morgan at Ebbets Field two years ago was the greatest catch I'd ever seen,' said the usually conservative Carl Erskine. "But that was before this one. This was greater."

Describing Snider's catch in the 12th inning which ended the game and preserved a 5–4 victory for the Dodgers is almost impossible. It was spectacular beyond description.

Neither Snider or Don Thompson, who was closest to him at the time, knew exactly what happened. All either could say was that within a split second Duke leaped against the wall and with the webbing of the glove managed to spear the ball just as before it bounced off the wall.

There were two men on and two out at the time and the Dodgers were leading by one run on Gil Hodges' 13th homer in the top half of the 12th. Jones got hold of one of Labine's serves and gave it a tremendous ride out towards the left center field wall and high.

Breaking with the crack of the bat, Snider ran and ran and ran and at the last second leaped high up against the wall. The next thing anyone knew the ball disappeared out of sight for a second and then Snider came down with a bounce, holding his gloved hand high to signify the catch.

"As I leaped I felt it hit my glove and the speed of the drive turned my glove around," Snider said. "I felt my right side hit the wall and then my knee, that's how much it spun me around."

Snider had his cap stolen in the wild, milling mob on the field but he managed to hold on to the ball for a souvenir. "It was the greatest I've ever made," the Duke grinned.

"I've seen some great diving catches in the past but this was the greatest because he had to fight the wall as well," Alston smiled.

"Say," he said, turning to announcer Vince Scully, "how could you guys describe that one?" And come to think of it, how could they?

The *Brooklyn Eagle's* main headline was: "Snider's Catch Called the Greatest." Above that the headline writer placed, "THEY'RE STILL TALKING ABOUT IT." The *Eagle's* Dave Anderson wasted no time telling where the Dodgers thought the catch ranked.

To a man, the Dodgers insist that Duke Snider's pogo-stick pinch of Willie Jones' liner hit against the left-center field wall in Philadelphia was the greatest, absolutely the greatest, catch in baseball history.

That takes in a lot of catches and a lot of history. And it brings up an interesting point on why Snider may make the Hall of Fame and why Pete Reiser didn't. Also, why Duke Snider's the best centerfielder in baseball these days. And that means you, to Willie Mays, and especially you, Mickey Mantle.

Snider has a gift of climbing walls, not splattering his brains against them as Reiser did.

"That was the same type of ball Pete would have hit the wall running for," Pee Wee Reese said between superlatives on Duke's catch. Not only was it a catch. It was the game, saving a 5–4 win for Clem Labine and the touring Dodgers.

Reiser, rated another Ty Cobb when he arrived in 1941, ruined his career because he never looked at a wall. Instead, he'd crash head-first. Result: fractured skull and constant headaches.

Not so with Snider, who says, "I saw Reiser hit the wall in 1947. He never took his eye off the ball." Duke admits, "I always take my off the ball just for a second. That way I judge where I am and how many steps it is to the wall. I've always done it.

"Yesterday, I figured I had about four steps to the wall. After four steps I jumped. My right foot dug into the wall. It's wood. Then my left knee scraped the wall and I turned my body.

"Aw, did I catch it? Honestly, I don't know. All I know is that the ball was in the webbing when I came down. Then everybody was running at me, players, fans. Some kid stole my cap."

Snider admitted he thought Jones' liner "might be a homer at first. At the last second, I changed my mind."

Don Thompson, playing left field at the time, verified Snider's glove was at the top of the wall, roughly 400 feet from the plate. The wall is 12 feet high.

That means Snider, in making a back-handed catch, was probably four feet off the ground. Figure the guy is six feet tall and his glove is two feet above his head. How does a man jump that high, especially when it appears he takes a step in mid-air?

Coach Ted Lyons, who said he could hear Snider's knee and torso bang the wall from the bullpen, brought out just why it was such a great catch. "It meant the game. If he misses it, we lose."

At the time Labine had walked Danny Schell and Bob Micelotta with two out. Then Jones clocked a sinker that didn't sink to left center. Then Snider made the catch. In the confusion, Gil Hodges' 13th homer provided the winning run in the 12th.

Labine was the third and luckiest Dodger pitcher. Preacher Roe, after five no-hit innings, gave a homer to Bobby Morgan in the seventh. Then Smokey Burgess crashed a three-run pinch homer off Jim Hughes in the eighth. Labine pitched the last four innings.

Roy Campanella also hit a homer, his first since April 15. And so did Snider. That gives him .356, 10 homers and 29 runs batted in. Please no more nonsense about Mays and Mantle.

Dodger coach Ted Lyons pitched for the Chicago White Sox from 1923 until 1946, excepting 1943 through 1945 when he was in the service, and was elected to the Hall of Fame in 1955. He was a teammate of the outstanding centerfielder Johnny Mostil during most of the 1920s. Lyons was a teammate of Bib Falk's in 1924 when Falk made his great catch while skidding across the dirt. Lyons and Dodger coach Billy Herman, an outstanding second baseman who began his major league career in 1931 with the Chicago Cubs, had seen many outstanding catches by outfielders, but not one that topped Snider's Memorial Day leaping grab.

Dave Anderson's comments about Willie Mays and Mickey Mantle were part of a rivalry among some baseball writers and among fans about who was the best centerfielder in New York, and therefore, in their minds, the best in baseball. The players themselves stayed out of this "rivalry," but fans and some writers in New York had their favorites. The *New York Daily Mirror* even had a special box during part of the 1954 season which compared Mays' previous day's performance with Snider's.

In his book *Bums*, Peter Golenbock quoted Ralph Branca, who was a teammate of Snider's.

"Duke was something. He could fly, he could throw, he could hit, he had power, he could do it all. I'm prejudiced, but when they ask me who was better, Mays, Mantle, or Snider, there's no contest. Duke was a better outfielder than the other two guys by far. He got a better jump on the ball. He had a much more accurate arm than either one of them, and he played in the toughest ballpark. At Ebbets Field you have to worry about running into the wall, where the other guys could run all day to catch the ball...." [347].

The Philadelphia writers were equally taken by Snider's Memorial Day vault up the Connie Mack Stadium wall. Joe Greenday of the *Philadelphia Daily News* wrote:

The Phillies entrain tonight for a swing through the West and when they return home again on June 15 perhaps they will have nicer words to describe Duke Snider. For it was the Duke that sent the Phils home moaning yesterday when his catch—termed sensational, outstanding, and spectacular—robbed them of a last ditch victory and gave the Brooklyn Dodgers a 5–4 triumph in a single holiday game.

Duke's aerial antics, which snared Willie Jones' drive in the bottom of the 12th with the tying and winning runs on base, was the climax to an afternoon that saw 22,383 souls bound to their seats in a hammer-and-tong contest.

...

Jones, who had gone hitless all day, tagged a Clem Labine pitch and sent it sailing toward the 405 ft. sign in left-center and it looked like a sure extra base clout and perhaps a winner for the Phils. But, along came centerfielder Snider, gliding across the outfield, to make a leaping stab of the pellet, a good 10-feet up on the wall.

It was the third out and the game was over but the majority of patrons were pinned to their seats. Even Martians would have agreed that the catch was out of this world.

Carl Furillo, the Dodgers right fielder and another wizard in the art of hair-raising catches, commented after the game that Snider dug his spikes in the wooden wall to get that extra boost for the catch.

Some of the veteran sportswriters agreed that it rates with some of the top grabs in baseball.

Not to alibi, but some of the Phils thought Snider had trapped the ball against the wall. However, the umpires called it legit.

The issue of whether Snider actually caught the ball was not mentioned in the New York papers. Snider himself was not entirely certain he had. His comment in Dave Anderson's *Brooklyn Eagle* article was, "Aw, did I catch it? Honestly, I don't know." Things happened so fast, and in such an unusual way that either a catch or a trap may have occurred. The other two Philadelphia papers both gave him credit for the great catch, and mentioned the doubts of the Phillies' manager Steve O'Neill and some Phillies players.

Frank Yeutter of the *Philadelphia Bulletin* gave a sense of the drama of the game in his account.

The Phillies will never forget Memorial Day, 1954, and Brooklyn's Duke Snider. And Willie Jones will have the strongest of all memories of the lanky centerfielder who made perhaps the greatest and most disputed catch ever seen in the 45-year Connie Mack Stadium.

There were a lot of home runs. There were a lot of tense, dramatic moments. There were almost continuous cheers by the holiday throng of 22,386.

But the greatest moment was the last split second.

Rookies Danny Schell and Bobby Micelotta were on base. They got there on walks. There were two out. Then Jones connected. He hit a long high drive that seemed to be labeled "home run." Then it became apparent the ball wasn't going to reach the left-field seats at the 405-foot mark.

It was going to be good for extra bases, though. It wasn't quite high enough. Only about ten feet high but still flying. The two kid Phils were racing around the bases like wildfire. Micelotta was carrying the winning run. The Dodgers were ahead 5–4 at that moment.

The crowd was frenzied.

Then came the Duke. Striding across the outfield in long, easy, yet rapid strides, he went to the wall. But the ball was four feet over his six-foot pate. The Duke went up in the air. You could hear a thud against the wooden wall. Up went the Duke still higher. He stretched his glove as high as he could stretch.

And he came down with the ball.

Just to show the momentarily mute crowd that he had the ball when he bounced off the wall, he started on a run for the infield still holding the glove-clasped ball above his head.

Pee Wee Reese, Junior Gilliam, and winning pitcher Clem Labine and Billy Cox raced to the outfield to meet him. So did some of the fans.

It was like the last play of a game that decided the pennant. Like the crowd that pressed around Bobby Thomson the day he hit the home run in the Polo Grounds to win the pennant for the New York Giants. Like the day Dick Sisler hit the home run that won the pennant for the Phillies in 1950.

But on the Phillies' side was black doubt that Snider had caught the ball fairly. Manager Steve O'Neill ran out on the field and protested to umpire Jocko Conlan, contending that the ball had first hit the wall and was trapped before it could bounce back into the field.

"I'll never admit that the ball was fairly caught," Steve said. "Maybe right now Snider's happy about it, but if he's honest some day in the future he'll admit he got the ball off the wall. Why, you could hear the ball hit the wall. Conlan said the Duke's elbow that hit and made the noise. Had it been Snider's elbow, he would have never made the catch. I'll believe to my dying day that we lost a tough game on an improper catch."

No matter who's right in the matter, it was the most dramatic game the Phils have played this season....

The *Philadelphia Inquirer*'s Phillies writer Stan Baumgartner, who had a major league career as pitcher beginning in 1914, also wrote about the thrilling game and the great catch as a major part of that game.

While it was Hodges' 13th home run that sent Bob Miller to a disheartening defeat, his first after two victories, the play that will live for long in the eyes of the fans was Snider's catch.

It was one of the most, if not the most sensational catch the writer has ever seen under pressure. It was a spectacular climax to one of the most thrilling contests the writer has seen — three hours and 55 minutes of continual thrills.

Danny Schell, who had batted for Ted Kazanski and walked, was on second, and Bob Micelotta, who had pinch hit for Miller and walked, was on first when Jones hit a 1–1 pitch by right-hander Clem Labine on the fat of his bat.

The ball soared toward the left field stands and for a moment the thrill-tingled fans, who had sat of the edge of their chairs from almost the first pitch, let out a wild cheer, thinking it was a home run and a Phils' triumph.

But the ball dropped slowly toward the ground. Snider, one of the National League's greatest fielders, raced to the fence, watched it arc toward the concrete wall.

He sensed it would hit the wall at least five feet above his outstretched arms. He coiled himself and then with one mighty spring shot up the wall.

Three, four, possibly five feet his body went up the concrete abutment. His gloved hand stretched high above his head. At the tip of his stretch his glove closed around the falling sphere. At the same moment he twisted his body to keep clear of the concrete, held the ball aloft, dropped to the ground and ran toward the Dodger dugout as the fans gave him a thunderous ovation.

But he was a long time reaching safety. Labine, the winning pitcher, ran into center field to meet him. So did the other Dodger players and fans, who mobbed him....

No photographs of Duke
Snider's catch on Memorial
Day in Philadelphia seem to
exist, but these two drawings
depict him planting his foot
into the wood facing on the
wall and then show him at the
apex of his vault up the wall
(drawing by Darryl Swanson,
North Collins, N.Y.).

In the middle of Stan Baumgartner's article was a box within which the title read: "Did Snider Really Catch It?" The text in the box was:

Did Duke Snider actually catch the ball that ended yesterday's Phillies-Brooklyn game in the 12th?

The fans thought he did and his Brooklyn teammates thought he did and, more important, Umpire Jocko Conlan, who called the play, thought he did. But the Phillies don't think so.

The Phillies bullpen crew of Coach Benny Bengough and pitchers Murry Dickson, Karl Drews and Steve Ridzik, to a man, state Snider grabbed the ball off the fence on a quick carom.

No protest is possible, however since it is a judgment play.

Almost fifty years later, on August 2, 2002, in a conversation I had with him, Steve Ridzik quickly recalled what he saw from his spot in the Phillies bullpen.

JA: One of the Philadelphia papers the day after Duke made the catch mentioned that you and the other players in the bullpen thought the ball was trapped.

Steve Ridzik: We did because we were sitting right there down the left field corner. When he caught that ball it was going away, and actually he hit the wall, but the ball hit the wall first. He had his glove going right into the wall. I remember the catch very, very well.

JA: The umpire didn't see it that way.

SR: The umpire is in around second base, and you couldn't tell. Don't forget, we were sitting right along the wall there, and the back of his glove was toward home plate. It was bing-bing, but it did hit the wall first because I remembered the play as soon as you mentioned it. It was a great catch, if you wanted to call it a catch. They called it a catch.

JA: How high up the wall was he?

SR: That wall was around 12 feet, and he was right at the very top of it.

JA: There was a little wire part of that fence above that.

SR: Right. It had about a foot or whatever of wire above the wall. He was actually right at the top of the fence and where the wire goes up.

JA : So Willie Jones's ball was a foot or two from going out?

SR: It was a good foot or two from going out. He caught it right at the top of the wall. It was a great play on Duke's part, I'll tell you that.

JA: How did Duke propel himself up the wall?

SR: He hit the wall with his foot and that kind of propelled him up to that height. He was a pretty tall guy. He was on the run coming over from center field at a little angle. I remember him hitting the wall and going up.

The back of Duke's glove hand was toward home plate. The umpire had no possible way of telling if that ball was caught or not. He just had to make a decision on it.

JA: But you guys all agreed that the ball was off the wall.

SR: Absolutely. Like I say, it wasn't something that was very noticeable. We're sitting 70, 80 feet, maybe a little more from where the play took place. So we're right along the wall and we have a perfect shot at looking at it. But, like I say, it was just about impossible for the umpire to make a call on that. When Duke came off the wall with the ball, naturally the umpire called it an out.

To others who have recalled Snider's Memorial Day 1954 catch, it has remained vivid. More than a year after the catch in Philadelphia, an article on Duke Snider by Al Stump appeared in the September 1955 *SPORT* magazine. Stump quoted the Dodgers' great catcher Roy Campanella about Snider and then went on to discuss the catch on Willie Jones's drive.

"Back of the plate," Roy says, "I see him get a jump on balls like no other outfielder gets. You take the catch off Jones at Philly last season—there's nobody, Mays included, who could have caught that one."

With two runners on base and the Dodgers leading, 5–4, in the 12th inning, Willie Jones drove a 405-footer up against the left-centerfield wall. Duke isn't a look-and-run outfielder like Mays. He prefers to keep the ball in view all the time if possible, and he was judging this one every step of his long run to the wall. There it seemed he was climbing the concrete—"on his knees," as awed Dodger coach Ted Lyons put it. Up and up he went like a human fly to spear the ball, give a confirming wave of his glove and fall backward to the turf. The wooden bracing on the wall showed spike marks almost as high as his head. It was such a catch that, although it saved the game for Brooklyn, admiring Philly fans swarmed on the field by the dozens. Duke lost his cap and part of his shirt and almost lost his belt.

Later Stump compared Snider with other men who were known for how they dealt with outfield fences.

Smaller, lighter off-the-wall operators, like Paul Waner, Mel Ott, Dom DiMaggio and Clyde Milan have made defensive baseball history, but among the big men there have been few with the catlike qualities of the thickly muscled Duke. "He's an acrobat, the same as Mays," Ralph Kiner says, "but with the difference that he scrambles only when it's necessary.... I'd say Duke covers more ground, wastes less motion and is more consistent than anyone since DiMaggio. And in playing the real tough ones, he's very close to Joe."

Manager Alston, who came by his admiration for Snider slowly ... is firmly convinced that Duke's outfield gymnastics are beyond compare. "I don't think I've ever seen an outfielder who can go so high for a ball while running at full speed," he commented after one of Snider's wall-climbing stunts at Ebbets Field. "I don't know how he does it. But he catches them, and he never seems to have trouble with the walls."

Without hesitation Carl Erskine, Duke's long-time friend and former teammate on the Dodgers, recalled Duke's climb in Philadelphia almost fifty years later. In an October 2001 telephone conversation with me, he said Duke could try to make that catch a thousand times and probably could not duplicate it. Carl Erskine considers that Memorial Day 1954 catch the greatest he ever saw.

Don Thompson was the left fielder when Snider made the Memorial Day catch, and was a fine fielder himself. In an April 6, 2002, conversation, he had no trouble recalling the catch and talking about it, almost as if it happened a week ago. He began by saying that, "If you saw that catch, you'd never forget it."

Don Thompson: Puddin' Head Jones hit a long fly to left center. Duke was coming over from center field, and running toward the fence. His right shoulder, the right side of his body was sort of turned to the fence. When he got to the fence he stuck his cleats in the fence, jumped up, and twisted.

JA: He was running full speed. He wasn't loping along.

DT: He was running full speed to get the ball.

JA: And he was pretty quick, wasn't he?

DT: Duke was pretty quick. I was coming over from left field and he went right in front of me. He was a little ahead of me. Then he turned right straight at the fence. He jumped up and caught it.

JA: Do you think you had a chance on the ball?

DT: I don't think I could have gotten it. I was playing this guy to pull. I was toward the left field foul line.

JA: Was his glove at the top of the fence?

DT: Yes. If it wasn't at the top it was close. It might have been a little above it.

What made Duke's catch so great was he was running full speed toward the fence, and turned his body sideways.

JA: And had to contend with the fence.

DT: Yes.

JA: Where did Duke put his cleats in the fence?

DT: I can't tell you how high up he jumped, but he jumped as high as he could. He really jumped. I was amazed when he caught it. I told him, "Duke, I never will forget that catch. That was one of the greatest I've ever seen."

Don Thompson said he saw Duke Snider in New Jersey several years ago, and again expressed to Snider his amazement over Snider's catch against Willie Jones in 1954.

On July 8, 1954, in a column he wrote about Snider for the *Brooklyn Eagle*, Harold C. Burr wrote: "The Duke is a ball hawk, climbing outfield walls like a human fly scaling a building. He made a catch in Philadelphia this year that was rated as the best of all time by eyewitnesses. It was as if he had springs in his spikes that he released in his necessity."

Similarly, on September 16, 1956, Charles Hoff of the *New York Daily News* took a photo showing Snider climbing up the Ebbets Field wall on a drive by Cincinnati's Gus Bell. In the next day's *News* the title above the caption was: "Human Fly."

And what about the victim of Snider's catch? After telling of Snider's recent hitting binge, Roscoe McGowen, in the June 23, 1954, *The Sporting News*, wrote:

> Even this kind of ball-belting was, if not exactly over-shadowed, at least given tremendous competition by The Duke's fielding feats. Capping them all, of course, was the extraordinary game-saving catch he made high off the left-center field wall at Connie Mack Stadium for the last out in the twelfth inning. Willie Jones hit the ball and he still cannot believe it was caught.

Two weeks later, in the July 7, 1954, *The Sporting News*, McGowen again returned to Snider's catch on the Willie Jones shot on Memorial Day 1954. His comments were part of a page devoted to comparing Snider and Willie Mays. Joe King made the case for Mays as the better player, while McGowen made the case for Snider. After briefly re-capping the catch on Willie Jones, McGowen wrote: "The Duke made a lot of other fine catches before and since but that one probably was the greatest of his career. Your agent, after recalling others that he has seen during almost three decades of watching major league baseball, is almost willing to put it at the top of the list."

July 30, 1954—Larry Doby

The Cleveland Indians' Larry Doby was widely regarded as one of the premier outfielders in the game by the time he made his catch on Washington's Tom Umphlett at Cleveland Stadium.

The *Cleveland Plain Dealer*'s Harry Jones first called Doby's catch "breathtaking," then later told about the catch.

> But the loudest cheer raised by the crowd of 17,504 was accorded Doby in the third inning when, with the Indians leading 5–3, and a Washington runner on base, he made a sensational catch of Tom Umphlett's bid for a home run.
>
> Umphlett's drive headed for the Washington bullpen canopy in left center. Doby raced over, scaled the fence and made the catch while suspended in mid-air.
>
> He then crashed into the top of the fence and was thrown to the ground, badly shaken.
>
> All Cleveland players, plus Manager Al Lopez and Trainer Wally Bock, rushed to his side as he lay there. He was on his feet a few minutes later and remained in the game though he reinjured his left shoulder and had the wind knocked out of him.

The next day, in his "BATTING AROUND" column, Harry Jones again commented on Doby's catch.

Larry Doby's breathtaking catch Friday night was still the chief topic of discussion before yesterday's game and even some of the Nats were saying it was something.

"Best catch I've ever seen," was Manager Bucky Harris' terse comment.

Both Frank Gibbons of the *Cleveland Press* and Hal Lebovitz of the *Cleveland News* were unreserved in their praise of Doby's great effort, and both quoted Dizzy Dean, who gave the catch legitimacy as one of the best ever. Under the title "Doby's Catch One of Greatest of All Time," Frank Gibbons began by mentioning Dean.

Dizzy Dean says he'll be a skunk's uncle if a catch Larry Doby made last night at the Stadium wasn't the greatest he has ever seen in his many years as a baseball, radio and television pitcher.

Old Diz, here to do a national television job on today's game, has seen most of the top-flight centerfielders in his 25 years around the circuits, and one of them played behind him in the person of Terry Moore.

"I seen them all," he maintains. "Moore, DiMaggio, and this here fellow named Mays. But I never seen a catch as good as this one and that pitcher ought to pay that Doby a month's salary.

Everybody who saw Doby launch himself like a rocket, soar above the five-foot fence in left-center, then bounce off the bullpen awning with a ball hit by Tom Umphlett of Washington, went along with Diz. If this wasn't the greatest catch of the century, it must be at least a match for any other.

Doby didn't remember much about what happened or how.

The Cleveland Indians' Larry Doby was a powerful hitter, a fast runner, and an excellent, strong-armed fielder.

"I just went for the ball, same as I did for Jackie Jensen's home run a couple of days ago, the one I missed. The fellows in our bullpen told me my right hand went through the awning before I bounced off. If it did, I didn't notice.

"I didn't get hurt much. Knocked the wind out of me and my left shoulder gave me a jolt, where I hurt it before. Maybe it hit a nerve."

Right fielder Al Smith was the best witness. He was there and took the ball out of Doby's glove after Umpire John Flaherty made the catch official without hesitation.

"Larry really took off and most of him was over the fence when he backhanded that ball. He bounced off that awning like a rubber ball. I thought he broke his back until he held up his glove with the ball in it."

The *News'* title over Lebovitz's article was: "Doby's Catch Greatest!" Lebovitz devoted his whole column to Doby's catch.

Man, that was the greatest.

That catch of Larry Doby's was out of this world... and almost out of the park. Ask Dizzy Dean, the great one, who rarely raves about baseball feats other than his own. "That," he declared emphatically, "was the greatest catch I ever saw, as a player or as a broadcaster.

"It was the greatest catch I ever saw in my whole life. I saw Terry Moore and Lloyd Waner make some great ones. But they were routine compared to this one. If I was the pitcher," drawled Diz, "I'd go up to Doby and say, 'Podner, here's half of my month's salary. You deserve it.'"

And that's how Art Houtteman, the pitcher in this case reacted. Oh, he didn't split his salary with Doby. But when the final out was made to give the Indians an 8–3 victory over Washington Art went to the dugout and waited for Larry to come in from center field.

"I wanted to talk to you alone," said the pitcher. "I wanted to thank you for that catch. As long as I live I'll never forget the greatness of that play."

Larry grinned. "We're all in this together," he replied.

Everything about the game was anti-climax to THE CATCH. When the Indians scored five runs in the second inning to overcome the Nats' three-run advantage there was much applause. The doubles by Jim Hegan and Al Rosen in this rally were royally greeted.

So was a later homer by Hegan and another by Doby.

But after Larry made THE CATCH the reaction of the fans was historic. When he loped off the field, most of the 17,504 customers STOOD UP and gave him a spine-tingling ovation.

THE CATCH was unbelievable. It was so spectacular mere words cannot do it justice.

It came in the third inning, with the Tribe ahead 5–3, Jim Busby on first and Tom Umphlett at bat. It must be remembered that Umphlett is labeled a scratch hitter, not one with power. The outfield rarely plays him deep.

But this one he hit. The ball sailed toward the canopy behind the fence on left center ... a certain homer to tie the score. Doby chased it on the dead run. He leaped, crashed the fence, seemed impaled on it, his body seemingly suspended in mid-air, his back acting as a fulcrum, his head over the fence, his feet dangling on the playing side.

Then he fell. From a distance there was the illusion that he had fallen over the fence, just as he did the other night in a futile attempt to steal a homer, but actually he had fallen back into the playing field. He lay prone on his back, unable to move. Did he still have the ball?

Left fielder Al Smith raced to his fallen roommate. He looked down, grabbed the ball out of his glove. Umpire John Flaherty, racing toward the fence for a better look, threw up his right hand. The batter was out. Doby had made THE CATCH.

Busby hurried back to first just ahead of Smith's throw. That was the Nats' last threat.

Doby, although badly shaken, finally got to his feet. His neck and shoulder muscles pained him, but he refused to allow Manager Al Lopez to take him out of the game. Later he made another fine catch and hit a homer.

And, Houtteman, who would have gone to the showers if Larry hadn't made THE CATCH, settled down to a steady finish for his tenth victory, one that put the Indians 2 ½ games ahead of the losing Yanks.

Harold Bossard, Tribe groundskeeper, was near the fence at the time of THE CATCH. He describes it, "I saw it but can't believe it. The ball was at least two feet above the fence and two feet on the other side of it when Larry caught it. He jumped so high and leaned back so far his knees seemed to hook the top of the rail."

Larry has made some super ones this year, some previously called the greatest. There was the one he grabbed after a belly-slam in Boston eight days ago to save a game for Bobby Feller. There were others, here at the Stadium, where he challenged the fence and won.

But last night's belongs in the Hall of Fame ... all by itself. It was THE CATCH. There may never be an equal.

Too bad Tris Speaker, his chief rooter, wasn't there to see it. Speaker, who calls Larry the best centerfielder in the game today—better than Willie Mays and Duke Snider—is in Lakeside Hospital recovering from a heart condition.

But when he heard THE CATCH on the radio, he grabbed the phone at his bedside and called the press box.

"Tell Larry," said the Gray Eagle, "he gave this old man a great big lift."

The August 11, 1954, *Sporting News* had an article on Larry Doby's spectacular catch on Tom Umphlett's long drive. The uncredited article included: "All players, fans and press box observers unanimously agreed with Manager Al Lopez that Larry Doby's catch, robbing Tom Umphlett of a home run July 31, was the greatest they had ever seen."

Although not as expansive as the accounts by the Cleveland writers, the writers for the *Washington Evening Star* and the *Washington Post* had high praise for Doby's superior effort. The *Evening Star's* Burton Hawkins wrote: "Busby singled to start the third and Tom Umphlett made a brave bid to tie the score with a booming smash to left-center. But Doby contributed possibly the finest defensive play of his career when he leaped against the 5-foot-6 fence to haul in the drive while draped against the barrier." Bob Addie of the *Post* ranked Doby's catch at the highest level.

> Doby made probably one of the greatest catches ever seen. It must stand no better than a tie with the great ones made in baseball history.
> It happened in the third inning when Tom Umphlett lashed a long drive to left center. Doby leaped just in front of the five-foot fence and came crashing down into the wire netting. For one awful moment, it seemed as if he had been impaled. He was out cold but revived after a couple of minutes and not only made a couple more great fielding plays, but also hit his homer after his thorough shakeup.

April 14, 1955—Duke Snider

The catch which is most remembered from 1955 is the Brooklyn Dodgers' Sandy Amoros's dramatic running catch in the left field corner on a ball hit by the Yankees' Yogi Berra in the last game of the World Series. Sandy Amoros's catch enabled the Dodgers finally to defeat the New York Yankees for a Series title.

However, perhaps the best catch of 1955 was Duke Snider's catch on a drive hit by the Giants' Monte Irvin in the home opener for the Giants, which the Dodgers won 10 to 8. The Dodgers' Roy Campanella and Carl Furillo each hit three-run homers, and the Dodgers' starting pitcher, Don Newcombe, hit two home runs. The highlight of the game was Snider's catch.

Jim McCulley of the *New York Daily News* set the scene and described the catch.

> Jim Hughes got the call out of the busy Brook bullpen when Newcombe was forced out and Walt Alston's ace fireman quieted down the eighth-inning uprising by the champions. But he needed a sensational catch by Duke Snider to escape in the ninth.
> Monte Irvin, who had been slamming the ball hard all afternoon, drove deep to center field leading off the Polo Grounders' last time around. When the ball left Irvin's bat there was some doubt whether it would remain in the playing field.
> Snider started chasing it, looking back over his shoulder. It looked for sure as if the ball would clear the short wire fence protecting the left field bleachers and go for another historic home run such as Joe Adcock hit here two years ago.
> But Snider never gave up and at the last moment, jumped high in the air, backhanding his glove toward the ball. The ball connected with the glove and stuck there as Snider crumpled to the ground, rolled over, and came up with the white pellet still in his mitt.
> It was a nab for the books....

After describing the Snider catch, Rud Rennie of the *New York Herald Tribune* wrote:

> Willie Mays could not have been more spectacular and the Duke can now be called "Say-Hey" Snider.

This catch of Snider's was poetic justice, because Irvin had climbed the leftfield wall and made a one-handed catch of a ball Snider hit there in the third.

The *New York Times*' John Drebinger called Snider's catch on Irvin "electrifying," and said the catch would start the Snider-Mays debates again. He was right. Three other New York sportswriters jumped in with articles having the debate as the central feature. This time the "debate" seemed fueled by some Dodger players.

In his *Long Island Press* article, Charley Feeney began his article with:

As the Dodgers today were shouting "say-hey Duke Snider," the World Champion Giants were wondering who altered last season's script.

... it was the Dodgers who were stealing the Giant thunder in the rain-swept afternoon before 29,124 shivering fans.... It was the Dodgers who were talking about Snider's amazing leaping catch of Monte Irvin's 440-foot drive in front of the centerfield bleachers.

...

Snider wasted no time showing the Giants there would be no ninth-inning dramatics. His sensational grab of Irvin's lead-off smash stunned the Giant fans among the crowd and brought the Brooklyn followers to their feet, cheering Flatbush's very capable answer to Willie Mays.

Snider's catch, rated one of the best ever made at the Polo Grounds (are you listenin' Willie), took the starch out of the Giants and gave Brook reliefer Jim Hughes some breathing room.

...

But it was Snider who they surrounded in the Brook dressing room. Some kidded him ... some soberly congratulated him. The players took the opportunity to show writers that Duke was their boy, Mays notwithstanding.

Newcombe, who did more hitting than pitching, cracked, "Nuts to Willie Mays. Snider is the best centerfielder. And don't forget to quote me."

Across the way in the Giant dressing room, Leo Durocher, surprisingly, wore a smile. "Yeah, it was a truly great catch," he said. "Anytime an outfielder runs full speed toward a wall and has to watch the wall and the ball it's a great catch."

Leo refused to be put on the spot in the growing Snider-Mays controversy. "It was a great catch," repeated the Giant skipper when a writer asked him to compare it with Mays' catch of Vic Wertz' drive in the World Series.

The title of Feeney's article was "Brooks, Shouting Say-Hey Duke, Steal Giant Thunder." Both the *New York World-Telegram* and the *New York Daily News* had similar headlines. The title over Bill Roeder's *World-Telegram* article was: "Bums Beat Drums for Duke As King of Center Fielders." The title over Dick Young's *Daily News* article was: "Snider's Sensational Grab Sparks New Mays Debate."

Bill Roeder's article, like Charley Feeney's, took its cue from the Dodger players' unmistakable appreciation for the talents of their centerfielder.

It was a remarkable catch Duke Snider made, all right, and the Dodgers played it for all it was worth. They sounded like publicity men, and maybe that was the idea.

In the Brooklyn clubhouse, all within earshot were informed by one player after another that the Duke had won the first round from Willie Mays.

Whether it was spontaneous or a step in a planned campaign it's hard to say, but there seems to no question that the Dodgers have decided they've heard enough about Willie and will begin pushing their own man.

"Curseword Mays," said Don Newcombe. "Snider's still the best center fielder." ... Jackie Robinson strolled through the clubhouse seemingly talking to himself, but making sure it was heard. "They can talk about Mays all they want," he was saying, "but that catch was a humdinger. I never saw a better one."

Except for Snider himself, who can't abide the endless comparisons with Mays, the only one who refrained from drawing Willie into it was Walt Alston.

"I'm in enough controversies," said the man who had the temerity to turn Roy Campanella into an eighth-place hitter. "I just thought it was a hell of a catch, but I don't know if Duke would take it over the one in Philadelphia last year."

Duke said he'd take the Philadelphia catch because he had to climb a wall to make it, while at the Polo Grounds he was on open ground, although not by much. He said the drive by Monte Irvin would have hit the bleacher screen if it hadn't been caught.

In his article, Dick Young of the *Daily News* also quoted Dodgers Don Newcombe and Carl Erskine, who, as might be expected, favored Snider over Mays as a fielder. Young also quoted the Dodgers' backup catcher, Rube Walker: "Rube Walker, who had a closeup view of yesterday's grab from the nearby bullpen, voted for this one. 'Best I ever saw,' he said. 'It was directly over his head, and they're always tougher.'"

From the opening sentence, Young moved directly into the debate.

Here it was just the second game of the season, and the great Snider-Mays debate had already erupted. Not between them, but about them. It was touched off by Duke's spectacular grab of Monte Irvin's shot to within a few feet of the left-center bleacher sector on the ninth inning.

Some thought it was the greatest possible catch. Other were more restrained, among them Snider himself.

"I think the one in Philly was tougher. I had to battle the wall on that one."

He was referring to the Memorial Day game of last year when he had dug his spikes into the wall, on the full run, and had backhanded the blast for the final out. That one was the ball game. If Duke hadn't caught it, two runs would have crossed, and Philly would have won.

This catch was similar—not quite as much to left-center, and no wall to contend with because there's more running room in the Polo Grounds. Duke streaked back to the edge of the grass, shot straight up, backhanded the drive, and rolled onto the gravel pathway—some three feet from the base of the bleacher wall.

...

In the Giant clubhouse, Leo Durocher was asked for his opinion. "Great," said Leo, which virtually is faint praise from him.

Durocher was asked if he's seen better. Diving catches for low liners. "They're harder," he thought for a moment, and said: "The one Duke made in the series at Yankee Stadium, that was harder."

This was a reference to Snider's leaping grab near the bleacher screen in right-center during the '52 series.

Willie Mays was asked for his opinion. "Pretty good," he said. "Great. He got it, didn't he?"

Leo Durocher's reference to catches of low liners may have meant diving catches in general, or he may have been thinking of the diving catch Mays made on Bobby Morgan in 1952, the catch Mays himself, and the one Tom Sheehan, considered Mays' greatest. Durocher's reference to Snider's 1952 World Series catch probably was the leaping one Snider made of a liner off Yogi Berra's bat.

Michael Gaven of the *New York Journal-American* and Milton Gross of the *New York Post* both compared the Snider catch on Irvin to the Mays catch on Wertz in the 1954 World Series. Gaven wrote:

Long after other features of the 1955 pennant race are forgotten the 29,124 fans who saw the inaugural at the Polo Grounds will remember the catch Duke Snider made on Monte Irvin in the ninth inning.

If the National League race is typically close it could well decide the pennant. Naturally this leaping stab in front of the centerfield bleachers was compared to the catch made by Willie Mays on Vic Wertz in the World Series.

One small voice says there was no comparison. All Mays had to do was run out, turn and there was the ball over his shoulder. A great catch, to be sure. But Snider had to run out, cross, leap and make a backhanded catch with his feet fully two feet off the ground. Snider, who resents comparison with Mays because too much has been made of it, compares his catch with another made off Willie Jones in Philadelphia last season. He climbed the wall fully three feet, made the Statue of Liberty, and grabbed it in his outstretched glove.

"The Philadelphia catch was much more difficult. It was my best," said the Duke.

"Both the Snider and Mays catches were made on the cinder paths," said Roy Campanella. "That's going beyond the realm of duty, isn't it? Let's say they were both great catches."

"Snider made a terrific catch," said Leo Durocher, who refused to compare it with the Mays catch in the World Series. So one vote for the Duke.

In his column in the *Post*, Milton Gross wrote that he considered Snider's catch "far greater" than Mays' catch on Wertz in the 1954 Series.

It didn't have the excitement because it didn't have the setting. The newsreels didn't record it for posterity. It was only the first out in the ninth inning with nobody on base in a free-hitting 10–8 game, and when the inning ended that was the score with the Dodgers winning.

But the play should be the thing in baseball as it is on the stage. If these two plays can be divested of the trimmings, then Snider, for the Polo Grounds opener, at least, has it over Willie.

You remember Willie's catch, of course. In the months which have passed since Mays made it, it's become known as The Catch. Cleveland's Larry Doby and Al Rosen were on second and first in the eighth, score, 2–2. Vic Wertz, who had gone three for three, belted a towering fly into center. Willie ran and ran and caught the ball still going away from the plate. After that, it seemed, the Indians were done.

The Giants were done, too, after Snider caught his yesterday, but this was only the second game of the season played in a gloomy setting of rain and mud that must add to the brilliance of Duke's performance. Footing in center was perilous.

Like Wertz, Irvin had been hitting the ball solidly all afternoon. This time, with Jim Hughes pitching, he sent a screamer that was more a liner than a fly ball deep and slightly to Snider's right. Duke turned and ran and then with the green shade of the wall almost at his back, he turned again, jumped, backhanded the ball, fell, rolled and his arm came up with it to show the fair catch.

In the Dodger dressing room after the game the conversation was of little else but that out.

"I took my eye off it just when it was hit," Snider said. "I ran about five-six steps in the general direction and then saw it again and held it until I caught up with it."

"Did you think it was better than Willie's in the series?" a reporter asked Duke.

"I only saw his on TV," Snider answered. "What made his catch so spectacular was that he made it over the shoulder. From what I saw, he caught his on the grass and when he wheeled to throw he was on the cinders. I caught mine on the cinders. I know this ball would have hit the screen if I didn't catch it."

Gross also quoted Campanella, who said: "I'd take this one over the one in Philly."

May 27, 1955 — Chuck Diering

Chuck Diering played a total of nine major league seasons for three different teams — the first five with the Cardinals, the sixth with the Giants, and the last three with the Baltimore Orioles. He was a swift runner and an outstanding fielder. His highest batting average for a year was .263 in 131 games as a St. Louis Cardinal in 1949. When he finished his last year in the major leagues in 1956, his career average was .249, which indicates why he was not a more highly publicized player and not one with a longer career. Of the nine years he played in the majors, he topped 100 games played in just four of those years.

In his "Daniel's Dope" column in the March 18, 1947 *New York World-Telegram*, Dan Daniel indicated how impressive Diering was as a fielder.

Mel Ott's effort to purchase outfielder Elvin Adams from the Cardinals, initiated during the world series last October, is likely to prove successful. And all because of Charley Diering, a native of St. Louis, who is making an amazing showing in the field with the world champions.

Diering hit only .266 with Rochester last season, but his defensive skill is superlative. He reminds me very much of Jigger Statz, when he starred for the Cubs and Dodgers, after a failure with the Giants.

"Though Diering does not impress me as a likely .285 hitter in the National League, he is so spectacular in the field that I am very likely to keep him," said Eddie Dyer. The boss of the Cardinals is very much worried about Terry Moore's knee, which was operated on this past winter. Terry is nearing his 35th birthday.

In early December 1951, the Cardinals traded Diering to the New York Giants. Just before the trade was made, Dan Daniel wrote about the proposed deal. About Diering, Daniel said: "Diering, perfectly willing to join the NL champions, is no slugger. He batted a measly .259 and drove in just eight runs in 64 games last season, but as a defensive center fielder, Chuck has no master."

Just as the Giants' training camp was to begin in 1952, James P. Dawson of the *New York Times* used the opportunity to praise Diering's fielding and talk about his troubles at the plate: "Diering, 29, is considered one of the most gifted defensive outfielders in the business. He hopes the change will help his batting average, which never was higher than .263 in five years as a Cardinal."

One of Chuck Diering's greatest defensive days came in a Cardinals-Dodgers game on July 16, 1950, in St. Louis. The *New York Times*' Roscoe McGowen commented on Diering's fielding: "Diering made three great catches, robbing Reese in the second, Van Cuyk in the fourth, and Furillo in the seventh."

The *St. Louis Post-Dispatch*'s Bob Broeg went further about Diering's work in the 10 to 2 pounding the Dodgers gave the St. Louis pitchers.

Then an outfield that had pitched a helluva fine game, with Chuck Diering giving an amazing exhibition in center, couldn't range high wide and handsome to pull down drives any longer.

...

Diering nearly made an out-of-this-world barehanded stab of Snider's first-inning drive to the flagpole and from then on Chuck, the deerfoot hometown kid, played brilliantly. He dove to his left for a one-handed snatch of Pee Wee Reese's liner in the second, ran back for a leaping grab of Van Cuyk's sharp drive in the fourth and made a running over-the-head catch of Furillo's leadoff belt in the seventh.

Chuck Diering, shown here as a Baltimore Oriole about 1955, was long recognized as a defensive standout during his major league career.

... Diering skidded on his side for his superlative catch against Reese....

In his *St. Louis Globe-Democrat* article, Martin J. Haley praised Diering's superlative fielding on July 16, 1950.

> The Brooklyn hit and run total would have been even higher but for sensational Cardinal fielding, especially by Center Fielder Chuck Diering.
>
> To begin with, Diering almost made a bare hand catch of Snider's far-flung first-frame triple. He did get his bare mauley on the ball but could not hold it as he subsequently dodged around the flagpole.
>
> Then in the second, Diering made a running, diving catch of Pee Wee Reese's liner in right center. Van Cuyk was his next victim, in the fourth. This time Diering, running fast with his back to the plate, leaped up for a glove grab of Van Cuyk's high liner dead to center. Furillo's long liner in the seventh toward left center was turned into another glove catch by Diering.

On May 28, 1955, Diering made a catch on Mickey Mantle that was compared to Willie Mays' catch on Vic Wertz in the 1954 World Series just eight months earlier. The title above Ben Epstein's *New York Daily Mirror* article was: "Diering's Catch On Mantle Rated Tops." Epstein wrote:

> Up to now, Mickey Mantle's distance plans have provided all the talk. But in this town, they're talking about the guy who caught one of the distance shots Friday night that The Switcher hit.
>
> Chuck Diering pulled the Barnum & Bailey, snaring it after being bumped by Hoot Evers in right center some 440 feet from the plate. Paul Richards hailed it a slicker piece of robbery than that performed by Willie Mays off Vic Wertz in the first game of the last World Series.
>
> Casey Stengel, who certainly has seen his share of this sort of act over the years, wouldn't know if it was the greatest he ever saw or not but in the perfesser's eyes it did provide an oddity. Casey recalled he had seen hundreds of crash plays by outfielders but never before had he viewed one so far out. He pointed out, however, that "Diering and Evers got a head start on Mantle by backing up 50 feet deeper than they normally play before he went to bat."

In the *Baltimore Sun*, under the sub-heading "Diering Makes Great Catch," Bob Maisel told more about Diering's catch on the Mantle drive.

> The little centerfielder belted his third homer of the season in the second inning, then with two Yankees on base and two out in the ninth, he made one of the most sensational catches seen in the Stadium since the Birds returned to the majors.
>
> Mickey Mantle leaned into one of Erv Palica's pitches and sent a towering drive to center which looked for awhile as though it might hit the right corner of the scoreboard on the fly.
>
> As soon as the ball was hit, Diering turned his back and ran as hard as he could. Still heading toward the fence at full speed, Chuck grabbed the ball at least 440 feet from the plate, and hardly more than 10 feet in front of the scoreboard.
>
> Hoot Evers, coming over from right field, tripped over Diering, and for a moment both fell to the ground, but Chuck held on to the ball as Mantle was rounding second.
>
> It seemed to take the little gardener five minutes to trot all the way back to the dugout, and by the time he got there the crowd was on its feet roaring its approval of the tremendous catch.

Louis Effrat of the *New York Times* called the catch "spectacular," and it helped stop Mantle's hitting streak at 16 games. Effrat made what was becoming a familiar comparison: "This Diering fellow is endearing himself to Baltimore fans with his sensational defensive work. In last night's game he 'robbed' Mantle with a catch that was comparable to the one Willie Mays made on Vic Wertz in the world series."

In the *Baltimore News Post*, Hugh Trader led with Diering's catch on Mantle, under the titles "Diering's Catch Tops Mays'" and "Richards Calls It 'Greatest,'" Trader wrote:

For all the publicity, and deservedly so, that the Giants' Willie Mays received for his famous '54 World Series catch, the feat doesn't compare to Chuck Diering's spectacular run and grab last night of Mickey Mantle's tremendous 440-foot wallop, says Paul Richards.

"I'm not even sure the Polo Grounds could contain Mantle's drive," adds the Bird boss. "It was a breathless play by Diering."

Nothing like it has ever been seen here before, that's for sure, and the fleet little Oriole centerfielder was a standout last night even as the Yanks overpowered our side, 6–2.

Not only did Diering pull off the aforementioned brilliant catch, he cut off another Mantle blast in the eighth and held Mick to a double which otherwise would have been an inside-the-park homer. Then Chuck poled a homer of his own and added a single for his night's work which had a throng of 21,150 cheering him constantly.

Further down in the article Trader returned to Diering's grab off Mantle's long drive.

... the evening's highlight was Diering's stupendous catch.

As Mantle unloaded his blast, which looked as if it might clear everything, Diering was off to the races and so was Hoot Evers, as the drive was in right center. On the last step Diering hauled in the ball and at the same instant Evers collided with Chuck. Both went sprawling but miraculously Diering held the ball.

Diering is now hitting .275 and has pushed his RBI's up to 20, which is sufficient slugging the way Chuck covers center field defensively. If there are better flyhawks, you name 'em.

Paul Richards's major league career began in 1932. He was a catcher for eight seasons in the big leagues. He began his twelve-year managing career in the big leagues in 1952.

June 29, 1955—Willie Mays

During the 1955 season Willie Mays continued to make many outstanding catches, but his greatest catch of 1955 was on a ball the Dodgers' Rube Walker hit at Ebbets Field on June 29. After telling about Willie's two home runs in the game, Joe King of the *New York World-Telegram* described the catch.

In addition, Willie made one of his celebrated catches as he climbed and leaped high up the centerfield wall for Rube Walker's liner in the seventh.

Don Mueller, who was covering on the ball also, said he couldn't imagine how Willie made the catch. The right fielder stated: "It seemed to me the ball had to carom high off the wall, and I cut out into the field to handle the rebound. I had turned away from Willie and didn't see him catch the ball, but when there wasn't any rebound I had to wonder whether this fellow had sprouted a pair of wings."

Barney Kremenko of the *New York Journal-American* compared the catch to Mays' catch on Vic Wertz in the previous year's World Series.

Last night's game undoubtedly was Mays' biggest of the year. He shone not only at bat, but in the field too.

In the eighth inning, young Say Hey climbed high on the Bulova sign in right center to make a sensational catch of Rube Walker's bid for an extra-base hit.

It didn't look possible, but there was Willie with the ball. This easily was his best fielding play of the season.

It also was fully in a class with his famous catch off Vic Wertz in the 1954 World Series.

This tendency to compare centerfielders' catches, including catches by Mays, against Mays' catch on Vic Wertz began with the Snider catch on the ball Monte Irvin hit on April 14, 1955, just two games into the season after Willie made the World Series catch. Willie's catch on Vic Wertz established a standard against which great running catches have been measured. This became the case even though, in the estimation of others and of Mays himself, he made better catches and plays even before he made the play on Vic Wertz's drive. The image repeatedly shown of the catch in the 1954 World Series became the standard which others, who didn't see Willie's or other outfielders' greatest catches, could make a comparison. Those, like Leo Durocher or Tom Sheehan or Russ Hodges, who did see some of Mays' catches which were better than the catch on Vic Wertz, had a higher standard for great catches.

Roger Kahn of the *New York Herald Tribune* devoted his June 30 article on the Giants-Dodgers game to the superlative game Mays had at Ebbets Field, especially making a catch that Kahn termed "beyond belief." Kahn led off with:

> Willie Mays was the greatest player in all baseball last night and the Giants relived a bright page out of their past. At Ebbets Field it was Willie driving a grand slam home run into the centerfield seats and it was Willie slashing another homer deep into the upper left centerfield stands and it was Willie singling home a sixth run and it was Willie catapulting to a catch beyond belief and the Giants won, of course. They beat the Dodgers, 6–1.

Kahn went on to tell of Willie's batting exploits through the top of the seventh before writing about the catch on Rube Walker.

> Two men were out in the seventh when Rube Walker, the left-hand hitting catcher who is filling in for Roy Campanella, came to bat. He walloped a long drive to right center. Don Mueller loped over, then turned to play the ball off the wall. Willie, with his great speed and instinct, raced over and stood at the base of the wall for perhaps a second while everyone wondered whether the blow would be a double or just a tremendous single for the leaden-legged Walker. Willie didn't wonder. He went up, feet, yards, higher than it seemed any human being could propel himself. His glove shot above his head, closed, then Willie fell, slamming the wall and crumpling to the ground.
> Lee Ballafant, the second base umpire, had run into center. He flashed his right hand up in the classic "out" sign, only then was it known that Willie had caught the ball. It was not believed.

Writing in the *New York Times*, John Drebinger had the following to say about Mays' effort on the Walker ball.

> Mays ... turned in one of his most spectacular catches of the season. In the last of the seventh, Rube Walker, subbing for the injured Roy Campanella, hit a powerful drive toward the deepest sector of the playing field in right center.
> Climbing the wall with the agility of a Rocky Mountain goat, the Say Hey Kid collared the ball with his gloved hand. He came down sprawling, but the ball stuck in the glove.

As his catch on Walker shows, Willie Mays had a facility for scaling outfield walls.

Just two weeks later, at the All-Star game on July 12, 1955, in Milwaukee, Mays made another catch that drew favorable notices. The *New York Times'* Arthur Daley told how, in a twelve-inning, 6–5 National League win, Mays robbed Ted Williams of a home run: "Ted shot a towering blast over the fence in right center. But Willie Mays leaped up, reached over the parapet and made a miraculous one-handed catch to rob the Boston slugger of a sure homer."

May 29, 1956—Duke Snider

On May 28, 1956, the 6-foot-4-inch, 215-pound, left-handed-batting Pirate first baseman, Dale Long, hit a homer in his eighth consecutive game, a major league record since tied by Don Mattingly of the Yankees (1987) and Ken Griffey Jr. (1993) of the Mariners. Long broke the old mark of homers in six consecutive games.

In the fifth consecutive game of his streak Long hit the homer out of Forbes Field at a place which had never before been reached. According to the *Pittsburgh Post-Gazette's* Jack Hernon (writing after Long hit the homer in his eighth consecutive game): "There had been no homers hit to the left of the light tower in right center since the park was opened, then there were two in two games, Long's and Snider's."

In Long's May 28 record-setting eighth straight game, Snider himself had hit a monumental home run off Pittsburgh pitcher Bob Friend in a 3–2 Pirate win. Jack Hernon again:

> The Buc ace walked Jim Gilliam and, after one out, Duke Snider hit a tape measure homer to run his hitting streak through 17 games.
> The drive carried over the fence in center beyond the spot where Long hit his homer last Wednesday night, the ball moving some 500 feet.

Hernon also mentioned Snider's fielding in that game: "Snider took extra base hits away from Walls and Bill Virdon with running, one-hand catches in deep left and right-center."

Les Biederman of the *Pittsburgh Press* wrote: "Duke Snider's monumental first inning homer that left the park between the Dreyfuss Memorial and the 436 foot sign on the right center wall ... was a new distance mark for that sector ... that even surpassed Long's shot in that direction last Wednesday."

In his "The Scoreboard" column elsewhere on the front sports page, Biederman related something Long told him.

> It was Long who offered the juicy news morsel that Duke Snider asked him before the game where his (Long's) record-breaking home run had gone over the right center wall last Wednesday. Long described the spot it left Forbes Field and Snider shook his head.
> "I've played here nine years trying to hit one over that wall but never have succeeded," Snider commented.
> In the first inning Snider achieved his ambition.

On May 29, batting all day against Don Newcombe in a 10–1 win for the Dodgers, Dale Long went homerless and hitless. However, he did pound one Newcombe pitch that at first looked as if it might make it out of the park. The *New York Times'* John Drebinger reported on Long's drive at Forbes Field.

> Although he went hitless, Long gave the crowd at least one big thrill. That occurred on his second time up, when he hit a tremendous smash just left of dead center in the third inning. For a moment it appeared the ball would clear the ivy-covered wall. Unfortunately, the Buc first sacker was making his bid in the spot farthest from home plate in spacious Forbes Field. Also, in hot pursuit he had one of the game's greatest center fielders, Duke Snider going at full speed. After a hard run, the Duke pulled down the ball with his gloved hand directly in front of the 470-foot marker.

In his June 10, 1956, *New York Times* article on a Dodgers' 8–5 win in Cincinnati, Drebinger, who had watched a number of great outfielders in his thirty years as a baseball writer, reflected on Snider as a fielder.

> It is too bad Brooklyn fans, because of the Ebbets Field layout, get so little opportunity to see their Duke Snider perform at his best as an outfielder. Even in Crosley Field, where the longest distance from home plate measures only 390 feet, the Duke has plenty of room to roam either to the right or left of center.
> However, it is in such spacious outfields as they have in Pittsburgh and Chicago that the

rangy Californian gets a chance to make those amazingly graceful catches comparable to those Joe DiMaggio used to make in the Yankee Stadium.

In the 1956 World Series against the Yankees, Snider continued his clutch fielding. Just after Mickey Mantle blasted a fourth-inning homer to give the Yankees their first run and enough for the final margin of victory in Don Larsen's perfect game win on October 8, Snider made a another great catch on a ball Yogi Berra hit. John Drebinger of the *New York Times* described the catch: "A moment later Yogi Berra appeared to have connected for another hit as he stroked a powerful low drive toward left center. However, Duke Snider tore over from center field and snared the ball with a headlong dive."

Snider's catch was overshadowed by one that saved Don Larsen's perfect game: the catch by Mickey Mantle.

October 8, 1956—Mickey Mantle

Although he has not received the accolades as a fielder that Duke Snider and Willie Mays have, Mantle's blazing speed enabled him to run down balls in spacious ballparks that others would not have caught. He also had a powerful throwing arm.

Tony Castro, in his book *Mickey Mantle: America's Prodigal Son*, discusses how the rookie Mantle worked with the veteran Yankee outfielder Tommy Henrich on developing better methods of fielding. How well Henrich's lessons were learned was evident early in Mantle's first season. Castro writes:

> Jim Busby of the White Sox was tagging up on a fly ball to Mickey in right field. Mantle caught the ball at the same instant that he planted his right foot the way Henrich had taught him. In almost the same motion, Mantle fired a strike to the plate; Busby was forced to stop halfway home and retreat to third. The Yankees in the dugout came to their feet, and Henrich walked over to Stengel. "That's the best throw I've ever seen anyone make," Henrich said. "I don't think I have anything else to teach him. He's got it down pretty good." [85]

In addition to being an outstanding baseball player at Texas Christian University, Jim Busby was a sprinter on the track team, and thus was a very fast runner.

Henrich had played next to Joe DiMaggio for years. DiMaggio was a superior thrower, and made many outstanding throws that Henrich saw. Still, Henrich called Mantle's throw "the best" he had seen.

In his perfect game in the 1956 World Series, Don Larsen was helped by several outstanding defensive plays in the infield, but especially by Mickey Mantle's catch of Gil Hodges's long ball to deep left center in the fifth inning. The *Times*' John Drebinger described Mantle's effort: "He tore across the turf to make an extraordinary glove-hand catch."

The *New York World-Telegram and Sun*'s Lou Miller wrote: "Hodges came close to spoiling Larsen's show in the fifth when Mickey Mantle, barely catching up with Gil's drive, had to reach his glove across his chest to make the catch at express-train speed."

In the book he wrote (with Phil Pepe) in 1991, *My Favorite Summer 1956*, Mantle said he considered the catch on the ball Hodges blasted into left center his best catch and the most important catch he ever made.

As had happened many times, Mantle's speed enabled him to catch a ball that almost no other outfielder could have reached. Mantle's tremendous swiftness accounted for outs on many long balls hit deep and into the alleys during his peak years. His great efforts to haul down balls hit in the gaps may have been minimized by observers because, with his speed, it was expected he would make catches on those long liners.

At Yankee Stadium in the fifth game of the 1956 World Series, Mickey Mantle outspeeds Gil Hodges's well-hit liner to deep left center field to help preserve Don Larsen's perfect game (© Bettmann/COR-BIS).

By 1955 Mickey Mantle's talents as a baseball player were well known. On May 10, 1955, his fielding took precedence over his hitting. In a 9–6 victory by the Yankees over the Cleveland Indians, Mickey made the catch of the game. The *New York Times'* Louis Effrat wrote: "There were any number of outstanding plays, but the best was by Mantle. He robbed Doby of an extra-base hit with a gloved-hand snare in front of the bleachers in the second."

On May 22, 1955, the *Baltimore Sun's* Bob Maisel quoted questions by Casey Stengel about Mantle. Stengel was talking about how others seemed to be underappreciating Mantle's many abilities. Without mentioning Mantle's name, Casey rhetorically asked questions which Maisel quoted.

"Who hits the ball farther than anybody else in the league right-handed? Who hits the ball the longest ball in the league left-handed? Who is the fastest man in the league? Who covers the most ground in the outfield? Who has the best throwing arm in the league?"

Casey didn't answer his questions, but left little doubt that one Mickey Mantle was the boy about whom he spoke. And after the last two games here, it's hard to give him an argument.

Mantle has done everything a great ballplayer has to do right now.

"This is the first year he hasn't been crippled in spring training," declares old Case. "Right now he's a healthy young man and if he stays that way he should give us a real year."

A week later, after a Yankee victory over the Baltimore Orioles, Maisel himself "answered" Casey Stengel's questions about Mantle's power.

Mickey Mantle even has the Oriole players talking about his tremendous power. Again last night, when his hitting streak was stopped, Mickey hit a ball which Chuck Diering took on the cinder track just in front of where the sign reads 450 feet.

Of course, he has hit them farther, a lot farther. Les Moss and Billy Hunter both agreed last night they had seen Mantle hit a ball in St. Louis which would have cleared the left field bleachers in the Stadium. All the way out into the street, that is.

In fact, they claim it would have gone out of the Stadium at the first flag pole on the top edge of the stadium.

Sure it's hard to believe, but who can doubt it after they've seen Mantle propel a ball almost out of sight?

In his book *Mickey Mantle's Greatest Hits*, David S. Nuttall discusses the blast which Moss and Hunter probably saw on April 28, 1953. Mantle was batting right-handed against the left-handed St. Louis Browns pitcher Bob Cain. Nuttall noted that observers estimated that the ball traveled between 485 and 530 feet. From the descriptions Moss and Hunter gave the *Sun's* Bob Maisel, it appears the 530 figure might be too short.

May 10, 1957—Henry Aaron

Now most known for his hitting, especially the home runs he hit across his major league career, Henry Aaron was one of the best all-around players in baseball history. This included his fielding. What may have been his greatest catch occurred on May 10, 1957, in a game his Milwaukee team played in St. Louis against the Cardinals. Aaron's Braves defeated the Cardinals 10–5.

Writers for the *Milwaukee Sentinel* and the *Milwaukee Journal* both reported on the catch in their reports on the game. Red Thisted of the *Sentinel* wrote: "Henry Aaron was limited to a single in four trips, but made one of the most sparkling catches of the year in the sixth. He slipped to his haunches chasing Wally Moon's fly and while in a near prone position stuck up his bare hand and caught the ball."

The *Journal's* Cleon Walfoort rated Aaron's catch at a high level.

Aaron made a catch off Wally Moon that was strictly the stuff of which the Hall of Fame was concocted.

Henry, in his usual deceptively desultory style that he hopes to get around to copyrighting, had set out dutifully in pursuit of a long but routine fly. But he slipped on the gravel in front of the right field wall and fell flat on—well, on his aspirations so far as that particular ball was concerned. So he speared the hard hit drive in his bare hand a foot from the ground while skidding on his glove, thus maintaining the reputation he has established with those who know him best:

"As good as he has to be."

The *St. Louis Globe-Democrat's* Harry Mitauer commented on Aaron's catch: "Wally Moon was robbed of a hit in the sixth when ... Hank Aaron caught his fly as he fell to the ground." Harry Mitauer did not report an essential element, the bare-hand grab. The *St. Louis Post-Dispatch* writer for the game did not mention Aaron's catch.

Two days later the *Sentinel's* Lou Chapman wrote an article on Aaron's hitting and the possibility that he would win the National League's triple crown—the leader in batting, home runs and runs batted in. In the article, Chapman quoted Fred Hutchinson.

"That guy's just an unconscious hitter," was the left-handed compliment paid Aaron by Fred Hutchinson, Cardinal manager. "He's great both offensively and defensively. Who else but Aaron could fall down and then make a bare-hand catch?

"I can't see any reason in the world why he can't be a triple champion. He's capable of doing anything. That guy is just unconscious, that's all."

Two years earlier, on July 30, 1955, the *Milwaukee Journal's* Bob Wolf, in writing about the 5–2 Braves win over the New York Giants of the day before, reported about the

On May 12, 1963, at Connie Mack Stadium in Philadelphia, Hank Aaron leaped high but could not reach the ball Johnny Callison of the Phillies hit for a triple (AP/Wide World Photos).

outstanding defense of the Braves behind pitcher Ray Crone. He too referred to Aaron as Hutchinson later would.

As good as Crone was, he owed a large vote of thanks to his defense. Johnny Logan made a flock of exceptional plays, started both Milwaukee double plays and handled nine chances all told. Henry Aaron helped out, too, with one of his characteristic "unconscious" catches on a ninth inning line drive.

Bob Wolf's colleague, Sam Levy, in a separate column about the Braves, told of a catch by Willie Mays and of Aaron's sterling ninth-inning grab in the game against the Giants.

Willie took off for Joe Adcock's terrific drive to the center field boundary line in the first inning, leaped high and made a one handed catch. Even more spectacular was Aaron's play in the ninth inning. Henry picked Bobby Hofman's sinking line drive off a blade of grass with a backhand catch. The ball was about an inch off the ground. It was a perfect climax to a fielding extravaganza.

So, early in his career, Henry Aaron was already being called an "unconscious" hitter and an "unconscious" fielder. It was clear that Aaron had exceptional awareness, speed, and reflexes which made his feats on the field appear to others as "unconscious."

As a pitcher for the Braves during most of the 1950s, Ernie Johnson was Henry Aaron's teammate. Later he became a broadcaster for the Braves. In Curt Smith's *The Storytellers*, Ernie Johnson told that, while chasing the ball that Wally Moon hit near the right field wall and the bullpen where Johnson was, Aaron stopped abruptly to avoid running into the concrete wall. The grass was wet. He slipped and his feet went out from under him. While bracing his fall with his gloved hand, Aaron put his bare (right) hand up to catch the ball. Johnson said it was "The greatest catch I've ever seen" (186). What makes this catch all the more remarkable was that he was not only falling and bracing for his fall, but that "Hank's back was to home plate...." (Ernie Johnson, 2004 note to me) and he still was able to look back enough to see the ball and to adjust his bare hand into the path of the ball.

June 3, 1957—Willie Mays

In 1957, Willie Mays made a catch on Roberto Clemente that was one of his very best. This catch on Clemente in Pittsburgh may have surpassed all the other great running catches he made.

In a June 1961 *SPORT* magazine article, "The Willie Mays Decade," Arnold Hano gives long-time Giants broadcaster Russ Hodges's opinion about which was the greatest of all of Mays' great catches up to that time.

> If you ask another fan, or a writer, to recreate some play by Mays that sticks in memory, there is never any hesitation. Russ Hodges, who has seen every game Mays has played, says instantly it was the play Mays made on Roberto Clemente in Forbes Field, the ball headed for the light tower when Mays made the catch. Hodges says it was the greatest catch Mays ever made; he says it was the greatest catch any human being ever made.

The *New York Times*' Roscoe McGowen's account of the June 3, 1957, game refers to the catch Hodges was astounded by.

> In the first inning, with two Pirates on base and one out, Roberto Clemente whacked a terrific drive toward the screen surrounding the light tower in left center field, more than 440-feet from home plate.
> Willie astonished the players, as well as the fans, by leaping high against the screen and making glove-twisting catch....

Several New York papers included comments from others about Willie Mays' catch on Clemente. Leonard Koppett of the *New York Post*, after telling about St. Louis Cardinal players who were spectators at the Pirates-Giants game of the night before, including Wally Moon, Alvin Dark, and Hobie Landrith, described the catch.

> Then Roberto Clemente lashed a high line drive toward the wall in left center. The runners were heading for home when Mays, racing back at top speed, grabbed the ball with one hand just before running into the wall.
> "Wow!" yelled Dark, Moon, and Landrith and the crowd.
> Henrich's head popped up again. He held up a finger. "Is that no. 1?" he asked Alvin. "Is that the best he's ever made?"
> "He's remarkable," said Alvin, "but I've seen him make as good."
> "That's the greatest I ever saw," said Landrith.

"I've never seen anything better," said Moon. "He just reached in front as he ran to the wall and flipped his glove up to grab the ball. He had to, because if he held his glove flat the ball would have bounced out."

Frank Thomas struck out to end the inning.

Bill Rigney's head popped up over the dugout roof.

"Greatest I ever saw," he said to Dark.

The crowd gave Willie a standing ovation as he ran back to the bench.

Tommy Henrich, who was an outstanding Yankee outfielder during most of the time Joe DiMaggio played center field for the Yanks, was a coach for the Giants when Mays made this catch on Clemente. Bill Rigney was a former infielder for the Giants; in 1957 he was their manager. Alvin Dark had been the shortstop for the Giants during the first four and a half years Mays played, and had seen Willie's great catches through the first part of the 1956 season before being traded to the Cardinals.

The *New York World-Telegram and Sun*'s Bill Roeder devoted his whole article to the catch, under the title "Willie's Catch Eclipses DiMag's, Says Henrich."

If old reliable Tommy Henrich says so, and we'll take his word for it, Willie Mays made the best catch he ever saw.

Everybody else says so, too, but we checked first with Henrich. He is a man of considered opinions. His judgment is good and he has seen any number of outstanding catches, including some by Willie and a great many by Joe DiMaggio.

Up until last night, Henrich had not gone completely overboard on any phase of Willie's play. But then, in the first inning of what was to become a 6–5 loss to the Pirates, Willie did the impossible.

He caught a ball that everybody in the park had conceded, the only question being how many bases Bob Clemente would get on it when the ball bounced off the wall in left center, 440 feet from home plate.

It never got to the wall. Neither did Willie. He stopped a foot short, jumped up and picked off this line drive that had been hit over his head and hit about as hard as anybody hits a baseball.

This ball was over Willie's head before you could see Willie running for it. He must have outrun it. He not only got back there, but he had time to flick his head for a quick look so he could tell just where to put his hands. He says he caught it in both hands. Some thought it was a one-hand job. We couldn't tell because Willie had his back to the plate and seemed to have his hands below his head when he caught the ball.

"It was the best catch I ever saw," said Henrich. "DiMag's is now second best and I'm going to tell him so next time I see him whether it's tomorrow or a year from now. In other words, I'm not going to change my mind about this. DiMag's catch on Greenberg in the Stadium about 1938 or '39 was No. 1 with me until this. But that was a high ball that Joe at least had time to track down. Willie didn't have any time at all."

Whitey Lockman, Johnny Antonelli and other veterans of the '54 Giants agreed that it outdid the catch Willie made on Vic Wertz in the World Series. Willie agreed, too. "Darned if I know if this is the best I ever made," he said. "It's hard for me to rate my own plays, but I know this tops Wertz. I caught it the same way, but on Wertz I had the ball in sight all the way. This one I didn't have time to do nothin' but run."

Bucky Walters said the boys in the left-field bullpen had a beautiful view of the catch. "Greatest ever," Bucky said. "You'd swear the guy must have rubber in him. He actually goes the limit and then goes a little further. And how he could stop short without hitting that wall I'll never know."

We personally thought it was the best catch we'd ever seen. So did everyone we talked with except Red Schoendienst, who said at first that Willie makes so many great ones that you can't split them out. Later, though, even Red was weakening. "You don't see many, at that, where a guy is so close to the wall on a ball hit that hard," he said.

Tommy Henrich must have rethought his determination not to change his mind about ranking Willie Mays' catch on Clemente the greatest he'd ever seen, and putting it above the catch Joe DiMaggio made on Hank Greenberg in 1939. As quoted above under the section on DiMaggio's catch on Greenberg, Henrich, in his 1992 book *Five O'Clock Lightning*, called the DiMaggio catch "the greatest catch I've ever seen," and did not mention Mays' catch on Clemente in the book.

Bucky Walters began his major league career as a third baseman in 1931 with the Boston Braves, but was a pitcher for most of his 19 years in the big leagues. He also played for the Boston Red Sox, the Philadelphia Phillies, and the Cincinnati Redlegs.

Right from his first words in his article, the *New York Daily News'* Jim McCulley could not contain his enthusiasm for what Mays had done.

> Was it, or wasn't it Willie Mays' greatest catch—the one Say-Hey made here tonight in the first inning against Roberto Clemente as the Giants dropped their third straight to the Pirates, 6–5, and the five game set?
>
> To most press box observers, including this one, it was. To some visiting coaches from the Cardinals, including Terry Moore, one of the game's greatest centerfielders, they weren't sure. But to everybody in the park, it was nothing short of "amazing," "tremendous," "sensational."
>
> The final result, and the consequences of the game between two second division teams, will soon be forgotten by the 7,504 customers. But they'll talk about Mays' catch here this evening as long as great ones are talked about.
>
> Better than the one the Giants' fleet centerfielder made on Vic Wertz in the '54 World Series at the Polo Grounds? Easy.
>
> Let us describe it. Rube Gomez started for New York and the first two men reached base on a single and a walk. Fondy flied to left, and then Clemente ripped a line drive to center.
>
> Clemente is a right-handed hitter, but his power is to right-center and that's where Mays was playing the Bucs' right fielder. But Roberto crossed up everybody by pulling the ball to left-center, deep on a line toward the 440-foot mark.
>
> It looked like a sure triple, two runs and possibly an inside-the-park homer. But Mays kept speeding right after it, wouldn't give up and gloved it over his shoulder, one hand, using the other to keep himself off the ivy-covered bricks. It was a 60-yard dash for a line drive Willie expected would go in the other direction.
>
> The crowd buzzed with excitement, as did the press box. Some didn't wait to consider all the other great grabs Willie had made. Almost everybody in the press box, including some observers of 50 years' standing, yelled: "Greatest catch I've ever seen anywhere." The crowd gave Willie a standing ovation as he trotted in after the inning ended.

The writers for the Pittsburgh papers were no less enthused. The *Pittsburgh Post-Gazette's* Jack Hernon wrote:

> It was a game which Willie Mays kept close with an "impossible" catch in the opening inning. He went to the light tower in center to reach up and glove Bob Clemente's line drive. Had he missed, it meant two runs at the time, and probably another as it was almost a surefire triple.

The *Pittsburgh Press's* Lester J. Biederman began his column on the game enthusing about the catch, and devoted most of his "The Scoreboard" to Willie's fielding. Under the title "Mays' Catch Dwarfs Buc Victory," Biederman began his article on the game:

> Willie Mays came up with a catch last night that he himself described as "the best I ever made" and it was so breath-taking and spectacular that the feat overshadowed the Pirate 6–5 victory over he Giants.
>
> Everybody raved about Mays' highway robbery on Roberto Clemente in the first inning with two Pirates aboard, because it was so downright sensational. And everybody included

Mays' own teammates, the victimized Pirates, the 7504 cash customers and the Cardinals, who were spectators, prior to opening a series with the Bucs tonight.

Gene Freese opened the first inning with a scratch single and Bill Virdon drew a walk off Ruben Gomez. Dee Fondy flied out and then Clemente stroked a drive that headed toward the left-center wall near the light tower.

Mays turned his back and started running. It didn't appear he had a chance. Freese was almost to third and Virdon beyond second when Mays, still running toward the wall, threw up his glove, grabbed the ball in the webbing, pushed himself off the wall and threw toward the infield.

The runners backtracked in a hurry and Clemente stood at first base and looked in astonishment. When Frank Thomas fanned and Mays came into the dugout, his teammates applauded him and the fans stood and gave him a salvo, too.

Biederman titled his "The Scoreboard" column "Mays Adds to Legend."

Willie Mays almost tried to treat it as routine, but neither his Giant teammates nor the Pirates would allow it. This was something special and everybody—except Mays, apparently—knew it.

Mays was busy removing his uniform in the Giant clubhouse last night as he went over the details of his fabulous catch on Roberto Clemente in the first inning.

When he finished, he agreed "it was the best catch I ever made." But he seemed to do so reluctantly. Had to get warmed up to do it.

"Yeah," Willie admitted, "it was the best all right. Better than the one against Bob Skinner in 1954 and better than the one against Vic Wertz in the 1954 World Series. I almost waited for those two to come down. This one I had to chase."

"As soon as Clemente hit it, I knew I had some work ahead. I started out for the wall and looked up and there was the ball. It seemed to be going straight for the wall and I stabbed it and it stayed in the webbing of my glove.

I took the ball in my left hand on the dead run, pushed myself away from the wall with my right hand and threw back to the infield. To tell the truth, I didn't get a good look at the catch. But I knew it was a good one. I'd have to say it was the best I ever made. I had to work for this one."

Willie was reminded of a bare-handed catch he made at Forbes Field a few years ago. "I remember," he laughed, "Rocky Nelson hit it and I was running to my right but couldn't get my glove around. So I just stuck out my bare hand and the ball stuck."

Everybody had endorsements ready for the Mays saga.

Tommy Henrich, the old Yankee who is watching Mays daily as a Giant coach and has his eyes opened more each game, called it the best catch he ever saw.

"I always thought Joe DiMaggio's catch of a ball Hank Greenberg hit about 1938 was the best," Henrich volunteered. "DiMag turned as soon as the ball was hit and was going at top speed when he caught the ball near the monument in centerfield at Yankee Stadium. But DiMaggio's catch is now No. 2. I've just seen No. 1.

"To give you an idea of what Mays beat and with what respect DiMaggio's catch was held, the Tiger bench waved towels at DiMaggio as a mark of esteem.

"But that Mays. He makes the impossible catches."

Bill Rigney didn't think Mays had a chance to catch it.

"That ball was actually uncatchable," he declared, "but that's when Willie makes 'em. He amazes me every day."

Bucky Walters, who was in the Giant bullpen in left field and had a good view of Mays making his fantastic catch, said, "Willie simply out ran the ball."

In the Pirate clubhouse, the boys tried to work up a head of steam about their third straight victory but it all simmered down to Mays.

Clemente, who was victimized, was rather reluctant to talk about the catch. He didn't seem to be in the mood. But he did admit it was the best catch he ever saw.

Bobby Bragan, who has been a Mays booster all along, gave Mays the supreme accolade.

"Mays," Bragan said, "is the only player who ever would have caught that ball. I don't see how he did it. He probably makes 25 of those a season, but unless you're a pennant winner like the Dodgers or the Yankees, you don't get the recognition you deserve."

The *Pittsburgh Sun-Telegraph*'s George Kiseda devoted almost all his article on the game to Mays' catch on Clemente's drive, and did so under the title "Willie's Catch 'Greatest.'" Kiseda wove one superlative after another into his article.

Giants Manager Bill Rigney said it was "uncatchable." Pirate Manager Bobby Bragan thought it was superhuman. Giants Coach Tommy Henrich said it was "impossible."

Willie Mays, who made the catch that Rigney, Bragan, Henrich and 7,000 others were buzzing about at Forbes Field last night, didn't know about the adjectives. Said Willie when asked if it was his greatest:

"I don't have time to compare my catches.... You can't describe those things."

He may have something there. You can't describe Willie's catches and do justice to them.

This one obscured the fact that the Pirates won 6–5 and put together a three-game winning streak for only the second time this year.

It came in the first inning with one out, Gene Freese on second, Bill Virdon on first and Roberto Clemente at bat. Clemente hit a blast to the left of dead center and when Mays turned in full flight the only question seemed to be whether he could hold it to a double or a triple.

"You don't think about a thing," Willie said later. "You don't know you're going to catch the ball 'till the second you catch it. It was still going—I just reached up.

"I'll say this: That ball was really hit."

Without turning around, Willie put his glove out and up in a desperate stab as he reached the base of the light tower and stopped abruptly like a man who had run into a wall.

A yard or two more and he would have run into a wall. He was so close that he put his right hand up to cushion the crash just in case. He was 440–450 feet from home plate.

Henrich, the ex–Yankee who used to play alongside a centerfielder named Joe DiMaggio, announced that he was revising his ratings of centerfielders.

"That wasn't ONE of the best catches I've ever seen," he said. "It's THE best. DiMaggio is No. 2.

"This is an impossible thing.

"When I see DiMaggio I'm gonna tell him why I put him in second place."

Rigney thought it was "the best" Willie has ever made and Willie makes plenty of impossible-looking catches. Said Rigney:

"That ball was uncatchable—I think. I never thought he had a chance, but then that's Willie. Give him an inch....

"There isn't a man in the world—go back to 1900, I don't care—there isn't a man in the world who could have caught that."

Bragan agreed with Rigney, a startling development in itself.

"I didn't think it was humanly possible to catch," Bragan said. "He's the only ballplayer that ever played baseball that could have caught that ball.

"Virdon's a pretty good fielder, isn't he? When he went out to take his position he couldn't take his eye off that spot. He kept looking over there measuring it. He couldn't believe the guy caught it."

As for Mays, he didn't know if it was his best catch but agreed with some of the witnesses that it was tougher than his most famous catch—the one on Vic Wertz in the 1954 World Series.

"This ball was hit on a bullet," Willie said. "The one Wertz hit looped a little."

The catch saved two runs, but the Pirates won anyway. Relief pitcher Nellie King got the win, his first, and it was his squeeze bunt that brought Johnny O'Brien running home with the winning run.

The Pirates won the series, three games to two, and they're ready for the Cardinals tonight. They don't have to look at Willie Mays again until July 5.

In Bill Roeder's June 5, 1957, article in *The Sporting News*, evidently written before Mays made the catch on Clemente, Tommy Henrich told of another impressive aspect of Mays' fielding.

> Tommy Henrich, now coaching for the Giants, says it's too early to compare Mays with Joe DiMaggio. "I don't think Willie has been around long enough for that kind of comparison," Henrich said, "but I know that Willie can do at least one thing better than anybody I ever saw."
>
> And what would that be?
>
> "It's his way of playing a ball that he's not sure he can catch," Tommy said. "He goes after it until the last split second, and then, when he decides that he can't catch it, he's still able to grab it on the bounce before it can get by him.
>
> "I've seen him go up in the air trying for a catch with his left hand, miss it, then turn in the air and pick the ball off the wall with his right hand, all set for the throw. How anybody could have that kind of coordination I don't know, but Willie has it."

July 7, 1957—Willie Mays

In his last year as a New York Giant in 1957, Willie Mays continued to be a defensive wonder. On April 20, he made a spectacular running catch of a long drive by the Phillies' Harvey Haddix at the Polo Grounds, a catch the *New York Times'* John Drebinger called "his first great catch of the season." On consecutive days (June 19 and 20, 1957) at Milwaukee's County Stadium, Willie Mays made outstanding catches on balls Hank Aaron belted, the first being a high leap at the 402-foot mark at the fence, and the second being on a run far to his left.

On July 7, Mays made two outstanding plays in the first of two games against the Pirates at the Polo Grounds, one being on probably the longest ball he ever caught. The *New York Daily Mirror's* Ken Smith described both plays.

> Willie Mays provided the fans their money's worth. The great centerfielder raced at breakneck speed onto the cinder path in dead center not far from the Eddie Grant Monument for a drive by Dick Rand in the eighth, probably the longest catch of his career, close to 470 feet.
>
> In the preceding inning, Willie made an even more illustrious play as he grabbed a bounding hit by Mejias and whipped it to Dan O'Connell for a rundown of Baker who was trapped between second and third on Mays' wizardry.

About the catch on Dick Rand, the *New York Times'* Roscoe McGowen wrote: "Mays came up with another 'greatest' catch in the eighth inning of the opener. Willie was going toward the Eddie Grant monument between the clubhouse stairways when he gloved Rand's long drive—nearly 470 feet from the plate."

Barney Kremenko of the *New York Journal-American* was even more glowing about the catch on Rand's drive.

> The catch he made off Bucco catcher Dick Rand while running full speed with his back to the plate in deepest center was one of his best.
>
> In this book, it surpasses the catch on Vic Wertz in the 1954 World Series even though Willie, in typical modesty, insisted: "It wasn't too tough."

Leonard Koppett of the *New York Post* also quoted Willie about the difficulty of the catch on Dick Rand. Before doing that, Koppett first wrote about Willie's excitement about being the starting centerfielder for the National League in the All-Star game. Although he was on the All-Star team the previous three years he was not the starter. Koppett then paid homage to Mays.

This drawing is copied from a photograph in the *New York Times* of July 8, 1957. A negative or a good print from which to make a clear image no longer seems to exist. The photograph, taken by John Orris, shows Willie Mays with the ball just arriving at the top of his glove and in full stride near the end of a long sprint to make the catch. The ball was hit by the Pirates' Dick Rand and traveled almost 470 feet by the time Mays caught up with it (drawing by Darryl Swanson, North Collins, N.Y.; permission: John Orris/*The New York Times*/Redux).

In his fifth major league season Willie is playing for the second straight year on a team headed nowhere. He's older, more polished, more professional, more self-confident. But he still has all his basic childish excitement for playing baseball and for being thrilled by playing it in the most glamorous settings.

And as a player he's greater than ever.

More than any other big names, Willie has to be seen every day to be truly appreciated. It's the accumulation of unbelievable fielding plays, the sum of his extra bases taken, the damage of his hitting that add up to his true worth.

He made another catch, in yesterday's opener, that had people talking for the rest of the day. Still limping slightly, he ran way into the opening between the two halves of the bleachers, where the clubhouse is, to haul down Dick Rand's eighth-inning drive. It was probably the "longest" catch ever seen in dead center at the Polo Grounds.

"But that wasn't a real hard catch," he said. "I knew I could get back there and saw the ball good over my left shoulder. The one on Clemente in Pittsburgh was much harder."

What fewer people talked about, though, was a much greater play he made in the seventh inning of the same game. With Gene Baker on first and two out, he raced in for a looping ball in short left-center. Most fielders couldn't come close in the first place. But Willie, seeing only at the last minute that he couldn't get it on the fly, trapped it with his glove on a short hop while on the dead run.

Still on the run, he let go a perfect throw, not too hard or high to third baseman Danny O'Connell. The amazed Baker, rounding second, was hung up and run down.

Every day produces some new marvel from Willie and no one will be surprised if he produces one in St. Louis tomorrow.

Note that Willie mentions the catch he made on Roberto Clemente in Pittsburgh as "much harder."

Jack Hernon of the *Pittsburgh Post-Gazette* saw Willie's grab similarly to his New York counterparts, but did not compare the catch with any other catch Mays had made. It was Hernon who, after the 1954 season, felt the Mays catch on a ball hit by Bob Skinner of the Pirates was the best catch he had seen in 1954, including World Series catch on Wertz.

There was also a Willie Mays spectacular for the home crowd of 10,825 to cheer about. In the eighth inning against Bonus Pitcher Frank McCormick, Rand teed off to dead center field.

Willie took one look, turned and almost ran out of the park. When he hit the cinder path in front of the clubhouse, he reached both hands above his head and took down the baseball.

Hernon misidentified the pitcher. It was Mike McCormick, then an 18-year-old.

Dick Rand hit a home run in the first game of the doubleheader. The Pirates won both games. Rand's homer was the only one he hit in the sixty games he played for the Pirates that year. He also hit one other major league homer, that for the Cardinals in 1955. His major league career was relatively brief. In addition to the sixty games he played in 1957, Dick Rand played in nine games in 1953, and three in 1955.

As was the case for Mel Clark on the ball Mays caught off Clark's bat in 1954, it is very unlikely that Dick Rand ever hit a longer ball that was caught. It is likely that Mays was not playing Rand to hit a long ball, and thus had to run a great distance to catch the ball. The catch on Dick Rand was to be Willie's last "great" long, back-to-the-plate catch at the Polo Grounds.

Later, on July 16, the *New York Journal-American*'s Barney Kremenko wrote an article of appreciation about Willie Mays, and included quotes from Frank Frisch and Jimmy Dykes.

Thrill-a-minute Willie Mays is giving Polo Grounds fans a full quota of excitement, even if the Giants are not.

Hardly a day goes by that the famed Say Hey Kid doesn't draw raves—either with his thunderous bat, his flying feet, or his magic glove. And how about that arm?

"How about that arm?" repeats Frank Frisch. "It's the greatest I ever saw. Bob Meusel, of the old time Yankees, was good, too. But you can't beat Willie."

Frisch, a Hall of Famer who does a post-game Giant television show and thereby sees Mays every day, doesn't stop there.

"I would pay money just to see him play," the Fordham Flash says. "He brings back the old days for a fellow like myself. He and Joe DiMaggio are the greatest centerfielders I ever saw. But Joe couldn't run the bases as well; he wasn't as daring as Willie.

"Going from first to third on a single wins a lot of ball games. Mays is the only one I know who does that consistently."

Jimmy Dykes, another old-timer at the Polo Grounds this week-end as one of Birdie Tebbetts' Cincinnati coaches, joins Frisch in the Mays Booster Club.

"He is one of the greatest I ever saw," insists Dykes. "He's a better centerfielder than Tris Speaker, and I saw plenty of Speaker. Willie throws much better. I'll go a step further. I think Willie is a better all-around player than Ty Cobb. Ty couldn't field in Willie's class."

In my August 2, 2002, conversation with him, Steve Ridzik had a number of comments about Willie Mays, his teammate on the New York Giants in 1956 and 1957.

SR: Richie Ashburn was pretty consistent. He always got to the ball. He was like DiMaggio. I don't remember any one particular play Richie made, but it seemed he was always in front of the ball.

Like when I played with Mays for a couple of years, and he made so many great catches. One thing with Willie. It was like he was always going away. When he tapped his glove two or three times, you knew it was in the well.

I remember one play. A guy was on third base and the ball was hit to right-center field and Willie, on the dead run, caught the ball going toward right field and turned and threw a perfect strike to home plate. Not many guys are capable of doing that. He came flyin' over there, caught the ball, and had the capability of turning and half-stopping and falling down and he could throw the ball like that. That was Willie's greatest asset. He had a great arm and he was pretty darn accurate with it all the time.

JA: When you saw that kind of play, what did you say to him when he came back to the bench?

SR: I used to tell him, "I'd put you in the Hall of Fame, for crying out loud, for making all those great catches out there while I was pitching." I used to chase him all over the Polo Grounds when I was pitching. And I'd say, "You just chase down all my mistakes and I'll put you in the Hall of Fame." We used to laugh and kid about that all the time. He used to do so many things so easy that it was unreal.

JA: Armwise, who else had an arm like Willie Mays?

SR: Rocky Colavito had a great arm. He could throw the ball a mile. Clemente had a great arm. I played with him down in Puerto Rico when he was just a kid. He wasn't in the big leagues yet. And he just amazed me. He was only 18 or 19 years old. Playing in San Juan. But he could do it all. I put him in a close capacity to Mays to go and get that ball and throw it. He did throw with a great deal of accuracy, and with the same power as Willie. Rocky had a great arm that could be a little erratic, but his arm was as good as Willie's. Willie seemed to have that accuracy.

I also thought Willie was one of the fastest guys that I've ever seen. He could be standing still, but by the time he put his second foot down after he started to run he was wide open. He could have stolen a hundred bases a year like they did with Brock. Willie would try to steal 45 bases and he'd steal 43. If they ever turned him loose, there's no tellin' how many he would have stolen. Back then we were playing for one run. We used the bunt or the hit and run more than they do today to move a guy over one base. Today they play for the big inning. I loved to get up there and hit. I wasn't a great hitter, but I did hit well. I loved to bunt. You felt like you were in the game. You had to do your job. I can't believe watching some of these guys today try to bunt.

The Giants left New York for San Francisco after the 1957 season. Mays returned for games at the Polo Grounds against the expansion New York Mets in 1962 and 1963, but the Met hitters did not challenge him with many long clouts.

September 17, 1957—Bill Tuttle

In the last paragraph of his article on the New York Yankees–Detroit Tigers game on September 17, 1957, the *New York Times*' Joseph M. Sheehan noted Bill Tuttle's catch: "A slim crowd of 5,353 was treated to the best Stadium catch of the season when Bill Tuttle robbed Mickey Mantle of a triple—or inside-the-park homer—with a jumping, backhanded catch of Mick's 440-foot line drive to left center in the fourth."

Joe Trimble of the *New York Daily News* agreed with Sheehan.

The Yanks would have gone ahead in the bottom of the fourth but for the greatest catch at the Stadium this year. Centerfielder Bill Tuttle went away back to the running track in left-center for a one-hand, back-hand grab of Mickey Mantle's 440-foot screamer, tumbling and somersaulting as he held the ball.

It would have been a triple and a run, since Howard made the second of his three hits right after the magnificent catch. The crowd of 5,353, smallest of the year in the Bronx, cheered like 10 times that number.

Next to the story about the game, the *Detroit Free Press* had six Associated Press photos showing Tuttle's catch. The *Free Press*'s caption read:

OUR BOY! BILL'S GOT IT! New York observers called it one of the most brilliant catches in many seasons—the leaping grab of Mickey Mantle's 440-foot drive made by Tiger centerfielder Bill Tuttle in the fourth inning of Tuesday's game.

Bill Tuttle was no stranger to making great catches. On May 27, 1955, the same day Chuck Diering made his terrific catch on Mickey Mantle, Tuttle made a catch on the Chicago White Sox' Jim Rivera in Briggs Stadium that stirred memories of Jo Jo White's catch in the 1934 World Series. Hal Middlesworth of the *Detroit Free Press* called Tuttle's catch "a spectacular game-saving catch."

The title above the *Detroit News*' account of the game was: "Tuttle's Catch Greatest Since 1934, Says Rowe." The *News*' Sam Greene described the catch and gave Schoolboy Rowe's comments. In the game, catcher Frank House's solo home run was the margin of victory for pitcher Billy Hoeft's shutout.

Equally important to Hoeft was a sensational catch by Bill Tuttle which prevented Chicago from at least tying the score in the ninth.

With Jim Brideweser on second base and one out, Jim Rivera smashed a liner into right center. Tuttle chased it almost to the 415-foot mark for a one-handed stab that stirred the crowd of 31,236 to sustained hurrahs.

"I wouldn't have given a nickel for Tut's chance to bring that one down," said House in the locker room.

Fred Hatfield, playing shortstop, Ray Boone, watching from the dugout, and Jack Tighe, busy in the bullpen, were others who thought Tuttle's pursuit hopeless.

"At first I didn't think I could get it," said Tuttle, "but after a half-dozen steps, I figured there was an outside chance. The ball stuck so solidly in the glove that, even if I had fallen, I'd have held it."

If Tuttle had missed, Brideweser would have walked home with the tying run and Rivera probably would have reached third with a triple.

"It might have been a home run inside the park," said Schoolboy Rowe. "Anyway, it was the greatest catch I've seen since Jo Jo White robbed Pepper Martin in the '34 World Series."

Schoolboy Rowe began his major league career in 1933 with the Detroit Tigers, and pitched for them for nine full seasons before being traded in 1942. He played fifteen seasons in the major leagues.

In the mid–1950s, speedy centerfielder Bill Tuttle anchored strong Detroit Tigers outfields that included Al Kaline in right field.

May 30, 1960—Willie Mays

After mentioning several catches that he made, Willie Mays, in his book *My Life In and Out of Baseball*, discusses a catch he made on the Cubs' Ed Bouchee in 1960.

> Let me say just this: I can remember one ball I caught that I never hoped to catch. Maybe that should define it as "greatest." It was off Ed Bouchee of the Cubs, at Candlestick in 1960. He hit a sharp liner, good depth, to right-center. I ran to cut it off, knowing that, the way were playing him, I could afford that luxury. If it got past me, the right fielder, going deeper, would play it off the fence.
>
> And it was past me—not only past me, but bending ever farther away from me in the wind.
>
> At the last minute, I literally stuck out the glove and snatched it out of the air when it was past me. My whole body had cooperated.
> ...
> If I have to pick a number-one catch—and I'd rather not—I've got to go for that one on Bouchee. All the others, no matter how vital the situation or how terrible the complications, have come down to being there when the ball was. This one, though—the ball was there first and I still caught it.

The catch on Bouchee occurred on May 30, 1960, in the first game of a doubleheader against the Cubs in San Francisco. The *San Francisco Examiner*'s Walter Judge wrote about the catch.

> Mays had kept the club in contention with his best catch of the season, an all-out one-handed grab of Bouchee's liner while running full tilt in right center. The catch closed out the Chicago ninth with two runners heading for the plate.
>
> The crowd stood and cheered as Willie came to the dugout.

The *San Francisco Chronicle*'s Bob Stevens called Mays' catch on the Bouchee ball "unbelievable."

As good as Mays' catch on Bouchee's liner was, it played second fiddle that day to the way Mays ended the second game. The *Chronicle*'s Stevens described Mays' most outstanding play, which occurred after Willie was walked in the ninth inning of the second game.

> Morehead worked the count to 3 and 2 on McCovey, who was swinging all out for the fences, and then got one where the big boy could belt it. Mays tore for second at the precise second of McCovey's swing, and the ball whistled behind him, past the lunging Cub first baseman Eddie Bouchee, and on the ground to right fielder Will.
>
> Under a full head of steam, Willie rounded second, continued on to third, rounded it, glanced back and then blasted off when he saw second baseman Jerry Kindall take Will's throw.
>
> Kindall, unnerved by the audacity of the streaking Mays, who was only 20 feet down the line when Jerry looked toward the plate, rushed his throw and it landed in the dirt. Mays crashed into catcher Moe Thacker, the ball squirted to the backstop and Mays was home. Willie leaped immediately to his feet, clapping his hands in the ecstasy of his success and then fell into the arms of congratulating Giants as the six hours and 27 minutes of action ended.

Stevens's colleague at the *Chronicle*, Will Connolly, devoted much of his column on the game to Willie's dash to the plate from first base.

> A day to remember was yesterday's holiday doubleheader, split by the Giants with the Chicago Cubs. That was just ordinary but Willie Mays' heroics weren't commonplace. Chicago writers who have watched Mays for more years than the locals, pronounced it one of Willie's greatest days—perhaps his greatest in the variety of marvels he performed. He homered into the left field stands against the wind, he stole three bases, he singled twice, he made two running catches to either side and generally bothered the Cubs even in their 2–1 victory in the first game. Almost by himself, he won the second for his staggering colleagues, 5–4, by barreling from first to home on a single in the ninth."
>
> "You watched the real Willie Mays," chorused the visiting press, not envious of the fact that their side was deprived of a possible sweep of the bill by Mays' dash. Even Manager Lou Boudreau of the Chicagoans didn't seem to feel too badly about "losing to Mays."
>
> "That man is the greatest base runner in either league," Boudreau pronounced. "There may be some men who may be as fast, such as Vada Pinson of Cincinnati, but for instinct on the paths, nobody is Mays' equal. His daring, and his speed to make it work, can upset any defense."
>
> You'd expect Manager Bill Rigney to lyricize over his man, and he did.
>
> "Nobody in baseball could have done it. I knew that if the right fielder threw to second, Willie wouldn't stop at third but would barge in all the way. Homers you expect him to hit. Bases you expect him to steal, and marvelous catches are almost routine with him. But that stretching for the winner in the ninth just about sums up all that is Mays."
>
> Willie himself conceded he might have been thrown out at the plate. "The relay throw from second wasn't too good but I didn't know that when I rounded third," he said softly. "But I figured even if the throw was good, I still had a chance of knocking the ball out of the catcher's hand, so I went in."
>
> ...
>
> The first time he looked, Mays said, was when he saw out of the corner of his eye that right fielder Bob Will had thrown to second to keep Willie McCovey from moving up to second.
>
> "I decided then to round third and keep going. No, I didn't hesitate. I didn't slow down. I figured my run would make [Jerry] Kindall throw in a hurry. He did, and it wasn't very accurate. If Will had thrown directly to home instead of to second, I couldn't have gone home."

Even on a day when he made a catch he thought might be his greatest, possibly the most difficult, Mays did something else which upstaged the catch.

August 5, 1960—Roberto Clemente

There is little dispute that Roberto Clemente, a 12-time Gold Glove outfielder for the Pittsburgh Pirates, was one of the greatest all-around defensive players ever. Clemente's prime years, like Curt Flood's of the St. Louis Cardinals, continued into the late 1960s. In Clemente's case, he may have made his greatest catch on June 15, 1971, at the age of 37. That catch came in Houston on a drive by Bob Watson. Clemente sped to the wall and leaped high up to grab Watson's bid for a home run. He went face first into the concrete wall as he caught the ball, suffering ankle, knee and elbow injuries.

In his book *Roberto Clemente: The Great One*, Bruce Markusen wrote that Houston manager Harry Walker felt the that catch on the ball Watson hit was the greatest he'd ever seen in his 34 years in baseball, and that Clemente's long-time teammate Bill Mazeroski compared that catch to one Roberto made on Willie Mays in 1960.

The catch of August 5, 1960, was another where Clemente threw caution to the wind and pursued a ball into a concrete wall. Like Earle Combs and Pete Reiser, Roberto Clemente risked his career to make a play.

The August 5 game against the San Francisco Giants was a duel between the Pirates' Wilmer "Vinegar Bend" Mizell and the Giants' Sam "Toothpick" or "Sad Sam" Jones, with Mizell and his mates winning by a 1 to 0 score. The game also was marked by superlative outfield play by Clemente and his teammate, Bill Virdon, who, in center field, made three outstanding plays.

The *Pittsburgh Post-Gazette*'s Jack Hernon actually felt that one of Virdon's plays, on a ball hit to the left center field wall, was "one of the finest plays ever pulled off in Forbes Field." Bill Virdon raced out to the wall, leaped into the ivy, and appeared to catch the ball hit by the Giants' Andre Rodgers. The umpire ruled that the ball hit the wall first, but Virdon threw a strike to the third baseman who had ample time to apply a tag on Rodgers. Virdon said the umpire checking his play made the right call. He didn't catch the ball.

The *Pittsburgh Press*'s Lester J. Biederman called the Virdon trap and throw the "play of the season."

Walter Judge of the *San Francisco Examiner* and Bob Stevens of the *San Francisco Chronicle* both lauded Virdon's defensive work. Judge wrote: "Alou thumped a 2–0 pitch 'way, 'way out there. But Virdon, ranging like a Willie Mays, went back and caught the drive at the light tower. A 440-foot blast, it was just a long out." The "Alou" who drove Virdon to the light tower was Felipe.

Because the end result of Roberto Clemente's catch on the ball Willie Mays hit in the seventh inning was so scary, both the San Francisco and the Pittsburgh writers described the catch.

The *Pittsburgh Post-Gazette*'s Jack Hernon wrote:

> The Bucs lost Bob Clemente for a few days when he made a tremendous catch in right field, on a long drive by Willie Mays in the seventh inning. Clemente gloved the ball with one hand and almost immediately crashed the right field wall.
>
> Clemente came tumbling down in a heap and after a bit of aid walked off the field. Dr. Joe Feingold took five stitches for a deep cut in his chin and Clemente also suffered contusions of the left knee. He will be out at least for the remainder of the Giant series.

The *Pittsburgh Press*'s Lester J. Biederman focused on the high quality of play the two teams exhibited. He began: "Dick Groat called it the "Best game I ever played in" and to a greater portion of the 33,304 wild-eyed fans the Pirates' 1–0 victory over the Giants last night was the most thrilling spectacle they've ever witnessed." Later Biederman added:

Few finer games have ever been staged in the 51-year history of Forbes Field. This one was topped off with positively brilliant pitching by Vinegar Bend Mizell and Sam Jones, and Bill Virdon and Roberto Clemente turned in breathtaking defensive maneuvers that had the fans uproaring all night long.

Clemente slammed into the right-center wall chasing Willie Mays' line drive to start the seventh and after making the catch, fell in a heap. A stretcher was sent out but Clemente was revived and he walked off the field under his own power, though shaky.

The *San Francisco Examiner*'s Walter Judge told more about Clemente's catch and crash.

The exciting Clemente was injured in the line of duty, bouncing off the concrete wall in the right field after taking a double away from Willie Mays in the seventh inning. Roberto fell below the 385-foot marker and momentarily looked as if he could be seriously hurt for he ran smack dab into the wall as he reached over his head for a fantastic one-handed catch.
A stretcher was brought out after the Puerto Rican, never unconscious, got to his feet he walked under his own power as the near capacity crowd of 33,304 cheered mightily.

It was the *San Francisco Chronicle*'s Bob Stevens who most agreed with Bill Mazeroski's later assessment of the greatness of Clemente's catch on the ball Willie Mays hit on August 5, 1960.

... and in the seventh, right fielder Clemente crashed into the wall to glove a Willie Mays rocket but to play no more this night. Clemente smashed face-on into the concrete base of the right-centerfield stands, at the 385 foot mark, and then collapsed in the dirt warning track he had ignored in his pursuit of the "certain double."
It required five stitches to close a laceration on his chin and his left knee was sorely damaged. The catch had to rank with the greatest of all time, as well as one of the most frightening to watch and painful to make.

In his book, *Clemente: the Passion and Grace of Baseball's Last Hero*, David Maraniss noted that Clemente's manager Danny Murtaugh considered the catch on Mays the best one he ever saw. Murtaugh had seen many great catches in his time in the major leagues. He played second base for three National League teams between 1941 and 1951. He managed the team for which he last played, the Pittsburgh Pirates, for 15 years between 1957 and 1976.

May 17, 1961—Willie Mays

On May 17, 1961, Willie Mays made a catch on Chicago Cubs catcher Dick Bertell which again brought back memories of the Wertz catch.
After calling a catch by Felipe Alou in the first inning of the game against the Cubs "almost incredible," Curley Grieve of the *San Francisco Examiner* went further on Mays' catch on Dick Bertell's ball.

The one Willie Mays pulled in the seventh WAS incredible.
He caught a vicious drive by Dick Bertell over his shoulder almost in front of the 410 foot sign in centerfield that has to be ranked with his all-time greatest.

Opposite: **The Pirates' Roberto Clemente makes maximum extension to catch a ball hit by the Cubs' Bobby Thomson at Wrigley Field in an August 19, 1958, game the Pirates won. After the catch, he tries to keep from falling to the ground (AP/Wide World Photos).**

Grieve went on to mention comparisons four of Mays' former teammates made with other
catches Mays had made.

"In a way," said Manager Alvin Dark, "it was a finer catch than the one he made off Vic
Wertz in the 1954 World Series. That one he saw all the way. This one he turned his back and
raced for it. It had to be perfect judgment. He caught it like a football."

Dark was captain of the Giants in '54. He saw the Wertz play from shortstop. Also on that
team were Wes Westrum, Larry Jansen, and Whitey Lockman, now Giant coaches.

"This one was better or at least as good as Willie's World Series catch," said Westrum.

Lockman disagreed:

"It was not as tough and not as dramatic. But no other outfielder in the league could have
made it."

Jansen inserted:

"Mays made one in Brooklyn that was greater than either of them."

Charles Einstein of the *San Francisco Examiner* noted the catch Mays made on Bertell,
calling it a "Vic Wertz Special." He also commented on the catch Felipe Alou made: "On
the very first hitter of the game, Felipe Alou climbed the fence in right like a hypnotized
house painter to take a homer away from Bob Will."

An article in the *San Francisco Chronicle* of the next day was titled: "Did Mays Top
1954 Series Catch?" *Chronicle* writer Dick Friendlich seemed to be making the case that
the catch on Bertell was the better one.

On Sept. 29, 1954, in the first game of the World Series, Willie Mays of the New York
Giants made a back-to-the-plate, over-the-shoulder catch of a 440-foot smash to center by
Cleveland's Vic Wertz.

That play has gone down as one of the great bits of fielding in modern baseball, and the *St.
Louis Sporting News* voted it the top thrill of the entire 1954 season.

Yesterday afternoon in Candlestick Park, the same Willie Mays made a similar catch of a
400-foot drive to dead center by Chicago Cubs' catcher Dick Bertell to end the seventh
inning and cut off a certain Chicago run, for Ed Bouchee had singled ahead of Bertell with
two out.

... Mays had been playing fairly shallow on Bertell, and after one look, he simply turned
his back and ran. He caught it with hands outstretched five feet from the 410-foot marker on
the center-field fence. How he sensed where the ball was from the time he showed his No. 24
to the diamond and the moment he caught it, only Willie knows.

... Informed yesterday of Dark's comparison [of the Bertell catch to the catch on Wertz],
Mays stayed in character.

"Did he say that? I don't know, I just try to get that ball and throw it back to the infield."
Then he relaxed a little.

"The wind made a difference. If it was blowing the other way, the ball is out of here. That
wind changes all the time, makes it tough."

These articles indicate two things. First, Willie's comments about the wind at Candlestick Park gives some idea of the problems he and other outfielders playing there had
to confront on both routinely hit balls and on balls which were difficult to deal with when
they left the bat.

Second, Alvin Dark's mention of the analogy to a football catch is an apt one for
Willie Mays. Almost three years later, Jimmy Cannon had a conversation with Willie. In
Cannon's April 26, 1964, article in the *Los Angeles Herald-Examiner*, Willie makes clear
his debt as a fielder to Green Bay Packer end Don Hutson.

It is a fable of baseball that Willie Mays plays the outfield as a fish swims or a bird flies. Baseball, according to the popular theory, is a mindless act as Mays practices it. He works at being

the greatest of modern players. But the spectacular moves are generally praised as accidents of an infallible instinct.

"I always know what I'm doing out there," Mays said. "For instance, I never hit a fence."

This was said with the pride of a guy who runs to walls with what appears to be a mindless desperation. But if he clambers up a wall, he seems to be using an invisible rope. He will run with that rocking gait to the fence and stop without skidding and catch a ball that grazes the wall.

"You know Don Hutson?" Mays asked. "He was a football player."

"A great end with Green Bay," I said.

"I learned how to play fences watching Don Hutson," Mays said.

This was in the clubhouse of the Giants in Phoenix. He was sitting at his locker autographing baseballs.

"You were too young to see Hutson play," I said.

"I saw him in the movies," he said. "A friend of mine showed me him. I watched the way he caught a football. He would catch a ball and stop real fast. Go one way, go the other way. I watched what he did. I said if he can do that with a football, why can't I do that with a baseball? I studied what he did. Then I went out and would run hard at the fence, and stop. I kept doing it till I could do it good. I twisted just like he did. He'd catch the ball and twist away from the guy going to tackle him. I catch the ball, and twist away from the fence."

Jimmy Cannon's article appeared in April of 1964. Later that year, in August and in September, Mays was to make two more great catches, the second of which may rank with the very top catches he ever made.

Mention should be made of a catch which may have occurred in either 1958 or 1959, and which was presented in Donald Honig's book *Mays, Mantle, Snider*. Leon Wagner played his first two years in the majors in San Francisco in 1958 and 1959. Honig tells Wagner's story of the almost unbelievable play. According to Wagner, the Cubs' Ernie Banks hit a long ball in Chicago's Wrigley Field. Once Wagner got to the wall from his position in left field, he decided the ball was going for a homer. However, Mays came running after the ball and at Leon with the intention of catching the ball. When he got to Wagner, Mays propelled himself upward by planting his feet on Wagner's chest. Wagner said Mays caught the ball. Newspapers I checked of the Giants-Cubs games in 1958 and 1959, the years Wagner and Mays were teammates, did not mention the unusual event.

August 17, 1961—Curt Flood

Curt Flood is known mostly as the player who challenged baseball's "reserve clause" by taking the courageous step to file suit against major league baseball to be free to work where he chose to work. Flood lost his suit, but set the stage for later action that opened the era of free agency in which players could negotiate with other owners. The reserve clause dated back to 1879 and held that owners had the exclusive right to determine where the players worked. It also meant that players could not bargain on the open market to obtain more money for their services.

By the time he refused to accept a trade to the Philadelphia Phillies after his 1969 season with the St. Louis Cardinals, Curt Flood was one of baseball's best fielding centerfielders, if not the best, over the last half of the 1960s. In addition, he was one of the game's best all-around players. As the *St. Louis Post-Dispatch*'s Dan O'Neill noted in an July 27, 1995, article about Flood, it is no stretch to believe that the brilliant-fielding Curt Flood would have been a legitimate candidate for the Hall of Fame had he had a normal career well into his 30s. The legal action he took contributed greatly to the premature end of his career.

In his 1994 book *Stranger to the Game* (written with Lonnie Wheeler), Hall of Fame pitcher Bob Gibson called his teammate Flood "the best center fielder I ever saw" (52). Gibson played in the majors from 1959 through 1975.

In 1961 and 1962 Flood made a number of sensational catches to fully establish himself as an outstanding outfielder. In his May 9, 1962, article on Flood, Neal Russo, writing in *The Sporting News*, told of what Flood considered his greatest catch to date.

> Flood, who once made a "human fly" catch by scaling the Busch Stadium wall, rates the catch he turned in at San Francisco, August 17, 1961, as his greatest.
> With the Cardinals leading, 2 to 0, in the eighth and Orlando Cepeda on second base with one out, Hobie Landrith lined to right-center.
> Getting an amazing jump on the ball, Flood sped to within a few feet of the fence, leaped as high as he could and speared the ball over his head with his back to the plate. "I was playing Landrith relatively shallow because I felt I had a chance to throw out Cepeda at the plate," Flood explained. "Cepeda's not a very fast runner. I didn't think I had a chance to make the catch. The wind actually held up the ball a bit."

The *San Francisco Examiner*'s Curley Grieve had more to say about the Flood catch.

> Larry Jackson pitched a sparkling three hitter to give the St. Louis Cards a 2–0 victory over the Giants but he was modest to give credit where credit is due.
> "Curt Flood won that game with a helluva play," said Jackson in the locker room afterward.
> The fleet little Oaklander who attended McClymonds High School at the same time as Cincinnati's Frank Robinson and Vada Pinson and later played Legion ball with them for the Bill Irwin Post, made a "kangaroo catch" on Hobie Landrith's smash to right center following Orlando Cepeda's double in the eighth.
> The ball would have crashed the fence near the top and gone for at least a double except that Curt raced over and leaped with outstretched glove just in time.
> There has been no better play—although some as spectacular—all season. It pinned another low-run defeat on hard luck Mike McCormick.
> Flood, 140 pounder stretching 5-9, grinned as he related: "I thought it was going out when I went after it. Then I was afraid I wouldn't catch up to it. I took the best leap I could—I must have gone up two feet—and caught the ball going away in front of me. I crashed into the fence. I don't think it would have gone over but it would have been close."
> Flood, Robinson and Pinson were all signed by Bobby Mattick, Cincy scout. Curt went to the Cards in a trade—and they were glad they had him yesterday.
> "That was a great clutch play," said Manager Johnny Keane. "I didn't think he would get it. I thought sure it was gone."
> Flood may not have been in a position even to run for it except for some towel-swinging in the Cardinal dugout. When Landrith came to bat, at least three Red Birds grabbed towels and signaled Flood to shade farther to right. He took five steps and needed every one of them.

Another factor affecting Flood's grab of the long Landrith drive was noted by the *St. Louis Globe-Democrat*'s Jack Herman. He also mentions another recent and rousing catch by Flood.

> The wind started up just as Hobie Landrith sent a fly toward right-center. Flood, who made a once-in-a-lifetime catch against the Phillies two weeks ago, did it again. He raced to the fence and leaped for another incredible back-handed grab, saving Jackson's first shutout in 28 starts.

Like the *San Francisco Examiner*'s Grieve, the *St. Louis Post-Dispatch*'s Neal Russo quoted Cardinal manager Johnny Keane and Larry Jackson about Flood's catch. Russo also quoted Cardinal coach Harry Walker.

Coach Harry Walker, a former outfielder, said that in the National League only Willie Mays or Bill Virdon would have had a chance to match Flood's catch.

"And I'm not so sure even Flood could make the same catch again—that's how tough it was," said The Hat.

The big play came with one out in the eighth inning after Orlando Cepeda had become only the second baserunner on the game with a double to left. The other man who reached base, Jose Pagan with a single in the third, was erased in a double play.

After Cepeda doubled in the eighth, Hobie Landrith connected with a high fast ball. Later he said, "I hit that ball as hard as I've ever hit any." Flood took off with his back to the infield all the way. About one step from the fence he timed his high leap perfectly and speared the ball.

Curt Flood's catch of a long ball hit by the San Francisco Giants' Hobie Landrith in San Francisco on August 17, 1961, was one of the greatest catches in his career (© Bettmann/CORBIS).

Flood rates this latest spectacular among his top three or four catches. He likes a diving catch this season as his No. 1 even though he climbed the Busch Stadium wall to make a great catch a few years ago.

"When the ball left Landrith's bat I thought for sure the ball was going out, but suddenly it stopped carrying so much," Flood said. He doubted that the drive would have cleared the eight-foot fence.

In his May 9, 1962, article in *The Sporting News*, Russo tells that in August of 1961 alone Flood made four "fancy" catches while playing behind pitcher Larry Jackson. Five years later, in the May 20, 1967, *The Sporting News*, Russo returned to Flood's prowess as a fielder. This time he included a number of quotes by and about Flood.

Roger Craig, a teammate of Flood just one year and now a special scout for the Dodgers, had this capsule size-up of Flood: "Flood is the best defensive outfielder in the big leagues."

From Lou Boudreau, player-manager turned broadcaster, came this encomium: "Flood is the most underrated outfielder. I haven't seen a thing Flood can't do. He gets as good a jump on a ball as Mays does. He has absolutely no fear of walls. His first thought is simply to get to the ball and catch it."

Said Pete Reiser, Cub coach and a top outfielder who challenged a few walls too many:

"Curt plays center field just the way you like to see it played. Every pitch means something to him. Some outfielders will get lazy and careless if the pitcher is wild. Not Flood. He's always ready."

Flood ... credited George Powles, his coach from his Little League days through high school, with helping him most with his fielding.

The surehanded Terry Moore was a coach on the Cardinals in Flood's first year with the Birds.

"Terry helped me with the biggest thing a center fielder needs—getting a good jump on the ball," Flood said.

From center field Flood keeps a wary eye to see whether a pitch is inside or outside.

"I can almost always tell whether the batter is going to pull the ball, so I shift my weight accordingly," he said. "Sometimes the difference in making the play or not is in going in the right direction even BEFORE the ball is hit."

The catch on Landrith's drive was among many Flood made to rob opposing batters of extra base hits. Three years later, on May 12, 1964, Flood made a catch at Connie Mack Stadium in Philadelphia which was compared to the catch on Landrith. The Cardinals beat the Phillies 4 to 2, and Flood's grab was a key play. The *Philadelphia Inquirer*'s Allen Lewis called the catch "miraculous," and went on to describe the situation.

Simmons might have been relieved sooner had it not been for Flood's acrobatics in the third. With Tony Taylor on third and Richie Allen on first after two were out, Roy Sievers smashed a long liner that had all the earmarks of a two-run double or triple. Flood raced back and over. Just as it seemed that the ball would go over his head and crash against the wall, the Redbird centerfielder leaped, gloved the ball and bounced off the fence with his glove held high, the ball still in it.

The *Philadelphia Daily News*' Stan Hochman told more, including Cardinals pitcher Curt Simmons' reaction.

The Phillies got seven hits off him, and it took a tremendous catch by Curt Flood in the third inning to stifle a big inning....

"I struggled," he admitted. "I'd get going pretty good, and then I'd walk a lefthander. But I was lucky, and Flood made a great play. That was the big one."

The Cardinals had blistered Art Mahaffey for three runs by the third inning. But the Phillies got two men on in the third and then Roy Sievers lashed a ball towards the leftfield fence. Flood chased it, and you could hear the thump when he banged into the fence as he caught the ball.

"It was an all-timer," Gene Mauch said afterwards. "It looked like Pete Reiser, who didn't know there was anything in the ballpark except the ball."

Flood must have gone to the same motto school as Simmons. He wasn't ga-ga about the catch. He said, "You're conscious of the wall. I didn't think the ball was hit hard when he hit it. These wooden walls ... they're a pleasure to run into."

Jack Herman of the *St. Louis Globe-Democrat* gave an idea about the consistently high level of Flood's play in the field.

In the previous inning he saved Simmons and the Cardinals with another of his unbelievable catches. With Phillies on first and third and two away the little guy raced to the wall in left-center for Roy Sievers' drive.

At the last instant, Flood crashed into the wall but somehow picked off the ball with a back-handed grab.

How good was the catch which Flood himself was not "ga-ga" over? The *St. Louis Post-Dispatch*'s Neal Russo tried to assess the catch's merit by asking others.

With two men on base in the third inning, Roy Sievers lashed a drive that was headed for the fence on left-center. Flood gave chase, leaped and made an unbelievable backhand stab. He crashed against the plywood fence when he came down, and the 14,412 gave him a standing ovation.

Leo Ward, the Cardinals' traveling secretary for so many years, yelled, "That's the greatest catch I've ever seen!"

Back in 1961, Flood dashed madly for the centerfield fence at Candlestick Park, made a tremendous leap and hauled in a drive with his back to the plate.

Would Flood compare catches?

"Nothing will ever compare with that one in Frisco," he said.

Ken Boyer dissented.

"I've always felt that catches made going into a fence are the greatest because the timing is tougher," Boyer said.

Philly coach George Myatt, who has been around the majors 23 years, rated a catch by Larry Doby in Cleveland as the only one that might be superior to Flood's.

"But I'm not so sure that Flood's wasn't tougher," Myatt said.

Flood's road roommate, Bob Gibson, said, "Flood's catches are like pretty girls. Every one's the prettiest you ever saw until you see the next one."

The *Philadelphia Bulletin*'s Ray Kelly wrote:

... the Cardinals held on for a 4–2 decision before 14,412 spectators who wondered if they'd ever seen a better catch than the one Flood made on Roy Sievers.

"It has to rate with the greatest I've ever seen," said Phillies coach George Myatt.

"I didn't think he had a chance for the ball," said coach Peanuts Lowrey.

Flood made his spectacular grab in the third inning. The Phillies, trailing 3–0, had runners on first and third when Sievers unloaded a terrific smash towards left center.

"I thought it was out of here," Roy said.

Flood, shading Sievers to left, had a long run. Just as the ball neared the wall, Curt went into the air on the run. He speared the ball as he crashed into the wall, and held it to end the inning.

"That was the ball game," Sievers said.

"I didn't think the ball was hit that hard," Flood recalled. "I thought I had it all the way. I used my right foot on the wall to get up, but I thought I hit the fence on my way down."

"You have to be an acrobat to play the outfield when I'm pitching," Simmons said.

In his "Man About Sports" column on the same day Ray Kelly's article appeared, the *Bulletin*'s Sandy Grady wrote about Flood and the catch on Sievers's ball. Grady began:

At least the Phils could send Curt Flood a bill for kicking a hunk out of their dog-food sign. Flood's spikes beat a cha-cha rhythm up the left-center signboard to make a play you only see in a jai-lai fronton. He also left some cleat marks on Roy Sievers' heart.

"Was that the all-time, four-star, most super, gigantic catch of your career?" people were asking Flood later.

"Yep. Any time you have to hit a wall, it's a good play," said Flood, a brisk, wiry, bird-like man. "I knew if I couldn't catch it, well, it's a two-base hit for Sievers and maybe two runs."

"Gee, you mean you rate that better than the catch you made in Candlestick Park?" challenged a St. Louis type.

"No. This one didn't make me run as far as the one in San Francisco," Flood said. "I guess I better do like Mays—catch 'em, not rate 'em."

A few paragraphs later Grady quoted John Quinn, the Phillies' general manager, who said, "I can't think of anybody but Willie Mays who could have made that play."

June 27, 1963—Al Luplow

Al Luplow played major league baseball in seven seasons, 1961 to 1967. The first five were spent with the Cleveland Indians, the sixth with the San Francisco Giants, and the last split between the Giants and the Pittsburgh Pirates. He played the outfield, and his best batting season was 1962 when he knocked 14 home runs and hit .277 in 97 games.

His .977 fielding average in 346 major league games in the outfield was a respectable figure. However, on June 27, 1963, Al Luplow made a catch which had the writers in Cleveland and Boston scurrying around for superlatives.

The *Plain Dealer*'s Bob Dolgan, in his first sentence on the Indians-Red Sox game at Fenway Park, called Luplow's catch "one of the all-time great catches in baseball history." He went on to describe the scene.

> Luplow's breath-taking catch came with the Tribe leading, 6–3. The Red Sox had men on first and third with one out. Dick Williams, the veteran utilityman, was the batter.
>
> Williams swung at a pitch thrown by Ted Abernathy and sent it rocketing to deep right center.
>
> Luplow flashed toward the fence. Going full speed he leaped high at the fence. He jumped so high his knees cracked the top of the five-foot barrier.
>
> The spring carried Luplow over the fence and as he flew through the air he stuck up his glove and the ball went in it.
>
> The force of Luplow's momentum continued him over the fence. He landed on his shoulder in the Boston bullpen.
>
> At first nobody was sure Luplow had hung on to the ball. But in the next instant he popped up from behind the fence and held the ball aloft. The crowd was stunned.
>
> A run scored after the catch to make it 6–4. But Red Sox manager Johnny Pesky wasn't satisfied. He wanted the play called a home run, claiming the ball had been caught in home run territory. The umpires didn't see it that way.
>
> Pesky protested the game, but there is no chance that he will win the protest.
>
> "It looked to me as if he was the ball," said a disgruntled Pesky afterwards.
>
> "It was the greatest catch I ever saw."
>
> ... Loop had a bruise about two inches long on his knee, where he hit the top of the fence.
>
> "The ball was about three feet past the fence when I caught it," said the kid from Zilwaukee, Mich.
>
> Joe Adcock, Jerry Walker and Birdie Tebbets and just about anybody else you wanted to ask said it was the finest catch they'd ever seen.

Joe Adcock, then a player for the Indians, had been a major league player of distinction since 1950. Having played mostly in the National League, he had been robbed of extra base hits on outstanding catches by Duke Snider and Willie Mays, and had seen his teammates Henry Aaron and Bill Bruton rob other batters with terrific catches. Birdie Tebbets, then the manager of the Indians, began his major league career in 1936. Tebbets was with the Detroit Tigers in 1939 when Joe DiMaggio made his remarkable catch on the drive Hank Greenberg hit. Jerry Walker was a pitcher with the Indians who began his major league career in 1957.

The title over Regis McAuley's *Cleveland Press* article was: "Those Who Saw It Agree—Luplow's Catch Greatest." McAuley's first sentence essentially reiterated the title.

> It was the most spectacular catch I've ever seen in baseball.
>
> Birdie Tebbets says he has seen catches that were made after harder runs but never one so sensational as this one.
>
> Umpire Joe Paparella, whose ruling on the catch caused Red Sox manager Johnny Pesky to finish the game under protest, said:

"I've seen only one other catch close to it and that was in Yankee Stadium when I first started to umpire. Johnny Lindell caught a ball in front of that low wall in front of the seats, flew into the stands and knocked himself cold. I looked in and he still had the ball and I called the batter out."

McAuley went on to describe the catch much as the *Plain Dealer*'s Dolgan did. He also gave the rule which made Al Luplow's catch an out: "The rule is that a batter is out if the catch is made before the fielder lands outside the playing field. Also the ball must be held after the fielder lands."

The Sporting News' writer on the Indians was Hal Lebovitz. In the July 7, 1963, edition, Lebovitz wrote of his high ranking of the Luplow catch: "And Al Luplow, who hasn't been able to push his average above .200, doesn't brood about it in the outfield. He has made two of the greatest catches these eyes have ever seen. One, against the Red Sox, is chronicled elsewhere in this issue." Lebovitz did not say what the other catch was, but it may have been a catch

While with the Cleveland Indians, Al Luplow's all-out effort led to two catches that caused one veteran writer to call them among the greatest he had ever seen.

Luplow made in Kansas City on September 18, 1962. The *Plain Dealer*'s Bob Dolgan called the running, diving, and tumbling catch at the left field line on fourth inning liner by John Wojcik "as spectacular a play as we have seen all year...." The *Kansas City Times*' Joe McGuff called the catch "sensational." Unfortunately, Al Luplow suffered a separated left shoulder while making the catch and was out for the rest of the 1962 season.

The sportswriters for the Boston papers concurred with the Cleveland writers on the greatness of Luplow's grab of the ball Dick Williams hit. The *Boston Herald*'s Arthur Sampson gave another view of the catch.

Lou Clinton had singled with one away and Dick Stuart had poked an under-hand curve by relief pitcher Ted Abernathy into right field for a single sending Clinton to third.

In this spot Williams smashed a soaring drive that sailed with the wind toward the Red Sox bullpen in right-center. Luplow, who had replaced Gene Green in right field for defensive purposes after Green lifted a sixth inning homer into the net for his first hit since May 30, raced after the ball in what appeared to be a hopeless chase.

Reaching the low barrier in front of the bullpen, the former Michigan State half back Luplow timed a leap and with a back-handed stab got the ball in his raised glove.

While in the air with his flying leap, Luplow's thigh hit the top of the fence and he flipped into the bullpen, took a football player's roll and appeared again holding the ball in his glove.

Clinton scored after the catch and Stuart went to second on the sacrifice fly. But this one run was small return for such a gallant home run bid that would have tied the score at 6–6 had not Luplow made such a courageous grab.

Jimmy Piersall, during his years with the Red Sox, used to rob visiting players of homers by pushing himself into the air with his right hand on top of the rail and snaring the ball as it sailed over the barrier with his extended glove. But Luplow didn't spring from the barrier. He leaped from the ground and toppled over the fence from his own momentum and that provided by the contact.

In some ways this was a similar catch to the one Harry Hooper made in the World Series of 1912 except that the former Red Sox right fielder made the grab with his bare hand as he toppled over a low fence and into the crowd.

It would be difficult to convince those at Fenway yesterday that Luplow's daylight robbery wasn't the greatest they'd ever seen and perhaps the greatest ever made at the park. It was, at least, the most sensational since Hooper's.

The *Herald*'s Ed Costello focused on the rule indicating that Luplow's leaping catch was an out, and not a home run as Red Sox manager Johnny Pesky contended, but not vociferously. As Costello wrote about the play, even the members of Pesky's own Red Sox bullpen saw Luplow's grab as a fair catch.

The four occupants of the Red Sox bullpen at the time—Coach Al Lakeman, Bob Tillman, Jack Lamabe and Chet Nichols-showed no signs of protest on Paparella's call. In fact, Nichols later said, "Al made a good catch, a great one, and acted like a seasoned football player when he fell into the bullpen. He landed on his shoulder and rolled prettily to his feet still with the ball."

Later in the article Ed Costello quoted Luplow about the catch.

A similarity between Cleveland and Boston walls helped Luplow make his once-in-a-lifetime catch, he said afterward. "The wall really didn't phase me, it has real good padding like ours in Cleveland," said Al. "Getting the ball was my main concern."

Declared Al, "When I got the ball, it was actually over the fence. My knees hit the fence as soon as the ball hit the glove and I just flipped over. I tucked the ball in when I went over, then I rolled over in the bullpen.

"I spiked myself on the knee," he related on his crash landing. A three-inch spike wound was the extent of the spiking.

So outstanding was Luplow's catch that the *Boston Globe* had three writers do articles featuring it. The morning *Globe*'s front page even had a picture of Luplow behind the fence after he lifted his glove with the ball in it, with an article by Harold Kaese under the photo. Over the picture at the left top of the front page were the words "FENWAY PARK EPIC," and over Harold Kaese's article the title was "Luplow's Catch Greatest." Kaese began his article by comparing the Luplow catch with catches by Jimmy Piersall.

Jim Piersall made many sensational catches while playing right field for the Red Sox in 1953, but he never made a catch at Fenway Park like the one that cost the Sox the final game of their series with Cleveland.

That is, he never disappeared, never became invisible, while making a catch. But Al Luplow did—as far as umpires, players and most fans were concerned—when he stole a game-tying home run from Dick Williams in the eighth inning.

Running full speed, Luplow made a leaping backhand catch of Williams' wind-helped drive, then vanished from view behind the padded fence of the home bullpen.

It was the best catch of a ball over a fence I have ever seen at Fenway Park.

It was a better catch—more reckless, more acrobatic—than Willie Mays' over-the-head gem off Vic Wertz in the 1954 World Series.

A second after he disappeared into the Boston bullpen, Luplow popped up holding the ball triumphantly in his glove, and Joe Paparella, umpire at second, immediately called Williams out.

Shades of Harry Hooper!

Johnny Pesky finished the game under protest, arguing that Luplow left the field to catch the ball, but the Sox manager was essentially trying to relieve his acute frustration.

The protest cannot be logically upheld. Taking this catch from Luplow would be like taking the Mona Lisa from DaVinci, the Gettysburg Address from Lincoln.

Exactly where the ball was in relation to the fence when it hit Luplow's glove, few people were in position to tell, but the ball did hit his glove a fraction of a second before he hit the top of the fence and flipped out of sight.

The first reaction of Boston players in the bullpen seemed to be to applaud, not to protest. It was that kind of catch. Two young Sox rooters sitting in the first row behind the bullpen, 30 feet away, saw it the umpire's way.

"There's no doubt he caught the ball before he went over the fence," said Fred Hanna of Natick. Allan Joy of North Quincy, his companion, added, "The ball was in his glove all the time, even when he hit the ground."

A former Michigan State halfback, used to being jackknifed by tacklers when catching forward passes, Luplow was airborne when he caught the ball, in no position to take his latitude and longitude at the moments of contact.

"It wasn't how I caught the ball, but when," said Luplow, whose first joy was that he had saved a victory for the struggling Indians.

As for Dick Williams, who hit the ball, instead of emerging as another in a long line of 1963 Red Sox heroes, he only got credit for a sacrifice fly. At least it was a sacrifice fly that should never be forgotten by those who saw it, knocking both the ball and the guy who caught it clean off the playing field.

The *Globe*'s Roger Birtwell wrote about the legality of the catch.

Did Luplow—while out of sight—hang onto the ball?

Second base umpire Joe Paparella, with the wisdom of Solomon, ruled that he did.

The reason? Luplow tumbled into the Red Sox bullpen. If he had dropped the ball on his way to the ground, a jury of Red Sox players would have leaped to its feet and screamed.

Testified a Red Sox bullpen pitcher: "As Luplow went down sidewise, he tucked the ball close to his body—like a football player. He tumbled on his shoulder and head like a football player. And he was up on his feet—fast.

"It was a wonderful catch, but the ball was beyond the fence—and over the bullpen—when he caught it."

Boston manager Johnny Pesky argued with Ump Paparella and announced he was playing the game under protest. Pesky's reason: "The ball was out of the field of play when Luplow caught it."

This cartoon, drawn by "PB" of the *Boston Globe*, shows Al Luplow's catch of a bid for a home run by the Boston Red Sox' Dick Williams during the June 27, 1963, game in Fenway Park. Luplow went up and over a five-foot-high fence.

But, and this was the view of the umpires, Luplow's feet were still within the field of play—just as were the feet of right fielder Harry Hooper of the Red Sox when he made his back-to-the-plate, barehanded catch off Captain Larry Doyle of the Giants when Hooper plunged into the third row of the temporary seats in the eighth game of the 1912 World Series.

Will McDonough of the *Globe* put the Luplow catch into a different framework of greatness by quoting Boston's power-hitting first baseman, Dick Stuart. The title above McDonough's article was: "Stuart on Luplow's Catch, 'Greatest If Mays Or Piersall Did It.'" Stuart had just come over to the Red Sox for the 1963 season after playing five years with the Pittsburgh Pirates. With the Pirates he saw great outfielding on his own team from his centerfielder Bill Virdon, and especially from his right fielder Roberto Clemente. In addition, he saw Mays make some outstanding catches against his team. His observations of wonderful fielding over his previous five years in Pittsburgh makes him a valid judge despite his own misadventures as a fielder, misadventures that led to his being referred to as "Dr. Strangeglove." McDonough begins with Stuart's quote.

"If Willie Mays or Jimmy Piersall had made that catch," said Dick Stuart, "it would go down as the greatest in history.

"But Al Luplow made the catch, and who's Al Luplow—just another ballplayer."

Who is this Al Luplow, the guy who made the sensational catch that caused such a stir at Fenway Park Thursday?

"Luplow," says Birdie Tebbetts, "is a guy that's going to be a helluva ballplayer when somebody gets across the point to him that baseballs are for hitting and catching—not biting.

"He's one of those former Big Ten football players and I think they train those guys by having them bite baseballs."

Fortunately for Birdie and the Indians Thursday, Al still looked as though he wanted to bite the ball as he robbed Dick Williams of a three-run homer in the eighth inning.

Luplow, called by some one of the best halfbacks ever to play at a pretty good football school named Michigan State, defied self preservation to make the catch.

Starting from his right field position, he raced full speed, and he can move pretty good, directly toward the barrier in front of the Red Sox bullpen. About two strides from the five foot fence he left his feet in a diving lunge and caught the ball as he went tumbling over the fence.

"I didn't think about the wall at all," said Luplow. "It has good padding like the one in Cleveland so I wasn't worried about it.

"The only thing I was concerned about was catching the ball. All I kept telling myself was 'I've got to catch this ball or they're going to tie the game up.'

"The ball was actually over the fence when I caught it. As soon as it hit my glove my knees hit the fence and I just flipped over.

"Rather than put out my bare-hand to brace myself, I tucked it in and rolled over. I spiked myself here," said Luplow pointing to his knee that bore a three-inch scrape, "when I landed."

Manager Johnny Pesky protested the call, feeling it should have been ruled a home run instead of an out. However, after scanning the rule book in his office later, Johnny knew that the protest is all but a hopeless call.

"The way the rule reads, I guess we've had it," said Pesky. "I wasn't going to protest the game but Billy Gardner told me he had seen the same type of play called a home run before and Billy's the type of guy that knows what he is talking about."

Billy Gardner was a veteran infielder. His last year as a major league player was in Boston in 1963. Johnny Pesky began his major league career as a shortstop with the Red Sox in 1942, was a lifetime .307 hitter, and three times led the American League in hits.

In *The Sporting News* of July 13, 1963, Hy Hurwitz told about Luplow's catch. He also quoted Johnny Pesky: "Pesky eventually conceded that it was the greatest catch he'd ever seen. "I've seen both DiMaggios [Joe and Dom] make some great ones. But nothing better than this," declared the Red Sox pilot."

In his book *Tribe Memories: The First Century*, Russell Schneider, a long-time sports-writer for the *Plain Dealer*, included the Luplow catch among the memories. He wrote: "But anyone who saw Luplow steal what would have been a three-run, game-winning homer by Dick Williams—or even read about it—will remember the catch as one of the best ever made in baseball" (84). Later, when Johnny Pesky returned to the Boston Red Sox as a coach and on a visit to Cleveland, Schneider said Pesky admitted that Al Luplow's catch "still was the greatest catch I ever saw" (84).

August 24, 1964—Willie Mays

Willie Mays dazzled another baseball gathering at Dodgers Stadium at Chavez Ravine in Los Angeles. The headline in the August 25, 1964, *Los Angeles Herald-Examiner* sports page read: "Mays Catch in Ravine Better Than '54 Series." The *Herald-Examiner*'s Bob Hunter was mightily impressed by Willie's effort.

> Barnum and Bailey has to have three rings to do what Willie Mays does all by himself.
>
> The 33-year-old super star, without the aid of a life net, executed the most dazzling catch of the year last night to save a 4–2 victory for the hard-boiled Giants.
>
> It came off Tommy Davis, with Ron Fairly on base in the eighth. Mays streaking from left center to right center to, somehow, outrun and catch a baseball earmarked for "triple."
>
> How he ever got to the ball, Willie himself said he doesn't know, and the standing ovation he was accorded was the greatest ever given a transient in Dodger Stadium.
>
> ... Willie M declined to list his feat among his most astounding catches, but it'll do until some outfielder grabs off a 550-foot tape measure job with his teeth.
>
> To him it was more or less of a routine spectacular.
>
> Alvin Dark, who still has his Giants scratching and biting in a brave effort to run down the Phils in the stretch, described another of Mays' catches:
>
> "If he had left his feet, dove for the ball two feet off the ground, backhanded it, rolled over and slid into the fence as what would have been the tying run crossed the plate, I would have said it matched his best."
>
> Dark was describing a circus act Mays put on against the Dodgers in old Ebbets Field when Dark was playing shortstop.
>
> The skipper thought last night's sleight-of-hand was more miraculous, however, than even Willie's celebrated catch on Vic Wertz in the 1954 World Series.

Alvin Dark's mention of the catch made in Ebbets Field refers to the catch Willie Mays made on Bobby Morgan in 1952.

The *San Francisco Examiner*'s Harry Jupiter put the catch on Tommy Davis on a higher plane.

> Tom ... drilled a long, long liner to right center. Mays, playing in left center for the right-handed slugger, got on his horse again and what a gallop!
>
> Paul Revere, passing the word about the fellows with red coats, didn't move any faster than Willie. He ran as hard as he could, stretched as far as he could, and made the glove-tip grab that was breathtaking. It was the best catch Mays has made this year, one of the finest of his great career.

In the same August 24 game, Mays made another fine running catch on a diving, slic-ing ball the Dodgers' Ron Fairly hit in the first inning. The *San Francisco Chronicle*'s Bob Stevens gave more details about Mays' fielding against the Dodgers:

It required a little help, such as two of Willie Mays' routine "miracle" catches, but Jim Duffalo hung on bravely to hurl his first complete game since 1961 last night for a 4–2 Giants victory over the Dodgers.

Mays, a wraith in the outfield, twice hauled the Hawk out of the soup to dazzle a shirt-sleeve crowd of 36,034....

Mays' heroics were spread out between two innings, the first and the eighth.

In the first, he ranged far to his right and behind left fielder Harvey Kuenn to backhand a sinking line drive by Ron Fairly.

But that catch was nothing compared to the one Willie made seven innings later to prevent a triple, the scoring of a run, and a 4–4 deadlock.

There was one out. Fairly singled and Tommy Davis ripped one.

Willie, playing in left-center, raced toward a ball no human had any business getting a glove to. Mays ranged to his left, searching, digging in, pouring on the speed, as the crowd screamed its anticipation of a triple.

At the last possible second, Mays leaped two feet off the ground, his left arm shot out and the ball slammed into his glove. He missed doubling the unbelieving Fairly off first base only because his momentum made it impossible for him to set himself for the throw.

Had it gone through, Davis would have had a triple, Fairly would have scored, and John Roseboro's ensuing fly, again to Mays and again deep, would have tied the score.

As Willie trotted in at inning's end, the crowd gave him a standing ovation and the first Giant to meet him at the dugout steps was, naturally, the beaming Hawk who shook his hand, took another look out to where Willie made the catch, and wagged his head in awe and wonder.

The crowd took the Dodger loss with kindness after seeing The Catch. It had received its reward for attending.

Not only had the fans seen the two catches by Mays, but they also saw the Dodgers' Willie Davis climb and bang into the centerfield fence to take an extra-base hit from Mays in the fifth.

In a separate column, Bob Stevens quoted Willie Mays as saying the catch on Tommy Davis "definitely was a better one than the ball I caught against Vic Wertz in the '54 World Series." Stevens also quoted Jim Duffalo.

... if Willie liked it, winning pitcher Jim Duffalo was crazy about it.

"That catch Willie made behind me in the first inning was the greatest I ever saw," said Duffalo. "But that one he made in the eighth? Well, you describe it. I'm not a writer."

In the next day's *Chronicle*, Stevens wrote an article titled "Even L.A. Lauds Mays' Catch," and gave quotes from several Los Angeles sportswriters, including ones noted above by Bob Hunter. The article gave Stevens another opportunity to express his own amazement with Willie's catch on the ball Tommy Davis hit.

This city admirably proved its provincialism a little transparent Monday night when the magic of Willie Mays reached out and touched it.

The incomparable Giants center-fielder made two of the most incredible catches of a career abundantly graced with the impossible, and he was justifiably rewarded with: (1) a standing ovation by nearly 40,000 fans at Dodger Stadium, and (2) headlines and eulogies compatible with the miracles he wrought.

Stevens was not done thinking about Willie's catch on Tommy Davis. In the September 5, 1964, *Sporting News*, Stevens told how excited members of the media were about the catches: "Forty-eight hours after Mays' amazing thefts had been written into the books, telecasts and radiocasts throughout Southern California still were viewing them, reviewing them, and evaluating them."

Three days after the great catches Mays made in Los Angeles, the *San Francisco Chronicle* ran a picture of the Polo Grounds being demolished. The picture showed seats strewn all over the field. In the center of the photo, the tall clubhouse at the end of center field still was standing. The title above the photo was: "Where Willie Roamed."

September 4, 1964—Willie Mays

Not two weeks after the catch on Tommy Davis, Willie Mays made another electrifying catch. On September 4, 1964, at Philadelphia's Connie Mack Stadium, Willie Mays again thrilled people with his fielding inventions. Allen Lewis of the *Philadelphia Inquirer* called Mays' catch that night "one of his all-time greatest catches." Lewis described the fourth-inning catch on the Mexican player Ruben Amaro.

> With two on and Callison on first base after a single to left, Amaro hit a long drive to the right field side of the scoreboard.
> Mays, shaded to right-center, took off at the crack of the bat but seemed to have no chance to make the catch. At the last second, going at full speed, he jumped against the tin of the scoreboard, stuck out one foot to cushion the impact of the collision and made the catch, landing flat on his back on the ground.
> For a second or two, the crowd was hushed, unsure that Mays had held the ball. Then, when Willie jumped up and began trotting toward the dugout, the fans rose to give him an ovation.
> Callison, who was on his way home while Mays was on the ground, just stood a few feet from the plate looking out at Willie as if he couldn't believe he'd caught the ball. It was just one in a long line of great plays the Giant star has turned in since he made his major league debut in this park in May 1951, but this was surely one of the best.

Elsewhere on the *Inquirer* sports pages, Frank Dolson quoted the Phils' manager, Gene Mauch. "'I think you have to put that one into the first few pages of the book he's writing on how to play center field,'" said Mauch.

The *Philadelphia Bulletin*'s Ray Kelly devoted his whole column to Mays' catch.

> It was one of Willie Mays' greatest catches.
> Willie Mays said: "Shucks, I ain't worrying about catching the ball. It's the hitting that counts."
> Yet Wonderous [*sic*] Willie made a play last night that will go down as a memory book item—at least to the 28,149 viewers.
> "I heard some fans still talking about the catch two innings after it happened," said Ed Roebuck, who was out in the Phillies right field bullpen.
> "The only way you can describe that catch is with a movie camera," said Phillies pitching coach Al Widmar.
> With John Callison on first base in the fourth inning, with two out and the Phillies trailing 1–0, Amaro let go with his "best batting bolt."
> The ball made a curving trail toward the scoreboard approximately 380 feet from home plate.
> Mays had been playing Amaro straightaway in center. At the crack of the bat, Willie took off and raced the ball toward the boarded lower part of the scoreboard.
> When it seemed he was going to run into the wall, Mays leaped into the air, grabbed the ball in his glove and then threw out his both feet to take the shock of the impact with the fence. He bounced off like a gymnast and fell flat on his back.
> "Don't ask me to describe it," Mays said. "You guys saw it better than I did. I went up for the ball. I knew the only way to keep from getting hurt was to use my feet against the fence. That's what I did."

**The New York Giants' Willie Mays is about to make a catch on a ball hit by the Cleveland Indians'
Vic Wertz in the second game of the 1954 World Series at the Polo Grounds in New York. Note that
the center field compartment has the Eddie Grant monument under and in front of the 483 feet sign**
(*New York Daily News*).

Gene Mauch, who admits he is never surprised at anything Mays does on a ball field, said,
"Willie could have done better—and made the catch bare-handed."

Amaro said: "That was the worst catch I ever saw. I'll always remember that catch because
it was the hardest ball I ever hit to right field—and he has to catch it."

"Anybody else would have broken their neck," Roebuck decided later.

The *Philadelphia Daily News'* Stan Hochman called Mays' catch "a once-in-a-lifetime
catch." After setting the scene, Callison on with two out when Amaro hit his drive,
Hochman gave his version of the catch.

Mays was playing a shallow centerfield, but he raced back on a collision course with the wall.
He reached up, caught the ball and it looked as though his momentum would send him
crashing through the Provident Tradesman advertisement. Instead, he thrust his leg up, and
climbed the wall for one wild, eerie step, then plunged to the gravel on his back.

"The greatest catch I have ever seen in baseball," Phillies' third base coach George Myatt said afterwards.

"Mays could have done it better," Mauch said wryly. "He could have caught it in his armpit."

"Man-oh-man," moaned Amaro. "It was my best bolt. It looked like he had to hit the wall. It had to be one of the best catches he's made."

Mays doesn't evaluate his catches, but there were plenty of people around who were willing. "Can you get one any greater?" Dark asked. "He's got to leap in the air, he's got the fence right there. There's no way it could be better."

Phillies coach George Myatt began his major league playing career as an infielder with the New York Giants in 1938 and concluded his days as a major league player in 1947 with the Washington Senators.

The *San Francisco Examiner*'s Harry Jupiter called Mays' catch on Amaro "marvelous ... one of his best."

The *San Francisco Chronicle*'s Bob Stevens called the catch "unbelievable," and went on to describe Willie's effort.

> The Phillies, with Callison on first and two down in the fourth, would have tied it but the incredible Mays dashed into right-centerfield to grab a twisting rocket off the bat of Amaro and hold it even though his momentum sent him crashing into the scoreboard. To soften the blow, Willie leaped, thrust both feet against the board and somersaulted to the ground, flat on his back.
>
> It was standing ovation time.

Five years before he made the catch on Amaro, Mays received high praise from a former adversary, Roy Campanella. In his book *It's Good to Be Alive*, Campanella told of how difficult Willie was to contain as a hitter. Campanella, who had seen great players in his days in the Negro League and throughout his time in the major leagues, put Willie on a higher level: "I miss Willie. I used to get a kick watching him play. He's the most exciting player I've ever watched—whether he's hitting, fielding, or running the bases.... The only other player who matched him in excitement on the ballfield was Jackie Robinson" (285).

In the dugout that night in Philadelphia was Mays' teammate Duke Snider, the former Dodger star centerfielder. It had been over ten years since he vaulted up the left center field wall in Connie Mack Stadium (Shibe Park) to make his greatest catch. Duke Snider finished his career as a baseball player in 1964.

Willie Mays' catches on Tommy Davis and Ruben Amaro in the 1964 season were among his greatest, and therefore among the greatest in baseball history. In 1964, the oddly shaped Polo Grounds, the scene of Joe Jackson's great poke in 1913, of Babe Ruth's emergence as a batting terror, and of many of Willie Mays' astounding fielding plays, was demolished. The proliferation of fields with blandly uniform outfield distances was to accelerate through the mid- and late 1960s and made it more difficult for wonderful outfielders to show the range of their abilities.

The New York Mets were the last occupants of the Polo Grounds before it was demolished. In those two years, 1962 and 1963, although a number of good outfield catches were made, none of them approached the level of the outstanding catches Willie Mays made during his years with the New York Giants.

Appendix:
A Great Catch That Wasn't

One catch that was submitted to *Baseball Digest* and printed in the June 1950 edition was a bare-handed catch and throw to the plate that the writer said the Boston Beaneaters' left fielder Hugh Duffy made on August 6, 1897. Unfortunately, the catch did not happen. Accounts of the game note that Duffy made a great throw to get the Baltimore runner out at home plate, but the sharply hit ball was already rolling on the ground when he got to it. The *Boston Daily Globe* writer T.H. Murnane wrote in his August 7, 1897, account of the game, "Then came the play of the day. Jennings cracked one safe to left and Quinn was on his way home like a flying mackerel. Duffy took the ball on the run and sent it true for Bergen. Quinn was caught by several feet and the game was over." The *Boston Evening Record* account said, "Jennings cracked a sharp bounder between Long and Collins and Quinn made a break for the plate for the tying run."

Bibliography

Alexander, Charles. *John McGraw*. New York: Viking, 1988.

The American Game of Base Ball: How to Learn It, How to Play It, and How to Teach It. New York: George Munro, 1868.

Anderson, Dave. *Sports of Our Times*. New York: Random House, 1979.

Auker, Elden, with Tom Keegan. *Sleeper Cars and Flannel Uniforms*. Chicago: Triumph Books, 2001.

The Baseball Encyclopedia: The Complete and Official Record of Major League Baseball. 8th ed. New York: Macmillan, 1990.

Benson, Michael. *Ballparks of North America*. Jefferson, North Carolina: McFarland, 1989.

Bready, James H. *Baseball in Baltimore: The First Hundred Years*. Baltimore, Maryland: Johns Hopkins University Press, 1998.

Buck, Jack, with Rob Rains and Bob Broeg. *Jack Buck: "That's a Winner!"* Champaign, Illinois: Sagamore Publishing LLC, 1997.

Campanella, Roy. *It's Good to Be Alive*. Boston: Little, Brown, 1959.

Castro, Tony. *Mickey Mantle: America's Prodigal Son*. Washington, D.C.: Brassey's, 2002.

Chadwick, Bruce. *The Cincinnati Reds: Memories and Memorabilia of the Big Red Machine*. New York: Abbeville Press, 1994.

Chadwick, Henry. *The Art of Pitching & Fielding*. Chicago: A.G. Spalding, 1886.

Curran, William. *Mitts: A Celebration of the Art of Fielding*. New York: William Morrow, 1985.

DiMaggio, Joe. *Lucky to Be a Yankee*. New York: Bantam Paperback, 1949.

Drebinger, John. "Eternal Infant of Flatbush." In *Best Sports Stories of 1945*. Edited by Irving T. Marsh and Edward Ehre. New York: E.P. Dutton, 1946.

Durocher, Leo, with Ed Linn. *Nice Guys Finish Last*. New York: Simon and Schuster, 1975.

Evers, John J., and Hugh S. Fullerton. *Touching Second*. Jefferson, North Carolina: McFarland, 1989. (Originally published in 1910.)

Faber, Charles F. *Baseball Ratings: The All-Time Best Players at Each Position*. Jefferson, North Carolina: McFarland, 1995.

Feller, Bob, with Bill Gilbert. *Now Pitching, Bob Feller*. New York: HarperCollins, 1990.

Fleming, G.H. *Murderers' Row: The 1927 New York Yankees*. New York: William Morrow, 1985.

Frommer, Harvey. *Shoeless Joe and Ragtime Baseball*. Dallas, Texas: Taylor Publishing, 1992.

Gershman, Michael. *Diamonds: The Evolution of the Ballpark*. Boston: Houghton Mifflin, 1993.

Gibson, Bob, with Lonnie Wheeler. *Stranger to the Game*. New York: Viking, 1994.

Golenbeck, Peter. *Bums: An Oral History of the Brooklyn Dodgers*. New York: Putnam's, 1984.

_____. *Fenway: The Unexpurgated History of the Boston Red Sox*. New York: Putnam's, 1992.

Gowdy, Curt, with Al Hirshberg. *Cowboy at the Mike*. Garden City, New York: Doubleday, 1966.

Gowdy, Curt, with John Powers. *Seasons to Remember: The Way It Was in American Sports, 1845–1960*. New York: HarperCollins, 1993.

Halberstam, David. *Summer of '49*. New York: William Morrow, 1989.

Hano, Arnold. *A Day in the Bleachers*. Cambridge, Massachusetts: Da Capo Press, 1995. (Originally published in 1955.)

_____. *Willie Mays*. New York: Grossett & Dunlap, 1970.

Harwell, Ernie. *Tuned to Baseball*. South Bend, Indiana: Diamond Communications, 1985.

_____, with Tom Keegan. *My Sixty Years in Baseball*. Chicago: Triumph Books, 2002.

Heinz, W.C. "The Rocky Road of Pistol Pete." In *The Second Fireside Book of Baseball*. Edited by Charles Einstein. New York: Simon and Schuster, 1958.

Henrich, Tommy. *Five O' Clock Lightning*. New York: Birch Lane Press, 1992.

Hoban, Michael. *Baseball's Complete Players*. Jefferson, North Carolina: McFarland, 2000.

Hodges, Russ, with Al Hirshberg. *My Giants*. Garden City, New York: Doubleday, 1963.

Holmes, Tot. *Brooklyn's Babe: The Story of Babe Herman*. Gothenburg, Nebraska: Holmes Publishing, 1990.

Holway, John. *Blackball Stars: Negro League Pioneers*. Westport, Connecticut: Mecklermedia Corporation, 1988.

_____. *The Complete Book of Baseball's Negro Leagues: The Other Half of Baseball History*. Fern Park, Florida: Hastings House Publishers, 2001.

Honig, Donald. *A Donald Honig Reader*. New York: Simon and Schuster, 1988.

_____. *Mays, Mantle, Snider: A Celebration*. New York: Macmillan, 1987.

Irvin, Monte, with James A. Riley. *Nice Guys Finish First*. New York: Carroll & Graf, 1996.

Jacobson, Sidney. *Pete Reiser: The Rough-and-Tumble Career of the Perfect Ballplayer*. Jefferson, North Carolina: McFarland, 2004.

Johnson, Dick, and Glenn Stout. *DiMaggio: An Illustrated Life*. New York: Walker, 1995.

Kaplan, Jim. *The Fielders*. Alexandria, Virginia: Redefinition, 1989.

Kelley, Brent. *The Early All-Stars: Conversations with Standout Baseball Players of the 1930s and 1940s*. Jefferson, North Carolina: McFarland, 2001.

_____. *In the Shadow of the Babe: Interviews with Players Who Played With or Against Babe Ruth*. Jefferson, North Carolina: McFarland, 1995.

_____. *Pastime in Turbulence: Interviews with Baseball Players of the 1940s*. Jefferson, North Carolina: McFarland, 2001.

_____. *They Too Wore Pinstripes: Interviews with 20 Glory-Days New York Yankees*. Jefferson, North Carolina: McFarland, 1998.

Klink, Bill. "Our Friend Willie," in *The Ol' Ball Game: A Collection of Baseball Characters & Moments Worth Remembering*. New York: Barnes & Noble, 1993.

Liberman, Noah. *Glove Affairs: The Romance, History, and Tradition of the Baseball Glove*. Chicago: Triumph Books, 2003.

Lieb, Frederick. *Baseball as I Have Known It*. New York: Coward, McCann & Geoghegan, 1977.

Linn, Ed. *Hitter: The Life and Turmoils of Ted Williams*. New York: Harcourt, Brace, 1993.

Lowry, Philip J. *Green Cathedrals: The Ultimate Celebration of All 271 Major League and Negro League Ballparks Past and Present*. New York: Addison-Wesley, 1992.

Mantle, Mickey. *The Quality of Courage*. Garden City, New York: Doubleday, 1964.

_____, with Mickey Herskowitz. *All My Octobers*. New York: HarperCollins, 1994.

_____, with Phil Pepe. *My Favorite Summer 1956*. New York: Doubleday, 1991.

Maraniss, David. *Clemente: The Passion and Grace of Baseball's Last Hero*. New York: Simon and Schuster, 2006.

Markusen, Bruce. *Roberto Clemente: The Great One*. Champaign, Illinois: Sports Publishing, 1998.

Marzano, Rudy. *The Brooklyn Dodgers in the 1940s: How Robinson, MacPhail, Reiser and Rickey Changed Baseball*. Jefferson, North Carolina: McFarland, 2005.

Mays, Willie. *My Life In and Out of Baseball*. New York: E.P. Dutton, 1972.

_____, as told to Charles Einstein. *Born to Play Ball*. New York: Putnam's, 1955.

_____, with Lou Sahadi. *Say Hey: The Autobiography of Willie Mays*. New York: Simon and Schuster, 1988.

McGraw, John. *My Thirty Years in Baseball*. Lincoln: University of Nebraska Press, 1995. (Originally published in 1923.)

Moffi, Larry. *This Side of Cooperstown: An Oral History of Major League Baseball in the 1950s*. Iowa City: University of Iowa Press, 1996.

Moore, Terry. *Covering the Outfield*. Chicago: Ziff-Davis Publishing, 1948.

Nuttall, David S. *Mickey Mantle's Greatest Hits*. New York: SPI Books, 1998.

Rhodes, Greg, and John Erardi. *Cincinnati's Crosley Field*. Cincinnati: Road West Publishing, 1995.

Rickey, Branch, with Robert Riger. *American Diamond: A Documentary of the Game of Baseball*. New York: Simon and Schuster, 1965.

Riley, James A. *The Biographical Encyclopedia of the Negro Leagues*. New York: Carroll & Graf, 1994.

Ritter, Lawrence. *The Glory of Their Times*. New York: Macmillan, 1966.

_____, and Donald Honig. *The Image of Their Greatness*. New York: Crown, 1979.

Roberts, Robin, with C. Paul Rogers III. *The Whiz Kids and the 1950 Pennant*. Philadelphia: Temple University Press, 1996.

Schneider, Russell. *Tribe Memories: The First Century*. Hinckley, Ohio: Moonlight Publishing, 2000.

Seymour, Harold. *Baseball: The Golden Age*. New York: Oxford University Press, 1971.

Smith, Curt. *The Storytellers: From Mel Allen to Bob Costas: Sixty Years of Baseball Tales from the Broadcast Booth*. New York: Macmillan, 1995.

Smith, Ira. *Baseball's Famous Outfielders*. New York: A.S. Barnes, 1954.

Smith, Ken. *The Willie Mays Story*. New York: Greenberg Publishers, 1954.

Snider, Duke, with Bill Gilbert. *The Duke of Flatbush*. New York: Kensington Publishing, 1988.

Solomon, Burt. *Where They Ain't: The Fabled Life and Untimely Death of the Original Baltimore Orioles, the Team That Gave Birth to Modern Baseball*. New York: Free Press, 1999.

Starr, Bill. *Covering the Bases: Baseball Then and Now*. New York: Michael Kesend Publishing, 1989.

Stein, Fred. *Mel Ott: The Little Giant of Baseball*. Jefferson, North Carolina: McFarland, 1999.

Stout, Glenn, and Richard A. Johnson. *Red Sox Century: The Definitive History of Baseball's Most Storied Franchise*. New York: Houghton Mifflin, 2004.

Thorn, John, and Pete Palmer, eds., with David Reuther. *Total Baseball*. Boston: Warner Books, 1989.

Wescott, Rich. *Philadelphia's Old Ballparks*. Philadelphia: Temple University Press, 1996.

Zimmer, Don. *Zim: A Baseball Life*. Kingston, New York: Total Sports Publishing, 2001.

Zingg, Paul J. *Harry Hooper: An American Baseball Life*. Urbana: University of Illinois Press, 1993.

Index